I0048349

BUDGETING IN NORTH CAROLINA LOCAL GOVERNMENTS

2ND EDITION

EDITED BY WHITNEY AFONSO

FEATURING:

★ AFONSO ★ ALLISON ★ AMMONS ★ BRADFORD ★
★ DELLA VALLE ★ EDMUNDSON ★ JOHNSON ★
★ MCLAUGHLIN ★ MILLONZI ★ MORGAN ★ PASCHAL ★
★ PETERSON ★ RIVENBARK ★ ROENIGK ★ ROESLER ★

UNC | SCHOOL OF GOVERNMENT

The School of Government at the University of North Carolina at Chapel Hill works to improve the lives of North Carolinians by engaging in practical scholarship that helps public officials and citizens understand and improve state and local government. Established in 1931 as the Institute of Government, the School provides educational, advisory, and research services for state and local governments. The School of Government is also home to a nationally ranked Master of Public Administration program, the North Carolina Judicial College, and specialized centers focused on community and economic development, information technology, and environmental finance.

As the largest university-based local government training, advisory, and research organization in the United States, the School of Government offers up to 200 courses, webinars, and specialized conferences for more than 12,000 public officials each year. In addition, faculty members annually publish approximately 50 books, manuals, reports, articles, bulletins, and other print and online content related to state and local government. The School also produces the *Daily Bulletin Online* each day the General Assembly is in session, reporting on activities for members of the legislature and others who need to follow the course of legislation.

Operating support for the School of Government's programs and activities comes from many sources, including state appropriations, local government membership dues, private contributions, publication sales, course fees, and service contracts.

Visit sog.unc.edu or call 919.966.5381 for more information on the School's courses, publications, programs, and services.

Michael R. Smith, DEAN
Aimee N. Wall, SENIOR ASSOCIATE DEAN
Jennifer Willis, ASSOCIATE DEAN FOR ADVANCEMENT

FACULTY

Whitney Afonso	Norma Houston (on leave)	David W. Owens
Trey Allen (on leave)	Cheryl Daniels Howell	Obed Pasha
Gregory S. Allison	Willow S. Jacobson	William C. Rivenbark
Lydian Altman	James L. Joyce	Dale J. Roenigk
David N. Ammons	Robert P. Joyce	John Rubin
Maureen Berner	Diane M. Juffras	Jessica Smith
Frayda S. Bluestein	Dona G. Lewandowski	Meredith Smith
Kirk Boone	Adam Lovelady	Carl W. Stenberg III
Mark F. Botts	James M. Markham	John B. Stephens
Anita R. Brown-Graham	Christopher B. McLaughlin	Charles Szypszak
Peg Carlson	Kara A. Millonzi	Thomas H. Thornburg
Connor Crews	Jill D. Moore	Shannon H. Tufts
Leisha DeHart-Davis	Jonathan Q. Morgan	Emily Turner
Shea Riggsbee Denning	Ricardo S. Morse	Jeffrey B. Welty (on leave)
Sara DePasquale	C. Tyler Mulligan	Richard B. Whisnant
Jacquelyn Greene	Kimberly L. Nelson	Brittany L. Williams
Margaret F. Henderson	Kristi A. Nickodem	

© 2021

School of Government

The University of North Carolina at Chapel Hill

Use of this publication for commercial purposes or without acknowledgment of its source is prohibited. Reproducing, distributing, or otherwise making available to a non-purchaser the entire publication, or a substantial portion of it, without express permission, is prohibited.

Printed in the United States of America

29 28 27 26 25   2 3 4 5 6

ISBN 978-164238-021-7

Contents

Part III: Financial Management and Planning

Chapter 8
Fund Balance and Budgeting for Local Governments

Chapter 9
Capital Planning

Chapter 10
Performance Measurement and Performance Management

Part IV: Communicating with Stakeholders

Chapter 13
Citizen Engagement through the Budget Process

Chapter 14
The Role of Local Elected Officials in the Budget Process

Chapter 15

Communicating Financial Condition to Elected Officials in Local Government

Chapter 16

Budget Presentation: How Format Can Improve Decision-Making

Introduction

"We must consult our means rather than our wishes."
— GEORGE WASHINGTON

"Budgets are blueprints and priorities."
— KEVIN MCCARTHY

"The budget is not just a collection of numbers, but an expression of our values and aspirations."
— JACOB LEW

"Like mothers, taxes are often misunderstood, but seldom forgotten."
— LORD BRAMWELL

The budget is a government's most important policy document. It reflects what governments do and do not do, often including a great deal of the *why*. More formally, it is a contract between the government and the public about the government's fiscal plan for the following year. It needs to reflect EVERYTHING that the government will be doing in the next fiscal year. Many perceive the budget as exclusively a technical document or an accounting exercise. While those elements are critical to proper budgeting, they are by no means what defines the process. This textbook introduces many of the elements that are a part of modern-day budgeting for local governments.

The chapters contained in this textbook, which emphasize the laws governing the North Carolina budget process, are intended to serve as resources for those who work with budgets in local government. While the book is designed to be able to be used independently of other resources, it has been designated as the primary textbook for the University of North Carolina at Chapel Hill School of Government's course, "Budgeting in Local Government," which is the second course in the School's finance curriculum.

The "Budgeting in Local Government" course is intended for managers, budget officers, budget analysts, and, more broadly, those who work with budgets in local government. It covers a range of topics, from the technical, e.g., calculating the revenue-neutral property tax rate as required by law in North Carolina, to the more philosophical, e.g., determining how to evaluate revenue policies from the lenses of economic efficiency and equity. The chapters in this textbook were written by School of Government experts in numerous fields, including local government law, public administration, environmental finance, and economic development. Additionally, new in the second edition are chapters from well-regarded practitioners in North Carolina who share their expertise, experience, and perspectives as various positions, including a budget director, town and county managers, and the deputy treasurer of the State and Local Government Finance Division of the North Carolina Department of the State Treasurer. The second edition boasts sixteen chapters of important and relevant information and insights for local government budgeting, and nine of those chapters are new to the second edition, making this edition much more robust and comprehensive than its predecessor.

Thank you to everyone who contributed to the text. Your contributions make this an incredible resource for the profession, and I appreciate your generosity. I would also like to thank the publications team at the School of Government, particularly the editors who took the lead: Hana Haidar and Melissa Twomey. Lastly, thank you to those who continue to attend the "Budgeting in Local Government" course, reach out with questions and suggestions, and help us at the School to understand the needs, concerns, and challenges facing the field of local government budgeting. Those interactions have helped to shape the course and the research informing this publication and other work.

Whitney Afonso, PhD
Associate Professor
Public Administration and Government

About the Authors

Whitney B. Afonso is an associate professor at the University of North Carolina at Chapel Hill (UNC-CH) School of Government. Whitney's research focuses on state and local public finance, with an emphasis on local sales taxes. Her work has appeared in journals such as the *National Tax Journal, Public Budgeting & Finance, Public Finance Review, Public Administration Review,* and the *Journal of Public Policy.* Whitney won the Burkhead Award for best manuscript published in *Public Budgeting & Finance* in 2015. She also has served on the executive committee of the Association for Budgeting and Financial Management since 2018. Additionally, she is an Academic Fellow at the UNC-CH Tax Center at the Kenan Institute of Private Enterprise.

In addition to traditional research and teaching, her position at UNC-CH engages her with elected officials and practitioners within the state. She is the liaison for the North Carolina Local Government Budget Association and collaborates and consults with the North Carolina General Assembly's fiscal research staff on issues of tax policy.

Gregory S. Allison, CPA, is a teaching professor at the University of North Carolina at Chapel Hill School of Government. Greg has been on the faculty of the School of Government since 1997, where he lectures and provides technical support in the field of governmental accounting and financial reporting. Greg is also director of the School's "Municipal and County Administration" course. He is a coauthor of the eighth, ninth (original and revised versions), and tenth editions of *Governmental and Nonprofit Accounting,* published by Prentice Hall. Greg was recognized as the Albert and Gladys Hall Term Lecturer for Teaching Excellence for 2002–2004, and received the Term Faculty Achievement Award for 2010–2012.

David N. Ammons is a professor at the School of Government at the University of North Carolina at Chapel Hill. He is a recipient of the Joseph Wholey Distinguished Scholarship Award for work in the field of public sector performance (2014 and 2020); the A. John "Jack" Vogt Lifetime Achievement Award for outstanding commitment to the advancement of local government budgeting and evaluation in North Carolina; and the Paul Posner Pracademic Award for lifetime academic and practitioner achievement in the field of public budgeting and finance. He served on the National Performance Management Advisory Commission and is currently a member of the North Carolina Governor's Advisory Committee on Performance Management. He is a fellow in the National Academy of Public Administration. His books include *Performance Measurement for Managing Local Government* (Melvin & Leigh, 2020) and *Municipal Benchmarks* (M.E. Sharpe/Routledge, 2012).

Emily H. Bradford has been the budget director for the Town of Hillsborough since 2007. She has also worked for the City of Gastonia, Town of Matthews, City of Charlotte, and City of Concord.

Jen Della Valle is the assistant to the town manager/deputy budget director for the Town of Hillsborough. Her prior professional experiences include working for the Town of Lake Lure, the North Carolina League of Municipalities, and Catawba County.

Sharon G. Edmundson, MPA, CPA, is currently the secretary of the Local Government Commission and a deputy treasurer for the State and Local Government Finance Division (SLGFD) of the North Carolina Department of State Treasurer. She has over twenty-five years of experience in government finance, all with the SLGFD. She also currently serves as an adjunct instructor for the School of Government at the University of North Carolina at Chapel Hill.

Sharon received her undergraduate degree in accounting from the University of North Carolina at Chapel Hill and a master's in public administration from North Carolina State University. When she can, she spends time in Emerald Isle, North Carolina, with her husband, Drew, and their three dogs.

Bertha T. Johnson is the director of budget and management services for the City of Durham, North Carolina. In this role, she is responsible for the development and management of the city's operating and capital budget, totaling over $500 million. Bertha is also responsible for oversight of the city's strategic planning, process improvement, and performance management programs, as well as the Bloomberg Innovation Team (I-Team). Bertha is also a member of the city's Executive Leadership Team. Bertha joined the City of Durham in 2005 as a senior budget analyst responsible for the oversight of the city's capital improvement plan. She was promoted to assistant budget director in 2006 and director in 2008. Bertha is also an adjunct professor at North Carolina Central University, located in Durham.

Bertha began her public service career in 1993 as the director of finance for the City of Roxboro, North Carolina. She has over twenty years of budget and finance experience in local and state government.

Bertha earned a bachelor of science degree in accounting from Elon University and a master of public administration from North Carolina Central University. She is also a graduate of the Public Executive Leadership Academy (PELA) and the Municipal Administration program at the University of North Carolina at Chapel Hill School of Government. She is also a recent graduate of the Bloomberg Harvard City Leadership Initiative (BHCLI). This program is a collaboration between Harvard Kennedy School, Harvard Business School, and Bloomberg Philanthropies to train mayors and senior city officials to tackle complex challenges in their cities and improve the quality of life of their citizens. Her cohort consisted of eighty leaders selected from cities across the world.

Bertha is a member and former president (2009–2010) of the North Carolina Local Government Budget Association (NCLGBA). In 2015, Bertha was awarded the A. John "Jack" Vogt Lifetime Achievement Award for outstanding commitment to the advancement of local government budgeting and evaluation by the NCLGBA. The award recognizes budget professionals who are committed to professional development and innovation in budgeting and evaluation and are committed to nurturing, mentoring, or educating others in the field.

Chris McLaughlin joined the University of North Carolina at Chapel Hill School of Government faculty in 2008 and specializes in local government tax and finance law. He is an honors graduate of the Wharton School of Business at the University of Pennsylvania and Duke University Law School.

Kara A. Millonzi, Robert W. Bradshaw Jr. Distinguished Professor of Public Law and Government, joined the University of North Carolina at Chapel Hill School of Government in 2006. She specializes in local government finance law, general county law, school finance, utilities finance, development finance, and incorporation. She is the lead faculty for Lead for North Carolina, a fellowship program that aims to recruit, train, and place the state's most promising young leaders in paid local government fellowships as a means of strengthening public institutions, supporting local communities, and cultivating a new generation of public service leaders in North Carolina.

Jonathan Q. Morgan is a professor of public administration at the University of North Carolina at Chapel Hill School of Government, where he teaches, advises public officials, and conducts applied research on economic development. His research has focused on industry cluster-based development; the role of local government in economic development; business incentives; development impact analysis; and innovative, homegrown approaches to job creation. Jonathan's articles have been published in leading journals, such as *Economic Development Quarterly, Policy Studies Journal,* and *Community Development.* Prior to joining the School of Government, he worked for Regional Technology Strategies, Inc., an economic and workforce development consulting firm. He has also served as director of economic policy and research for the N.C. Department of Commerce, and Research and Policy Director for the N.C. Institute of Minority Economic Development. Jonathan holds a BA in economics from the University of Virginia, an MPA from Clark Atlanta University, and a PhD in public administration from North Carolina State University.

Renee Fuller Paschal's interest in local government began during her senior year of high school nearly thirty-seven years ago when she covered city council and county commissioners' meetings for her hometown's newspaper. A college internship with the City of Burlington fueled her desire to attend the Master of Public Administration program at the University of North Carolina at Chapel Hill School of Government and work in local government. She spent the bulk of her career in Chatham County, where she worked with a superb team of professionals to build the county's operating and capital budgeting processes. The capital budget led to numerous construction projects, such as a new agriculture and conference center, courthouse, and detention center, giving Renee much real-world, if sometimes painful, experience with capital budgeting and construction projects. In 2014, Chatham County achieved an AAA bond rating from S&P's Global Ratings, becoming the smallest county at that time in North Carolina to do so. In 2018 Renee retired as Chatham County's first female manager to take care of her elderly father. She continues to teach capital budgeting classes for the School of Government and is currently assisting Harnett County with its operating and capital budgets. Renee credits the works she was able to do in Chatham to the county's incredible team of employees and now-retired School of Government faculty member Dr. A. John (Jack) Vogt, whom she called every week for a couple of years for help in producing the Chatham's first Capital Improvements Program. She dedicates this chapter to Dr. Vogt and to several wonderful mentors for their generosity in showing her the local government ropes, especially Mike Dula, Ben Shivar, Charlie Horne, and Vicki McConnell. Finally, Renee would like to thank Rebecca Joyner, Partner, Parker Poe Adams & Bernstein LLP, for reviewing and editing the entire debt section of her chapter.

Eric J. Peterson has worked for five municipalities since his career started in 1987. He has been the town manager of Hillsborough since 1997 and was the manager of Topsail Beach from 1991 to 1997. Special acknowledgment goes to Kai Nelson for his help with Eric's chapters as well as his decades of mentorship in the areas of budgeting, finance, and management. A huge thank you and recognition goes to all the amazing co-workers, employees, and elected officials who have been part of teams that have worked through major challenges over the years. Their successes and lessons learned are the ones shared in Eric's chapters.

William C. Rivenbark is a professor of public administration at the School of Government at the University of North Carolina at Chapel Hill, specializing in performance and financial management. He has published in numerous academic journals and has coauthored two books. He is also a Fulbright Scholar.

Dale J. Roenigk joined the University of North Carolina at Chapel Hill School of Government in 2005 and took over the directorship of the North Carolina Benchmarking Project in 2006. He helped develop the web-based County and Municipal Financial Condition dashboard tool hosted by the North Carolina Treasurer's Office to help North Carolina local governments assess their fiscal condition. Prior to joining the School of Government, he worked for the State of North Carolina Department of Health and Human Services doing program evaluation and quality monitoring for mental health services. He began his career in public service working for a policy consulting firm in Washington, D.C. Roenigk earned a BA from Duke University and a PhD from the University of North Carolina at Chapel Hill.

Patrice C. Roesler is the manager of elected official programming for the Center for Public Leadership and Governance at the University of North Carolina at Chapel Hill School of Government.

Roesler joined the School of Government in January 2018. She is responsible for the strategic development of governance training and education programs for local elected officials. Her responsibilities include research and analysis of local elected official programming needs, collaboration with faculty and staff in the design of curricula that address the requisite leadership skills and behaviors for effective local governance, and identification of resources to help expand capacity to deliver programs and services.

Prior to joining the School of Government, Roesler's career spanned over forty years with the N.C. Association of County Commissioners, where she served as deputy director for twelve years, after having served for twenty-eight years as director of intergovernmental relations and as a registered lobbyist for the organization's advocacy group. Her advocacy focus included laws and policies related to intergovernmental relationships, public health, social services, mental health, and criminal justice. She holds a BA in English from Atlantic Christian (now Barton) College.

PART I

BUDGET PREPARATION AND ENACTMENT

Chapter 1

Local Government Budgeting: Insights from a Budget Director

Bertha T. Johnson

Downtown Durham, North Carolina

Introduction

A budget is a fiscal policy by which priorities are funded and resources are allocated. In determining its budget, how does an organization decide the allocation of resources and evaluate if the resources are used effectively? To understand the resource allocation process, a broader vision of how all the components of the process connect is needed.

Overview of the Resource Allocation Process

Figure 1.1 Overview of the Resource Allocation Process

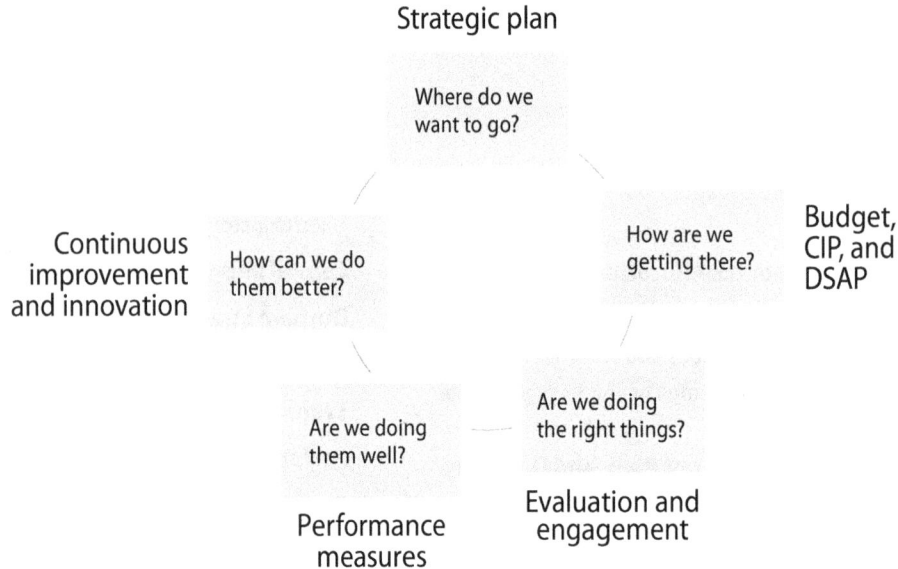

Strategic plan

Where do we want to go?

Continuous improvement and innovation

How can we do them better?

How are we getting there?

Budget, CIP, and DSAP

Are we doing them well?

Are we doing the right things?

Performance measures

Evaluation and engagement

Strategic Plan

The first question for an organization conducting its resource allocation process is "Where do we want to go?" The answer is an organization's "strategy."

Decisions about the allocation of resources start with setting priorities, which can be formulized in a strategic plan (see Figure 1.1), determined by preference, or simply agreed upon. If an organization decides to create a strategic plan, then the plan should be developed with elected officials, employees, and residents. (The same collaboration should occur for setting priorities.) A strategic plan serves to translate a long-term vision into present and future organizational efforts, and it identifies the resources that align with that long-term vision in order to achieve priorities.

The strategic planning process begins with the development of a vision statement and a mission statement. A vision statement expresses what an organization ultimately wants to become. The City of Durham, North Carolina's vision statement is, "Durham is the leading city in providing an excellent and sustainable quality of life."[1] A mission statement describes what the organization is currently doing to achieve its vision. Durham's mission statement is "to provide quality services to make Durham a great place to live, work and play."[2] It is important for the employees of an organization to understand how they are contributing to the realization of the organization's vision and mission. Ideally, new hires should be oriented on the organization's strategic plan during employee orientation.

---

1. City of Durham, *Durham's Got It! Strategic Plan*, https://durhamnc.gov/DocumentCenter/View/343/Council-Vision-and-Mission-Statements-and-Goals-PDF?bidId=.
2. Ibid.

Durham City Council's Priorities and Strategic Plan Goals

While a strategic plan is an organization's vision for the future, the annual budget is the organization's plan for how to achieve that vision. Durham's Budget and Management Services Department aims to align the city's annual budget with its strategic plan. It is expected that departments align their departmental budgets with the strategic plan. The following are five goals outlined in Durham's strategic plan:

1. **Innovative and High Performing Organization**
   Provide professional management that encourages a culture of innovation, collaboration, and transparency in order to deliver quality services through an exceptional workforce.
2. **Creating a Safer Community Together**
   Build a community that allows residents to live, work, and play safely, free from harm and hazards.
3. **Shared Economic Prosperity**
   Enable an environment in which human and workforce development and business growth occur to encourage an inclusive economy.
4. **Connected, Engaged, and Diverse Communities**
   Foster cohesive, engaged, and diverse communities where residents have equitable access to community resources and the opportunity for a high quality of life.
5. **Sustainable, Natural, and Built Environment**
   Guide equitable, efficient, and environmentally sound investments in the city's built and green infrastructure assets.[3]

How to Keep Residents Informed of and Engaged in the Strategic Plan

To ensure accountability and keep residents informed of the progress made on initiatives, Durham features a dashboard for its strategic plan on the city's website. City departments update the outward-facing dashboard twice a year.[4]

---

3. "FY 2019-2021 Strategic Plan, Durham: What's Next?," City of Durham, https://durhamnc.gov/183/Envision---Strategic-Plan.
4. Ibid.

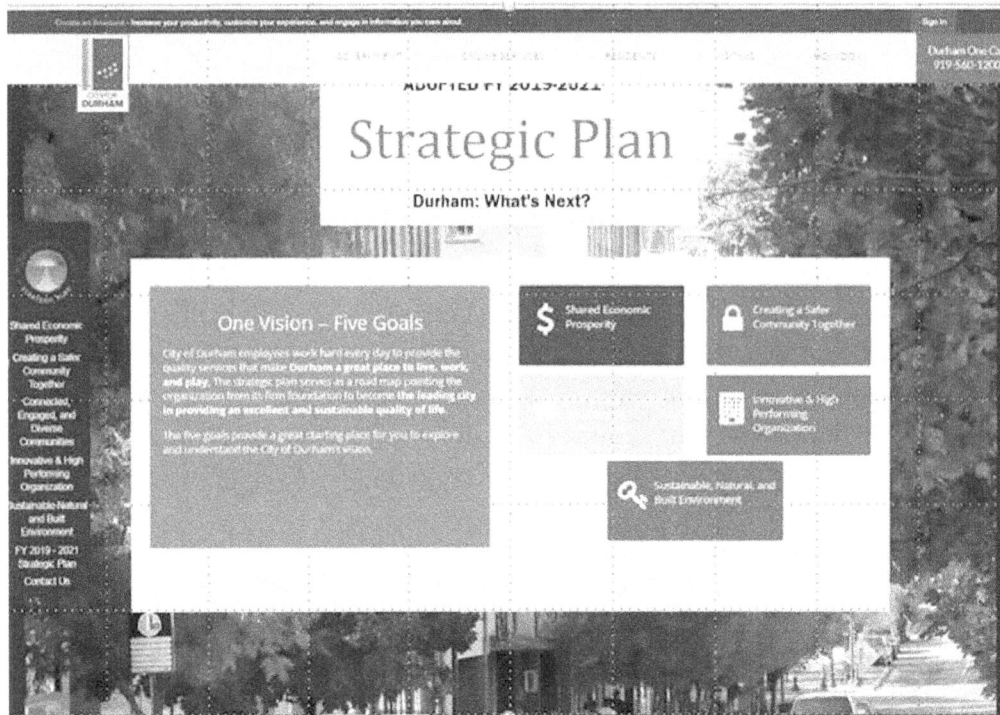

Online Dashboard for Durham's Strategic Plan

Budget, Capital Improvement Plan, and Durham Strategy and Performance

Budget Development Process

After a vision and priorities have been established, the next question for an organization to consider in its resource allocation process is "How are we going to get there?" The operating budget and the capital improvement plan (CIP) are the financial tools used to implement the priorities. The strategy is long-term; priorities are established annually. Once the operating budget and CIP are adopted, they serve as the financial plan for the upcoming fiscal year. Updating the CIP is part of Durham's annual budget development process.

The annual budget development process is the framework for communicating major financial operational objectives and allocating resources to achieve those objectives. This process is a complex undertaking involving the entire city government. The process begins in October and ends in June. By state law, the city must adopt an annual budget ordinance by June 30 of each year. Coordination between elected officials, the administration, and city departments during the process is essential to the development of the budget. To assist these groups with coordination, a general calendar of activities is provided below (see Figure 1.2).

Figure 1.2. City of Durham Budget Development Calendar

October	November	December
• Budget and Management Services (BMS) presents an update of the multiyear plan to the city manager. • Budget request pre-list opens for departments. • Budget manual updated	• Budget request pre-list due from departments • Meet with city manager to discuss pre-list items	• Personnel information is pulled from HR system to build department targets and organizational charts. • Durham Strategy and Performance (DSAP) meeting (12/12) • CIP/ Information Technology (IT) governance kickoff (12/17) • BMS presents update of multiyear plan to city manager.
January	**February**	**March**
• Budget kickoff (1/8). City manager and budget director present financial and operational objectives. • Departments verify and confirm personnel and operating targets. • DSAP meeting (1/16) • CIP submissions are due (1/31). • Public input on budget process begins.	• New budget requests and Add to Base need to be submitted by the first Monday in February (2/3).[a] • DSAP meeting (2/13) • Department budgets need to be entered into MUNIS by the last Monday in February (2/24).[b] • City council retreats.	• Public input on budget process continues. • First public hearing conducted at a regular city council meeting • BMS prepares revenue projections. • DSAP meeting (3/12)
April	**May**	**June**
• Departments present budgets to the city manager. • Balance expenditure requests with revenue estimates	• Preliminary budget and CIP prepared and formally transmitted to city council. • Departments present preliminary budgets to city council. • DSAP meeting (5/14)	• Second public hearing in accordance with state law • City council adopts the budget by June 30.

a. "Add to Base" refers to mandatory additional funding requests (i.e., contract escalation costs, rent increases, etc.)
b. MUNIS refers to the City of Durham's ERP system.

Durham's operating budget development process begins with projecting revenues and expenditures for the upcoming year. In Durham, multiyear financial plans are in place for all major funds to serve as a basis for future-year projections.

The annual budget has four basic functions. First, it expresses the policy of the Durham City Council. Through the budget, the city council exercises its authority to allocate resources. As part of the budget review process, the city council determines the tax rate for each fiscal year. Other fees, such as water and sewer rates, tipping fees, parking rates, and cemetery fees, may be reviewed and adjusted if necessary. During this process, the council also approves salary and benefit adjustments.

Second, the budget is a management and planning tool. The budget and subsequent accounting reports allow managers to isolate potential problems and ensure that city resources are used effectively and efficiently. The process of preparing the budget provides managers the opportunity to evaluate their operations and to formulate goals and objectives for the upcoming year. The budget system also provides a means of monitoring progress toward those goals throughout the year.

Third, the annual budget is a means of communicating the city's spending plan to the residents of Durham and others. The budget is a tangible expression of the city council's policy direction. To residents, the budget is a symbol of the policy of the city council and the actions of the city administration.

Finally, the budget is the foundation for the proper accounting of city funds. It expresses in financial terms the goals and plans of the city council.

Multiyear Financial Plans

A good practice for organizations to align funding with budgets is developing multiyear financial plans. Like the capital improvement plan (CIP), multiyear financial plans forecast revenues and expenditures for future years. The plan can be linked with the strategic plan to demonstrate the impact of current and future decisions on the tax rate and fund balance. Multiyear financial plans also show elected officials the impact of financial decisions on future years' budgets. For example, if the Durham City Council chose to implement a program mid-year in the current fiscal year, the full-year annualized cost would be programmed into the multiyear financial plan for future years. This shows the commitment of future years' funds.

Another example of the benefit of creating multiyear financial plans is when the Durham City Council accepted a federal community-oriented policing (COP) grant to fund the salary and benefits of twenty-five police officers for three years. Other costs not covered by the grant, including uniforms, technologies, vehicles, and weapons, needed to be budgeted for current and future years. The grant also has a non-supplanting clause and stipulates that the city is required to retain the officers for a certain number of years after the expiration of the grant. A multiyear financial plan can be used to demonstrate the total impact of accepting the grant on future years' budgets and can be used to capture future economic-development incentive payments and other commitments.

> "The multiyear financial plan is a modeling tool that helps demonstrate the consequences of decisions, rather than a tool that makes the decisions."
>
> —Tom Bonfield, City Manager, City of Durham (2008–2020)

Participatory Budgeting

Participatory budgeting (PB) is a process of democratic deliberation and decision-making in which ordinary people decide how to allocate part of a municipal or public budget. PB allows residents to identify, discuss, and prioritize public spending projects, and gives them the power to make real decisions about how money is spent.

In 2018, the Durham City Council approved guidelines and allocated funding to establish a PB program in Durham. And $2.4 million was allocated for projects.

The council also appointed a fifteen-member steering committee to establish the goals of PB and support the administration of the program, which is called "PB Durham." The $2.4 million was equally allocated among the three city council wards ($800,000 per ward). Residents were allowed to decide how to use the funding for one-time projects in the community.

Since its launch in November 2018, PB Durham has engaged over ten thousand residents and students. Over five hundred ideas were initially submitted during the idea collection phase in Fall 2018, with the second phase of proposal development taking place from January to April 2019. During the second phase, over one hundred students and residents from the community reviewed, vetted, analyzed, and developed more than forty project proposals using data, community research, and support from technical experts. The voting phase throughout May sought input from residents and students age thirteen or older regarding which of the top forty projects should move to the final implementation phase. The winning projects from PB Durham Cycle 1 are currently in the implementation phase, and some have been completed.

In response to feedback from the Cycle 1 evaluation[5] and to the COVID-19 pandemic, PB Durham Cycle 2 shifted its scope. A grant fund was established to support local efforts to strengthen the community's social and economic fabric by offering relief assistance to communities in Durham. Durham City Council approved $1 million for Durham-based nonprofit and community organizations that are directly serving residents impacted by the pandemic and/or addressing issues contributing to racial, economic, and social inequities in Durham to apply for funding to support community-rooted work.

Capital Improvement Planning

The CIP is a statement of Durham's policy regarding long-range physical development of the city. It is developed for a six-year period and updated annually; year one is the adopted CIP budget for the upcoming fiscal year. Project costs must be a minimum of $100,000 to be included in the CIP. Citizen input is solicited in the development of the CIP. The CIP process begins in August and is finalized with the adopted budget.

Durham Strategy and Performance

It is important that accountability is built into any resource allocation process. Stat meetings are a good way for an organization to hold departments accountable to ensure leadership is kept abreast of any issues related to implementing the organization's strategy in a timely manner. In Durham, these meetings are part of a program

---

5. This evaluation was conducted by North Carolina Central University's Master of Public Administration program.

Figure 1.3. Durham's CIP Development Process

August	Internal CIP administrative meetings held to begin discussing the current status of CIP projects.
October	Departments submit pre-list requests for funding to BMS for the upcoming CIP process.
November	All CIP forms and instructional materials are made available to departments. BMS meets with submitting departments to identify priority items and funding potential for pre-list projects.
December	CIP kickoff is held.
February–March	CIP submissions are reviewed, scored, and aligned with citywide strategic plan.
March	Citizen panel reviews projects/presentation.
April–May	Recommendations are made to city manager and council for adoption in June.

called Durham Strategy and Performance (DSAP). Each initiative in the citywide strategic plan participates in a semi-annual (at minimum) DSAP meeting to provide initiative teams an opportunity to share their current status, milestones, and related data and measures. These meetings are opportunities for initiative owners and leaders to gain clarity about the status of initiatives and scope changes and discuss issues and/or roadblocks to their initiatives' advancement.

Accountability is vital not just between city management and staff but also between residents and their elected leaders. Residents need to stay informed and hold elected officials accountable. As described in the "How to Keep Residents Informed of and Engaged in the Strategic Plan" section of this chapter, Durham has an outward-facing dashboard and strategic plan reports on its website for residents to monitor progress on a variety of initiatives and performance measures. This online dashboard is updated twice a year.[6]

Elected Officials

The role of elected officials in the budget process is to set policy and provide guidance. Adoption of the strategic plan and budget is setting policy. The strategic plan is the strategy, and the budget and CIP financially support the strategy. Sometimes, elected officials have budget requests they want to support that do not get funneled through a department. These requests may come from elected officials themselves, wards or districts, community groups, or individual residents. This is when there seems to be a conflict of interest. How do these requests get prioritized in the budget process? In Durham, the process for elected officials to submit budget requests parallels that for internal departments. Elected officials submit their requests through the city clerk's office. The city clerk compiles the requests, obtains the mayor's approval, and

6. City of Durham, "FY 2019-2021 Strategic Plan."

submits a summary of the requests to the budget department. The budget department analyzes the request and prioritizes it using a prioritization tool adopted by the city council, which then votes on the requests to be included in the budget.

Evaluation and Engagement

After the questions "Where do we want to go?" and "How are going to get there?" are answered (i.e., a strategy and budget have been developed, respectively), the next question for an organization is "Are we doing the right things?" Program evaluation and engagement are key tools to answer that question. Evaluation is systematically investigating the worth (value), merit (quality), or significance (importance) of a program. It can also be used as a method for collecting, analyzing, and using information to answer basic questions about a program.

It can sometimes be overwhelming to implement program evaluation in an organization, especially when there is limited capacity. One way to start is to apply it to new budget requests that relate to existing programs or services. For example, during the last budget process, the Durham Budget and Management Services Department received one hundred budget requests, and five of those requests were identified by the city manager as significant enough to require additional analysis. These requests represented 26 percent of the overall general fund requests, and they were all expansions of existing programs or services.

Program evaluation can help determine what issue a department is trying to solve and why it believes new funding is the solution. Program evaluation can also help determine if new funding is really the best solution and illuminate issues that can be resolved through process improvement or other means.

Equally important to program evaluation is engagement. It is important to engage employees and residents. An integral part of program evaluation is the engagement of stakeholders in the evaluation process itself. This can be through focus groups,

Figure 1.4. How Durham Applied Program Evaluation to New Budget Requests

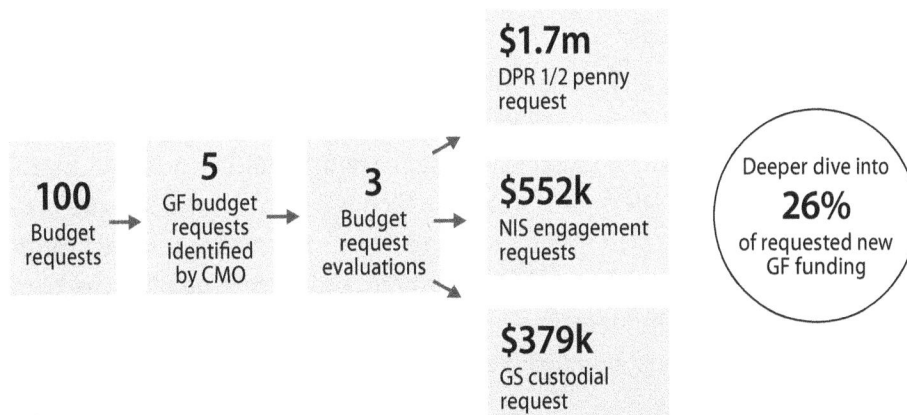

surveys, and more, which capture how residents are experiencing the service or program. Employee feedback is key to understanding if employees believe they are trained to do the work required of them; if they are receiving adequate direction and supervision; if they are satisfied with their pay and benefits; and if they are aware of the city's mission, vision, and goals; and how the city's mission, vision, and goals relate to their daily work. Residents need to be engaged in setting priorities and providing feedback on existing programs and services. There are many ways to achieve this type of engagement, including employee and resident surveys, community forums, and public hearings. In Durham, annual resident surveys and bi-annual employee surveys are conducted through an external consultant. The results are reported to the city council, elected officials, and the public by the independent consultant. Human Resources then coordinates with departments to develop action plans to respond to low-scoring service areas.

Performance Management

After an organization has determined whether its program is doing the right things, the next question for an organization to ask itself is, are we doing them well? In the budget context, this question relates to assessing the impact of resource allocation, which is achieved through performance management.

The performance management process involves the use of performance data to make operational and strategic budget decisions, as well as to frame strategic discussions about the future. This process also involves monitoring, reporting, and analyzing data in order to make changes to operations throughout the year and to drive budget discussions.

Using data to make resource allocation decisions contrasts with the use of anecdotal stories or "gut" feelings to make such decisions. In Durham, some groups often argue that because the city is growing, Durham needs more firefighters, police officers, and building inspectors. However, when the need for such resources is supported by data, alternatives to simply increasing the amount of personnel arise. The goal of performance data should be to show what would be different if the organization did X, Y, or Z. In this way, the desired outcome plays a pivotal role in the allocation of resources.

Performance management should be embedded in operational business practices. If possible, there should be a formal platform to track performance, and formal touch-point meetings for using and discussing performance data should be held. Durham's performance management platform is DataHub, which is a ClearPoint Strategies portal designed to track strategic plan initiative progress and performance metrics (both citywide and in individual departments). DataHub not only tracks quantitative data but also contains qualitative information (e.g., analysis and storytelling). It simplifies reporting, as users can view data and/or create and export reports on demand.

In Durham, it is expected that departments track performance data and review them daily, weekly, or monthly, depending on the type of measure. In his book, *The Practice of Management* (1954), Peter Drucker wrote, "What gets measured gets managed."[7]

In Durham, department directors discuss performance data quarterly with their deputy city manager. Departments provide performance updates to the city manager twice a year as part of the budget process. Departments present program and service performance data to the city council during the annual budget presentations prior to budget adoption.

A few important principles when engaging in strategic planning and performance management are as follows:

1. *Measure what matters.* Select measures that will help the organization understand whether initiatives/actions are helping achieve the goal or purpose. Measures that are aligned with the organization's strategy are valuable.

2. *Use data to inform.* The performance measure, related graph, and dashboard are not the end goal. They are part of the journey. The organization should continue to be curious, ask questions, discuss, and explore. In general, the organization should implement processes and structures that promote discussion, accountability, and support.

3. *Be flexible and periodically reassess.* Are you confident in the data integrity? Is the data meaningful? Is there a better or more relevant performance measure?

Continuous Improvement and Innovation

The City of Durham recently established an equity and inclusion department and hired its first equity and inclusion manager. The equity and inclusion manager collaborated with city leadership and the racial equity core team (comprising employees from all city departments) to develop a vision and mission for racial equity in Durham, as well as definitions to use as the foundation to develop a racial equity action plan.

The city's vision for racial equity is, "Durham is a vibrant community in which all residents and employees thrive with power and purpose. Racial equity is an embedded principle, shared economic prosperity is a reality, and race is not a predictor of outcomes."[8] The vision represents aspirational goals for Durham residents. The city also drafted a mission for racial equity that represents the way City of Durham employees work on behalf of Durham residents every day to advance racial equity.

---

7. Peter F. Drucker, *The Practice of Management* (New York: HarperCollins Publishers, 1954).

8. "Racial Equity and Inclusion Division," City of Durham, https://durhamnc.gov/4092 /Racial-Equity-Inclusion-Division.

The city's mission for racial equity is, "The City of Durham intentionally identifies racial inequities, engages the community, and uses a collaborative approach in creating solutions to ensure race no longer stands as a determinant of outcomes and opportunities" to normalize conversations about race.[9]

The city also adopted a host of defining terms, including one for racial equity, which is "when racial identity cannot be used to predict individual or group outcomes."[10] A critical part of the work of the racial equity core team has been the development and implementation of a racial equity action plan. One of the strategies in the city's racial equity action plan is to introduce tools for racial equity decision-making. One of the tools the organization decided to advance this year is a "Budget Equity Tool."

> City budgets are important places to prioritize racial equity through targeted investment. Acknowledging inequities and race-based root causes allows cities to make revenue, procurement, and contract decisions intended for improving local governance. Cities are both conducting regular racial equity assessments of budget decisions and making decisions driven by a desire to address inequities and systemic racism.[11]

Durham started the journey to incorporating racial equity in its budgeting during the budget development process for fiscal year 2020–2021.

The first step was to understand what city departments consider when making budget requests. Four questions were included on a budget request form that was distributed to the city departments:

1. How well does the budget request represent the needs of the population of Durham?
2. If you have involved community members or stakeholders in developing this request, please explain.
3. How would this impact the Durham community, and what results/outcomes are intended for them?
4. How would this impact your department, and what intended results/outcomes do you expect?

The questions provided departments the opportunity to discuss equity but did not mention equity specifically so that the responses to the questions could establish a baseline for how departments approach requests without leading them in a particular direction. The next step was to use the data to inform how racial equity could be incorporated in the next year's budget process.

Many local governments may not have the resources to incorporate racial equity into their budgeting processes, specifically the availability of personnel to analyze data from questionnaires. The Durham Budget and Management Services Department

---

9. Ibid.

10. "Racial Equity Terms and Definitions: Shared Language," City of Durham, https://durhamnc.gov/4346/Racial-Equity-Terms-and-Definitions.

11. "Budget Decisions for Racial Equity Impact," National League of Cities, https://www.nlc.org/resource/budget-decisions-for-racial-equity-impact/.

was able to hire an intern to assist in analyzing the information from the prior year's budget process in order to design the budget development process for fiscal year 2021–2022.

University of North Carolina at Chapel Hill master of public administration candidate Molly Gaskin served as that intern. She evaluated the ninety budget requests of fiscal year 2020–2021 for equity and performance measure usage. Across the fiscal year 2020–2021 budget requests, four to five general types of responses stood out as categories that became a coding structure for the four open-ended questions that were included on the budget request form sent to city departments. The coding structure also included an indicator for whether the overall request mentioned or evoked equity, as well as a grading scale for the way departments used performance measures in their requests.

The requests were evaluated for overall equity content by asking two questions: (1) did the request use the term "equity?" and (2) did the questions evoke equity? Requests were considered to evoke equity if they did one of the following: consider the impact of the work, consider community access or engagement, mention specific historical community issues or approaches to solving those issues, and/or mention an underserved or marginalized demographic.

Overall, twenty-six of the ninety forms addressed equity, either using the term itself or evoking equity through one of the methods mentioned. Based on the answers to the open-ended questions, between 40 and 53 percent of the requests focused on improving the level of service, and 13 percent of the requests discussed equity based on the same definition. The city ultimately funded $565,450 of requests that evoked equity, which is about 11 percent of what was funded in fiscal year 2020–2021.

Many of the requests that used the word "equity" or evoked equity were programs that already lent themselves to the issue, such as contracting support for Minority and Women Owned Business Enterprises (MWBEs), while many requests that did not involve equity were requests for equipment, hence the high number of requests concerned with improving the level of service.

Based this work, we knew going forward Durham would need to decide who should weigh in on addressing equity in the budget process, hold those discussions, and begin implementing the necessary changes. The questions remained: Where does an equity evaluation belong in the budget process, and who will conduct the evaluation? Should we change the questions asked on the request form to target equity more specifically? How do we address requests for equipment or requests that may be unrelated to equity concerns? How can the city determine if the equity-focused requests have equitable outcomes?

For the fiscal year 2020–2022 budget process, it is essential that departments understand the key concepts and definitions of racial equity espoused by Durham. These concepts and definitions were developed with employees across the organization led by the newly hired equity and inclusion manager, Sharon Williams.

The Durham Budget and Management Services Department provided the following criteria (in the form of questions) to all departments and the city council for considering equity in developing budget requests:

- Does this request impact a geographic area in Durham where residents are predominantly Black and/or Hispanic/Latino?
- Does this request create or establish the ability to track equity data (e.g., race/ethnicity, gender identity, geographic location) and/or assessments to determine if inequities exist within a current program, initiative, practice, or policy?
- Does this request improve outreach, communication, and/or engagement in geographic areas in Durham where residents are primarily Black and/or Hispanic/Latino?
- Does this request propose or change an administrative policy that creates a more equitable workplace environment?
- Does this request promote contracting and procurement opportunities for Black and/or Hispanic/Latino residents?

The Durham Budget and Management Services Department also shared with departments examples of funded budget submissions for the 2020–2021 fiscal year that advanced equitable outcomes:

- Minority- and Women-Owned Contract Support
  - Allocated $275,000 in Dedicated Housing Fund to increase the number of minority- and women-owned businesses (MWBE) that contract with the city and to track the number and monetary value of contracts awarded to determine and reduce inequities.
- Transitional Jobs Permanent Funding
  - Allocated $100,450 to permanently fund the Transitional Jobs Program, which provides justice-involved residents with up to twenty-six weeks of employment with the City of Durham, as well as job readiness training, ongoing skills training, and other supportive services.
- Go Durham Service Enhancements
  - Allocated $1,070,000 in the Transit Fund to expand transit night/Sunday service to three additional Go Durham routes.

Conclusion

As this chapter was initially being written, COVID-19 did not exist, in the United States at least. Now, there are over 12.4 million cases of COVID-19 and 257,000 deaths from the disease in the U.S. On a smaller scale, in March 2020, prior to the pandemic, the City of Durham experienced the Ryuk malware attack, which infected/encrypted files on individual workstations as well as on some external and cloud-stored files connected to the city's network or synced to the network during the attack. The entire city was shut down. Every single workstation and laptop used by city employees had to be wiped clean, re-imaged, and connected back to the city network. Then, COVID-19 hit North Carolina. City employees who were not essential employees were told to go home, and many of them did not have the adequate technology to do their jobs from home.

The focus pivoted in the middle of the budget process to revising revenue projections, securing funding to address issues related to the coronavirus pandemic, providing a safe work environment for city employees, and supporting small businesses that were struggling in Durham. The city

- provided 5 percent premium pay for frontline employees who were required to continue working;
- set aside a $5 million COVID-19 fund, of which $1 million will be allocated for a Small Business Recovery fund (Duke University matched at $1 million, and Durham County matched with $1 million);
- allowed employees who could to telework and awarded employees who could not COVID-19 leave;
- budgeted $7.8 million from fund balance to cover projected revenue losses in lieu of eliminating jobs;
- eliminated all pay adjustments for employees in the upcoming year;
- limited funding to requests required to maintain existing programs and services; and
- reduced travel and training budgets in all departments by 50 percent.

In March 2020, Durham City Mayor Steve Schewel and Durham County Commissioner Chair Wendy Jacobs assumed extraordinary powers under local declarations of emergency due to the COVID 19 pandemic. With these powers, they issued emergency stay-at-home orders and other declarations to keep Durham safe during this crisis. The next priority was to plan for how Durham would recover, renew, and reemerge, as well as accomplish the dual purpose of keeping the community safe while helping the economy reopen. In order to make best decisions about how to revise emergency declarations and stay-at-home orders, the Durham Recovery & Renewal Task Force (RRTF) was established to advise Schewel and Jacobs. Throughout the process, the RRTF's goal was to engage with community partners, experts, and local businesses in order to provide Durham's elected leaders with actionable guidance and advice. The advisory group was composed of community leaders from various industries, including public and private health care, universities, local businesses, and local government. To support this work, funding was allocated from the City of Durham's COVID-19 fund.

Durham's experience with the COVID-19 pandemic demonstrates that even the best strategies and plans must be agile. An organization should always be able to pivot to address the current environment. Having a strategic plan can be especially important during a crisis. Initiatives that were slated to be implemented at a later date, such as providing online services, digitizing files, and enhancing technologies, may become critical to implement earlier than originally planned to effectively serve a community experiencing a crisis. If these initiatives are already captured in a plan with an assigned department, cost estimates and proposed performance measures can be quickly evaluated and implemented.

Durham has also embarked on a citywide exercise to reimagine the future of service delivery models and program offerings based on lessons learned and insights gained from the COVID-19 pandemic. Crisis always brings opportunity to reflect and reimagine. For example, the City of Durham was on the brink of implementing a space allocation study; however, based on what was learned about employees' ability to telework effectively, the city will likely reconsider space allocation. According to Jina Propst, Director of General Services for the City of Durham, "As we reimagine where we physically work, we'll see more options for space. How that shakes out, will depend a lot on our philosophical and policy approach to teleworking. For example, will this pandemic show us that One-Call can operate remotely and we do not need a dedicated call center?"[12]

Another example is how Durham has found more ways to engage more residents through virtual platforms, which provides more opportunities for engagement to those who may be less likely or unable to attend an in-person meeting. Prior to the pandemic, only the Durham City Council's regular business meetings and the Durham City-County Planning Commission's meetings were televised on Durham Television Network and live streamed on four of the city's social media platforms. City council work sessions were only audio live streamed. Now, all city council work sessions are also televised on Durham Television Network and live streamed on the city's YouTube channel, which is where the real discussion about agenda items occurs.[13] Residents can now watch the work session discussions and city staff presentations before the city council members vote at the next city council regular business meeting.

Public administrators should always seek ways to achieve better outcomes for their residents, even in challenging times. Durham is no different than other cities; we want to achieve the best outcomes for all of our residents. However, we understand that during a time of crisis, underserved communities are disproportionately negatively affected, and we work to serve those communities in the best way possible.[14]

---

12. Jina Propst (General Services Director, City of Durham), email message to author, December 18, 2020.

13. The City of Durham's official YouTube channel can be found here: https://www.youtube.com/channel/UCHUDjJ4VIFaf3a9ap9s5qEA.

14. The majority of Latino (72 percent), Black (60 percent), and Native American (55 percent) households reported facing serious financial problems during the coronavirus outbreak, versus just 27 percent of Asian and 36 percent of white households reporting the same struggle; Kelly Anne Smith, "Covid and Race: Households of Color Suffer Most from Pandemic's Financial Consequences Despite Trillions in Aid," *Forbes Advisor*, September 17, 2020, https://www.forbes.com/advisor/personal-finance/covid-and-race-households-of-color-suffer-biggest-pandemic-consequences/.

Chapter 2

Budgeting for Operating and Capital Expenditures*

by Kara A. Millonzi and William C. Rivenbark

---

*This is a slightly revised version of Chapter 3 in Kara A. Millonzi, ed., *Introduction to Local Government Finance*, 4th ed. (UNC School of Government, 2018). Used by permission.

   As used in this book, the term "municipality" is synonymous with "city," "town," and "village."

Introduction

North Carolina counties, municipalities, and public authorities (collectively, local units) are required to budget and spend money in accordance with the Local Government Budget and Fiscal Control Act (LGBFCA), codified as Article 3 of Chapter 159 of the North Carolina General Statutes (hereinafter G.S.). In fact, a local unit may not expend any funds, regardless of their source, unless the money has been properly budgeted through the unit's annual budget ordinance, a project ordinance, or a financial plan adopted by the unit's governing board (these concepts are discussed in more detail in the sections below).[1] On the expenditure side, a local unit may spend public funds only for purposes specifically authorized by the state legislature, through general laws, charter provisions, or other local acts. Revenues and expenditures for the provision of general government services are authorized in the annual budget ordinance.[2] Revenues and expenditures for capital projects or for projects financed with grant proceeds are authorized in the annual budget ordinance or in a project ordinance.[3] Revenues and expenditures accounted for in an internal service fund are authorized in the annual budget ordinance or in a financial plan.[4]

This chapter describes the legal requirements for budgeting for operating and capital expenditures. It also presents common budget tools and techniques for both the annual (operating) and capital budgeting processes. The chapter is divided into three sections. The first discusses how to prepare, adopt, and amend a unit's annual budget ordinance and presents various tools available to assist local officials during the budgeting process. This is followed by a section focusing on the adoption of a project ordinance for capital projects and expenditures. It also discusses common strategies for capital planning. Finally, the third section briefly details the requirements for adopting and implementing a financial plan.

---

1. There is an exception to this inclusiveness requirement. The Local Government Budget and Fiscal Control Act (LGBFCA) permits the revenues of certain local government trust and agency funds to be spent or disbursed without being budgeted. Chapter 159, Section 13(a)(3) of the North Carolina General Statutes (hereinafter G.S.). Many counties and municipalities set aside and manage moneys in a pension trust fund, for example, to finance special separation allowances for law enforcement officers. The employees and retirees for whom the local government is managing these moneys have ownership rights. Although a county or municipality must budget its initial contributions on behalf of employees into the pension trust fund, once the moneys are in the fund, earnings on the assets, payments to retirees, and other receipts and disbursements of the funds should not be included in the local government's budget. Municipalities sometimes maintain perpetual trust funds for the care and maintenance of individual plots in the unit's cemetery.

Another example is when a county or municipality collects certain revenue for another governmental unit and records this revenue in an agency fund. Although the moneys are held temporarily by the county or the municipality, they belong to the other unit. The collections, therefore, are not revenues of the county or municipality collecting them and should not be included in its budget.

2. G.S. 159-13.

3. G.S. 159-13.1.

4. G.S. 159-13.2.

Annual Budget Ordinance

The annual budget ordinance is the legal document that recognizes revenues, authorizes expenditures, and levies taxes for the local unit for a single fiscal year. (Each unit's fiscal year runs from July 1 through June 30.)[5] The budget ordinance must be adopted by the unit's governing board. At its core, it reflects the governing board's policy preferences and provides a roadmap for implementing the board's vision for the unit. The LGBFCA, however, requires the board to include certain items in the budget ordinance and to follow a detailed procedure for adopting the budget ordinance.

Substantive Budget Ordinance Requirements and Restrictions

The LGBFCA imposes certain substantive requirements and limitations on the budget ordinance.

Balanced Budget

Perhaps the most important statutory requirement is that the budget ordinance be balanced. A budget ordinance is balanced when "the sum of estimated net revenues and appropriated fund balances is equal to appropriations."[6] The law requires an exact balance; it permits neither a deficit nor a surplus. Furthermore, each of the accounting funds that make up the annual budget ordinance (e.g., general fund, enterprise fund, etc.) also must be balanced.[7]

Estimated net revenues is the first variable in the balanced-budget equation; it comprises the revenues the unit expects to actually receive during the fiscal year, including amounts to be realized from collections of taxes or fees levied in prior fiscal years. (Typically, debt proceeds are not considered a form of revenue, but for budgetary purposes debt proceeds that are or will become available during the fiscal year are included in estimated net revenues.) The LGBFCA requires that the unit make reasonable estimates as to the amount of revenue it expects to receive.[8] The statute also places a specific limitation on property tax estimates. The estimated percentage of property tax collection budgeted for the coming fiscal year cannot exceed the percentage of collection realized in cash as of June 30 during the fiscal year preceding the budget year.[9]

---

5. G.S. 159-8(b). The Local Government Commission (LGC) may authorize a public authority (as defined in G.S. 159-7) to have a different fiscal year if it facilitates the authority's operations.

6. G.S. 159-8(a).

7. For a description of the purpose and function of accounting funds, see Gregory S. Allison, "Accounting, Financial Reporting, and the Annual Audit," Chapter 9 in Millonzi, *Introduction to Local Government Finance*, 4th ed.

8. G.S. 159-13(b)(7).

9. G.S. 159-13(b)(6). The statute provides for a different calculation when budgeting for property taxes on registered motor vehicles. The percentage of collection is based on the nine-month levy ending March 31 of the fiscal year preceding the budget year, and the collections realized in cash with respect to this levy are based on the twelve-month period ending June 30 of the fiscal year preceding the budget year.

Revenues must be budgeted by "major source."[10] This includes, at a minimum, property taxes, sales and use taxes, licenses and permits, intergovernmental revenues, charges for services, and other taxes and revenues. A unit is free to group revenues into more specific categories.

The second variable in the balanced-budget equation is *appropriated fund balance*. Only a portion of a local unit's fund balance is available for appropriation each year. The LGBFCA defines the fund balance available for appropriation as "the sum of cash and investments minus the sum of liabilities, encumbrances, and deferred revenues arising from cash receipts, as those figures stand at the close of the fiscal year next preceding the budget year."[11] Legally available fund balance is different from fund balance for financial-reporting purposes as presented on the balance sheet of a local government's annual financial report. It includes only cash and investments, not receivables or other current assets. Legally available fund balance results when any of the following occurs: unbudgeted fund balance carries forward from prior years, actual revenues exceed estimated revenues in the current fiscal year, actual expenditures are less than appropriations in the current fiscal year, or actual revenues exceed actual expenditures in the current fiscal year. A portion of this fund balance usually is legally restricted to certain expenditures. A unit's governing board may appropriate restricted fund balance only for those specified purposes.

The calculation for determining the amount of legally available fund balance that may be appropriated to cover new expenditures starts with an estimate of cash and investments at the end of the current year and subtracts from them estimated liabilities, encumbrances, and deferred revenues from cash receipts at the end of the current year. All of these figures are estimates because the calculation is being made for budget purposes before the end of the current year. If the estimate of available fund balance is for the general fund, typical liabilities are payroll owed for a payroll period that will carry forward from the current year into the budget year and accounts payable representing unpaid vendor accounts for goods and services provided to the local government toward the end of the current year. Encumbrances arise from purchase orders and other unfulfilled contractual obligations for goods and services that are outstanding at the end of a fiscal year. They reduce legally available fund balance because cash and investments will be needed to pay for the goods and services on order. (Note that the governing board is required to appropriate this portion of the fund balance to cover the encumbered amounts that will be paid out in the next fiscal year. That portion of the fund balance may not be used to offset new expenditures, though.) Deferred revenue from a cash receipt is revenue that is received in cash in the current year, even though it is not owed to the local government until the coming budget year. Such prepaid revenues are primarily property taxes. They should be included among revenues for the coming year's budget rather than carried forward as available fund balance from the current to the coming year.

---

10. G.S. 159-13(a).
11. G.S. 159-13(b)(16).

A unit's governing board is not required to appropriate all of the resulting fund balance, only that amount which is required, when added to estimated net revenues, to equal the budgeted appropriations for the fiscal year. The remaining moneys serve as cash reserves of the unit, to be used to aid in cash flow during the fiscal year. A unit also may use unappropriated fund balance to save money to meet emergency or unforeseen needs and to be able to take advantage of unexpected opportunities requiring the expenditure of money. Some units accumulate fund balance as a savings account for anticipated future capital projects.

The third variable in the balanced-budget equation is *appropriations for expenditures*. An appropriation is a legal authorization to make an expenditure. Only the unit's governing board may authorize appropriations. The LGBFCA allows a governing board to make appropriations in the budget ordinance by department, function, or project.[12] For example, a board may appropriate total sums to the finance department, public works department, law enforcement department, planning and zoning department, and so on. Each department then has flexibility to fund its operational and capital expenditures from its budget allocation. Alternatively, a board may appropriate moneys for each major expenditure category, such as salaries/benefits, utilities, supplies, insurance, capital, and the like. The budget officer/manager, department heads, and other staff may not exceed the amounts budgeted for each function. The same is true if a board appropriates by project. A governing board may not make appropriations by line item or by an individual object of expenditure in the budget ordinance itself. The budget ordinance is a summary document that, for ease of exposition, aggregates expenditures. Many governing boards require submittal of more detailed, line-item budgets by each department to justify expenditures being requested. A board may require that the manager or head of each department follow the more detailed budgets ("working budgets") during the fiscal year. The budget ordinance represents the legal appropriations of the unit, though.[13]

Required Budget Ordinance Appropriations

In addition to the balanced-budget requirement, the LGBFCA directs a governing board to include certain appropriations in its budget ordinance.[14] These requirements apply to the initial adoption of the budget ordinance as well as to any subsequent amendments.

---

12. G.S. 159-13(a).

13. This distinction is significant. For example, the statute governing disbursements of public funds requires that, before an obligation may be incurred by a unit, the finance officer or a deputy finance officer verify that there is an appropriation authorizing that particular expenditure. G.S. 159-28(a). The statute refers to an appropriation in the budget ordinance, not in more detailed, working budgets.

14. Note that the budget ordinance requirements discussed in this chapter generally are limited to those imposed by the LGBFCA. Units must be mindful that other statutory provisions may place additional requirements or restrictions on the budget ordinance.

Debt Service

A governing board must appropriate the full amount estimated by the local government's finance officer to be required for debt service during the fiscal year.[15] Each year during the spring, the Local Government Commission (LGC) notifies each finance officer of his or her local government's debt-service obligation on existing debt for the coming year. If a county or municipality does not appropriate enough money for the payment of principal and interest on its debt, the LGC may order the unit to make the necessary appropriation; if the unit ignores this order, the LGC may itself levy the local tax for debt-service purposes.[16]

Continuing Contracts

A governing board must make appropriations to cover any obligations that will come due during the fiscal year under a continuing contract, unless the contract terms expressly authorize the board to refuse to do so in any given budget year.[17] Continuing contracts are those that extend for more than one fiscal year.

Fund Deficits

A governing board must make appropriations to cover any deficits within a fund. A deficit occurs if the amount actually encumbered exceeds appropriations within the fund. If a unit follows the provisions on expenditure control in the LGBFCA, a deficit should not occur. However, should a deficit occur, a governing board must appropriate sufficient moneys in the next fiscal year's budget to eliminate that deficit.

Property Taxes

If a local unit levies property taxes (which it is not required to do), the governing board must do so in the budget ordinance.[18] The property tax levy is stated in terms of rate of cents per $100 of taxable value.[19]

Encumbered Fund Balance

If a local unit incurs obligations in the prior year that have not been/will not be paid during the prior fiscal year, the unit must appropriate sufficient amounts to cover those expenditures in the new fiscal year. Once the fiscal year expires, there is no budget authority to disburse funds under the prior year's budget. The moneys must be included in the new budget ordinance before they can be disbursed. This often occurs when a unit orders goods or enters into service contracts toward the end of the fiscal year.

---

15. G.S. 159-13(b)(1).

16. G.S. 159-36. Note that the LGC may not require a unit to make appropriations for repayment of installment financing debt incurred under G.S. 160A-20. The provision also does not apply to contractual obligations undertaken by a local government in a debt instrument issued pursuant to G.S. Chapter 159G, unless the debt instrument is secured by a pledge of the full faith and credit of the unit.

17. G.S. 159-13(b)(15).

18. G.S. 159-13(a).

19. The property tax levy process is described in greater detail in Kara A. Millonzi, "Revenue Sources," and Christopher B. McLaughlin, "Property Tax Policy and Administration," Chapters 4 and 5, respectively, in Millonzi, *Introduction to Local Government Finance*, 4th ed.

Limits on Appropriations

The LGBFCA places upper or lower limits on certain appropriations in the budget ordinance. The statute also specifies the types of funds that may (and sometimes must) be used.

Contingency Appropriations

A governing board may include in each fund a contingency appropriation, that is, an appropriation that is not designated to a specific department, function, or project. The contingency appropriation may not exceed 5 percent of the total of all other appropriations in the fund, though.[20] The governing board may delegate authority to the unit's budget officer to assign contingency appropriations to specific departments, functions, or projects during the fiscal year.[21]

Tax Levy Limits

If a unit levies property taxes, the proceeds must be used only for statutorily authorized purposes. A governing board may not include an appropriation of property tax revenue that is not authorized by law. In addition, there is a $1.50 per $100 property valuation aggregate property tax rate cap.[22] Furthermore, the estimated percentage of collection of property taxes used in the rate calculation may not exceed the percentage of the levy actually realized in cash as of June 30 during the prior fiscal year.[23]

Required Funds

Each unit must maintain funds applicable to it according to generally acceptable accounting principles.[24]

Limits on Interfund Transfers

The annual budget ordinance sometimes includes appropriations to transfer money from one fund to another. The LGBFCA generally permits appropriations for interfund transfers, but it sets some restrictions on them, each designed to maintain the basic integrity of a fund in light of the purposes for which the fund was established. In addition, the LGBFCA prohibits certain interfund transfers of moneys that are earmarked for a specific service.

Each of the limitations on interfund transfers discussed below is subject to the modification that any fund may be charged for general administrative and overhead

---

20. G.S. 159-13(b)(3).

21. *See* G.S. 159-15.

22. G.S. 159-13(b)(4). Note that G.S. 160A-209 and 153A-149 authorize a municipality and a county, respectively, to seek voter approval to levy property taxes for purposes not authorized under general law. If a unit receives voter approval to expend property tax proceeds for such a purpose, the total of all appropriations for that purpose may not exceed the total of all other unrestricted revenues and property taxes levied for the specific purpose. G.S. 159-13(b)(5). Voters also vote on levying tax rates for one or more purposes such that the combined total rate exceeds the $1.50 per $100 valuation cap.

23. For more information on calculating the property tax rate(s), see McLaughlin, "Property Tax Policy and Administration."

24. G.S. 159-26.

costs properly allocated to its activities, as well as for the costs of levying and collecting its revenues.[25]

Voted Property Tax Funds

Proceeds from a voted property tax may be used only for the purpose approved by the voters. Such proceeds must be budgeted and accounted for in a special revenue fund and generally may not be transferred to another fund,[26] except to a capital reserve fund[27] (if appropriate).

Agency Funds for Special Districts

A special district is a unit of local government, other than a county or municipality, "created for the performance of limited governmental functions or for the operation of a particular utility or public service enterprises."[28] Some units collect moneys on behalf of special districts. These moneys must be budgeted and accounted for in an agency fund and are not part of the local unit's annual budget ordinance.[29]

Enterprise Funds

A governing board may transfer moneys from an enterprise fund to another fund only if other appropriations in the enterprise fund are sufficient to meet operating expenses, capital outlays, and debt service for the enterprise.[30] This limitation reflects the policy that enterprise revenues must first meet the expenditures and the obligations related to the enterprise. (Note that other statutory provisions further restrict or prohibit a unit from transferring moneys associated with certain public enterprises.)

Although transferring money from an enterprise fund to another fund is legally allowed, it may result in negative consequences. It may, for example, negatively impact the local unit's credit rating or disqualify the unit from certain state loan and grant programs.[31]

Service District Funds

A service district is a special taxing district of a county or municipality. Although a service district is not a separate local government unit, both the proceeds of a service district tax and other revenues appropriated to the district belong to the district.

---

25. G.S. 159-13(b).

26. G.S. 159-13(b)(10).

27. A unit may establish and maintain a capital reserve fund to save moneys over time to fund certain designated capital expenditures. G.S. 159-18. For more information on capital reserve funds, see Kara A. Millonzi, "Financing Capital Projects," Chapter 7 in Millonzi, *Introduction to Local Government Finance,* 4th ed.

28. G.S. 159-7(b)(13).

29. G.S. 159-14(b).

30. G.S. 159-13(b)(14).

31. *See* G.S. 159G-37; *see also* Kara Millonzi, "Transferring Money from an Enterprise Fund: Authority, Limitations, and Consequences," *Coates' Canons: NC Local Government Law* (blog), June 5, 2012, https://canons.sog.unc.edu/transferring-money-from-an-enterprise-fund-authority-limitations-and-consequences/.

Therefore, no appropriation may be made to transfer moneys from a service district fund except for the purposes for which the district was established.[32]

Reappraisal Reserve Fund

A reappraisal reserve is established to accumulate money to finance a county's next real property revaluation, which must occur at least once every eight years. Appropriations to a reappraisal reserve fund may not be used for any other purpose.[33]

Optional Budget Ordinance Provisions

The budget ordinance must contain revenue estimates, appropriations for expenditures, and, if applicable, the property tax levy. The ordinance must show revenues and expenditures by fund and demonstrate a balance in each fund. A unit's governing board, however, is free to include other sections or provisions in the budget ordinance. For example, it might include instructions on its administration. If a fund contains earmarked revenues and general revenues or supports a function for which property taxes may not be used, the ordinance might specify the use of the earmarked funds or direct which non–property tax revenues are to support the function in question. The ordinance also may authorize and limit certain transfers among departmental or functional appropriations within the same fund and set rates or fees for public enterprises or other governmental services.

Adoption of Budget Ordinance

In addition to imposing certain substantive requirements related to the budget ordinance, the LGBFCA also prescribes a detailed process for adopting the budget ordinance.

Role of Budget Officer

Before discussing the specifics of the budget process, it is important to understand the role of the budget officer. The North Carolina General Statutes mandate that the governing board of each unit must appoint a budget officer.[34] In a county or municipality having the manager form of government,[35] the manager is the statutory budget officer. Counties that do not have the manager form of government may impose the duties of budget officer on the finance officer or on any other county officer or employee except the sheriff or, in counties with populations greater than 7,500, on the register of deeds. Municipalities not having the manager form of government may impose the duties of budget officer on any municipal officer or employee, including the mayor if he or she consents. A public authority or special district may impose

---

32. G.S. 159-13(b)(18). This restriction also applies to any other revenues that the local unit has appropriated to the service district.

33. G.S. 159-13(b)(17).

34. G.S. 159-9.

35. In the manager form of government, the law delegates to the manager the authority to serve as chief administrator of the government. The manager is hired by, and works at the pleasure of, the governing board.

the duties on the chairperson or any member of its governing board or on any other officer or employee.

The LGBFCA assigns to the budget officer the responsibility of preparing and submitting a proposed budget to the governing board each year. Having one official who is responsible for budget preparation focuses responsibility for timely preparation of the budget, permits a technical review of departmental estimates to ensure completeness and accuracy, and allows for administrative analysis of departmental priorities in the context of a local unit's overall priorities. In many units, the statutory budget officer often delegates many of the duties associated with budget preparation to another official or employee, for example, the finance officer or a separate budget director or administrator. This is strictly an administrative arrangement, with the official or employee performing these duties under the direction of the statutory budget officer. Under the law, the budget officer retains full responsibility for budget preparation.

Once the budget ordinance is adopted, the budget officer is charged with overseeing its enactment. As discussed below, the governing board also may authorize the budget officer to make certain limited modifications to the budget ordinance during the fiscal year.

Budgeting Process

Before the budgeting process begins, the budget officer, often with guidance from the governing board, establishes an administrative calendar for budget preparations and prescribes forms and procedures for departments to use in formulating budget requests. Budget officers often include fiscal or program policies to guide departmental officials in formulating their requests. The LGBFCA specifies certain target dates for the key stages in the budgeting process, which should be incorporated into the budget officer's plan.

A budget officer's calendar often includes other steps that, though not statutorily required, are integral to an effective budgeting process. For example, many units kick off the annual budget process with one or more budget retreats or workshops for governing board members, department heads, and others. This allows governing board members to set policy for the coming year and provide directives to the budget officer and department heads about budget requests at the outset of the budget process.

Sometimes a budget officer will need to include other boards, organizations, or citizens in the budgeting process. Counties must provide funding for several functions that are (or may be) governed by other boards, such as public schools, community colleges, elections, social services, mental health, and public health. These boards have their own processes for formulating proposed budgets and requesting funds from the county. In addition, both counties and municipalities routinely receive requests from nonprofits, other private organizations, or citizens for appropriations to support certain community activities and projects. (A county or municipality generally does not have authority to make grants to private entities (including nonprofits). They may, however, enter into a contract with a private entity and pay it to perform a function on behalf of the local government.)[36] The budget officer often serves as the liaison between these other boards, private entities, and citizen groups and the governing board. The budget officer should work with the governing board to establish an organized process for the board to receive and evaluate these various requests.

Budget Calendar

By April 30: Departmental Requests Must Be Submitted to the Budget Officer

The LGBFCA directs that each department head submit to the budget officer the revenue estimates and budget requests for his or her department for the budget year. Each department, or the unit's finance officer, also must submit information about current-year revenues and expenditures. The budget officer should specify the format for, and detail of, these submissions.

By June 1: Proposed Budget Must Be Presented to the Governing Board

The budget officer must compile each department head's revenue estimates and budget requests and submit a proposed budget for consideration by the governing board.[37] Generally, the proposed budget must comply with all of the substantive requirements previously discussed. A governing board, however, may request that the budget officer submit a budget containing recommended appropriations that are greater than estimated revenues.[38] This affords the board a ready opportunity to discuss different expenditure options.

When the budget officer submits the proposed budget to the governing board, he or she must include a budget message.[39] The message should contain a summary explanation of the unit's goals for the budget year. It also should detail important activities funded in the budget and point out any changes from the previous fiscal year in program goals, appropriation levels, and fiscal policy.

If a revaluation of taxable real property in the unit occurs in the year preceding the budget year, the budget officer must include in the proposed budget a statement of the revenue-neutral tax rate, "the rate that is estimated to produce revenue for the next fiscal year equal to the revenue that would have been produced for the next fiscal year by the current tax rate if no reappraisal had occurred."[40] While the LGBFCA is silent on where the revenue-neutral tax rate must be included in the proposed budget, an appropriate place would be in the budget message. The rate is calculated as follows:

1. Determine a rate that would produce revenues equal to those produced for the current fiscal year.
2. Increase the rate by a growth factor equal to the average annual percentage increase in the tax base due to improvements since the last general reappraisal.
3. Adjust the rate to account for any annexation, de-annexation, merger, or similar event.

---

36. G.S. 153A-449 (counties); 160A-20.1 (municipalities).
37. G.S. 159-11(a).
38. G.S. 159-11(c).
39. G.S. 159-11(b).
40. G.S. 159-11(e).

After Proposed Budget Presented to Governing Board but before Its Adoption: Notice and Public Hearing

When the budget officer submits the proposed budget to the governing board, a copy must be filed in the office of the clerk to the board, where it remains for public inspection until the governing board adopts the budget ordinance.[41] The clerk must publish a statement that the proposed budget has been submitted to the governing board and is available for public inspection.[42] The LGBFCA does not specify where or when the statement must be published. The clerk should follow the general provisions for legal advertising in Article 50 of G.S. Chapter 1. The clerk also must make a copy of the proposed budget available to all news media in the county. It may be helpful, though it is not legally mandated, for a unit to also post the proposed budget on its website.

The governing board is required to wait at least ten days after the budget officer submits the proposed budget before adopting the budget ordinance. This is true even if the board makes no changes to the proposed budget.[43] This interim period affords citizens time to review the proposed budget and to voice their opinions or objections to governing board members.

The governing board also must hold at least one public hearing on the proposed budget before adopting the budget ordinance. During the public hearing, any person who wishes to be heard on the budget must be allowed time to speak. The board should set the time and place for the public hearing when it receives the proposed budget, if not before. This information is included in the notice published by the clerk. Sometimes a board holds a series of budget review meetings and briefings on each of the major budget categories.These do not satisfy the statutory requirement. The law requires that at least one public hearing be held on the entire budget. The statute requires no specific minimum number of days between the date on which the notice appears and the date on which the hearing is held; however, the notice should be timely enough to allow for full public participation at the hearing.

By July 1: Governing Board Must Adopt Budget Ordinance

After the governing board receives the proposed budget from the budget officer, it is free to make changes to the budget before adopting the budget ordinance. In fact, based on citizen input, as well as that from other boards and department heads, the governing board often makes adjustments to the proposed budget before finalizing and adopting the budget ordinance. When a board makes such changes to the proposed budget, questions often arise about whether and to what extent it must make the changes known to the public before adopting the budget ordinance. The statute requires only that the budget officer's proposed budget be made available for public

---

41. G.S. 159-12(a).

42. Ibid. The notice also must specify the date and time of the public hearing to be held on the budget.

43. G.S. 159-13. The ten-day period begins to run the day after the notice is published. Weekend days and legal holidays count toward the total number of days. However, the ten-day period may not end on a Saturday, Sunday, or legal holiday. It must instead end on the next weekday that is not a legal holiday. *See* Rule 6, North Carolina Rules of Civil Procedure, G.S. 1A-1, Rule 6.

inspection and that one public hearing be held after the proposed budget is submitted to the board. A unit is under no legal obligation to formally solicit public input of modifications to the proposed budget before its adoption.

The LGBFCA allows a budget ordinance to be adopted at any regular or special governing board meeting, at which a quorum is present, by a simple majority of those present and voting.[44] The board must provide sufficient notice of the regular or special meeting, according to the provisions in the applicable open meetings law.[45] The budget ordinance is entered in the board's minutes, and within five days of its adoption, copies are to be filed with the budget officer, the finance officer, and the clerk to the board.[46]

Once the board adopts the budget ordinance, it may not repeal it. Any modifications are made pursuant to G.S. 159-15 (discussed below). This is true even if the board adopts the budget ordinance before July 1.[47]

Interim Appropriations

Missing the April 30 or June 1 deadline does not invalidate the budgetary process or budget ordinance. There are some consequences to missing the July 1 deadline, though. After June 30, a unit has no authority to make expenditures (including payment of staff salaries) under the prior year's budget. If a board does not adopt the budget ordinance by July 1 and needs to make expenditures, it must adopt an interim budget, making "interim appropriations for the purpose of paying salaries, debt service payments, and the usual ordinary expenses" of the unit until the budget ordinance is adopted.[48] This is a stopgap measure. An interim budget should not include appropriations for salary and wage increases, capital items, and program or service expansion. It may not levy property taxes, nor should it change or increase other tax or user fee rates. The purpose of an interim budget is to temporarily keep operations going at current levels. An interim budget need not include revenues to balance the appropriations. All expenditures made under an interim budget are charged against the comparable appropriations in the annual budget ordinance once it is adopted. In other words, the interim expenditures eventually are funded with revenues included in the budget ordinance.

---

44. G.S. 159-17. Adoption of the budget ordinance is not subject to the normal ordinance-adoption requirements of G.S. 153A-45 for counties and G.S. 160A-75 for municipalities.

45. *See* G.S. 143-318.12. However, G.S. 159-17 specifies that "no provision of law concerning the call of special meetings applies during [the period beginning with the submission of the proposed budget and ending with the adoption of the budget ordinance] so long as (i) each member of the board has actual notice of each special meeting called for the purpose of considering the budget, and (ii) no business other than consideration of the budget is taken up."

46. G.S. 159-13(d).

47. *See* Kara Millonzi, "Amending a Newly Adopted Budget Ordinance before July 1," *Coates' Canons: NC Local Government Law* (blog), June 13, 2011, https://canons.sog.unc .edu/amending-a-newly-adopted-budget-ordinance-before-july-1/.

48. G.S. 159-16.

Local Government Commission (LGC) Action for Failure to Adopt a Budget Ordinance

At some point, if a local unit's governing board refuses or is unable to adopt its budget ordinance, the LGC may take action. State law empowers the LGC to "assume full control" of a unit's financial affairs if the unit "persists, after notice and warning from the [LGC], in willfully or negligently failing or refusing to comply with the provisions" of the LGBFCA. If the LGC takes this action, it becomes vested "with all of the powers of the governing board as to the levy of taxes, expenditure of money, adoption of budgets, and all other financial powers conferred upon the governing board by law."[49] LGC takeover will only occur in extreme cases, though. Most of the time, a unit's governing board is left to work out any differences and adopt its budget ordinance.

Budgetary Accounting

The LGBFCA requires local units to maintain an accounting system with applicable funds as defined by generally accepted accounting principles (GAAP).[50] Local units enter their adopted budgets into their accounting systems at the beginning of the fiscal year; this allows them to accurately track the difference between an appropriation and the accumulated expenditures and encumbrances applied against that appropriation. Budgetary accounting is considered a best practice for several reasons. It provides the foundation for budget-to-actual variance reports, providing critical information to departments for remaining within their budgets and to elected officials who possess the ultimate fiduciary responsibility of the organization. It provides the information needed for managing budget amendments and for complying with a statutory preaudit requirement.[51] Finally, budgetary accounting provides the needed information for following GAAP when local units issue their annual financial statements.

Amending the Budget Ordinance

The adopted budget ordinance encompasses the local government unit's legal authority to make all expenditures during the fiscal year. Before a unit may incur an obligation (order goods, enter into service contracts, or otherwise incur obligations of the unit), the finance officer or a deputy finance officer must ensure that there is an appropriation authorizing the expenditure and that sufficient moneys remain in the appropriation to cover the expenditure.[52] Events during a fiscal year may cause greater or less spending than anticipated for some activities, or needs may arise for which there is no appropriation or for which the existing one is exhausted. To address these situations, the local unit may need to amend the budget ordinance.

---

49. G.S. 159-181.
50. G.S. 159-26.
51. See G.S. 159-15 for budget amendments. See G.S. 159-28 for the preaudit requirement.
52. *See* G.S. 159-28(a).

The budget ordinance may be amended at any time after its adoption.[53] A governing board may modify appropriations for expenditures, recognize additional revenue, and/or appropriate fund balance to cover new expenditures. As amended, however, the budget ordinance must continue to be balanced and comply with the other substantive requirements previously discussed. Although not legally required to do so, a governing board also may amend the budget ordinance to reflect changes in revenue estimates during the fiscal year.

A budget ordinance may be amended by action of a simple majority of governing board members as long as a quorum is present. There are no notice or public hearing requirements. Alternatively, a governing board may delegate to the budget officer the authority to make certain changes to the budget. This authority is limited to (1) transfers of moneys from one appropriation to another within the same fund or (2) allocation of contingency appropriations to certain expenditures within the same fund. All other changes to the budget ordinance, including any revenue changes, must be made by the governing board.

Changing the Property Tax Levy

Local government units are limited in their ability to legally change the property tax levy or otherwise alter a property taxpayer's liability once the budget ordinance has been adopted. The property tax levy includes the general property tax rate plus any special taxing district rates. A board may alter the property tax levy only if (1) it is ordered to do so by a court, (2) it is ordered to do so by the LGC, or (3) the unit receives revenues that are substantially more or less than the amount anticipated when the budget ordinance was adopted.[54] A board may change the tax levy under the third exception only if it does so between July 1 and December 31.

Common Budgeting Tools and Techniques

Local government units may adopt any budgeting process that facilitates effective decision-making for adopting a balanced budget ordinance as long as it complies with the legal requirements of the LGBFCA. Local units, historically, have approached the budget process as a financial exercise, focusing primarily on the financial inputs and outputs of the organization. Today, however, local units often take a broader perspective of the budgeting process and include information derived from their strategic plans and performance measurement systems to help guide budgetary decision-making. The goal, as articulated by the reinventing government movement

---

53. G.S. 159-15. Sometimes a board adopts the budget ordinance before July 1. The budget ordinance is not effective until July 1; however, it may be amended at any time after its adoption subject to the limitations set forth in G.S. 159-15.

54. G.S. 159-15. This limitation applies once the budget ordinance is adopted, even if that occurs before July 1.

of the early 1990s, is for local units to make decisions that enable them to steer the boat rather than just row it.[55]

Line-Item Budgeting

Line-item budgeting places the focus of decision-making on revenue estimates by each revenue category and on appropriations by each expenditure account. This form of budgeting is often criticized for its incremental approach to decision-making, resulting in an adopted budget for the forthcoming fiscal year that merely reflects the current year's budget with slight adjustments, the assumption being that the group of services contained in the current year's budget should continue for the following fiscal year. Despite this criticism, line-item budgeting nonetheless provides the foundation for budgetary accounting. Local units prepare line-item budgets to accurately appropriate the necessary resources for each expenditure account contained in the categories of personnel, operations, and capital outlay; to record the line-item budgets in the local unit's financial management system to track budget-to-actual variances over the course of the fiscal year; and ultimately to document budgetary compliance as required by the LGBFCA.[56]

Strategic Budgeting

A management tool that local units often use to embrace long-term decision-making is the creation and adoption of a strategic plan. As previously mentioned, local units often begin their budgetary processes with budget retreats or workshops for elective officials. At these events, officials from the local unit tend to focus on how the forthcoming budget will help advance the long-term goals contained in the unit's strategic plan. For example, a local unit may want the annual budget process to focus on infrastructure because economic development is a long-term, community goal. Broadening the budget process to include the organization's strategic plan enables the local unit's leadership to shift the focus from individual line-item accounts to long-term strategic goals that impact the direction of the community.

Performance Budgeting

Another common management tool used by local units to track service efficiency and effectiveness is performance measurement, wherein individual programs adopt mission statements, goals, objectives, and performance measures to demonstrate the outputs, efficiencies, and outcomes of service delivery. For example, a major output for public safety is the number of service calls. A major outcome is the timeliness of these service calls as tracked by response time. An advantage of performance budgeting, or the incorporation of performance measurement information into the budget, is that it enables the local government unit to make resource allocation decisions based

---

55. David Osborne and Ted Gaebler, *Reinventing Government* (New York: Penguin, 1992).

56. G.S. 159-26(a).

on efficiency and effectiveness measures.[57] Returning to the public safety example, performance budgeting represents the process of deciding whether or not to add an additional officer based on the objective of responding to 95 percent of service calls within four minutes rather than solely on the local unit's ability to afford an additional position.

Zero-Based Budgeting

A technique that is commonly cited for its advantage of eliminating or reducing incremental budget decisions is zero-based budgeting. This budgeting technique, in theory, requires that every line item be reviewed and justified from a base budget of zero rather than from the current-year budget. Zero-based budgeting, in practice, requires each department to submit three budget packages for review: its current-year budget, a reduced budget, and an expansion budget.[58] Departments are ranked based on the priorities of the organization and, based on that ranking, assigned one of the three budget packages, thereby reducing the probability that all departmental budgets reflect current year budgets with slight adjustments. However, reviews on the effectiveness of zero-based budgeting for eliminating or reducing incremental decision-making have been mixed.

Balanced Scorecard

The balanced scorecard is designed specifically to help a local government unit translate its vision and mission into tangible objectives and outcomes.[59] Originally designed for the private sector, the balanced scorecard was adopted in the public sector as part of administrative reform and is now used as a management tool that helps local units broaden their budgeting processes during the preparation, implementation, and evaluation stages of the budget. The balanced scorecard requires a local unit to track the collection of metrics within the four quadrants of citizens, operations, financial resources, and employees, thereby providing local units with a broader, more balanced context in which to make budgetary decisions.

Capital Budgeting

In North Carolina, local units may budget revenues and expenditures for the construction or acquisition of capital assets (capital projects) or for projects that are financed in whole or in part by federal or state grants (grant projects) either in the annual budget ordinance or in one or more project ordinances. A project ordinance

---

57. Janet M. Kelly and William C. Rivenbark, *Performance Budgeting for State and Local Government*, 2nd ed. (Armonk, N.Y.: M. E. Sharpe, 2011).

58. Robert L. Bland, *A Budgeting Guide for Local Government*, 2nd ed. (Washington, D.C.: International City/County Management Association, 2007).

59. F. Stevens Redburn, Robert J. Shea, and Terry F. Buss, *Performance Management and Budgeting* (Armonk, N.Y.: M. E. Sharpe, 2008).

appropriates revenues and expenditures for however long it takes to complete a capital or grant project rather than for a single fiscal year.[60]

Capital Projects

The LGBFCA defines a capital project as a project that (1) is financed at least in part by bonds, notes, or debt instruments or (2) involves the construction or acquisition of a capital asset. Although a capital project ordinance may be used to recognize revenues and appropriate expenditures for any capital project or asset, it typically is used for capital improvements or acquisitions that are large relative to the annual resources of the unit, that take more than one year to build or acquire, or that recur irregularly. Expenditures for capital assets that are not expensive relative to a unit's annual budget or that happen annually usually can be handled effectively in the budget ordinance.

Grant Projects

A grant project ordinance may be used to budget revenues and expenditures for operating or capital purposes in a project financed wholly or partly by a grant from the federal government, state government, or a private entity. However, a grant project ordinance should not be used to appropriate state-shared taxes or other federal or state revenue or aid provided to a unit on a continuing basis. Such revenue or aid, even if earmarked for a specific purpose, should be budgeted in the annual budget ordinance.

Creating a Project Ordinance

A governing board may, at any time during the year, adopt a project ordinance at any regular or special meeting by a simple majority of board members as long as a quorum is present. The ordinance must (1) clearly identify the project and authorize its undertaking, (2) identify the revenues that will finance the project, and (3) make the appropriations necessary to complete the project.

Each project ordinance must be entered in the board's minutes, and within five days after its adoption copies of the ordinance must be filed with the finance officer, the budget officer, and the clerk to the board.

The budget officer also must provide certain information about project ordinances in the proposed annual budget submitted to the governing board each year. Specifically, the budget officer must include information on any project ordinances that the unit anticipates adopting during the budget year. The proposed budget also should include details about previously adopted project ordinances that likely will have appropriations available for expenditure during the budget year.[61] This is purely informational. The board need not take any action to reauthorize a project ordinance once it is adopted.

---

60. G.S. 159-13.2.
61. G.S. 159-13.2(f).

Balanced Project Ordinance Requirement

The LGBFCA requires a capital or grant project ordinance to be balanced for the life of the project. A project ordinance is balanced when "revenues estimated to be available for the project equal appropriations for the project."[62]

Estimated revenues for a project ordinance may include bond or other debt proceeds, federal or state grants, revenues from special assessments or user fees, other special revenues, and annually recurring revenues. If property tax revenue is used to finance a project ordinance, it must be levied initially in the annual budget ordinance and then transferred to the project ordinance. Other annually recurring revenues may be budgeted in the annual budget ordinance and transferred to a project ordinance or appropriated directly in a project ordinance.

Appropriations for expenditures in a project ordinance may be general or detailed. A project ordinance may make a single, lump-sum appropriation for the project authorized by the ordinance, or it may make appropriations by line item, function, or other appropriate categories within the project. If a capital project ordinance includes more than one project, the revenues and appropriations should be listed separately and balanced for each project.

The key characteristic of a project ordinance is that it has a project life, which means that the balancing requirement for such an ordinance is not bound by or related to any fiscal year or period. Estimated revenues and appropriations in a project ordinance must be balanced for the life of the project but do not have to be balanced for any fiscal year or period that the ordinance should happen to span.

Amending a Project Ordinance

A project ordinance may be amended at any time after its adoption but only by the governing board. If expenditures for a project exceed the ordinance's appropriation, in total or for any expenditure category for which an appropriation was made, an amendment to the ordinance is necessary to increase the appropriation and identify additional revenues to keep the project ordinance balanced. A governing board also may amend a project ordinance to change the nature or scope of the project(s) being funded.

Closing Out a Project Ordinance

Unlike the annual budget ordinance, a project ordinance does not have an end date. It remains in effect until the project is finished or abandoned. There are no formal procedures for closing out a project ordinance when a project is done. Projects sometimes are completed with appropriated revenues remaining unspent. Practically speaking, such excess revenues are equivalent to a project fund balance. The remaining moneys should be transferred to another appropriate project, fund, or purpose at the project's completion. Annual revenues budgeted in a project ordinance that remain after a project is finished may be transferred back to the general fund or to another fund included in the annual budget ordinance. Bond proceeds remaining

---

62. G.S. 159-13.2(c).

after a project is finished should be transferred to the appropriate fund for other projects authorized by the bond order or to pay debt service on the bonds. Note that any earmarked revenues in a project ordinance retain the earmark when transferred to another project or fund.

Justification for Capital Budget

The National Advisory Council on State and Local Government Budgeting encourages the adoption of a comprehensive policy to successfully implement and manage the various aspects of capital budgeting.[63] A common question in local government is why local officials need to manage two budgeting processes, one for the operating budget and another for the capital budget. There are several reasons for implementing and managing a separate capital budgeting process.[64]

The first reason involves the lasting impact of decisions. For example, a decision to expand bus routes during the operating budget process can be changed during the operating budget process for the following fiscal year. A decision to expand a police station, however, is more permanent in nature, requiring a level of review beyond incremental adjustments to the operating budget.

A second reason, which builds on the first, is that debt financing is often used to acquire capital assets. The issuing of debt has a long-term impact on a county or municipality because the law requires that debt-service payments be appropriated as part of the budget ordinance.[65] The processes and procedures for capital budgeting can provide a more structured review for a critical decision, such as issuing debt, where additional debt service payments may impact the organization's financial condition and possibly reduce future operating budget flexibility.

A third reason for implementing and managing separate capital budgeting processes can be traced back to state law. The budget ordinance adopted by counties and municipalities in North Carolina covers a single fiscal year beginning July 1 and ending June 30.[66] The acquisition of major capital assets or the completion of infrastructure projects often extends over multiple fiscal years from approval to completion. State law allows local units to adopt their capital budgets with a capital project ordinance, which authorizes all appropriations necessary for project completion and prevents project proceeds from having to be re-adopted in subsequent fiscal years.

A final reason is the variation in assets and costs as compared to the operating budget, wherein decisions are often incremental from one fiscal year to the next. In any given fiscal year during the capital budgeting process, local officials may be faced with using cash reserves for anything from purchasing a new fire truck for $750,000 to issuing $20 million of debt for infrastructure improvements. Capital budgeting allows for the use of specific techniques for evaluating and prioritizing capital requests in terms of organizational need, capacity for acquisition, and community impact.

---

63. National Advisory Council on State and Local Government Budgeting, *Recommended Budget Practices* (Chicago: Government Finance Officers Association, 2003).
64. Bland, *A Budgeting Guide for Local Government*, 2nd ed.
65. G.S. 159-13(b)(1).
66. G.S. 159-8(b).

Capitalization and Capital Budget Thresholds

The establishment of a capitalization threshold, which dictates how the costs associated with the acquisition of capital assets are reported in the annual financial statements as required by G.S. 159-25(a)(1), is an important policy decision for a local government unit. The Government Finance Officers Association (GFOA) defines "capital assets" as tangible items (e.g., land, buildings, building improvements, vehicles, equipment, and infrastructure) or intangible items (e.g., easements and technology) with useful lives that extend beyond a single reporting period.[67] The GFOA recommends that local governments adopt a capitalization threshold of no less than $5,000 for any individual item, which means that capital assets costing $5,000 or less are reported as expenditures or expenses in the period in which they are acquired. Capital assets costing more than $5,000 are reported on the balance sheet and depreciated based on their estimated useful lives.

It is a professional practice for counties and municipalities also to establish a financial threshold to determine what capital requests are considered part of the operating budget process and what capital requests are considered part of the capital budget process—referred to as the capital budget threshold. This threshold is often based on the size of the local government. For example, a smaller local government with a population of approximately 20,000 might establish a capital budget threshold of $50,000, meaning that capital assets costing $50,000 or less would be part of the operating budget process and capital assets costing more than $50,000 would be part of the capital budget process. An additional criterion often used in determining this threshold is the estimated useful life of the capital asset; capital assets with longer estimated useful lives are more appropriate for the capital budget than for the operating budget. A reason for applying this additional criterion is that debt is often used to finance capital assets, and debt payments should never exceed the estimated useful life of the asset.

Common Capital Budgeting Tools and Techniques

As with the annual budgeting process, a local unit may adopt any capital budgeting process that facilitates effective decision-making as long as it complies with the legal requirements of the LGBFCA. An essential component of any well-designed capital budgeting process is planning. Many units have adopted formalized capital improvement programs (CIPs) to facilitate the planning process, and, increasingly, units are relying on more sophisticated analyses relating to the financial condition of the unit to make accurate budget forecasts.

---

67. Government Finance Officers Association (GFOA), "Establishing Appropriate Capitalization Thresholds for Capital Assets," approved by the GFOA executive board on February 24, 2006.

Capital Improvement Program (CIP)

A CIP is a forecast of capital assets and funding sources over a selected period of time. While local officials often refer to the capital budget and CIP as one and the same, they are separate management tools. The capital budget covers one fiscal year and is adopted by ordinance.[68] The CIP, which commonly contains five years of proposed capital assets and funding sources beyond the capital budget, is approved as a long-term plan that local officials update on an annual basis.

There are numerous reasons why local officials prepare and approve a CIP in conjunction with their unit's capital budget. It provides a schedule for the replacement and rehabilitation of existing capital assets, which is fundamental to all capital improvement programs. It allows time for project design and for exploring financing options, both of which are critical to evaluating the merits of a capital asset from a cost-benefit perspective. It also is the primary vehicle for providing the necessary infrastructure to support economic and community development in a coordinated manner, which is fundamental to land use and master plans. As well, a CIP has the potential to help a local government maintain or improve its bond rating due to the premium that bond-rating agencies place on planning.

Table 2.1 provides an example of a capital budget for a local government. The capital budget of $900,000 is adopted by ordinance for fiscal year 2016, appropriating the necessary financing sources to fund the capital assets aggregated by functional area. The major capital project for fiscal year 2016 is the expansion of the unit's public safety building, which is funded by $100,000 from annual operating revenue and $400,000 from general obligation (GO) bonds. The $200,000 of asphalt maintenance (streets and transportation) is funded from the remaining GO bonds, and revenue bonds will be used to fund an expansion of the unit's water and sewer system.

Table 2.1 also provides an example of a five-year CIP for the local government, beginning with fiscal year 2017. While the CIP represents a plan and is updated on an annual basis as new requests are considered, it gives local officials time to prepare for future events. In fiscal year 2018, for example, $100,000 is allocated for a new park, giving local officials the time required to negotiate with multiple landowners to secure the necessary property. And in fiscal year 2019, $400,000 is allocated for GO bonds, giving local officials time to prepare for a bond referendum. These two examples highlight another critical reason why local officials prepare CIPs: doing so allows them to anticipate how the funding of capital assets will impact future operating budgets. Once the park is functional, adequate proceeds must be appropriated in the annual operating budget for additional park maintenance. The operating budget also must appropriate the debt-service payments for the issuance of the GO bonds as required by G.S. 159-13(b)(1). Preparing CIPs enables departments to consider the impact of proposed capital assets on their operating budgets when evaluating and submitting capital improvement requests.

---

68. The phrase *capital budget* refers to appropriations for capital outlay in a single fiscal period. A government board may make these appropriations in the annual budget ordinance or in a project/grant ordinance.

Table 2.1   Capital Budget and Capital Improvement Program (CIP)

Item	Capital Budget FY 2016	CIP FY 2017	FY 2018	FY 2019	FY 2020	FY 2021
Capital assets by function						
Public safety	500,000	50,000	50,000	50,000	50,000	50,000
Environmental services			250,000			250,000
Streets and transportation	200,000			400,000		
Parks and recreation			100,000			
Water and sewer	200,000	50,000			200,000	
Total	900,000	100,000	400,000	450,000	250,000	300,000
Financing sources						
Operating revenue	100,000	50,000	50,000	50,000	50,000	50,000
Capital reserve fund		50,000	250,000			250,000
Grants			100,000			
General obligation bonds	600,000			400,000		
Revenue bonds	200,000				200,000	
Total	900,000	100,000	400,000	450,000	250,000	300,000

Financial Condition and Forecasting

As discussed above, the CIP is a management tool that facilitates long-term planning for the acquisition of capital assets in local government. There are two additional management tools that support the capital budgeting process from a financial perspective: financial-condition analysis and financial forecasting. Such tools are critical, given the ways in which the acquisition of capital assets can impact an organization's current financial condition and future operating budget flexibility.

Financial-Condition Analysis

The first of these additional management tools, financial-condition analysis, allows officials in a local government unit to move beyond reporting on the financial position of the organization with an unqualified audit opinion of its annual financial statements to actually analyzing and interpreting the financial statements in order to determine and report on the financial condition of the organization. The reason financial-condition analysis is so important to capital budgeting and finance is that acquiring and financing capital assets has the potential to drastically change the financial condition of a county or municipality; therefore, it is imperative to monitor these changes on an annual basis for the financial sustainability of the local government.

Fortunately, local officials have access to two web-based dashboards that provide key financial ratios for analyzing the financial condition of any county or municipality in North Carolina. The fiscal analysis tool dashboard, which is located on the North

Carolina Department of State Treasurer's website (www.nctreasurer.com), provides selected financial ratios for governmental activities, the general fund, the water and sewer fund, and the electric fund. The tool calculates the ratios over a five-year period and benchmarks them against other local governments. The North Carolina water and wastewater rates dashboard, which is located on the Environmental Finance Center's website at the University of North Carolina at Chapel Hill School of Government (www.efc.sog.unc.edu), provides selected operations, debt-service, and liquidity financial ratios for water and wastewater activities.

While the details of financial-condition analysis are beyond the scope of this chapter, two financial ratios associated with the general fund and two financial ratios associated with an enterprise fund are discussed below to highlight the critical connection between acquiring financial capital assets and the financial condition of a local government.[69]

General Fund Financial Ratios

A financial ratio from the general fund's statement of revenues, expenditures, and changes in fund balance is the *debt-service ratio*, which is calculated by dividing principle and interest by total expenditures. This ratio provides feedback on the percentage of annual expenditures being committed to annual debt service, which impacts service flexibility. The International City/County Management Association cautions local governments not to exceed 10 percent;[70] however, counties in North Carolina often exceed this percentage because of school financing. This ratio plays an important role when local officials are deciding whether to issue additional debt for capital assets. Another financial ratio from the general fund's balance sheet is *fund balance as percentage of expenditures*. This ratio provides feedback on the solvency of the general fund, which is extremely important to monitor, as cash reserves often are used to finance capital assets.

Enterprise Fund Financial Ratios

Two critical ratios calculated from the financial statements of an enterprise fund are the *debt-coverage ratio* and the *capital-assets-condition ratio*. The enterprise fund's debt-service ratio is calculated by dividing net income of the enterprise by annual debt service—for example, a ratio of 1.25 means that net income exceeded debt service by 25 percent. This ratio is an important indicator of the financial condition of an enterprise fund. It is important also to creditors and bond-rating agencies, particularly when local officials seek to issue revenue bonds. The capital-assets-condition ratio provides feedback on the accumulated depreciation of the capital assets assigned to an enterprise fund (the ratio is 1.0—accumulated depreciation divided by capital assets being depreciated). A high ratio suggests that a county or municipality is investing in

---

69. For more information on financial-condition analysis, see William C. Rivenbark, Gregory S. Allison, and Dale J. Roenigk, "Communicating Financial Condition to Elected Officials in Local Government," Chapter 15 in this book, at 331–47.

70. International City/County Management Association, *Evaluating Financial Condition*, 4th ed. (Washington, D.C.: International City/County Management Association, 2003).

its capital assets; a low ratio, that a local unit needs to review its annual investment in capital assets.

Financial Forecasting

Financial-condition analysis provides extremely important information about capital budgeting and finance; however, financial ratios are typically calculated from audited financial statements (historical data). The second management tool, which is more aligned with the CIP, is financial forecasting—a projection of revenues and expenditures (expenses) over a selected period of time to show the future operating results of a fund on the basis of an agreed-upon set of assumptions.[71] Research has shown that a five-year model is standard in local government, which reconciles with the typical CIP.[72] The implementation of a capital budget and a CIP, as previously discussed, addresses the operating results of the respective funds based on additional debt-service payments, changes in positions and operating expenses, and additional revenue. Financial forecasting provides local officials with a methodology to estimate how the acquisition of capital assets contained in the CIP will affect the relationship between the inflow and outflow of resources in a fund over the selected forecast period.

Table 2.2 presents an example of a five-year financial forecast for the general fund. The forecast of all revenues and expenditures is based on a 2 percent growth rate, with the exception of property taxes and debt service. The forecast for property taxes is based on a 3 percent growth rate, and the forecast for debt service is based on amortization schedules. The current fiscal year (CFY) balance, as noted, is an estimate based on nine months of annualized data; however, the estimate shows that revenues are expected to exceed expenditures by $5,449 for the CFY, increasing fund balance by that amount. The forecast shows that estimated revenues are expected to exceed estimated expenditures for the following two fiscal years, increasing fund balance to $134,947 at the end of fiscal year 2018. The forecast then shows that estimated expenditures are expected to exceed estimated revenues for the remaining three fiscal years, reducing fund balance to $79,935 at the end of fiscal year 2021. The reason for the reverse in trend is that the local government expects to double its debt-service payment from $50,000 to $100,000 in fiscal year 2019 due to the implementation of its CIP.

The five-year financial forecast shown in Table 2.2 gives local officials time to begin discussing how the county or municipality can afford the additional debt service payment schedule for fiscal year 2019. Changes can be made to operating revenues and expenditures, for example, or to the capital budget and the CIP to reduce the impact of taking on more debt. Local officials need information on the different ways counties and municipalities in North Carolina can use pay-as-you-go strategies to acquire capital assets and on how they can issue and structure debt to accommodate the needs of their organizations and communities.

---

71. Larry Schroeder, "Local Government Multiyear Budgetary Forecasting: Some Administrative and Political Issues," *Public Administration Review* 42, no. 2 (1982): 121–27.

72. William C. Rivenbark, "Financial Forecasting for North Carolina Local Governments," *Popular Government* 73, no. 1 (2007): 6–13.

Table 2.2 Five-Year Financial Forecast for General Fund

Item	CFY* FY 2016	Forecast FY 2017	FY 2018	FY 2019	FY 2020	FY 2021
Fund balance, beginning	$100,000	$105,449	$117,006	$134,947	$109,551	$91,112
Revenues						
Property taxes	500,140	515,144	530,598	546,516	562,911	579,799
Local option sales taxes	101,985	104,024	106,105	108,227	110,391	112,600
Permits and fees	52,444	53,492	54,562	55,653	56,767	57,902
Intergovernmental	50,000	51,000	52,020	53,060	54,121	55,204
Sanitation fees	74,785	76,280	77,806	79,362	80,949	82,568
Total	779,354	799,940	821,091	842,818	865,139	888,073
Expenditures						
Administration	100,691	102,705	104,759	106,854	108,991	111,171
Public safety	246,123	251,045	256,066	261,188	266,411	271,740
Environmental services	182,654	186,307	190,033	193,834	197,711	201,665
Transportation	98,585	100,557	102,568	104,619	106,712	108,846
Parks and recreation	95,852	97,769	99,724	101,719	103,753	105,828
Debt service	50,000	50,000	50,000	100,000	100,000	100,000
Total	773,905	788,383	803,150	868,214	883,578	899,250
Difference	5,449	11,557	17,941	(25,396)	(18,439)	(11,177)
Fund balance, ending	$105,449	$117,006	$134,947	$109,551	$91,112	$79,935

*Current fiscal year (CFY) balance is an estimate based on nine months of annualized data.

Financial Plans for Internal Service Funds

An internal service fund may be established to account for a service provided by one department or program to other departments in the same local unit and, in some cases, to other local governments. If a local unit uses an internal service fund, the fund's revenues and expenditures may be included either in the annual budget ordinance or in a separate financial plan adopted specifically for the fund.[73]

Adopting a Financial Plan

The governing board must approve any financial plan adopted for an internal service fund, with such approval occurring at the same time that the board enacts the annual budget ordinance.[74] The financial plan also must follow the same July 1 to June 30

---

73. G.S. 159-8(a); 159-13.1.

74. At the same time that he or she submits the proposed budget to the governing board, the budget officer must also submit a proposed financial plan for each intragovernmental service fund that will be in operation during the budget year.

fiscal year as the budget ordinance. An approved financial plan is entered into the board's minutes, and within five days after its approval, copies of the plan must be filed with the finance officer, budget officer, and clerk to the board.

Balanced Financial Plan Requirement

A financial plan must be balanced. This is accomplished when estimated expenditures equal estimated revenues of the fund.[75]

Internal service fund revenues are principally charges to county, municipality, or authority departments that use the services of an internal service fund. These charges are financed by appropriated expenditures of the using departments in the annual budget ordinance. Internal service fund revenues or other resources also may include appropriated subsidies or transfers unrelated to specific internal service fund services, which would come from the general fund or some other fund and be shown as transfers-in rather than revenues for the internal service fund.

Expenditures from an internal service fund are typically for items necessary to provide fund services, including salaries and wages; other operating outlays; lease, rental, or debt-service payments; and depreciation charges on equipment or facilities used by the fund.

In adopting the annual financial plan for an internal service fund, a governing board must decide what to do with any available balance or reserves remaining from any previous year's financial plan. The law permits fund balance or reserves to be used to help finance fund operations in the next year or, if the balance is substantial, to fund long-term capital needs of the fund. Alternatively, fund balance may be allowed to continue accumulating for the purpose of financing major capital needs of the fund in the future, or it may be transferred to the general fund or to another fund in the budget ordinance or to a project/grant ordinance for an appropriate use. A unit should avoid amassing in its financial plans large fund balances that are unrelated to the specific needs of the internal service fund.

Amending a Financial Plan

A financial plan may be modified during the fiscal year, but any change must be approved by the governing board.[76] Any amendments to a financial plan must be reflected in the board's minutes, with copies filed with the finance officer, budget officer, and clerk to the board.

---

75. G.S. 159-13.1.
76. G.S. 159-13.1(d).

Summary

Local government units in North Carolina are required to budget and spend money in accordance with the LGBFCA, which provides a comprehensive legal framework for preparing, adopting, and amending the annual budget ordinance, project ordinances, and financial plans. The majority of this chapter, as a result, focused on interpreting the numerous statutes in the LGBFCA, including those addressing the definition of a balanced-budget ordinance, the limits on appropriations and interfund transfers, the adoption and amending of the budget ordinance, and the use of project ordinances and financial plans. After a brief overview of budgetary accounting, the chapter presented management tools and processes used by local government officials to make budgetary decisions within the broader context of their organizations.

Chapter 3

Balancing the Budget

Eric J. Peterson, Emily H. Bradford, and Jen Della Valle

Introduction

Line items and lots of numbers usually come to mind when thinking about budgets. Cutting requests, raising taxes or utility rates, funding new projects, and choosing between two well-justified needs, knowing only one can be afforded, are other typical experiences we think of. Numbers are a big part of budgeting, but they are just one piece. The bigger challenge is digging into the stories behind those numbers to learn why requests are being made, develop alternatives and backup plans if there is not enough money to fully fund a request, understand competing interests, determine what requests have better long-term value, and figure out how to pay for everything in a fiscally responsible way. Converting that information into priorities allows organizations to stretch public dollars as far as they can go. The concept of developing a balanced budget in which revenues must equal expenditures seems like a math exercise, but budget development is just as much about the process itself, which involves collaborating, searching for options, considering "what-if" scenarios, and engaging in creative and strategic thinking to ensure that well-informed decisions are made.

What process should you follow to develop your local government's budget? The answer is whatever works best for your organization in addressing the challenges and opportunities it is facing. Because there is no one right path to follow, this chapter shares concepts, examples, options, and questions for you to consider in designing an approach that works best for your situation.

Getting Started: Annual Budgetary Planning Retreat

Most local governments hold an annual budget meeting early in the budget development process to provide direction on key issues. The meeting, often referred to as a "retreat," is intended to guide the manager and staff in developing a budget that aligns with the governing board's goals. Ideally, meeting in a different location than your organization's regular facility encourages creative and fresh thinking. Some governing boards prefer to get out of town to meet and see this as an opportunity for relationship building that leads to more in-depth discussions about issues they are facing. This can be especially helpful when elected officials and staff have strongly differing views on issues. Due to the criticism that often accompanies the expense of an overnight trip out of town, governing boards are more likely to retreat to a different location in or near their community.

During the retreat, the governing board provides direction to the manager on what they want to see in the upcoming budget. This is usually described in terms of priorities, changes, new initiatives, and solutions to issues that are significantly impacting the community. While many priorities fall on the expense side of the budget ledger, determining how to pay for current operations plus new initiatives is another major policy choice that rises to the forefront of deliberations on the revenue side. In addition, consideration of raising property taxes, fees, and utility rates, along with adopting new charges, are often thoroughly discussed during the retreat.

The budget is the "go-to" resource document for most organizations, as it contains such a wide range of information. The Government Finance Officers Association's (GFOA) Distinguished Budget Presentation Awards Program captures the breadth of budgets by conceptualizing budgets as four functions: financial plan, policy document, operations guide, and communications device. In these four categories, budgets are rated on twenty-seven different criteria.[1]

With many people involved in developing a complex document, it is essential that when the starting gun goes off the organization is running in the right direction. The importance of clear direction, as well as considering questions and concerns from everyone in the organization, cannot be overstated. Therefore, a successful budget process starts with designing the budgetary planning retreat.

---

1. For more information about the Government Finance Officers Association's (GFOA) Distinguished Budget Presentation Awards Program, see https://www.gfoa.org /budget-award.

Traditional Components of an Annual Budgetary Planning Retreat

The following are questions a governing board, manager, and staff typically ask during a budgetary planning retreat in order to assess where the organization is currently, what its limitations are, what opportunities it has, and where it wants to go. This must be done before the task of setting priorities can begin.

- ☑ Financial overview: How are things looking for the current year, budget year, and beyond?

- ☑ Strategy review and updates: What are the organization's mission, vision, values, goals, objectives, and priorities?

- ☑ What would a successful year look like in terms of accomplishments?

- ☑ Are current priorities and operations congruent with governing board expectations? If not, what changes does the board want to see?

- ☑ What requests for new programs, services, projects, personnel, capital, and equipment should be prioritized?

- ☑ What are the challenges, gaps, issues, needs, and concerns? And what are the options to improve those areas?

- ☑ Is raising taxes and/or rates an option? Is charging new fees an option?

- ☑ Pending debt retirements, how might you want to use or save those funds?

Clear Direction Early in the Process

Many retreats end with the governing body and staff walking out the door excited about the many great things they are going to accomplish over the next year, such as building parks, hiring more employees, and replacing old equipment. Too often reality strikes a couple of months down the road after staff update revenue estimates and totals all the departments' expenditure requests for the upcoming fiscal year. The governing body, manager, and staff realize that there is far less money than they expected. In addition to being demoralizing, this wastes a lot of time and energy. Therefore, it is important to provide a reality check to the board and staff early in the process so everyone has a feel for what the budget picture might look like by the time the manager's recommended budget is presented.

Reality Check Case Study: Knowing Limitations Early Improves Decision-Making

The town manager and budget director in Hillsborough knew the upcoming budget was going to be tough and would likely require a significant tax rate increase. They worried the traditional financial overview that would be presented at the beginning of the annual budgetary planning retreat would not effectively paint a clear picture of the cuts and rate increases that would be needed. Most managers are cautious when describing the financial condition for an upcoming year. Thus, the town manager and budget director were aware that hearing the manager's warning that "this is going to be a tight year" understandably might not resonate with the board and staff.

Reality Check, *continued*

They decided to prepare a preliminary version of the budget showing each department's draft expenses, financial summaries by fund, multiyear fund balance projections, and other key information. The preliminary budget was given to the board two weeks before the retreat. Seeing the bottom-line deficits, decreasing fund balance projections, and significant cuts quickly set the tone that this was a serious situation. The board and staff focused their energy and problem-solving skills on the most important issues. Time was not wasted pursuing projects that were not financially feasible that year.

When the board, manager, and staff walked out the door of that retreat they had agreed on several critical steps. First, there was consensus on funding items to ensure daily operations continued to run smoothly. Early agreement on that portion of the budget freed up time and allowed everyone to focus on several other key issues: repaving streets, exploring options to better control employee health insurance costs, cutting the projected deficit, and working to minimize the pending tax rate increase. Because the retreat was in mid-February, there was plenty of time to explore options, as well as communicate and engage with the community, which was especially important because a big tax rate hike would not be popular with the community. Waiting until May, when proposed budgets are usually presented to the board, to deliver such news would have made a bad situation worse. A shorter time frame builds pressure, which is not conducive to good decision-making.

Hillsborough's approach made time an ally, reduced pressure that frequently builds up near budget adoption, allowed for more options to be explored during the following four months, and avoided surprising the board and public. The result was approval of a six-cent tax rate increase to fund a four-year street repaving surge to catch up on the maintenance backlog. This investment put the town on a twenty-year replacement cycle, repaving about five percent of the streets each year.

Public input, suggestions, and frustrations were shared early in the process. In communication to the public, an effort was made to clearly indicate where the additional funds were going to be spent and why. Internally, this is referred to as the "restaurant menu" approach. Even if something is more expensive than one would like, it is more acceptable when one knows what they are getting for their money. Minimal opposition was expressed at the public hearing and the meeting where the budget was adopted.

Designing the Retreat: Key Questions and Decisions

A successful budget process requires early planning and feedback from key stakeholders. This helps ensure critical issues are deliberated in a thoughtful manner that results in clear direction being provided to staff so they can develop a proposed budget that addresses the governing board's priorities. Attention must be paid to small logistical items to make this early planning session productive.

☑ **Facilitator.** When practical and affordable, having a facilitator is preferred. Having an independent party guide the meeting, ask questions, make observations that move the deliberations forward, and keep the group on track is often the difference between a successful and unsuccessful day and budget process. Facilitators are especially helpful in navigating boards through complex and emotional decisions. They can use exercises and techniques to focus the board, think through issues, add perspective, see the big picture, and identify opportunities and gaps, all while building camaraderie. There may be occasions when it is more practical to have the mayor, manager, assistant manager, or budget director facilitate the retreat. However, mayors and managers will likely feel that they are better able to listen, learn, understand, and participate when a facilitator leads these sessions.

☑ **Setting the agenda.** Most years bring unique challenges, and adjustments to the retreat format may be needed. Many local governments have a standard format to cover certain areas and then leave time for whatever issues may require the most attention. One year it may be relationships and communications with advisory boards. Another year it may be updating the objectives for the strategic plan, addressing capital needs, navigating through the COVID-19 pandemic, a recession, a downtown redevelopment project, or affordable housing. Whatever the format, the first step in the process is often the mayor or chair and manager informally discussing what they see as key issues and topics requiring board direction, as well as updates and information. The next step is the mayor or chair and manager seeking guidance from the board to hear their thoughts and suggestions on what they want to accomplish. Once that feedback is received, a draft agenda can be developed for the board to consider. At this point the facilitator may then get involved, helping refine the design of the retreat to address everyone's interests.

- **Advance information**. Providing information to the board well before the meeting (e.g., status of goals, issues faced, financial information, progress updates on current-year goals or strategic plan, operational reviews from departments, and capital needs) is a time saver by either eliminating or streamlining presentations to free up time for critical discussions. Board members are required to read a lot of information, so it is essential to give them plenty of time to prepare.

  It is easier to provide information or progress updates in advance on initiatives, goals, and programs that are funded in the current year's budget cycle compared to new issues for the upcoming fiscal year. Therefore, providing detailed information in advance of the retreat may not be reasonable to accomplish, or is rushed at the eleventh hour, depending on the topics the governing board wants to explore at the retreat. Ideally, providing advance information is the goal, but flexibility to allow for high-level strategic and conceptual discussions is necessary for exploring options at a retreat.

- **Homework assignment: priority-ranking key issues**. Ranking budget issues, such as new positions, capital projects, items, equipment, programs, possible tax rate increases, and previously unfunded items, can be given to board members as a homework assignment. Hillsborough often uses a format where board members rate each proposed budget issue by checking one of three boxes: support, do not support, or not sure/ want more information. They can also comment about what additional information they want to have. This prioritizes how the limited time available will be used. There is little benefit to talking for a long time about something everyone agrees upon. Everyone has limited attention, so it is essential that this be managed by narrowing discussion topics to those that are pivotal to the organization or where there are differing views that need to be deliberated. Boards often spend too much time on issues that do not make a difference and then do not have the energy to adequately tackle the big issues. Items on which the board is not unanimous and especially those on which they are split get discussed first to ensure there is adequate time to work through these key decisions. While this approach has been successful in Hillsborough, other communities may find that the priority ranking exercises are more effective if they are conducted at the retreat (as opposed to completed as homework assignments) following manager/staff providing information on the key issues (see Appendix A, "Budget Retreat—Issue Rating Form: Example from Hillsborough Fiscal Year 2017," at the end of this chapter).

☑ **Location.** Finding a place that is comfortable, free of distractions, and ideally different from the regular meeting room helps provide a fresh perspective and energy. If a regular meeting room must be used, consider re-arranging the setup to give it a different feel.

☑ **Seating.** The members of Hillsborough's board of commissioners sit in different locations for every board meeting. They started this practice over twenty years ago, believing it promotes engagement and allows them to see issues, as well as their colleagues, from different perspectives. Consider mixing up the seating assignments for the retreat if this is not something you already do. If possible, arrange the seats so everyone is positioned to easily see one another, such as in a horseshoe, circle, or rectangle, as this facilitates good discussions.

☑ **Staff involvement.** The Hillsborough board has always invited the management team (department heads and other key staff) to participate in the retreat. Staff and board member seating is intermingled to encourage free-flowing discussions, when it is appropriate for staff to participate. Having staff attend, listen, participate, and provide information on the spot has multiple benefits:

- Because staff carry out the board's directives, they walk out of the retreat with a better understanding of what needs to be accomplished and why. Much can be lost in translation from reading the minutes or listening to someone else describe the meeting.
- Questions, ideas, and requests for information regularly come up. The best time to respond to these board inquiries is immediately to keep the momentum of conversations going.
- A major threat to good decision-making is having tunnel vision, or an insider's view. What might sound good among a small group in a

meeting room on a Saturday morning may not be practical or affordable, and it could suffer from other terminal flaws. Companies testing products often seek outside perspectives to identify possible concerns. Staff can provide that type of valuable feedback, as well as share thoughts to make successfully carrying out the board's goals more likely.

- For this to work, staff and the board must reasonably stay in their lanes and respect each other's roles. The staff's job is to advise, recommend, and ultimately implement the board's direction. The board provides overarching policy and direction, as well as identifies key goals and objectives. There is always some overlap in these two lanes, more so in smaller local governments. If there is a level of comfort and respect for the lines, it can be helpful to have input from the board and staff into each other's lanes (i.e., the policy and operations worlds, respectively).

☑ **Financial overview.** This lets the board and department heads know what they can anticipate in terms of capacity for new additions going into the new fiscal year. Is this going to be a good year for expansions, lean with some new requests being funded, hold the line, or be severe enough that cuts to the base will be needed? It is helpful to remind everyone of high-priority unfunded needs. These can be expensive to fund, especially if cuts were necessary to get through the current year, such as replacements of vehicles, equipment, information technology items, and maintenance projects. Addressing a backlog of needs can be very expensive. This is a common problem that occurs as local governments emerge from recessions. Depending on the capacity of budget/finance staff, building financial models capable of incorporating "on-the-fly" adjustments to revenue and expense (incorporating new key issues from the governing board) assumptions can be great tools to facilitating retreat deliberations to arrive at a new "bottom line."

☑ **Showing the "bottom line" with just a continuation budget.** Just continuing what is being done today with nothing new other than essential priorities, such as regular replacement of vehicles, equipment, and infrastructure maintenance, is an easy way to show how much capacity the local government generally has for taking on new expenses. Seeing the available funds, or lack thereof, adds clarity to the process of prioritizing, identifying alternative or more affordable ways to address needs, and considering whether revenue increases should be considered.

☑ **Take plenty of breaks.** People's attention spans are limited, and others need to get up and move to stay alert. Taking breaks keeps people feeling fresh and provides opportunities for everyone to interact, get to know each other better, and have sidebar discussions without disrupting the group. Every retreat has at least one moment when upon restarting the meeting, someone speaks up and says they were just talking with another participant and they had some additional thoughts or ideas they want to share with the group. These breaks also allow the facilitator to assess how things are going and touch base with the mayor, chair, and/or manager to check in and make mid-course adjustments.

☑ **Closure and confirmation.** Before everyone walks out the door at the end of the day, make sure there is clarity on what is to be accomplished as well as the information and options that need to be brought back to the board. This seems obvious, but it is a regular occurrence when staff or the board are unsure or have differing interpretations of what was decided. Writing down key decision points and follow-up items for everyone to see during the meeting is critical. The inclusion of those points in the minutes or summary of the meeting will be a reference guide that is returned to later when working on the budget, as well as when preparing for the next year's budget retreat. The last task of the day is to identify lessons learned that can be applied to make future retreats better.

Initial Budget-Balancing Steps

Once the board provides direction at the retreat, it is time to get working on developing the budget. Again, there is no one right way to develop a balanced budget. New challenges or circumstances often call for a revised approach. The steps listed below provide a general baseline that can be adjusted.

1. **Project revenues.** Forecast estimate revenues for the upcoming year initially without the use of rate increases or savings (fund balance or retained earnings).

2. **Total expenditure requests**. There are two basic approaches for how this can be done:
   - Option 1: Include all requests. The initial deficit will be much larger with this approach.
   - Option 2: Continuation budget approach. Only include items that would be part of keeping currently funded operations funded; thus, expenses for new programs, capital, and personnel will be left out. The "continuation budget" prioritizes taking care of what is needed to responsibly run the operations, such as replacing worn-out vehicles and equipment, maintaining assets, training employees, and ensuring salaries and benefits are competitive for retaining and recruiting talent. Any request that is not part of the continuation budget is considered an expansion item and initially placed on a department's "unfunded" list.

3. **Forecasting approach for revenues and expenditures**. The safest and most common method for developing a balanced budget is slightly underestimating revenues and overestimating expenses. Find the balance between being reasonably conservative and avoiding excessive padding, because ending the fiscal year with an excessive surplus or deficit can hurt your credibility due to the lack of forecasting accuracy. That credibility is put to task at fiscal year-end when audited financials reflect favorable/unfavorable variances between budget and actual revenues and expenditures adding to

or subtracting from fund balance; when an organization consistently misses those year-end projections by material amounts, a board's confidence in the budgetary forecasts may wane. This can result in critical needs not being funded. Capital purchases and projects can occur more than a year later, so often cost more than projected. Providing a little extra buffer for these and similar types of expenses avoids having to find money mid-year, which can be problematic. If the year ends better than expected, then surplus funds go to fund balance, which is always a challenge to maintain or build, so that is a good problem to have. There may be a significant decline in some revenue sources or unexpected expenses, such as having to replace a fire or garbage truck that gets totaled. Cutting the margins too close limits the budget's ability to absorb surprises. Finding the right balance between overly cautious and overly optimistic is always an ongoing struggle. This is further complicated when developing a balanced budget relies on expense reporting from so many different people in departments and divisions throughout an organization.

4. **Determine the bottom line (i.e., size of projected deficit or surplus).** After projecting revenues, determine how much fund balance, if any, can safely be appropriated, as well as any other funding sources, such as capital reserve fund allocation. That will identify the expenditure limit or what the "cost of government" will be for each fund. Show the impact on the fund balance or savings levels: both the net dollar amount and percentage. (See Appendix B, "Town of Hillsborough General Fund Summary," at the end of this chapter for an example. The "Fund Balance Appropriation Needed to Balance the Budget" and "Available Fund Balance Remaining" values are indicated with red arrows.) Hillsborough uses a three-year format, so when working toward balancing the budget its focus is not just on developing a fiscally responsible plan for the upcoming budget (referred to as Year 1), but also for the long term (i.e., the budget needs to look acceptable by Year 3). This helps avoid surprises, discourages making decisions with a short-term view, and provides more time for problem-solving.

5. **Learn more about requests**. This is done by thoroughly reading the justifications and meeting with departments to understand their needs, opportunities, problems, and alternatives being considered; identifying collaboration opportunities between certain departments; observing trends; and seeing the challenges from the departments' point of view.

6. **Refinement**. On the expense side, refinement is done via cuts, deferments, phased implementations, and creative solutions. On the revenue side, refinement is usually done by exploring the impact of increasing property taxes, solid waste, water, sewer, electric, or other fees. The use of debt instruments to fund expenses, in lieu of using cash or a pay-as-you-go approach, can also be inputted at this time. After each round of adjustments, keep going back to the summary page for the fund to see the impact on the bottom line until the deficit and fund balance numbers are within target range or policy.

7. **Check financial parameters.** In addition to fund balance levels, it is important to consider some key financial metrics to ensure a fiscally responsible budget is being proposed. Some examples of financial parameters include the following:

☑ **Taxes and user charges.** If your local government already has a high property tax rate, increasing it may not be an option for generating additional revenue.

☑ **Multiyear impact.** How does the financial forecast look down the road? Just because you can "get by" this year does not mean the budget is fiscally responsible if Year 3 of the forecast is projecting serious challenges.

☑ **Debt levels.** Check to ensure the debt load is within adopted policies, benchmark against other local governments, and verify that proposed new debt will not crowd out the ability to fund core services in the future.[2]

Benchmarking and Information Sources for North Carolina Local Governments

The "Financial Analysis Tools and Reports" page of the North Carolina Department of State Treasurer's website has links to key tools that provide helpful guidance regarding your budget preparation.[3]

☑ **Other sources are listed as follows:**

• **North Carolina county and municipal finance information.** This provides detailed financial information by governmental entity that comes from the Annual Financial Information Report (AFIR), which is reported to the Local Government Commission.

• **Benchmarking tool for North Carolina counties and municipalities.** This allows each governmental entity to generate a custom report comparing its performance on key financial metrics against as many as five other units.[4]

---

2. North Carolina Department of State Treasurer, State and Local Government Finance Division, *Analysis of Debt of North Carolina Counties at 6-30-2020* (February 4, 2021), https://files.nc.gov/nctreasurer/documents/files/SLGFD/LGC/LocalGovDebtMngmt/debtanalysisreport.pdf. This report provides ratios of total outstanding debt, per capita debt, and other summary debt-related data by county and municipality, as well as jurisdiction population. Additional debt comparison information can be found in the "Benchmarking and Information Sources for North Carolina Local Governments" section of this chapter; this information can help you assess the financial and budgetary conditions of your local government. If there is no one on your staff that can do these assessments, then contact your auditor; staff at the Local Government Commission; the University of North Carolina at Chapel Hill School of Government; or an experienced finance director from another town, city, or county.

3. "Financial Reports and Analysis Tools," North Carolina Department of State Treasurer: State and Local Government Finance Division, https://logos.nctreasurer.com/Reporting/Report/External?applicationCode=AFIR.

4. Ibid.

- **North Carolina Water and Wastewater Rates Dashboard.** This tool is prepared by the Environmental Finance Center of the School of Government at the University of North Carolina, Chapel Hill (hereinafter UNC School of Government). Benchmark information regarding rates, affordability, comparison of bills, cost recovery, debt service coverage ratio, quick ratio, days of cash on hand, cash flow, debt-to-equity ratio, and asset depreciation are all included, and other key metrics are all presented in an easy-to-understand format.[5]
- **North Carolina Stormwater Fee Dashboard.** This tool is prepared by the UNC School of Government's Environmental Finance Center.[6] This dashboard is a statewide stormwater fee survey that lists, compares, and analyzes the different fee structures across the state. These structures paint a picture of North Carolina's stormwater management priorities and can be used as an educational tool for communities across the state.

Funding Priorities—First, Take Care of What You Have!

How do you decide what stays and gets cut in the budget? The answer differs depending on the year, issues, economy, direction provided by the governing board at the budgetary planning retreat, and other factors. For many years in Hillsborough, the manager and budget team have used four priorities (listed below) as a guide during the first passes of the budget to determine what stays in. This priority list is regularly shared with the board, so board members are familiar with the manager's approach.

Before new items are added into the proposed budget, the funding needs that fall into the category of "take care of what we have" take precedence. This prevents essential needs from being crowded out by shiny new items. Failure to provide proper resources for operational and service needs ultimately costs more over the long haul. Over the years, Hillsborough's mayors and boards have adopted "take care of what we've got" as its unofficial budget motto. The phrase is included and explained in every budget message from the town manager, is frequently brought up during internal discussions among departments, and is regularly referenced by the board and some advisory boards during meetings throughout the year.

1. **Safety and legal mandates.** The most important part of a local government's operations is that all employees go home safely each day and that no citizens are hurt as a result of the way those operations are run. A few

---

5. "North Carolina Water and Wastewater Rates Dashboard," UNC School of Government Environmental Finance Center, last modified March 4, 2020, https://efc.sog.unc.edu/resource/north-carolina-water-and-wastewater-rates-dashboard.

6. "2019-20 North Carolina Stormwater Fee Dashboard," UNC School of Government Environmental Finance Center, https://efc.sog.unc.edu/resource/2019-20-north-carolina-stormwater-fee-dashboard.

examples include implementing guidelines for confined space entry equipment and providing personal protective equipment (PPE), driver safety training, automated external defibrillators (AED) at facilities, work zone safety equipment and training, Occupational Safety and Health Administration (OSHA) and industry standard practices, providing clean and safe water for the community to drink, and many other related needs. This also includes legal mandates the local government must comply with or implement. Funding legitimate safety needs and legal mandates is considered the "no option" plan when it comes to running local government operations.

2. **Maintaining current service levels.** Continuing daily operations and providing resources to ensure core service delivery is not compromised. Even a "base" or "continuation budget" should require some level of scrutiny. There should be a "check-in" on the efficiency/effectivenes of items that are currently funded to ensure they are still adding value and are still a higher priority than unfunded requests.

3. **Infrastructure, vehicles, equipment, and personnel.** These four items are the foundation of local government operations. A local government's mission, vision, strategic priorities, and objectives cannot be implemented if these basic items are not in working order. The longer a municipality waits to address, repair, or replace these assets (tangible and intangible), the more expensive the issues become over the long term. The American Society of Civil Engineers' (ASCE) Infrastructure Report Cards assign grades to how well assets are maintained. It is rare when governments receive higher than a C for maintaining the most important and expensive assets in their communities. The ASCE's most recent update gives the country's infrastructure an overall rating of a D-plus.[7] Infrastructure Report Cards are important reminders that the construction of new assets must be balanced with having skilled personnel, equipment, and organizational structure to operate and maintain these assets. Achieving that balance is critical in avoiding the overextension of resources.

    Finally, for employees to be efficient and effective in carrying out their duties it is essential they have the right tools to do the job. These include training, competitive pay, and benefits. If their vehicles and equipment are regularly in the shop, that wastes time and compromises service quality to the community. Ultimately, for tools and equipment to be effective the people operating them must be skilled and experienced; thus, retaining and recruiting talent is a priority.

4. **Efficiency improvements.** Taking advantage of opportunities to fund items that save money over the long term is a must. It is so easy to overlook the

---

7. For more information about the ASCE's 2021 Report Card, see https://infrastructurereportcard.org/infrastructure-categories/.

importance of life cycle costing in operations when trying to make cuts to balance the budget. Spending more on the initial upfront purchases, conducting more training, or performing additional maintenance can cost less and save money over time. The following are just a few examples to consider:

- ☑ **Vehicles and equipment.** Factor in reliability, frequency, and cost of repairs (time and dollars), fuel mileage, and re-sale value when sold as surplus. The American Public Works Association publishes a vehicle replacement guide that assigns points based on age, miles/hours, type of service, reliability, maintenance and repair costs, condition, and energy efficiency.[8] Many jurisdictions have tailored the guide's fundamentals to their circumstances.

- ☑ **Water tank construction or most other capital projects.** Life cycle costing, even at a rudimentary level, should be a part of capital cost analysis. Calculate the difference in maintenance costs. For instance, going the less expensive route up front to build a tank with four metal legs, cross-bracing, and a center pipe will require regular scrapping and repainting over the life of the tank. Have engineers assess the life cycle costs when building its most recent water tank. Taking the more expensive option with the near maintenance-free concrete base, instead of all the exposed metal supports and pipe, can be less expensive.

- ☑ **Roof repair.** The cost difference between twenty and thirty-year shingles is often not much, so the small additional dollar investment may be worth it.

- ☑ **Streets.** Studies have shown that repaving streets on a twenty-year rather than a thirty-year or more schedule is more cost-effective.

- ☑ **Driver safety training.** Providing driver safety training for police and other operations may seem like an unnecessary expense, but it may be a worthwhile investment when compared to the costs of increased insurance and lawsuit settlements. Reviewing your organization's risk or experience modifiers for workers' compensation and property and liability insurance coverage will help evaluate opportunities for long-term cost savings.

Deficit Management

Identifying the severity and reason for the deficit determines the approach used to balance the budget. If the deficit is modest, the usual tactics of trimming expenses by line items, tamping down expense projections that have too much padding, refining revenue projections, using a small amount of fund balance, or considering modest increases to rates and taxes frequently get the budget where it needs to be. Big deficits

---

8. The guide can be purchased at https://www.apwa.net/store/detail.aspx?id=PB.A1223.

> **Traditional Deficit Reduction Strategies**
>
> ☑ Trim expenses.
>
> ☑ Defer lower-priority requests to future years.
>
> ☑ Delay capital purchases.
>
> ☑ Structure debt so the first payment is pushed out to the next fiscal year or later in the budget year so only one payment is due instead of two.
>
> ☑ Spread projects over several years due to limited organizational capacity and funds.
>
> ☑ Raise property taxes, fees, and/or rates.
>
> ☑ Appropriate from savings.
>
> ☑ Use debt financing, such as a lease-purchase agreement to pay for a capital item that you would otherwise pay cash for.
>
> ☑ Reduce, delay, or eliminate employee raises.

require a strategy shift due to complexity and because so much is at stake for the organization and community. Eliminating a large gap is not going to be attainable by chiseling away at line items a few hundred dollars at a time, much like trying to bail out a ship taking on a lot of water by using a small bucket.

Use caution before implementing "across-the-board cuts" and "freezing vacancies." Some organizations use across-the-board cuts and freezing vacancies as deficit reduction strategies, such as implementing a 5 percent reduction to all departments. One problem with this tactic is that local government departmental operations vary greatly. For some departments, the arbitrary reduction figure will be easy to attain; they will not need to make much effort to improve efficiency. For others it will not be possible due to mandatory service requirements, debt payments, and other reasons. This approach also does not take organizational priorities into consideration. A process by which the organization validates vacant positions prior to posting and recruitment is a more effecitve approach than a simple blanket policy of freezing positions.

Is it wise to make the same level of cuts to an organization's highest priorities and services as to the lowest? Being effective requires thought, planning, and engagement with those most impacted by the actions to craft an approach that is practical and achieves the desired results.

Revenue increases. Raising property taxes, solid waste, recycling, and vehicle fees are options for balancing the general fund budget or at least reducing the deficit. In enterprise funds, increases to stormwater, electric, water, or sewer rates, as well as updating system development fees, are other options. Assuming that expenditures are reasonable and address critical needs, modest rate increases can often bring the budget into balance. It can be tempting to put off tax or rate increases, but if this is done for too many years then the local government can put itself in an even worse situation, often solved with large rate increases. Many utilities, as well as bond-rating agencies, prefer to see smaller but more frequent increases to avoid this trap.

Savings. If a local government has been disciplined in maintaining strong savings levels, then using fund balances, retrained earnings, or capital reserve moneys may be an option to help get the organization through tough times, particularly for non-recurring expenses. It should *not* be the only way to fill the deficit, and a plan must be developed to ensure the organization does not become dependent on savings to balance the budget in future years.

In the aftermath of a natural disaster, during or after a recession, raising taxes and rates may not be an option. This is another reason to protect the organization's reserves. When local governments become overly reliant on savings to balance the budget, the reserve level may drop so low that no more can be appropriated. Thus, when you need the funds the most, they are not available. Then, the problem has gone from bad to worse. Reserves and savings can be spent quickly but often take a long time to rebuild.

COVID-19, recessions, the loss of a major employer or industry, and natural disasters are reminders of how fast problems that affect budgets can hit. Having elected officials and staff both understand the importance of maintaining solid reserve levels for emergencies, economic crises, and special opportunities is critical. Saying no to using fund balance when things are going well can be hard, but it is worth it when times are tough to have enough money in the bank to help during a crisis. The Town of Topsail Beach, North Carolina, was disciplined about maintaining strong savings levels in all its funds (e.g., general, water, and erosion control). When Hurricanes Bertha and Fran hit, only seven weeks apart in 1996, the town was able to respond quickly and had more options at its disposal because officials had the resources to fund their recovery efforts.

Making difficult decisions today keeps your organization fiscally strong, preserves its flexibility, and prepares it for tomorrow's unforeseen challenges. Or, simply stated, it is easier to stay out of trouble than to get out of trouble. Therefore, developing policies to guide how much reserves to maintain is critical for local governments, such as fund balance percentage of operating expenses, days of cash on hand for enterprise funds, and others. This guidance is important for informing the public, newly elected officials, and staff about the best and safe practices for local government finance. Having and adhering to these policies are some of the core factors credit rating agencies consider when evaluating a local government for a bond issuance.

Prior to the town manager's arrival in Hillsborough in 1997, the town had deferred property tax and water and sewer rate increases for years. Fund balance and retained earnings were regularly used to balance the budget. This was done even though the finance director sent memorandums to the board cautioning against this practice. Months later, when preparing the budget using a three-year format, the new manager discovered the town was approximately eighteen months away from being bankrupt in both funds if the board continued to follow the same approach. To get out of this situation, the board had to raise property taxes by seven cents. Water and sewer rates were increased by 23.5 percent. Additional increases were needed in subsequent years to put Hillsborough back in good financial standing.

Big Deficit: More Complex Strategies to Balancing the Budget

When the organization finds itself in a predicament that cannot be solved with traditional approaches, such as expenditures cuts to lower-priority items and slight increases to revenues, then it is time to consider a more elaborate strategy. The areas below provide options to consider when organizations are facing significant deficits and crises.

☑ **Communication.** Sharing information to get out in front of the questions that will be raised during challenging situations is essential to make everyone aware of what is happening. When employees and elected officials are informed, involved, and given the opportunity to participate in coming up with solutions, that is often a key ingredient to success. Opening those lines of communication and inviting feedback should be done every year; this makes a crisis more manageable, as feedback is part of the way organizations best solve problems. The same is true when it comes to informing the public of unpopular deficit reduction strategies, such as service reductions, project delays, and rate increases.

Most organizations do a good job getting information to the board regarding key budget issues, especially during the budgetary planning retreat, workshops, and all the way through to adoption. The missing link is often not involving and informing employees at all levels of the organization. This is a missed opportunity as employees, especially at the line and supervisory levels, have the best vantage point for seeing what works, what does not, and what may be successful going forward. The Town of Hillsborough involves employees at all levels in two ways:

- **Departmental retreats**. These retreats involve all or most employees. They usually take place between November and February to prepare for the upcoming budget planning and submittals. During this time, departments conduct an operational review to identify broken functions or processes, non-value-added activities that should stop, operational challenges, and budget requests to address issues raised in the reviews.
- **Budget preview for employees.** Each year the manager gives a presentation for all employees about the budget to share key issues, decision points and funding items, and invite feedback. Depending on the year and issues, the preview may take place right after the council's budgetary planning retreat or just before the proposed budget is presented to the board. Knowing what is being proposed makes it easier for employees to share concerns and alternatives before adoption is considered. The presentation is also recorded so employees who cannot attend can watch the video at their convenience. During the COVID-19 pandemic, the manager made short videos to share information with employees, and email updates were provided.

Communication and Process Improvement: Navigating the Great Recession

In the early stages of the Great Recession, Hillsborough's town manager and budget director toured all of the town's governmental departments and divisions, sharing a presentation to describe the challenge facing the town. The presentation included examples everyone could relate to, not just deficit projections. For example, the presentation described how many new homes and/or millions of dollars in new development were required just to cover employee raises each year. This was at a time when almost no new construction was happening. Sharing benchmarking comparisons on staffing to other local governments, the cost to residents in taxes and rates each year, and other examples added context. Painting a clear picture in relatable terms got employees invested in the process of containing costs and redesigning operations to get the town through the crisis.

Guidelines from the Toyota Production System were shared (e.g., the five whys, root cause analysis, flowcharting), along with other principles.[a] "How-to" steps and forms were provided to all employees and departments, making it easier to identify, explain, and submit cost savings ideas. About 160 ideas were submitted the first year. Each idea was logged onto a spreadsheet so everyone could provide feedback and see the status of each proposal. Departments presented their cost containment and operational redesign ideas to the manager. The biggest changes were then reviewed at the budgetary planning retreat for further consideration. Many ideas were implemented and helped Hillsborough balance the budgets for the next several years. Over a two-year period, about 15 percent of general fund positions were eliminated. Fortunately, all but one position elimination was achieved through vacancies or reassignments.

---

a. Jeffrey K. Liker, *The Toyota Way, 14 Management Principles from the World's Greatest Manufacturer* (New York: McGraw-Hill, 2004).

☑ **Process improvement efforts.** These efforts, including lean production,[9] the Toyota Production System,[10] and similar approaches, emphasize waste elimination, streamlining, time savings, and simplification and can play a pivotal role in developing practical solutions during a budget crisis. To be successful in generating ideas and options, evaluating alternatives, and getting buy-in, organization-wide employee involvement is a must. Experts say that for most efficiency efforts to work, there must be known constraints to get buy-in to the initiative. There is nothing like a clearly acknowledged financial crisis to get everyone on the same page, such as the Great Recession, the COVID-19 pandemic, or a natural disaster. Businesses have the universally understood goal of making a profit. Local governments have so many diverse goals it is difficult to get everyone focused on the same mission. A budget crisis may be the closest thing local governments get to a unified vision. During these times, most understand the importance of streamlining to keep core operations going while minimizing layoffs.

---

9. *Wikipedia*, s.v. "Lean Government," last modified September 29, 2020, 22:38, https://en.wikipedia.org/wiki/Lean_government.

10. Jeffrey K. Liker, *The Toyota Way, 14 Management Principles from the World's Greatest Manufacturer* (New York: McGraw-Hill, 2004).

> **Great Recession—Town of Hillsborough: General Guidelines to Departments for Developing Cost Containment Options**
>
> - <u>Use a strategy map</u> for guidance in determining how to pursue priorities and which priorities to pursue.
>
> - <u>Plans should be practical and make sense over the long term.</u> Think investment (i.e., delaying needed asset maintenance or replacement is "robbing Peter to pay Paul.").
>
> - <u>Continue investing in employees</u> via providing training, growth, and experience opportunities.
>
> - If eliminating positions becomes necessary, <u>keeping current personnel employed will be a top priority.</u> Thus, not filling vacant positions and developing transitional strategies are ways to save money to protect employee jobs. Employees have the knowledge and creativity necessary to refine operations. Therefore, <u>if personnel are expected to develop viable cost containment options today, they must have the comfort of knowing they will have a job tomorrow!</u>
>
> - Staffing reductions can be done through (1) natural attrition, (2) transfers, (3) severance agreements for employees interested in early retirements or career changes, and (4) assistance in finding career or growth opportunities with other organizations. Also, if the position of an employee in good standing is eliminated, then the individual will be given six months' advance notice of the elimination.
>
> - <u>Use benchmarking data and other sources to seek out examples</u> from other local governments and businesses that could succeed in Hillsborough.

☑ **Departmental budget targets.** When there is not enough time to ramp up a formal process improvement initiative, simply letting departments know how much money they have in their budget can generate effective results. For this approach to work, departmental budgets need to be reviewed in advance by the budget, finance, or manager's office to determine if the target amount is reasonable. For example, the public works department may be assigned a target of $3.2 million. It is then up to the director to submit a budget that does not exceed that amount. Hillsborough used this approach with great success for several years during the Great Recession. It was also popular with the department and division heads, town manager, and budget director for the following reasons:

- Control: Departments have more control and a voice in the changes being made to their budgets.
- Creativity: Decision-making is pushed to those most impacted by the cuts, as they are best equipped to prioritize cuts and generate innovative solutions.
- Engagement: The approach involves more levels of the organization because those that are most affected, frontline staff and those delivering services, play a key role in collaborating to develop ideas and options, as well as prioritizing what stays in the budget and what gets cut, reduced, modified, or delayed to a future year to stay within the allocated resources.

- Time savings: The approach allows for less back and forth with the manager and budget team.
- Flexibility: Mid-year changes were allowed when opportunities and new ideas emerged, which spurred creative solutions year-round, not just during budget development.
- Results: Employees regularly went to department heads and management with new and creative ideas year-round. There were so many ideas implemented that the town created an "Employee Innovation, Customer Service, and Endurance Awards" program to recognize these efforts, as well as encourage this mindset in the organization's culture.

☑ **Identifying strategic "bridges" and "band-aids."** These ideas can turn into long-term efficiency improvements or just serve as short-term patches to get through a crisis. The terms "band-aids" and "bridges" have become part of Hillsborough's lexicon during times of crisis when it comes to finding solutions to closing budgetary gaps. There are always far more wants, needs, and opportunities than funding, so stretching available dollars is a constant priority. Instead of building a new police station estimated to cost millions of dollars, in 2020 Hillsborough repurposed a vacant building it owned adjacent to the police department headquarters for about $300,000. For a small fraction of the cost of a new building, this bridge likely deferred the need for a new station another ten years, thus freeing resources to address other high-priority needs. A similar approach is being pursued to meet the need for a new public works facility, but with a much longer life span. Implementing the ideal or best solution is often not possible. Finding an approach that meets many needs opens up many options that are far more affordable; these are often referred to as "80 percent solutions."

☑ **Free up time for critical thinking and analysis.** Working through budget challenges can be overwhelming for everyone involved. It is critical that leaders, such as the mayor, board, management, and department heads, encourage everyone to find significant blocks of quiet time so staff can focus without interruptions to make progress on these critical decisions. It is almost impossible to be creative and do tedious analytical work when there are regular interruptions.

Decision-Making Reminders

It is easy to get impatient and want to move on to the next issue in the budget process, especially if most people appear to agree. Reviewing key traits involved in good decision-making can avoid big mistakes. The three steps below are frequently referenced in decision-making guides. While it is nice to have all key decisions made before the budget is adopted in June, that is not always possible.

Generate Options

☑ Exploring even one or two other ways to approach a situation greatly improves the odds of success. Critical thinking and brainstorming allow an organization to explore if there is a better and/or more efficient solution available. This helps avoid tunnel vision and missing out on better options or modifications that would improve the original proposal.

☑ What is the opportunity cost? Or, what are you giving up to fund a given item? When debating whether to include an item in the budget, consider if there are other items that would make a bigger impact on the organization or community. Too often we get fixated on one item, program, or request and forget about all the other needs or opportunities that could be funded. For example, if the request under consideration is to fund a new full-time position, the debate can easily get focused on whether to add this position. Pulling back from that item and looking at other unfunded requests often adds critical context. It may be that building a small section of sidewalk to address a long-standing pedestrian safety hazard turns out to be more important. Replacing a piece of equipment that is regularly breaking down is just another example.

Verify

☑ Confirm the information, analysis, data, and assumptions are correct. This helps counter confirmation bias, halo effects, or horn effects by more objectively evaluating issues regarding requests we initially view favorably or unfavorably. Bad or worst-case scenarios are too often glossed over or not even considered.

☑ Obtain an accurate cost picture. Identify the longer-term cost, such as five years or even the full life cycle if it is a capital item. For example, in the case of a position, after totaling the salary, benefits, vehicle, maintenance, fuel, insurance, equipment, computer, training, workers' compensation, and other expenses, it turns out what appeared to be a $50,000 salary per year is really $80,000 annually over the next five years, or $400,000. Then, the debate can expand to looking at what other unfunded items would benefit the organization or community even more given those financial parameters.

Time to Reflect: Slower Is Faster

☑ Using baking a cake as a metaphor for the evaluation process, a previous assistant town manager frequently said, "we need to let it bake," meaning that the process should not be rushed. This reduces emotion and helps avoid impulse purchases, such as when shopping. During the budget process, it is rare that there are urgent matters that must be decided on the spot. Continuing a discussion to the next meeting or some later time allows for reflection, additional research or data gathering, and new options to be developed.

☑ If more time is needed to make a well-informed decision, evaluate options, and consider how a project could go wrong, then delay action on those items. A common phrase used in the racing or motorsports world applies to budgeting: "Slower is faster!" It is much easier to avoid a mistake than to do damage control and clean up a mess afterwards, especially when public dollars are involved. Budget amendments are easy enough to make later in the year, so definitely take advantage of the ability to stretch out the window of time needed to evaluate requests.

What Makes a Good Budget Request?

A local government can have excellent strategies, goals, performance measures, and tactics on how to balance the budget, but ultimately the foundation that determines how effective the organization is at evaluating its priorities, needs, risks, and opportunities boils down to the quality of the justifications for budget requests. Some departments and individuals excel at preparing requests that make compelling cases. Their forms and supporting documents are well-written; integrate pictures and graphics; cite studies, performance measures, and statistics; and refer to your organization's mission, vision, value, and goals. Other departments and individuals are going to struggle to make a good case, but that does not mean their request is not as or more important than ones presented in a more polished fashion.

The goal is to fund the highest priorities, not the priorities that were presented in the best manner. Still, to help management and ultimately the board make a well-informed decision, requests need to effectively anticipate and respond to key questions (i.e., the why, what, when, where, how, and how much, as well as "What happens if you do not fund this?"). Therefore, it is critical the organization provide support to ensure most requests, especially critical ones, state a strong and clear case describing the need. This is a key part of the teamwork that is needed to run a successful organization.

Everyone has different skill sets and areas of expertise. Departmental staff are the subject matter experts, and they know the intricacies of how equipment, processes, and service delivery work in actual practice. The manager, budget office, or finance office are often not familiar with the technical details surrounding operational requests to do an effective job stating the case. However, their familiarity with the budget process, key decision-making factors, and presentations allows them to be a good resource to partner with departments to develop strong justifications to review and base decisions. As budget and operational staff work together, they become more effective in learning about operations, issues, needs, and how to get things done. Over time, this improves communication, increases knowledge, encourages appreciation of everyone's roles, helps work get done faster, and ultimately provides better information for everyone.

Appendix A. Budget Retreat—Issue Rating Form: Example from Hillsborough Fiscal Year 2017

Budget Planning Worksheet, Part I: General Fund and Personnel

#	Issue/Proposal	Cost	Support	Don't Support	Not Sure: Want Alternatives or Additional Information
	Projects/Facilities/Initiatives				
1	*Street Repaving* – Funding keeps streets on 20-year or 5% cycle.	$350,000			
2	*New Town Hall Annex & Meeting Room/ Town Barn retrofit* to Clerk/HR/Other offices. Also provides space for additional planner, stormwater staff, and mayor. Billing & Collections from Water Fund contributes $200,000. Should provide room for Town Engineer, utility analyst, and utility inspector in new Annex.	$750,000			
3	*Skateboard park:* annual debt service or funds for land acquisition or other related use starting FY18.	FY18+: $15,000			
4	*Pedestrian improvement engineering studies* US70 and Churton Street from Corbin to US70. Local match allows the Town to leverage DOT funding.	$25,000			
5	*Fiber Loop* – connect all town facilities, create backbone that can serve as next step in bringing high-speed internet to Hillsborough.	$1,000,000			
6	*Public Works facility relocation*: facility in flood plain, small, old, & poor condition. Moves PW to NC86N facility + vehicle shelters. Design: $50,000 (FY16), $10,000 design (FY17). Debt starts FY17 with ½ payment, full payments start in FY18.	FY17: $10,000 FY17: $32,376 FY18+: $64,752			
7	*Public Safety Station* (police, fire, fire marshal, & EOC) – **delay** start of design from FY18 to FY19.	$500,000 split over two years			
8	**Historic Properties Coffee Table Book (UNFUNDED)**. $5,000 for first phase in FY17 is funded. The remaining $62,500 for FY18-19 is unfunded.	$5,000			

Budget Planning Worksheet, Part I *(continued)*

#	Issue/Proposal	Cost	Support	Don't Support	Not Sure: Want Alternatives or Additional Information
	Projects/Facilities/Initiatives				
	Vehicles/Equipment				
9	*Police vehicles*: $70,000 to replace 2 aging patrol vehicles + equipment. *Replacing 17- & 18-year-old Crown Vics.*	FY17: $70,000			
10	*Public Works equipment:* all will be purchased via a combined 5-year master installment purchase/loan. • *Knuckle-boom truck* replaces 18 yr. old unit. • *Dump truck* replaces 1991 unit. • *Vibratory roller* replace 15 year old unit, and vibrating roller superior for patching.	$140,000 $110,000 $52,000			
11	*Parks & Public Lands Crew* – Truck, mowers, trailers, and other equipment.	$86,850			
12	*Police:* replace outdated in-car video systems Page 170.	$48,000			
	Personnel (All departments)				
1	*Merit Pay* 3.25% average raise (up to 4.0% max + up to two 1/3rd bonus points for noteworthy achievements. Mgt. Team <u>not</u> eligible for bonus pts.	$70,000 (GF) $50,000 (WSF)			
2	*ORFD Personnel Transfer + Full-time fire chief*	$150,000			
3	*Compensation & Classification Study* – essential if ORFD personnel transfer looks as if it may occur. HPD salaries are out of line, hurting recruiting, possible retention issues, other positions need evaluation compared to market, and multiple positions are being considered for re-class due to taking on responsibility beyond the job description.	$100,000 (GF) $35,000 (WSF)			
4	*Re-organization/Create Parks & Public Lands Div.* – Move project planner over new Parks & Public Lands Division, hire planner to replace her position, add three-person grounds maintenance crew. Add supervisor position in FY19. New planner would not start until late in FY17 (May 2017).	**New planner** FY17: $7,000 in FY18: $55,800 **3-person crew** FY17: $57,766 FY18: $137,654			
5	*Accounts Payable Clerk* (Finance) – address workload and cross-training/back-up needs. Starts mid-FY17. Full cost in FY18.	FY17: $20,461 FY18: $43,561			
6	*Stormwater Program Coordinator* – to replace current coordinator who will be promoted to Stormwater Manager. FY17 costs will be less than projected costs since position won't start until approx. Sept 1.	$72,038.			

#	Issue/Proposal	Cost	Support	Don't Support	Not Sure: Want Alternatives or Additional Information
	Projects/Facilities/Initiatives				
7	*Equipment Operator (Stormwater)* – assigned to public works but represents the amount of time, in projected personnel hours, the department will spend on stormwater maintenance.	$48,344			
8	*Water Plant Operator (part-time)* – uses retired operator to fill in when other operators are out due to sick, vacation, or training.	$26,913			
9	*Training Manager (part-time) Police* – uses veteran officer on reserve that is certified instructor to coordinate HPD training and continue implementation of "make every day a training day" initiative.	$25,000			
10	*Fire Inspector* – requested for FY17, **not funded** due to potential transfer of ORFD personnel to town that can assist with inspections. If transfer does not occur, then inspector position may be added back for FY18 or FY19.	$80,783 (includes vehicle)			
11	*Management Analyst* (Administration) – requested for FY17, **delayed to FY19.**	FY19: $61,275			
12	*Police Officers* – 2 requested for FY18, **delayed to FY19.** This would add 4 officers in FY19.	$114,000			
13	*Debt Management Analyst* (Finance) – request for FY18, **delayed to FY19.**	FY19: $58,831			
14	*Park Superintendent* –requested FY17, **delayed to FY19**. Supervises 3-person crew, focuses on parks and public lands, reports to new Parks & Public Lands Mgr.	FY19: $77,353			
15	*Property Maintenance Workers (2)* – Distr. & Collect. Requested for FY17, **delayed to FY19.**	FY19: $82,000 + Vehicle: $35,000			
16	*Water Plant (2)* – Operator and Mechanic: **delayed to FY18 and FY19.**	$97,469			

Budget Planning Worksheet, Part II
Water and Sewer Fund, All Revenues, New Additions and Cuts

#	Issue/Proposal	Cost/Savings	Support	Don't Support	Not Sure: Want Alternatives or Additional Information
	Projects/Facilities/Initiatives				
1	NC86 Water line improvements – critical link to south zone, assists central pressure zone, conx from Hampton Pt, to Meadowlands, to Forest Ridge area.	$90,000			
2	_Reservoir Phase II – Construction._ $8.3 million, 15 – 20-year loan.	FY18: annual debt $638,072			
3	_Northern Zone Loop_ – eliminates system gaps, greater pressure to Orange HS & Churton Grove.	FY17: $50,000			
4	_Inflow & Infiltration_ (I&I) – sewer line/system repairs, reduce flow into the system & WWTP. On-going line item.	$50,000 annually			
5	_Effluent Aeration Equipment_ at WWTP – increase oxygen levels, avoid violations, save energy.	$253,000			
6	_Generator permanently mounted at raw water intake_: Eliminates need to move/connect large portable unit during outages so water plant can get water from intake at Lake Ben Johnson for treatment.	$80,000			
7	_Old Water Plant/Line Crew Ops Facility Expansion:_ additional space for staff as the town grows. Currently only one bathroom for about 18 staff, lack of adequate heating and cooling.	FY18: $50,000 (design) FY19: $330,000			
8	_Water Plant Expansion – Design:_ **Delayed**, won't start until FY20.	FY20: $50,000 FY21: $400,000			
	Vehicles/Equipment				
9	_Misc. truck replacements_. • Meter readers • Line crews – 2 trucks.	$28,000 $70,000			
10	_Tractor_ w/ enclosed cab, addresses safety issues, shared with line crews and public works.	$64,000			
11	_Jet-Vac Truck_ replaces old mounted vacuum & jet machines. Major upgrade, eliminates some contracted services and cost shared with stormwater for cleaning storm drains. Total lease, company resp. for maintenance, repairs, OTW requires $342K purchase.	$70,000 annual lease payments			
12	_Mini-excavator:_ replaces 10 year old unit.	$45,000			

	REVENUE DECISIONS (ALL FUNDS)	Cost/Savings	Support	Don't Support	Not Sure: Want Alternatives or Additional Information
1	**Property Tax** – No increases projected FYs 17-19				
2	**Stormwater Fee** – Sets up stormwater as separate utility fund. Proposed residential fee of $50/year. Proposed non-residential fees/tiers being updated and will get to board ASAP.				
3	**Water Rates** – No increases proposed FYs17-19				
4	**Sewer Rates**: No increases proposed FYs17-19				
5	**Decreasing Minimum Water/Sewer Rate:** Complete last step, lower from 2600 to 2500.				
	Town Board: Space below to 1) add items missing from budget that should be included, and 2) items to cut, reduce, or defer that are not in the lists above				

Source: Adapted from Town of Hillsborough, N.C. By permission.

Appendix B. Town of Hillsborough General Fund Summary

FINANCIAL SUMMARY - GENERAL FUND

Budget Unit	FY18 Actual	FY19 Estimate	FY20 Budget	FY21 Projected	FY22 Projected
Contingency	0	0	250,000	250,000	250,000
% Change	0%	0%	0%	0%	0%
Governing Body	130,200	134,817	138,713	137,037	141,117
% Change	-11.3%	3.5%	2.9%	-1.2%	3.0%
Administration	535,310	646,595	733,470	738,159	754,194
% Change	-2.2%	20.8%	13.4%	0.6%	2.2%
Local Government Channel (PEG)	40,292	9,570	0	0	0
% Change	31.8%	-76.2%	0.0%	0.0%	0.0%
Accounting	348,651	289,543	287,760	292,054	296,478
% Change	39.8%	-17.0%	-0.6%	1.5%	1.5%
Planning	394,441	417,431	464,820	464,601	469,020
% Change	-4.6%	5.8%	11.4%	0.0%	1.0%
Ruffin-Roulhac	12,669	193,939	181,786	190,041	176,066
% Change	-90.7%	1430.8%	-6.3%	4.5%	-7.4%
Public Space	724,928	866,873	766,574	751,913	746,531
% Change	11.2%	19.6%	-11.6%	-1.9%	-0.7%
Safety & Risk Management	85,831	76,854	87,242	73,672	74,560
% Change	-6.0%	-10.5%	13.5%	-15.6%	1.2%
Information Services	372,295	254,606	278,614	290,993	290,102
% Change	238.7%	-31.6%	9.4%	4.4%	-0.3%
Police - Administration	607,871	672,142	744,960	757,719	759,486
% Change	1.1%	10.6%	10.8%	1.7%	0.2%
Police - Patrol	2,141,235	1,893,411	1,896,778	1,898,732	1,884,297
% Change	35.1%	-11.6%	0.2%	0.1%	-0.8%
Police - Investigations & Community Services	674,064	660,383	752,527	762,487	781,660
% Change	2.9%	-2.0%	14.0%	1.3%	2.5%
Fire Marshal & Emergency Mgmt	134,247	151,992	224,268	188,125	190,479
% Change	-5.1%	13.2%	47.6%	-16.1%	1.3%
Fire Protection	1,214,363	1,310,635	1,228,641	1,224,351	1,221,955
% Change	1.3%	7.9%	-6.3%	-0.3%	-0.2%
Fleet Maintenance	241,535	326,751	361,944	362,649	365,139
% Change	-17.8%	35.3%	10.8%	0.2%	0.7%
Streets	877,061	941,448	778,093	803,731	760,434
% Change	45.4%	7.3%	-17.4%	3.3%	-5.4%
Powell Bill	183,434	199,965	185,000	185,000	185,000
% Change	-27.6%	9.0%	-7.5%	0.0%	0.0%
Solid Waste	609,234	462,446	547,867	521,560	569,219
% Change	16.9%	-24.1%	18.5%	-4.8%	9.1%
Cemetery	10,038	9,457	13,994	13,164	3,164
% Change	-83.1%	-5.8%	48.0%	-5.9%	-76.0%
Economic Development	473,164	477,864	490,396	498,610	507,719
% Change	0.0%	1.0%	2.6%	1.7%	1.8%
Special Appropriations	613,513	727,029	186,041	337,434	485,826
% Change	86.6%	18.5%	-74.4%	81.4%	44.0%
TOTAL EXPENDITURES	**10,424,375**	**10,723,750**	**10,599,488**	**10,742,032**	**10,912,446**
% Change	15.5%	2.9%	-1.2%	1.3%	1.6%
Surplus / (Deficit) at Current Tax Rate	567,473	(720,921)	(346,733)	(131,177)	83,209
Surplus / (Deficit) w/Tax Rate Increase	567,473	(720,921)	(346,733)	(131,177)	83,209
Tax Rate [1]	0.62	0.62	0.62	0.62	0.62
Fund Balance Appropriation Needed to Balance Budget	567,473	720,921	346,733	131,177	0
Available Fund Balance Remaining [2]	4,975,820	4,254,899	3,908,166	3,776,989	3,860,198
Fund Balance as % of Operating Expenditures	48%	40%	37%	35%	35%

[1] A property tax revaluation is scheduled for FY21, which will likely result in a downward adjustment of the tax rate.

[2] The town's Fund Balance Policy recommends maintaining an undesignated fund balance of between 20 to 60 percent of annual operating expenditures and a "target" of 33 percent.

Source: Town of Hillsborough, N.C.

Chapter 4

Budgeting in Economic Downturns for Local Governments

Whitney B. Afonso

Introduction

Budgeting in economic downturns is a difficult task for local governments. The literature that examines the budgeting behaviors of local governments and analyzes the choices that they have, as well as the possible short- and long-term impacts of those choices, is often referred to as *cutback management*. Cutback management can be understood as the process of managing an organization during a period when lower levels of resources are available.[1] The strategies evaluated in the cutback management literature are typically analyzed using a framework of efficiency and equity. In this framework, efficiency cuts, or what can be referred to as rational cuts, are often considered costly because of their focus on "weeding out" fat. Efficiency cuts search for where cost savings can occur without disruption (often with the goal of increasing long-term efficiency) but are less politically palatable than across-the-board cuts, and in many cases and can take a great deal of time. Unlike efficiency cuts, equity cuts are equitable or fair because they typically "spread the pain" with across-the-board cuts, where the majority of departments receive similar reductions in their budgets. These cuts, while not efficient, are often easier to make both in terms of the time to implement them and the political capital costs involved. Within these two broad perspectives on making cuts to budgets, there are several strategies for implementing those cuts. This chapter discusses the different strategies that local governments employ to balance their budgets during economic downturns, highlights North Carolina local governments' strategies in the Great Recession and the Great Lockdown, shares what are often considered best practices, and concludes with providing additional resources available to local governments.

---

1. Charles H. Levine, "More on Cutback Management: Hard Questions for Hard Times," *Public Administration Review* 39.2 (1979): 179–83.

Background

The two stages of a business or economic cycle are *boom* and *contraction. Boom* is essentially a period of economic expansion or growth, as defined by GDP, and *contraction* is the subsequent period of economic decline (or downturn) (see Figure 4.1). While these two periods make up the "business" cycle, they also impact local budgets tremendously—not just businesses. Of course, the business cycle impacts federal and state budgets as well, but differently. The federal government is not required to adopt a balanced budget, allowing it to deficit spend during the "trough," or lowest point, of an economic downturn (see Figure 4.1). State governments, like local governments, must adopt balanced budgets but are typically less constrained than their local counterparts. Local governments are often in a more challenging position than states because they are subject to tax and expenditure limits (TELs), they are more limited in the taxes and fees they are able to levy and implement, and a high percentage of their expenditures are mandatory rather than discretionary (especially for counties).

Figure 4.1. The Business Cycle

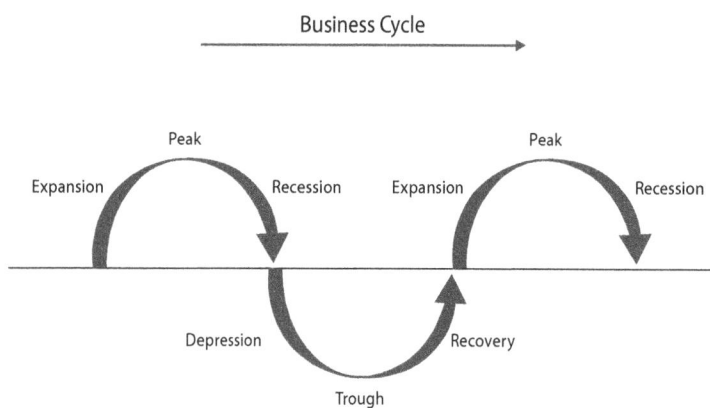

These limitations leave local governments in the position of having to make very hard budgeting decisions during economic downturns. Within the fields of public administration and public financial management, there is a literature referred to as *cutback management,* which was pioneered in the late 1970s and early 1980s. It not only explores what governments do to balance their budgets during these troughs, but also tries to understand the impacts of those choices. While the Great Recession and the COVID-19 pandemic are hopefully "100-year floods," economic downturns come every few years and are inevitable, but that does not make them easy to cope with. "Every public manager faces the challenge of cutback management. Real resources are declining (though demand for public service is not). Cutbacks are a reality. Consequently, public managers have the responsibility to make their agencies smaller while, simultaneously, fulfilling their organizations' missions."[2] Thus, the challenge is how to be as efficient and effective (if not more so) with fewer resources. Behn (1996) highlights the six primary roles of a manager in a cutback environment: (1) decide

---

2. Robert D. Behn, "Cutback Management: Six Basic Tasks," *Governing* (March 1996): 68.

what to cut, (2) maintain morale, (3) attract and keep quality employees and staff, (4) engage and rally key stakeholders in the process, (5) encourage innovation, and (6) avoid disasters.[3] Clearly these roles extend outside of just the budget and/or finance department, but it is helpful to keep in mind that these six different roles need to be working together in order for your organization to best navigate the economic downturn. This chapter focuses on the first step laid out by Behn (1996).

Clearly, the largest challenge of cutback management is deciding what to cut when the decision to cut has been made. This is not only because local governments and their respective departments are often already running on lean budgets, but also because deciding what to cut is a visible and controversial task that involves both internal and external stakeholders with differing preferences, needs, and values. Often governments simply choose to make across-the-board cuts, which seem straightforward and fair and are not as difficult politically as targeted cuts that look for efficiencies. However, across-the-board cuts are also typically less efficient than targeted cuts and take resources from departments with less flexibility and greater or even counter-cyclical spending needs (meaning that in times of economic downturn, their expenditures increase), rather than departments with more "fat," or ability to absorb the cuts without disruption to services. If across-the-board cuts are like taking a hatchet to the budget, then targeted cuts are like taking a scalpel to it.

No matter the strategy you lean toward or believe is most appropriate for your government, you should consider the importance of where you start. Before deciding what cuts to make, revisit your organization's strategic plan, performance data, and values/mission. Organizations should be asking themselves what their core functions are, what future are they working toward for the community and for themselves, what are the guiding values of the organization, and what would happen if they did not perform their services.[4] Organizations should also be considering what opportunities this period of downturn (or even crisis) presents and what risks it presents. There are always opportunities. A crisis is often an opportunity to rethink and reimagine a process, service, etc.[5] Recessions are often a prime period for innovating and asking departments to think outside the box for ways to deliver services more efficiently and effectively.

There are many strategies that local governments employ to balance budgets. Common strategies include reducing staffing (through attrition, hiring freezes, furloughs, layoffs, etc.), reducing the scope of programs, eliminating programs, reducing professional development opportunities, and making efficiency improvements. Of course, expenditures are only one side of the balanced-budget equation. Local governments can also consider increasing taxes or fees, introducing new taxes or fees, selling off assets, privatizing services, or identifying new sources of revenues. However, given the

---

3. Ibid.

4. Edwin C. Thomas, *The Challenges of Cutback Management,* (Public Policy, 2002), https://citeseerx.ist.psu.edu/viewdoc/download?doi=10.1.1.500.8492&rep=rep1&type=pdf.

5. It is said that the Chinese character for crisis is composed of opportunity and danger. Evidently that is not true of the Chinese character, but the wisdom still is!

nature of the cutback management literature and the history of choices made by local governments in economic downturns, this chapter focuses on expenditure reductions.

Using a fund balance, or what is often referred to as a "rainy-day fund," is another option. In North Carolina, the Local Government Commission (LGC) encourages local governments to maintain a fund balance of at least 8 percent of their operating costs, and the majority of local governments maintain at least that much. In fact, local government solvency (the percentage of operating costs maintained in the fund balance) was 26.77 percent for counties and 148.91 percent for municipalities in 2017. Generally, smaller jurisdictions will maintain a higher level of fund balance than large jurisdictions.

Lastly, one of the most common strategies employed to balance budgets is to defer capital costs, whether they are construction, repair, or maintenance. While a mix of these four basic areas of budget-balancing strategies (reducing expenditures, finding new revenue sources, allocating fund balance, and deferring capital costs) is often employed over the course of the recession, typically the least common is to increase revenues (other than intergovernmental transfers from the state and federal government, over which there is little control).

Cutback Management Literature

The cutback management literature emerged in the 1970s, thrived through the 1980s, and has seen a resurgence in the past decade. This section presents an overview of the literature, the groundwork upon which it is built, and some of the most common findings and lessons. The section begins with a discussion of the tension between targeted or rational cuts (those that focus on efficiency) and across-the-board cuts (those that focus on equity). To be clear, equity is assessed on an intragovernmental level, meaning the fairness between departments. It is not equity, necessarily, from the perspective of employees or citizens/service recipients. The section then proceeds with an overview of what is observed in the field and concludes with some cautions for local governments in the midst of a retrenchment period, where retrenchment is defined as "the reduction of costs or spending in response to economic difficulty."[6]

Within the literature, many scholars indicate the strengths and weaknesses of both targeted cuts and across-the-board cuts. Generally, most scholars argue in favor of a targeted, or rational, approach,[7] though there are those who approach cutback management from a more pragmatic perspective and recognize that targeted cuts

---

6. *Oxford Languages Dictionary*, s.v. "retrenchment (*n.*)," accessed December 13, 2020, https://languages.oup.com/.

7. Ringa Raudla, Riin Savi, and Tiina Randma-Liiv, "Cutback Management Literature in the 1970s and 1980s: Taking Stock," *International Review of Administrative Sciences* 81.3, (2015): 433–56; Charles H. Levine, "Police Management in the 1980s: From Decrementalism to Strategic Thinking," *Public Administration Review* 45 (1985): 691–700.

may not always be feasible and that across-the-board cuts are advisable.[8] Those who advocate for the pragmatic across-the-board cuts note that these cuts reduce decision-making costs, can minimize conflict, and are perceived as equitable.[9] Advocates of across-the-board cuts do not argue, however, that these cuts necessarily lead to better outcomes than those produced by targeted cuts. Across-the-board cuts do remove an important element of targeted cuts, which is analysis of where cuts can be made and the costs, both financial and temporal, associated with the cuts. Across-the-board cuts also remove what can be viewed as the stigma associated with being presented as one of the wasteful or less necessary departments. In fact, because all departments serve someone, being singled-out can cause conflict among stakeholders in a period when the public sector will need support for the tough decisions being made. Lastly, across-the-board cuts seem fair and equitable among departments, as everyone is sharing the pain.

However, advocates of targeted cuts point to the many weaknesses associated with across-the-board cuts, such as the following: across-the-board cuts may not accurately reflect the needs and preferences of citizens; they penalize the departments that are already operating efficiently with little fat to trim; they are agnostic to the actual needs of departments; and they may lead to a decline in service provision (levels and quality). Advocates of targeted cuts state that "across-the-board cuts would be a reasonable response only if the present budget reflects perfectly the community's desired mix of government services."[10]

Given the conflicting perspectives, is there any sort of consensus about or best practice for budgeting in economic downturns? In general, the advice from the literature that most scholars advance is a combination of a preference for targeted cuts with a dose of pragmatism. The result is recognition that for small deficits and short-term cuts, across-the-board cuts may by appropriate, but in longer periods of retrenchment and with larger deficits, it is important to use a targeted approach.[11] Levine (1984) suggests that small deficits can be defined as those of 7 percent or less of the budget in a single year or 15 percent or less over a three-year period.[12]

There are several recommendations from the literature for budgeting practices, but what do we observe in practice? The vast majority of studies, at the local level, suggest that local governments do a mix of across-the-board cuts and targeted cuts and

---

8. Christopher Hood and Maurice Wright, eds., "From Decrementalism to Quantum Cuts?" in *Big Governments in Hard Times* (Oxford: Martin Robertson, 1981), 199–227.

9. See Raudla, Savi, and Randma-Liiv, "Cutback Management Literature," 433–56 for more information and additional resources.

10. Carol W. Lewis and Anthony T. Logalbo, "Cutback Principles and Practices: A Checklist for Managers," *Public Administration Review* 40, no. 2 (1980): 184–88.

11. Charles H. Levine, "Retrenchment, Human Resource Erosion, and the Role of the Personnel Manager," *Public Personnel Management Journal* 13, no. 3 (1984): 249–63; Allen Schick, "Incremental Budgeting in a Decremental Age," *Policy Sciences* 16, no. 1 (1983): 1–25; Raudla, Savi, and Randma-Liiv, "Cutback Management Literature," 433–56.

12. Levine, "Retrenchment," 252.

that no one strategy dominates.[13] So what cuts are actually made? Most cuts can be put into one of three categories: the running costs or operational costs, the program costs (transfers and public services), and capital expenditures. Operational costs are considered in two categories: personnel and non-personnel. Local governments can cut personnel costs through reduction of overtime, furloughs, wage freezes, layoffs, and hiring freezes. Examples of non-personnel cuts are freezes on training, limits on utilities and supplies, and reduction of equipment budgets. For program costs, managers are presented with the choice of reducing the quantity of services being offered (such as reducing service hours, restricting access to the service, and reducing the frequency of the service) and the quality of those services. Lastly, capital expenditures can be reduced or cut. In the extreme, local governments can temporarily eliminate capital spending, or simply defer maintenance, freeze spending for new projects, and postpone nonessential projects. The evidence shows that cuts to capital expenditures are the dominant strategy used in periods of retrenchment, followed by cuts to operating costs, specifically to personnel costs via hiring freezes.[14]

While all of these cuts can create short-term savings, there are many ways that these choices can create long-term costs. For example, layoffs can be costly due to decreased employee morale and productivity as well as the future costs of hiring someone new for those positions.[15] Another example is how deferring capital costs (through maintenance and replacement) can lead to much larger costs in the future and lead to the "infrastructure crisis" many are facing.[16] Therefore, it is critical to consider both the short-term benefits and the long-term costs of these strategies and ensure that you are continuing your jurisdiction on a path of sustainability.

The Great Recession and the Great Lockdown

As of the writing of this chapter in early 2021, there have been two major economic disruptions in this century: the Great Recession in 2008 and the Great Lockdown caused by the COVID-19 pandemic in 2020. While these two economic downturns

---

13. See Raudla, Savi, and Randma-Liiv, "Cutback Management Literature," 433–56, for an overview.

14. For an overview of these findings, see Raudla, Savi, and Randma-Liiv, "Cutback Management Literature," 433–56.

15. Leonard Greenhalgh and Robert B. McKersie, "Cost-Effectiveness of Alternative Strategies for Cutback Management," *Public Administration Review* 40, no. 6 (1980): 575–84; Charles H. Levine, "Organizational Decline and Cutback Management," *Public Administration Review* 38, no. 4 (1978): 316–25.

16. Carol W. Lewis and Anthony T. Logalbo, "Cutback Principles and Practices," 184–88; William C. Rivenbark, Whitney Afonso, and Dale J. Roenigk, "Capital Spending in Local Government," *Journal of Public Budgeting, Accounting & Financial Management* 30, no. 4 (2018): 402–14; Whitney B. Afonso, "Local Government Capital Spending during and after Recessions: A Cause for Concern?" *International Journal of Public Administration* 37.8 (2014): 494–505.

were extremely different, local governments responded to the crises in similar ways. The large amount of overlap in tactics used by local governments to respond to the Great Recession and to the Great Lockdown suggests that there are "go-to" strategies. The Great Lockdown was, in many ways, unprecedented in terms of its severity, speed, and impacts on the economy. Compared to the Great Recession, different elements of the economy were impacted during the Great Lockdown, but there was more confidence about the sectors and taxes being impacted. Despite these differences, the same cutback management tools were wielded during both crises. In fact, I argue elsewhere that the Great Lockdown is a unique example of being able to budget for a recession in advance of it—and governments made largely the same choices.[17]

Pulling information from a survey conducted by the North Carolina Local Government Budget Association and the North Carolina League of Municipalities,[18] the strategies employed by local governments for fiscal year 2021 (FY21) to balance the budget are not surprising. The most common strategies employed by counties were using fund balance, reducing capital improvements, and increasing fees. Only one reporting county (of the twenty-nine that completed the survey) reported plans to increase taxes, and only three reported plans to cut public services. The most common strategies reported by municipalities were to close facilities, appropriate fund balance, and increase fees. Furthermore, almost all jurisdictions reported adjusting staffing strategies. Over 80 percent of municipalities reported that there would be no new positions added in FY21; this was followed by a majority of local governments reporting plans to institute a hiring freeze.

Figure 4.2. Strategies to Balance the Budget in Response to Projected Revenue Shortfall: Counties

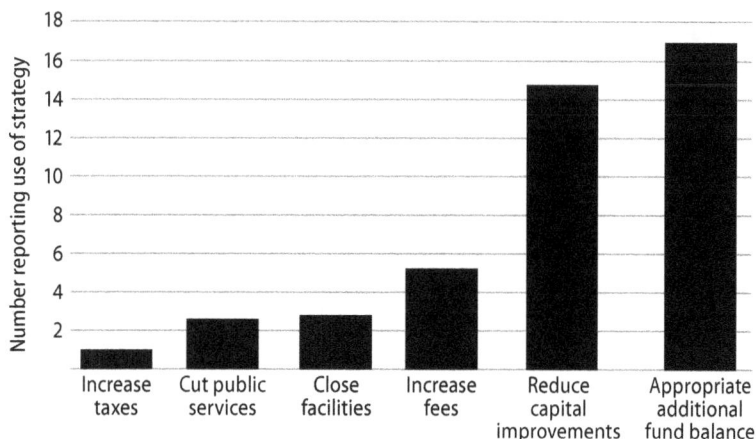

17. Whitney B. Afonso, *Budgeting Strategies Being Employed by County and Municipal Governments for Fiscal Year 2021 during the COVID-19 Pandemic*, Local Finance Bulletin 55 (UNC School of Government, June 10, 2020), https://www.sog.unc.edu/publications/bulletins/budgeting-strategies-being-employed-county-and-municipal-governments-fy-2021-during-covid-19.

18. Data from this survey were presented in Afonso, *Budget Balancing Strategies*.

Figure 4.3. Strategies to Balance the Budget in Response to Projected Revenue Short-fall: Municipalities

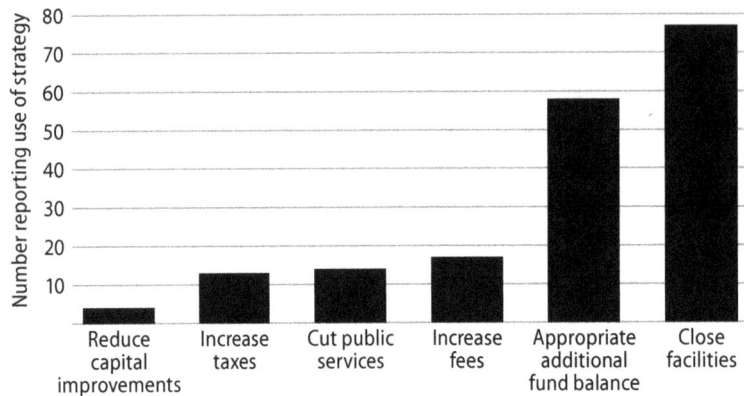

Figure 4.4. Percentage of Jurisdictions Utilizing Staffing Strategies in Response to Projected Revenue Shortfalls

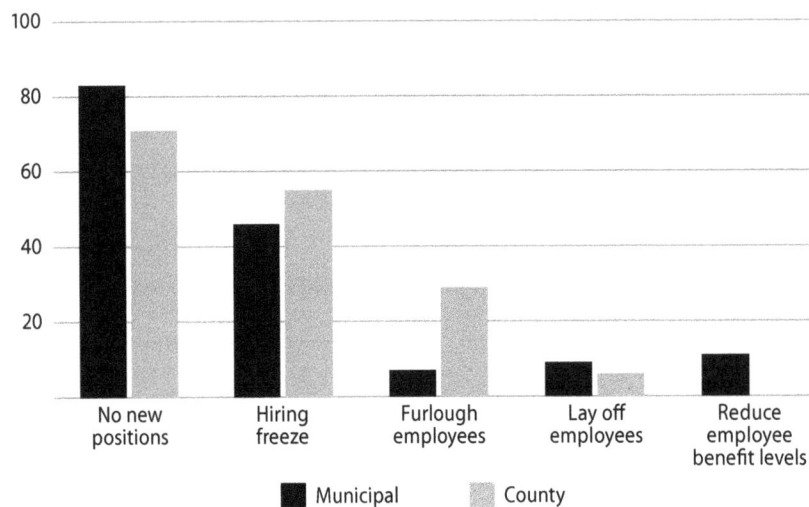

So how do the responses to the Great Lockdown compare to those of the Great Recession? Well, responses to the Great Recession tell a similar story. For fiscal year 2009, local governments reported using many of the same strategies.[19] Sixty-five percent of municipalities reported no pay raises, which was the most common strategy reported. Sixty percent reported reductions to capital spending, and less than 10 percent reported reducing services levels. Similarly, almost half reported intending to increase fees, while only 3 percent reported the intention to raise the tax rate.

These responses to crises are not unique to North Carolina, as North Carolina presents the same trends as the rest of the country. While there are differences in

---

19. David N. Ammons and Trevor Fleck, *Budget-Balancing Tactics in Local Government* (Chapel Hill, NC: UNC School of Government, February 1, 2010), https://www.sog.unc .edu/publications/reports/budget-balancing-tactics-local-government.

what local governments can and cannot do, the same basic patterns of preferring to reduce operational or staffing costs, reduce capital costs, and increase fees rather than taxes has been true almost universally.[20] Of course, different states have different tax and expenditure limits that significantly impact local government responses, different revenues available, and different roles and responsibilities for municipalities, counties, and special districts. These differences, and others, shape how local governments respond to crises and economic downturns, but despite these differences the strategies are very similar across states.

Additional Resources and Perspectives

It can feel overwhelming to think about how to start when faced with balancing a budget during a recession. This chapter has presented information to use and important considerations when starting this process, but there are also many helpful practitioner-focused research studies and guides that highlight best practices and common tactics for balancing budgets during downturns. In fact, just in the first few months of the COVID-19 pandemic, groups such as the International City/County Management Association (ICMA) and Government Finance Officers Association (GFOA) released blog posts and white papers on cutback management.

For example, in an ICMA blog post (June 1, 2020), Professor Kurt Thurmaier highlighted three principles for local cutback management during the COVID-19 pandemic. First, follow strategic plans and priorities. The top priorities that have been identified should help guide the choices made when dealing with reduced revenues. Second, use the rainy-day funds that have been developed during stronger economic periods. Third, do not put off capital improvement projects and do consider debt when interest rates are low.[21]

Similarly, the GFOA updated its "Fiscal First Aid" resources and presented a "COVID-19 Special Selection" white paper on balancing the budget in bad times. It highlights many management and leadership strategies as well as short-term budget-balancing strategies. It presents strategies under six primary categories: control personnel costs, enhance purchasing practices, review ongoing expenditures, pool resources and find partnership opportunities, better manage capital costs, and enhance revenues. The paper also highlights techniques that it indicates should be used with "extreme caution" and techniques that are labeled as "inadvisable" treatments.

20. Christopher W. Hoene and Michael A. Pagano, *City Fiscal Conditions in 2008 Research Brief on America's Cities, Issue 2009-2* (Washington, D.C.: National League of Cities, September 2009).

21. Kurt Thurmaier, "Three Principles and a Sim: Guidance for Cutback Budgeting in the Covid-19 Recession," *ICMA* (blog), June 1, 2020, https://icma.org/blog-posts/three-principles-and-sim-guidance-cutback-budgeting-covid-19-recession.

These techniques include strategies such as underfund pension obligations, default on debt, shift operational costs to capital budgets, and sell off assets.[22]

There are also many other resources available to local governments (many of them are listed at the end of this chapter for recommended further reading). One such resource is a report published in 2010 by David Ammons and his student, Trevor Fleck, on the budget-balancing strategies employed by local governments in North Carolina at the start of the Great Recession.[23] This is a very helpful resource that presents a multitude of options available to local governments in the state, as well as a notion of how common those options are. It is worth noting that the literature suggests that different strategies are taken at the start of an economic downturn from later on in a downturn. The longer the downturn lasts, the more severe and targeted the strategies adopted will be (raising taxes, layoffs, etc.); these actions reflect strategies from early in the recession.

Other useful resources are three bulletins I have written on the theory and practice of coping with economic downturns. Two of the bulletins examine the literature and the strategies employed in the states of California and Georgia during the Great Recession, present useful discussion and concerns, and act as a good supplement to this chapter.[24] Additionally, there is a more recent bulletin that goes further into the data presented here on coping strategies employed by local governments when crafting the fiscal year 2021 budget in the Spring of 2020.[25] It provides more detail on these strategies and delves more deeply into the severity of the economic crisis caused by the COVID-19 pandemic from the perspective of local governments.

Conclusion

Economic downturns are inevitable. Public servants must be prepared to deal with these periods of contraction while still thriving to provide high levels of services and keep government running efficiently, effectively, and equitably. Unfortunately, there is no one right answer. Cutback management provides a lens by which to consider multiple options for facing cuts, including across-the-board cuts and targeted cuts.

---

22. Shayne Kavanagh, *Balancing the Budget in Bad Times* (Government Finance Officers Association, August 2020), https://www.gfoa.org/materials/balancing-the-budget-in-bad-times-gfr.

23. Ammons and Fleck, *Budget-Balancing Tactics.*

24. The two bulletins are as follows: Whitney Afonso, *Theory and Practice for Coping with Economic Downturns at the Local Level: Part I,"* Local Finance Bulletin 48 (UNC School of Government, September 2014), https://www.sog.unc.edu/publications/bulletins/theory-and-practice-coping-economic-downturns-local-level-part-i; Whitney Afonso, *Theory and Practice for Coping with Economic Downturns at the Local Level: Part II,* Local Finance Bulletin 56 (UNC School of Government, June 2020), https://www.sog.unc.edu/publications/bulletins/theory-and-practice-coping-economic-downturns-local-level-part-ii.

25. Afonso, "Budgeting Strategies."

However, there are still many ways to implement those cuts once the initial strategy is decided upon, including reductions in personnel costs, capital expenditures, and service provisions. Additionally, there are ways to increase revenues through fees and taxes and seeking out alternative revenues like grants and intergovernmental aid. These decisions must all be navigated carefully with thought to the short-term savings and the long-term costs to both the unit and the citizens it serves.

Recommended Further Reading

Afonso, Whitney. *Budgeting Strategies Being Employed by County and Municipal Governments for FY 2021 During the COVID-19 Pandemic.* Local Finance Bulletin 55. UNC School of Government, June 12, 2020. https://www.sog.unc.edu/publications/bulletins/budgeting-strategies-being-employed-county-and-municipal-governments-fy-2021-during-covid-19.

———. *Theory and Practice for Coping with Economic Downturns at the Local Level: Part I.* Local Finance Bulletin 48. UNC School of Government, September 2014, https://www.sog.unc.edu/publications/bulletins/theory-and-practice-coping-economic-downturns-local-level-part-i.

———. *Theory and Practice for Coping with Economic Downturns at the Local Level: Part II.* Local Finance Bulletin 56. UNC School of Government, June 2020, https://www.sog.unc.edu/publications/bulletins/theory-and-practice-coping-economic-downturns-local-level-part-ii.

Ammons, David N., and Trevor Fleck. *Budget-Balancing Tactics in Local Government.* Chapel Hill, NC.: UNC School of Government, 2010. https://www.sog.unc.edu/publications/reports/budget-balancing-tactics-local-government.

Kavanagh, Shayne. *Balancing the Budget in Bad Times.* Government Finance Officers Association, 2020. https://www.gfoa.org/materials/balancing-the-budget-in-bad-times-gfr.

Miller, Gerald G., and James H. Svara, eds. *Navigating the Fiscal Crisis: Tested Strategies for Local Leaders.* White paper prepared for the International City/County Management Association, 2009. https://icma.org/sites/default/files/302108_alliance_icma_crisis.pdf.

Stenberg, Carl W., *Coping with Crisis: How Are Local Governments Reinventing Themselves in the Wake of the Great Recession?* Policy issue white paper prepared on behalf of the International City/County Management Association Governmental Affairs and Policy Committee, 2011. https://icma.org/sites/default/files/303228_GAPC%20-%20coping%20with%20crisis%20white%20paper.pdf.

PART II

REVENUES

Chapter 5

Evaluating Government Tax Policy through the Lenses of Efficiency, Equity, Adequacy, and Feasibility

Whitney B. Afonso

I. Introduction

A *revenue instrument* is a tool used by governments—including local governments—to raise moneys to fund the services provided to citizens. Revenue instruments turn budgeting decisions into reality. Understanding the different revenue instruments used by governments—not just the legal limitations and restrictions that are in place around these instruments but also the strengths, weaknesses, and consequences of each one—is critical for local government leaders and citizens alike. This chapter will focus on revenue instruments over which local governments have autonomy, chiefly, on taxes and fees.

The revenue streams adopted by local governments are heavily constrained by state laws, especially in states, like North Carolina, that do not have *home rule*.[1] There are no perfect revenue instruments, and local leaders often have little influence in shaping their communities' tax and fee policies, but being aware of the effects—both good

---

1. "*Home rule* describes the scope of authority that some states delegate to local governments. . . . In a home rule state, cities are granted broad powers over matters of local concern. . . . [The term] refers to the power the local government has to make its own rules." Frayda Bluestein, "Is North Carolina a Dillon's Rule State?," *Coates' Canons: NC Local Government Law* (blog), October 24, 2012, http://canons.sog.unc.edu/?p=6894 (discussing North Carolina's structure in detail).

and bad—of different revenue choices can improve decision-making and enhance the government's communication with its citizens.

> Home rule jurisdictions do not look to state statutes to determine what actions they are permitted to take. Rather, these units of government are limited in their actions by what state statutes have prohibited them from doing. For example, if a city is a home rule city and the state has not prohibited occupancy taxes, then the city may adopt such a tax, regardless of whether the state has enacted a statute authorizing it to do so.

This chapter, which is aimed primarily at local government public administrators (but which is, I think, useful for all readers), will explore some of the larger revenue instruments relied upon by local governments. It will also provide in-depth discussions of four key criteria to be used by local administrators to examine the appropriateness of a given revenue instrument and the implications of its use, along with analyses of how the revenue instruments highlighted fare when viewed under these criteria (e.g., are there cases when some of the criteria are in conflict regarding a certain revenue stream?). The chapter aims not only to present the technical definitions of the concepts discussed, but also to provide different perspectives on them and to give local government administrative staff, on top of a set of essential terms, tools to employ when engaging with citizens, elected officials, and fellow staff members.

II. Criteria for Evaluating Tax Policy

The question at the heart of this chapter is this: How does one decide if a particular local government tax policy is, on balance, a positive (and not a negative) thing? As the chapter progresses, you will discover that there is no easy (or even correct) answer to this question. The decisions underlying tax policies are made after consideration of competing values and concerns, and often these decisions are subjective and personal. Measuring the "goodness" or "badness" of a given tax policy can be a thorny endeavor. However, there are four basic criteria that can—and should—be used to make such assessments: efficiency, equity, adequacy, and feasibility. While application of the criteria is a uniform proposition, how you, as local administrators, weigh and balance them is not a one-size-fits-all exercise. The weight accorded some tax decisions and not others will reflect the values of your communities and of yourselves.

> Remember, taxes are not voluntary things. They are intentional policy decisions. User fees are also policy decisions, but they are considered voluntary in nature; you don't have to pay them if you don't engage in certain behaviors. Of course, some user fees are more avoidable than others. For example, park facility rentals are more easily avoided than water bills.

A. Efficiency

Efficiency, in the context of economics, refers to the "economic state in which every resource is optimally allocated to serve each individual or entity in the best way while minimizing waste and inefficiency. When an economy is economically efficient, any changes made to assist one entity would harm another. In terms of production, goods are produced at their lowest possible cost, as are the variable inputs of production."[2] In everyday language, this translates into the price and quantity at which the market (if left alone) would have supplied a particular good (i.e., the *efficient point*). When the market does not supply the good at the efficient point, a *market failure* results. A *monopoly* is an example of a market failure. The problem with taxes, from an efficiency perspective, is that they move us away from the efficient point. Let's look at this within a case example and through the use of figures.

> Example: *Company A manufactures pens (goods) and offers them for sale. Purchaser B needs to buy the type of pens produced by Company A for its own operations. Company A, as a business, is interested in profiting from those sales. Purchaser B, also a business, is interested in its own bottom line and, as a result, wants to pay as little as possible for the pens produced by Company A.*[3]

Figure 5.1. Basic Supply and Demand Curve—Goods

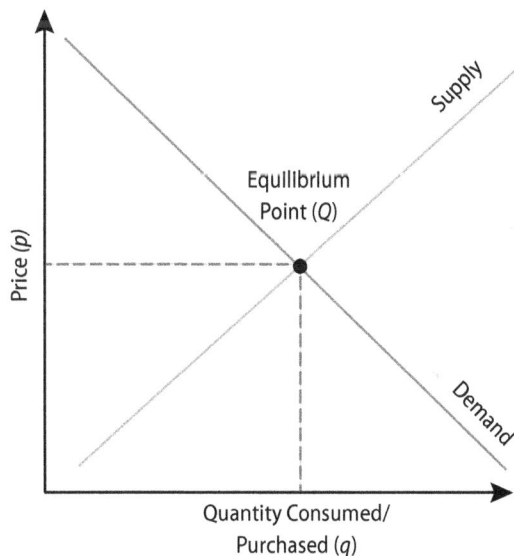

---

2. "Economic Efficiency," Investopedia, last modified February 28, 2020, https://www.investopedia.com/terms/e
/economic_efficiency.asp#ixzz539kZwBqz.

3. This example is an extreme simplification of how markets work. The reality is that there are typically numerous and varied producers and consumers of/for a given good or service. Were you to actually have just one producer or consumer of a good/service, you would end up with a market failure and you would not reach the efficient point or outcome. The most well-known example of this outcome is the only-producer failure, which is also called a monopoly. These concepts, touched upon in the text above, are discussed in greater detail in the text below.

Figure 5.1 depicts the classic, basic supply and demand curve that some of you may have seen before. Given that producers of goods want to maximize their profits (and achieve what is often referred to as *producer surplus*), and that consumers want to minimize their costs and maximize what is known as *consumer surplus* (which is the money they would have spent for a particular good but did not have to, which makes them happy), the efficient point in this situation is called Q, which represents the most efficient outcome given these competing demands. For purposes of our case example, the equilibrium point in Figure 5.1 represents the situation where Company A is selling and producing pens at a level in keeping with its profit demands/preferences, given what Purchaser B is willing to pay for a specific quantity of the goods.

Figure 5.2 depicts the same supply and demand curve as is set out in Figure 5.1, so Q is still the efficient point. However, this figure displays an additional scenario where taxes have been added to the goods for sale, which results in a shift in the quantity of goods purchased/consumed. You can see that fewer goods are being purchased after taxes are added, consumers are paying more for those goods, and producers are being paid less for each unit sold. This means that both consumer surplus and producer surplus have decreased when compared to the pre-tax scenario shown in Figure 5.1. Of course, this second scenario has generated tax revenue for the government (which is the very reason the tax was imposed in the first place). The unfortunate reality, though, is that the loss in consumer surplus and producer surplus is greater than the tax revenue generated. This outcome is called *dead weight loss*; it is displayed in the portion of the graph to the right of tax revenue and is labeled "DWL." To maximize efficiency, we want to minimize dead weight loss because it harms all parties—it reflects a loss on the part of consumers and producers and is of no benefit to the government.

Figure 5.2. Supply and Demand Curve—Goods + Taxes; Dead Weight Loss (DWL)

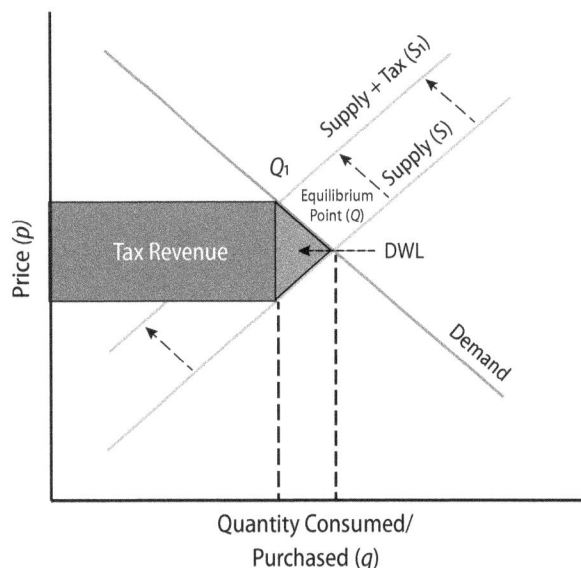

Figure 5.3. Supply and Demand Curve—Goods + Low-Rate Taxes; Dead Weight Loss (DWL)

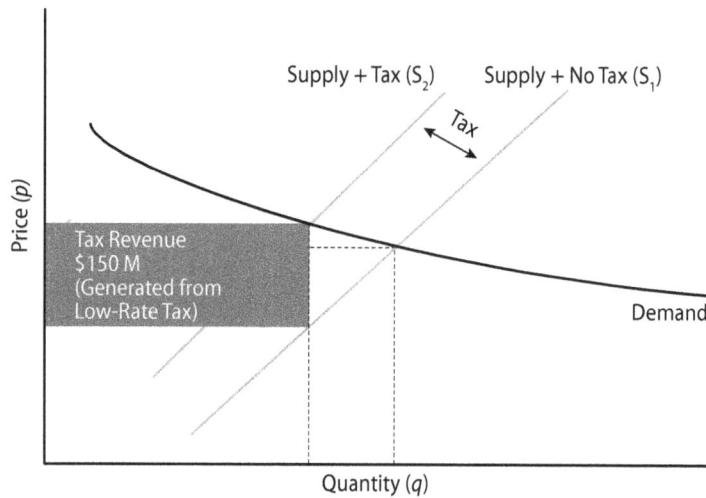

Figure 5.4. Supply and Demand Curve—Goods + Higher-Rate Taxes; Dead Weight Loss (DWL)

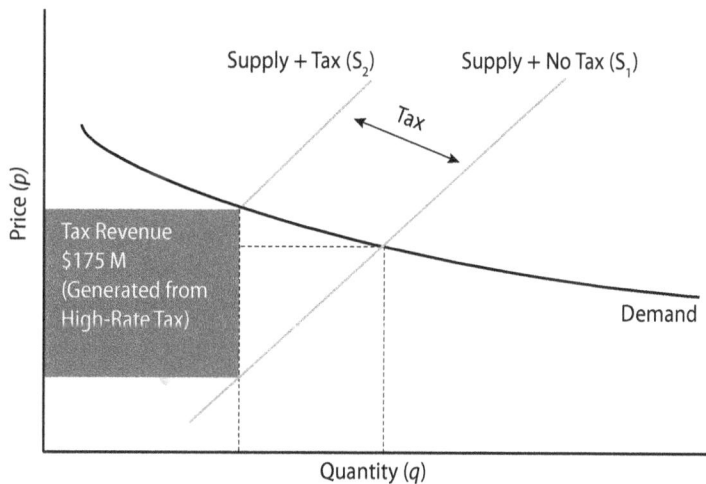

To refer to our example of the pen market, Purchaser B is paying more per pen and buying fewer pens because of the increased cost, and Company A (the producer/manufacturer) is making fewer pens because of the reduced demand and because it is now selling them for less per unit. The reason A is making less money per pen and B is spending more money per pen is because of the portion of the price that represents tax revenue going to the government.

Dead weight loss is an almost inevitable outcome of government taxation of goods, services, etc. But there are ways it can be minimized. The first tactic for attacking dead weight loss is to make tax rates low. Figure 5.3 presents a supply and demand curve featuring a relatively low-rate tax, whereas Figure 5.4 presents that same curve featuring a higher-rate tax. It is plain from even a quick glance at both figures that, while tax revenue is greater in Figure 5.4, the dead weight loss is greater (significantly so), too. Figure 5.5 shows that if the tax rate is raised high enough, up to a certain

Figure 5.5. Supply and Demand Curve—Goods + Highest-Rate Taxes; Dead Weight Loss (DWL)

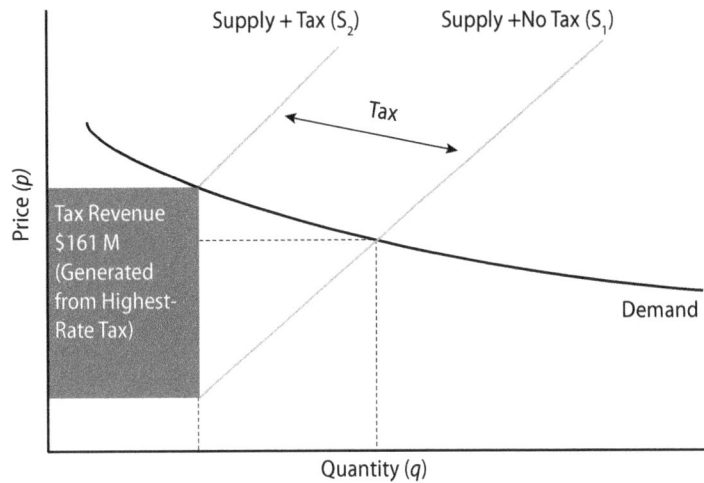

level, tax revenues will actually decrease. These figures demonstrate what would happen if the government were to consider imposing different rates of sales or excise taxes for the pen market. While we typically assume that higher taxes will always equate to higher tax revenues, these figures demonstrate that this is not always the case. At some point, Purchaser B will find an alternative to pens. In the case of an excise tax that is imposed exclusively on pens, this may mean switching to pencils or markers. Additionally, these figures demonstrate that even when higher tax revenues are achieved through higher taxes (see, e.g., the difference between Figure 5.3 and Figure 5.4), this comes at a cost, namely, increased dead weight loss.

A second method for minimizing dead weight loss involves taxing goods when the supply or demand for them is *inelastic*. Inelastic in this context means not sensitive to changes in price. Thus, when demand for a given good or service is inelastic, consumers will buy the good/service no matter what it costs. The majority of goods subject to inelastic demand can be put into two main categories: life-or-death necessities and goods to which people may be said to be addicted. Blood for a blood transfusion falls under the first category of goods. If you get into a terrible car accident and need a blood transfusion to survive, you are likely willing to pay almost anything for that blood. Given this, government could tax blood at a relatively high rate and create very little dead weight loss. Whether doing so is appropriate or moral is another question, but, for purposes of the present discussion, such a tax can properly be called efficient.

While life-or-death-type goods are not typically taxed at high rates, addictive goods, in contrast, often are. Cigarettes and alcohol are two of the most common examples of addictive goods. Governments often impose special excise taxes on these types of goods, which are often referred to as "sin taxes." The demand for these goods is far less sensitive to price changes than it is for other goods like shoes and DVDs. Figure 5.6 depicts an inelastic demand curve and illustrates the reduction in dead weight loss when demand is inelastic. It is important to note that, in the case of an

Figure 5.6. Inelastic Demand for Goods

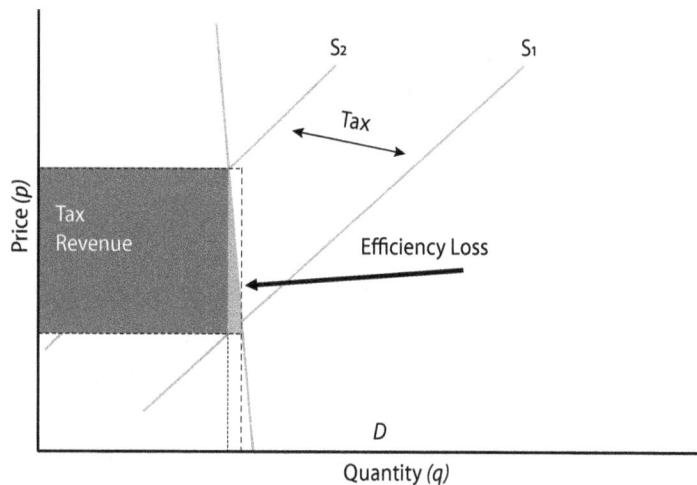

inelastic demand (as opposed to an inelastic supply) curve, the majority of the tax burden is borne by the consumer rather than the producer.[4]

There are fewer examples of inelastic supply scenarios. A common one involves rental apartments. No matter the changes in demand, there is a relatively fixed supply of existing apartments for rent. This inelastic demand for rental units means that property owners of rental units will be able to shift the costs of taxes largely to the renters, rather than pay them themselves. (This is the opposite of the situation in our pen market example, where the burden was shared between the producer and purchaser.) In contrast, if property taxes were to be raised and demand by consumers was sensitive to changes in price (perhaps because there was a large number of rental units available), then the majority of the property taxes would be paid by the apartment building owners.

Another way of looking at the negative implications of efficiency loss is to think about how people's behavior changes because of taxes. As the figures above show, the first and clearest change that results from higher taxes is that consumers buy fewer goods and producers make fewer goods (which also results in lower levels of both consumer and producer surplus, as discussed earlier in this subsection).

Other behavioral changes can be observed when the government treats, or taxes, different parts of the economy differently. A recent example of this involves short-term lodging rentals. Apartments and houses rented out through platforms like Airbnb were not, at the time of this writing, subject to occupancy taxes, whereas hotel and motel rooms in the same communities were. While there are many reasons why a person might want to stay in an Airbnb rental, the lack of occupancy taxes on

---

4. For more on exactly who is bearing the burden (also called "incidence") of taxes, see Whitney Afonso, "Let's Play 'Who's Paying That Tax?'" *Death & Taxes* (UNC School of Government public finance blog), January 23, 2017, https://deathandtaxes.sog.unc.edu/lets-play-whos-paying-that-tax/.

such accommodations made them less expensive, something that, as a rule, would make consumers more likely to choose an Airbnb lodging over a hotel or motel room.[5]

Another example that has gotten a great deal of attention over the past few years involves sales taxes. Historically, online retailers like Amazon.com did not have to collect sales taxes on goods sold, whereas their brick-and-mortar counterparts did. This made the same good offered at the same sales price less expensive on Amazon than at the consumer's neighborhood store. Arguably, this tax advantage encouraged many consumers to shift their purchasing patterns and negatively impacted the portions of the economy that were subject to sales taxes.

A more classic example of a behavioral change attributable to the fact that certain goods are taxed at different rates than similar goods involves excise taxes. Imagine if the government imposed a 6 percent tax on all beer sales and a 9 percent tax on all sales of wine and liquor. What would consumers do? Those who have a strong preference for wine or liquor might be willing to pay the higher cost, no questions asked. Others who prefer wine or liquor but who don't want to—or can't afford to—pay the higher cost (due to the higher tax) of the good might choose to buy beer instead.

Examples of the same or similar goods receiving differential tax treatment (which, in turn, might change consumer behavior patterns) abound. For example, if you buy a DVD of a movie at a retail store, you will pay taxes on it, but if you go to see a movie in a theater, in many states (including North Carolina, until recently) you will not be taxed on the ticket price. Or if you go to a barber shop for a haircut, you will not pay taxes on the service, but if you buy a Flowbee (the glorious haircutting vacuum device from the 1990s) or barber's scissors to cut your locks, you will be taxed on your purchase. Ideally, the government should not be seeking to change people's behaviors. It should instead want consumers to purchase the goods and services they prefer and not to substitute and shift buying habits because of taxes.[6]

As the foregoing discussion demonstrates, efficiency is a useful criterion for evaluating whether taxes (and fees) are "good." To this end, from an efficiency perspective, you as local leaders want your revenue instruments to minimize the dead weight loss they create and to change people's behaviors as little as possible. This is why taxes with large, broad bases—those that tax a larger share of the economy and do so at low rates—are often considered the most efficient ones. However, for various reasons, governments often choose to narrow the tax base and to increase the tax rate. One of the most common reasons for this is *equity*.

B. Equity

While *efficiency* may be the most complex concept discussed in this chapter, *equity* will likely be the most subjective and contentious. This is because equity, when used as a measure and in the present context, evaluates the fairness of a given tax or fee, and what you as a public administrator consider "fair" may be entirely different from

---

5. This is not to say that there are no other factors influencing the cost of both types of rentals.

6. The exception to this is the case of market failures (discussed earlier in this subsection). There are occasions when reducing or shifting consumption can lead to better outcomes.

what your town/city manager or council members, or even your citizens, consider fair. As discussed above, there are concrete ways to evaluate whether a tax is efficient or not. Assessing equity is a different story altogether. Not only are there are many ways to evaluate whether a tax is "fair," there are just as many definitions of what "fair" means. That being said, it is still possible to evaluate, applying basic methods, the fairness of a tax or fee; best practice is to consider other perspectives while doing so.

Because equity, as a rationale, often underlies the way the tax base is defined and how tax rates are set, and because it involves some important trade-offs not seen with the other criteria discussed in this chapter, understanding the many dimensions (and definitions) of equity in the tax realm is crucial. Also, you are more likely to have people come to you to discuss concerns about equity than concerns about any of the other criteria.

The discussion in this subsection will frame equity considerations according to two principles: the *ability-to-pay principle* and the *benefit principle*.

1. The Ability-to-Pay Principle

The *ability-to-pay principle* is what most people think about when considering the question of the equity of certain forms of taxation. Simply stated, this principle dictates that every person should pay taxes based on his or her ability to pay those taxes. While this seems straightforward enough, there are many nuanced elements to this equity principle. For example, how, exactly, does one define "ability to pay"? How does one assess whether this standard is being met and determine the way it should be applied? This chapter will discuss the ability-to-pay principle by referencing two types of equity: *horizontal equity* and *vertical equity*.

a. Horizontal Equity

The concept of *horizontal equity* states that individuals who have similar incomes and hold similar assets (i.e., who theoretically have the same ability to pay) should pay the same amount of taxes. This seems logical and reasonable at first glance. It grows more complicated, though, when you start asking questions like, "How does one determine 'ability to pay'?" The first things that come to mind when answering this question are wages and salaries. For some people, wages and salaries are the only items that should be considered when assessing a person's ability to pay taxes. Other people might want to factor in other things—such as the number of children a taxpayer has, the amount of student loan debt he or she carries, the cost of living where the taxpayer lives, and any tangible property owned by him or her (e.g., cars, boats, planes, van Gogh paintings)—into the ability-to-pay equation.

A second question that arises when one looks more deeply into horizontal equity is, "What does it mean, for tax purposes, to treat people in similar financial situations the same?" This question becomes especially difficult to answer when financially similar people behave differently. Let's use the example of the personal income tax. The personal income tax could, were it to be dramatically simplified by removing deductions and exemptions, treat similar people alike, because income would then be the only ability-to-pay consideration. However, personal income taxes, at both the state and federal levels in the United States, do not work this way; neither tax scheme is based only on income.

Marginal Tax Rate versus Effective Tax Rate

This chapter will discuss tax rates from an *effective tax rate* perspective. This term is often used interchangeably with the phrase "marginal tax rate." The two are dramatically different concepts, however, and for this reason (and others), it is important to distinguish between them.

A *marginal tax rate* is the rate at which the last dollar of income you make is taxed. An *effective tax rate* is the average tax rate at which your income is taxed. The clearest way to think about this is to use the example of the federal personal income tax.

Under 2018–2019 laws and regulations, if you made $150,000 a year and filed your return as a single taxpayer, then your marginal tax rate (or tax bracket) is 24 percent. However, your total income is not taxed at that rate because your income, no matter how much you ultimately make, is taxed under the same progressive schedule as is everyone else's income. This means that the first $9,525 you earn is taxed at a 10 percent rate, no matter how much money you make. Each time you change tax brackets, only the additional revenue that falls into that new range is taxed at that different rate. For this example, let's assume that you are taking the standard deduction and not claiming any other exemptions. After such adjustments, your effective tax rate is actually 18.3 percent.[a] This differential is even more stark at lower incomes. For example, for an income of $40,000 a year for a single taxpayer, the marginal tax rate is 12 percent and the effective tax rate is less than 8 percent.

The example above considers only federal personal income taxes. Often, an effective tax rate is arrived at after consideration of other taxes (such as state income taxes, sales taxes, property taxes, and excise taxes) paid by taxpayers, producing, ultimately, an *overall effective tax rate*. This overall effective tax rate is what is used to calculate the estimate for the annual Tax Freedom Day—the date that "represents how long Americans have to work in order to pay the nation's tax burden."[b]

---

a. This is not including standardized deductions or exemptions that many people would have in place and that would further lower the effective tax rate.
b. "Tax Freedom Day 2019 Is April 16th," Tax Foundation, https://taxfoundation.org/publications/tax-freedom-day/.

For example, the federal government chooses to tax capital gains differently than wages, gives parents child tax credits, allows taxpayers to claim exemptions for dependents, and permits those paying off school debt to deduct student loan interest payments. Arguably, some of these credits, exemptions, deductions, and separate tax treatments are in place because the federal government is taking a broad view of ability to pay in an effort to make the personal income tax more horizontally equitable.

Some of you may question the differential treatment of capital gains under the Internal Revenue Code (i.e., why they are taxed at a lower rate than income). Is this being done to encourage investment, perhaps based on a perception by the government that it will correct for under-investment (i.e., a market failure), thereby making it more economically efficient? Many would argue yes, though just as many would argue that the differential treatment creates horizontal inequity. There are almost always trade-offs where tax decisions are concerned, which is why it is so important to be mindful of the many considerations that go into such decisions. Section III,

"Discussion of Select Taxes and Fees," will explore some of the most common tax instruments used by governments and will address how each one fares when assessed under the criteria laid out earlier in this section. Horizontal equity, in particular, will be critical when considering tax instruments like the property tax.

b. Vertical Equity

Vertical equity dictates that people with differing abilities to pay taxes ought to pay different amounts in taxes. In some respects, this concept assumes that horizontal equity concerns (see the subsection immediately above) have been addressed and goes a step further by considering the share of the total tax burden that different populations "should" pay. While one might assume that vertical equity means that a person with a greater ability to pay more in taxes should in fact pay more, this is not actually what it means. Vertical equity merely considers a person's share of the complete tax burden based on his or her ability to pay. Vertical equity is manifested in three ways: *progressive tax burdens*, *proportional tax burdens*, and *regressive tax burdens*.

With progressive taxes, as the taxpayer's ability to pay (or as his or her income) increases, the effective tax rate also increases. With proportional taxes, the effective tax rate is consistent across differing levels of ability to pay. To be clear, this does not mean that the wealthy will not pay more in taxes in actual dollars with proportional taxes; it simply means that the percentage of their income they pay in taxes is the same percentage applicable to the less wealthy. With regressive taxes, as the ability to pay increases, the effective tax rate declines. In most cases, this will not mean that the actual dollar amount declines, just the percentage of income that is paid in taxes. All of these tax rate phenomena are shown visually in Figure 5.7.

The federal personal income tax system is a clear example of a progressive tax system. Currently available deductions and exemptions often have the effect of reducing progressivity, however.[7] Advocates of the so-called flat tax are calling for the federal personal income tax system to become proportional. Many states, including North Carolina, have proportional personal income tax systems.

2. The Benefit Principle

The *benefit principle* is another common method for conceptualizing the equity of taxes. Rather than measuring equity according to taxpayers' ability to pay taxes, this principle instead focuses on which persons or groups are using the services financed by the taxes and/or fees in question. Under the benefit principle, fairness involves

---

7. *See* "Who Gains Most from Tax Breaks," *New York Times*, April 13, 2012, http://www.nytimes.com/imagepages/2012/04/13/opinion/sunday/0415web-leonhardt2.html (easy-to-understand graphic based on Tax Policy Center data). Note that, in order to reduce one's tax burden, one must have a tax burden in the first place; 45 percent of Americans have no federal income tax liability at all. *See also* Tax Foundation, "The Income Tax System Is Progressive," https://files.taxfoundation.org/legacy/docs/The%20Income%20Tax%20System%20is%20Progressive-03.png (chart, based on data from the Joint Committee on Taxation, showing federal income tax rates for specific income groups); Heritage Foundation, "The Top 10 Percent of Earners Paid 70 Percent of Federal Income Taxes," *2011 Budget Chart Book, Federal Revenue Chart 2*, http://dailysignal.com/wp-content/uploads/top10-percent-income-earners-6004.jpg.

Figure 5.7. Vertical Equity—Different Tax Burdens

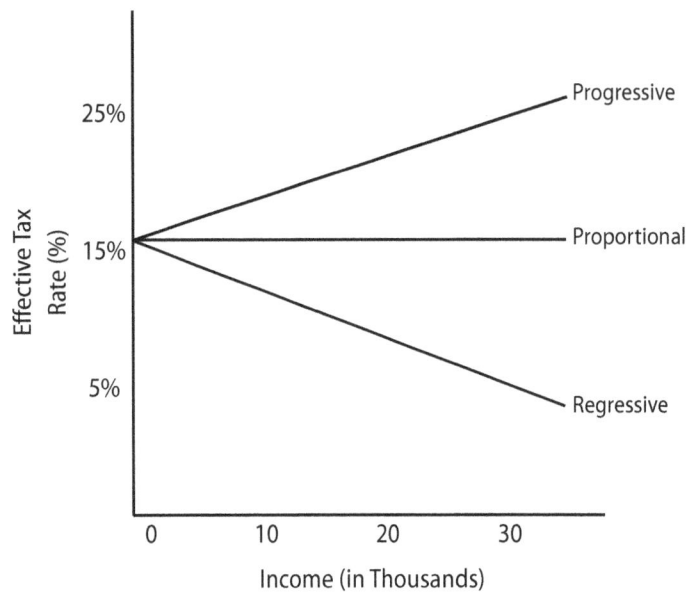

linking revenue streams from certain taxpayers to specific services being used by those taxpayers, resulting in a situation where the people who use a specific service pay more for it than those who do not (if those non-users pay at all). Ultimately, then, equity, under this principle, is based on a relationship between consumption and payment. This relationship often manifests itself as a direct payment for services received and, as part of a fair tax system, tends to works best when the services provided by the government closely resemble those provided by the private sector (such as water, electricity, and bus services).

In general, taxes are not structured and imposed according to the benefit principle (though many fees charged by governments are). How many of you have heard from citizens complaining about paying for schools through their property taxes even though they do not have any children (i.e., they don't use the schools their taxes are supporting)? These citizens are expressing their frustrations about the perceived unfairness regarding the lack of connection between consumption and payment (as discussed immediately above).

The benefit principle is frequently at odds with the ability-to-pay principle when determining the equity of a given tax. By basing the distribution of tax burdens on the question of which taxpayers benefit from a particular service and which do not rather than on the ability of taxpayers to pay for that service, you will almost always end up with taxes that do not satisfy both groups of taxpayers.

Unlike taxes, the majority of government-imposed fees (which are almost always imposed based on the benefit principle) are regressive. While a regressive tax burden is a form of vertical equity, most people do not view it as an equitable thing. By contrast, most people perceive proportional or progressive tax burdens as fair.

C. Adequacy

Adequacy, in the context of this textbook, simply refers to the question of whether there are sufficient (or adequate) funds available to finance government. The question of what an appropriate-sized government looks like, while relevant, is outside the scope of this chapter. This subsection will examine the concept of adequacy through the lenses of *revenue-raising capacity*, *tax elasticity*, and *stability.*

1. Revenue-Raising Capacity

Revenue-raising capacity refers to the ability of a revenue instrument to produce a significant amount of revenue at a reasonable tax rate. There are two embedded ideas in this definition, and both are somewhat subjective. The first is "significant amount of revenue." There are actual and political costs involved in adopting new taxes and fees. A so-called "good" tax or fee is one that will make those costs worthwhile, and it will do that by producing significant revenue. Clearly, a jurisdiction would not want to adopt a tax if it was going to generate a meager amount of revenue; doing so would earn the distinction of being "more trouble than it's worth."

The second idea embedded in the revenue-raising capacity definition is "reasonable tax rate." (This idea is also relevant to the efficiency criterion discussed in Section II.A and is also featured in Section II.D, which addresses feasibility.) If tax rates are too high—i.e., if they are unreasonable—it can actually lead to lower collection rates. This was shown in Figures 5.3 through 5.5 and discussed in the text surrounding those figures.

When various tax rates are kept at reasonable levels, this means, ideally, that the government is not taxing one or more parts of the economy at vastly higher rates than others. Allowing such noticeably higher, and perhaps unreasonable, tax rates to be applied to different sectors would likely lead to (1) substitution/efficiency losses (exemplified by the earlier example from our case study where increased taxation caused the consumer to switch from pens to pencils; Purchaser B may have preferred pens, but the excise tax imposed on pens made them too costly, compelling B to buy pencils instead) and (2) vertical inequity (see Section II.B.1.b) because similarly situated taxpayers making different choices would be bearing different burdens even though they have similar abilities to pay.

The *tax base* is the wealth of assets that are subject to a given tax. A broader tax base, one that includes more sources of wealth to tax, can have tax rates lower than those imposed on narrower tax bases and still produce the same amount of revenue. This explains why so many major taxes in the United States (e.g., the income tax, the sales tax, the property tax) have broad tax bases.

2. Tax Elasticity

Tax elasticity refers to how much a certain tax (or fee) is affected by changes in the economy, particularly by changes in personal or household income. An *elastic tax* is one that increases as income levels grow and rises at a rate that is faster than the level of income growth. An *inelastic tax*, by contrast, is sluggish in nature and changes less frequently than do personal income levels. *Unit elastic* is the term for a revenue instrument that keeps perfect pace with personal income.

Often, elected officials and other decision makers prefer elastic taxes over inelastic ones. This is because such taxes more than keep up with growth in the economy and in income levels, they outpace inflation, they require few adjustments to the existing rate structure, and they do not put leaders in the position of having to make the unpopular choice of either raising taxes or introducing new taxes as the economy grows. This preference for elastic taxes is based on the assumption—frequently a reality—that the economy will grow and is not currently in decline. When a recession hits or personal income declines within a jurisdiction, elastic taxes will fall faster than the loss in income.

3. Stability

Stability as used here refers to the desire for revenue raised over time to remain predictable and to stay at relatively constant levels. Stable revenues are easier to forecast, and having this sort of stability aids significantly with longer-term budgeting and planning. Note, however, that the preference on the part of government officials for elastic taxes that grow with the tax base and the economy, as described above, is in contrast with the desire for stable and predictable revenue streams. This tension has led most scholars to advise governments to rely on a full portfolio of revenue sources rather than to depend heavily on any one source for funds. As a result, many governments often have both elastic taxes (like sales taxes) and inelastic taxes (like the property tax) as major revenue sources.

D. Feasibility

Feasibility, much like *adequacy* (discussed immediately above), is an extremely pragmatic criterion for evaluating the pros and cons of a given tax or fee. The feasibility of taxes and fees is assessed according to two metrics: *administrative feasibility* and *political feasibility*.

1. Administrative Feasibility

Administrative feasibility refers to how easy it is to collect the tax or fee in question and how easy it is to fairly administer the tax/fee. The ease-of-collection aspect of administrative feasibility has two facets. First, taxes and fees that are considered "good" should not be costly to administer and collect. As public administrators, you do not want to spend a fair portion of the revenue generated by a specific tax or fee to finance the collection of that tax or fee. Second, taxes and fees should not be overly burdensome (financially or otherwise) for taxpayers to pay.

The goals of government, then, should be to impose taxes and fees with low administrative (internal) and low compliance (taxpayer) costs and to always be thinking of ways to lower these costs even further. The federal personal income tax is often criticized for not being underpinned by these goals. Many critics attack both the costs incurred by the Internal Revenue Service in overseeing this federal tax (administrative costs) and the costs borne by taxpayers, e.g., hiring tax preparers, in paying it (compliance costs).

While administrative feasibility is chiefly concerned with the costs of administering a tax or fee, the question of whether the tax/fee can actually be implemented sometimes arises. The classic example used in economics coursework is the idea of a tax on bad thoughts. This may be a popular idea and viewed as a form of sin tax, but how could you ever possibly implement it?

2. Political Feasibility

The second measure of feasibility, political feasibility, refers to the perceived likelihood that citizens are willing to tolerate a given tax. The literature on the willingness of elected officials to adopt unpopular positions, including those related to the imposition of new types of taxes and tax increases, tends to be either pessimistic or pragmatic in nature, depending on one's perspective. For example, during recessions, when government revenues are in decline, the majority of research shows that increases in tax and fee rates, along with the introduction of additional taxes and fees, are much less common than are decreases in service delivery and layoffs.[8] This reflects what is perceived to be the unwillingness of elected officials to increase taxes.

Citizens, for their parts, react to different taxes in different ways. Some taxes incite strong and passionate responses, while others go almost unnoticed. There are three types of citizen responses to proposed revenue increases. The first is *absolute tax intolerance*, where any increase in taxes is instantly rejected outright by taxpayers, who may as a group be viewed as anti-tax. The second is *sticker shock*, where the high rate/increased amount of the tax, once revealed, causes citizens to reject it. The third is *reasonableness*, where citizens assess the new tax (or a rate increase) in a reasonable manner, weighing the tax/increase's costs and benefits.

This third type of citizen response leads to an important question: How can governments get citizens to behave reasonably when it comes to taxes? Three methods have been suggested. Some may not be feasible; some are possibly unethical. The first tactic for soliciting a reasonable citizen response to a new tax/increase is to link the tax/increase to the services that will be funded by it, highlighting just how important new revenue is for service provision. Some services are obviously going to be more popular and visible than others. For example, in many states, local governments are authorized to earmark local sales taxes for specific purposes. This tends to make these taxes more popular. Citizens can see where their tax dollars are going and, if they support the services slated to receive funding, they are likely to be more willing to tolerate an increased sales tax. Earmarks for schools, stadiums, and economic development are viewed favorably by taxpayers and thus are fairly common. You see very few earmarks for landfills, though.

---

8. *See* Whitney B. Afonso, "Coping with the Great Recession: Theory and Practice for County Governments," *International Journal of Public Administration* 36, no. 11 (2013): 768–79 (reviewing the literature and providing examples).

The second way a government might foster a reasonable citizen response to proposed taxes/rate increases is contradictory to the approach listed just above and is ethically suspect. It has to do with the level of visibility of taxes. Less visible types of taxes tend to be more popular among taxpayers than those that are more overt, such as property and income taxes.[9] Many citizens do not realize the full extent of their tax burdens. Similarly, many are unaware of the precise cost to them of new taxes. This gap in information makes citizens less likely to reject new taxes.[10]

What makes a given tax or fee less visible to taxpayers? The two most common factors are (1) when the tax/fee is collected frequently and in small increments (making it difficult, without good recordkeeping, to keep track of total amounts paid) and (2) when the revenue instrument being used in a given situation is being used simultaneously by multiple governments (making payout amounts less visible to the individual taxpayer, since his or her reported taxes paid will be shown in the aggregate rather than broken down into specific levels of government to which the taxes are being remitted).

Sales taxes are a classic example of a less visible type of tax. You pay sales taxes on almost everything you buy. They cost you $0.30 here, $2.50 there—it is difficult to know how much you spend in total over the course of a year. Adding to the confusion is the fact that you pay both state and local sales taxes. Most people do not think about how much of their money is going to which level of government, making it difficult to hold those governments accountable for those outgoing funds. Some states have state, county, municipal, and special district sales taxes, further exacerbating this problem.

The third method for achieving reasonable citizen responses to taxes/rate increases involves exporting the tax burden to non-residents. Doing this makes taxes and fees more popular—or at least less objectionable—with citizens. A great deal of this depends on the revenue instrument used by the government and on the community. For example, in states like Florida, you can have local option fuel taxes. These taxes are much like the local sales taxes found in North Carolina, where the revenue raised stays in the local/taxing jurisdiction, except that they are excise taxes on fuel. Who bears the burden of these local option fuel taxes? It very much depends on the county imposing the tax. In rural counties with no major highways running through them, the local option fuel taxes will largely be borne by residents. However, in counties with universities, robust tourism industries, major highways, etc., it is reasonable to expect that non-residents will contribute a significant amount of revenue thanks to these fuel taxes. Other revenue instruments will result in the same outcome, with

---

9. Property and income taxes are some of the most visible taxes in this country, and they are also some of the least popular with citizens. For more on visibility and acceptability regarding taxes, see Whitney Afonso, "It Was an (Im)Perfect Illusion: Fiscal Illusion and You," *Death & Taxes* (UNC School of Government public finance blog), May 22, 2017, https://deathandtaxes.sog.unc.edu/it-was-an-imperfect-illusion-fiscal-illusion -and-you/.

10. For an overview of some of these issues, see Whitney B. Afonso, "Fiscal Illusion in State and Local Finances: A Hindrance to Transparency," *State and Local Government Review* 46, no. 3 (2014): 219–28.

the total revenue raised being dependent on the composition of the economy and location of the taxing jurisdiction.

III. Discussion of Select Taxes and Fees

This section will examine the four tax evaluation criteria—discussed in the sections above—in the context of property taxes, sales taxes, and various user fees. While these are critical sources of revenue for most jurisdictions in the state, they will not reflect all of the revenue sources relied upon by your community. Accordingly, the discussion in this section is not intended to be comprehensive. Instead, it is meant to be illustrative of the four criteria in action and to help the reader further understand how the criteria apply to actual revenue sources.

A. Property Taxes

The property tax has been at the heart of local government financing for a century now and has allowed for much local government autonomy. While it no longer makes up the percentage of total local revenue it once did, the property tax remains the largest source of own-source (meaning non–federal government) revenue for local governments nationwide, and North Carolina is no exception. The property tax is often viewed as a "good," though not very popular, tax because it satisfies many of the four evaluation criteria. This subsection will analyze how the property tax performs under those criteria in the following order: efficiency, equity, adequacy, and feasibility.

1. Efficiency

Judged under the first criterion, the property tax is a relatively efficient tax. It has a broad base and relatively low tax rates on average, which suggests that it will produce little dead weight loss. Additionally, the supply of land in most jurisdictions is relatively fixed (though annexation, which by definition adds to the land total in a jurisdiction, is an exception), making the supply also relatively inelastic. This inelastic supply leads to less efficiency loss. This is in part why many economists and scholars prefer the split rate property tax (or land value tax), where land is taxed at a different and higher rate than the structures on top of the land, which are more elastic or sensitive to change in rates than is the demand for land itself. Of course, not all property is taxed, which narrows the tax base and increases the necessary tax rate—leading to higher taxes and, subsequently, greater dead weight loss. What types of property go untaxed? Government-owned properties, Native American lands, and non-profit properties like churches are the most common examples. Clearly these properties are exempted from taxation for reasons other than efficiency.

2. Equity

Measuring equity, our second criterion, involves looking at how successfully and consistently property is assessed (and somewhat on how it is structured). In terms of horizontal equity, the property tax often falls short. This is in part due to the choices that people make, but, more importantly from a government perspective, it is connected to the fact that there are many ways the government can tax like properties differently. For example, if your jurisdiction has a cyclical assessment cycle,[11] as the economy grows (or declines), some taxpayers end up being taxed under the previous economy. This outcome is typically viewed as an issue tied to growth. If Property Owner A's home was assessed this year, and if the community in which she lives is growing, then her property tax bill will be much higher than the bill for the owner of a nearly identical home assessed five years ago. This scenario reared its ugly head during the Great Recession. Owners of homes that were assessed right before the housing bubble burst, during what was at the time a boom, saw their tax burdens increase, while those with property assessed during the recession, at values that were likely the same as or even lower than what they were pre-recession, saw their burdens decrease.

The extent of property assessment differentials depends in large part on the quality of the assessor. Does a house with an additional window in the third floor attic get assessed at a higher value than the same home without one? Ideally, the assessed value of a home should capture the home's market price. For homes that have not recently been on the market, however, arriving at this value can be challenging. In terms of vertical equity, the property tax is slightly progressive.[12] Many states try to make it more vertically equitable with circuit breakers[13] and exclusions.

In terms of our third criterion, the property tax can be called an adequate tax, as it generates a great deal of revenue at relatively low rates and is stable and inelastic. While property taxes do not grow with the economy, they also do not drop as much (typically) as do other taxes during economic downturns.

The property tax also satisfies our last criterion, feasibility. Its widespread use in this country leaves no question that it is administratively feasible, and there is little doubt about its political feasibility.

The administrative and compliance costs associated with property taxes are not overly burdensome. The political feasibility of these taxes may come into question when a government is considering increasing the property tax. While it is fairly straightforward from an administrative perspective to raise property taxes, tax and

---

11. An example of such a cycle is a county that is broken into six sections and that assesses one section each year.

12. Though our current focus is on who bears the burden of a tax on property, it is worth noting that if demand for rental units is very high, then property owners will be able to shift the burden of property taxes to renters, making it less progressive.

13. A "circuit breaker" in this context means a "targeted tax break . . . that limits or reduces property taxes for certain individuals." Tonya Moreno, "Property Tax Circuit Breaker Relief," *The Balance,* October 12, 2018, https://www.thebalance.com/what -is-a-property-tax-circuit-breaker-3193326.

expenditure limitations created by political concerns often limit what jurisdictions can do legally, and the political unpopularity of the property tax often restricts what elected and public officials can realistically do.

B. Sales Taxes

The sales tax has become the second-largest source of own-source revenue for local governments. Its growth over the past few decades has been tremendous nationwide, including in North Carolina. Because the sales tax is a fundamentally different tax than the property tax, it should come as no surprise that it performs differently when evaluated using our four criteria. In terms of efficiency, a pure sales tax (which is not common) would be assessed very differently than the type of sales taxes found in North Carolina (and in most states). If the entire set of goods (and services) in a jurisdiction were taxed at the same (low) rate, and if the sales tax in that jurisdiction resembled a consumption tax, then the sales tax would have an incredibly broad base and would be able to generate a good deal of revenue. This would lead to less dead weight loss. Additionally, there would be few substitutes for preferred goods under this paradigm, and people's consumption patterns would not change much.[14] However, in reality, we exempt most services and many goods (the most common being food, prescription drugs, and clothing) from the sales tax. These exemptions significantly narrow the size of the tax base, which, in turn, results in higher rates and greater changes in consumption patterns. This leads to higher levels of inefficiency.

Perhaps some readers are thinking, "We should exempt food from the tax base, it is only fair!" Many states, including North Carolina at the state level, have echoed those sentiments and allowed for this exemption. In terms of horizontal equity, a tax on the sale of food is reasonable and equitable. However, in terms of vertical equity, such a tax—which is a pure consumption tax—is highly regressive and places higher effective tax rates on lower-income consumers (even though all people are subjected to the same sales tax rate, the poor spend a greater percentage of their income on taxable goods). By removing key elements of the tax base, mainly those goods considered essentials, the sales tax becomes less regressive and is considered more equitable.

Sales taxes, like property taxes, do well when being evaluated on their adequacy—though they would do even better with broader and more inclusive tax bases. Unlike the property tax, sales taxes are elastic. This means that they are exciting sources of funding that generate revenue that outpaces the growth in the economy. However, they are also less predictable and stable than other taxes, which could lead to revenue shortfalls during economic downturns.

Sales taxes are also feasible taxes. The costs to administer them are low and are often borne by the retailers who are responsible for collecting taxes from consumers and remitting them to the state. The compliance costs associated with sales taxes are also low (while the compliance costs of use taxes are, in theory, higher for consumers,

---

14. A sales tax would still change consumption patterns to some extent because, for most goods, the increase in price brought on by the addition of the tax would lower consumption.

these taxes are not typically remitted by individuals). The political feasibility of sales taxes is also high. The rapid growth in their use demonstrates that many taxpayers prefer relying more heavily on sales taxes to fund services than on other forms of revenue. This is likely the case because sales taxes are less visible than many other revenue instruments and are perceived as being exportable to non-residents.

C. User Fees

Determining whether and how user fees satisfy the four criteria for assessing taxes and fees is much more challenging because there are so many different types of user fees. For simplification purposes, this section will focus on utility fees for water services and on park entrance fees. In terms of efficiency, these two fees are quite different. Water is a necessity, and so the demand for it is fairly inelastic. However, you can imagine that if the fees/rates for water were to get high enough, people might stop watering their lawns and would try to take faster showers. Thus, the amount of water fees might distort some consumer behaviors, but this is outweighed by the fact that there are no good substitutes for water and the base level of water consumption is inelastic. When it comes to measuring efficiency, park entrance fees are a different matter. Not all parks charge such fees, so it is not a fee imposed on the entire base. Further, there are substitutes for going to a given park, and visiting parks, unlike consuming water, is not a necessity, so demand is likely to be elastic. This means that there will be more dead weight loss and tax avoidance connected with park entrance fees (and more behavior changes among consumers) than with fees for water consumption.

In terms of equity, both water service fees and park entrance fees satisfy the benefit principle (though to different extents), in that those who most benefit from the particular service are the ones who finance it. Often, utilities are self-sufficient operations, and so they are almost purely satisfying the benefit principle. Parks, on the other hand, are rarely self-sufficient, so the benefit principle is only partially satisfied. In terms of the ability-to-pay principle, user fees are typically regressive, and water and park fees are no exception. Water bills are more likely to make up a larger percentage of income for low-income consumers than for their wealthier counterparts. The same is true for park fees, which may also "price out" lower-income consumers. This means that these fees are disproportionately paid by middle- and high-income earners, though, making them less regressive (but limiting access is not really the goal).

Water fees and park entrance fees also differ in terms of adequacy. As mentioned above, water (and sewer) fees are often sufficient to fund the utility provider in its entirety, making them adequate from a revenue-raising standpoint. They are also relatively stable because they revolve around a necessity. The same cannot be said for park entrance fees. While the revenue raised by these fees contributes to the cost of maintaining public parks, park entrance fees do not have the revenue-raising capacity of other taxes and fees. They are also elastic, so they will grow when the economy is doing well but suffer losses during economic downturns. Thus, they are not a stable source of income.

The feasibility of these two types of fees also varies. Water fees score relatively high on the administrative feasibility scale. They carry low compliance costs, which are borne by the consumer, and the costs associated with administering these fees make up a relatively small fraction of the taxing jurisdiction's revenue. Also, the administrative costs for water services are declining as the technology for tracking consumer use improves (with the advent of smart meters and the like). Park entrance fees, on the other hand, can have much higher compliance costs (depending on the park). This is one reason, of many, why most parks do not charge entrance fees. Determining the political feasibility of park entrance fees is dependent upon the community in which the park is located, among other things. Park fees are often exportable, and thus may receive higher support from citizens if there is a perception that non-residents will be paying the bulk of the fees. (Note that this exportability principle does not apply to water fees.) Both water and park entrance fees are relatively visible in nature. While consumers may not fully appreciate the extent of the taxes they pay out over the course of a year, water and park fees, which are paid either monthly or at the time of consumption, tend to not go unnoticed (like a sales tax might).

IV. Conclusion

It is critical for local government officials to understand the ramifications of their choices, even when they have little discretion over what those choices are. To best serve citizens, officials need to know how the taxes and fees they decide upon and impose burden different groups in different ways and how these decisions may affect citizen behavior. Officials also need to be able to communicate such issues with many different stakeholders. The four criteria examined in this chapter can be used to facilitate these conversations—both in terms of explaining decisions and learning to appreciate the perspectives of other parties.

As far as citizen concerns go, issues around equity will likely be the ones most commonly raised. Public officials will encounter people talking about the "fairness" of a given tax or fee. Citizen understanding of what is or is not fair, however, may be completely different from officials' views on the matter, leading to a great deal of frustration and confusion all around. The language, context, and perspectives presented in this chapter may not change how anyone actually internalizes what they think of as "fair," but the author hopes that this text will foster dialogue and provide insights into the value and legitimacy of considering equity in different ways. The four criteria discussed in the chapter are not always easy to understand, especially since they often contradict and compete with each other. Nonetheless, all four are equally important and should be considered by officials when updating, adopting, and understanding the revenue portfolios of their jurisdictions.

Chapter 6

Financial Forecasting for Budgeting

Dale J. Roenigk

Introduction

"Prediction is very difficult, especially if it's about the future."
—Niels Bohr

Local government budgets are required to be balanced between planned expenditures and expected revenues. The expenditure side of the equation is mostly under the control of the local government. After the new fiscal year starts there are a variety of ways a local government can control expenditures if adjustments are needed, such as cutbacks and hiring freezes, or spend more money if surpluses are high. But the revenue side of the balancing task has an important element of uncertainty and limited control. We can choose tax rates and fees and estimate expected revenues, but we cannot be sure of what the future year will produce. Sales taxes may fall short, occupancy taxes may come in low, and new property development expected to bring in new revenue may not occur. Moreover, we cannot change tax rates midyear if revenues are coming in low.

The simple reality of revenue forecasting is that you will almost certainly be wrong if being right is judged by ending up exactly with the total revenues forecast. Instead, our objective should be twofold. First, we should strive for a level of accuracy in our aim that will minimize the need for major adjustments when the forecasts are missed. Second, we should look for insights that good forecasting can produce that will support informed budget decisions in the forecast year and beyond.

This chapter will lay out a framework for carrying out the process of revenue forecasting needed for local government budgeting. It will break this framework into three steps:

- what you should do before you forecast,
- the actual forecasting If revenues, and
- the critical tasks that should take place after the forecast is made.

As part of this framework, the chapter will recommend six best practices that should be part of a good revenue forecasting effort by a local government.

Before You Forecast

While North Carolina state law does lay out requirements for setting up a local budget, it provides very limited guidance on how to forecast revenues. North Carolina General Statute (hereinafter G.S.) 159-13(b)(7) simply states that "[e]stimated revenues shall include only those revenues reasonably expected to be realized in the budget years, including amounts to be realized from collections of taxes levied in prior fiscal years."[1] Details about what is reasonable must be guided by practice and experience.

Figure 6.1. Range of Estimation Targets

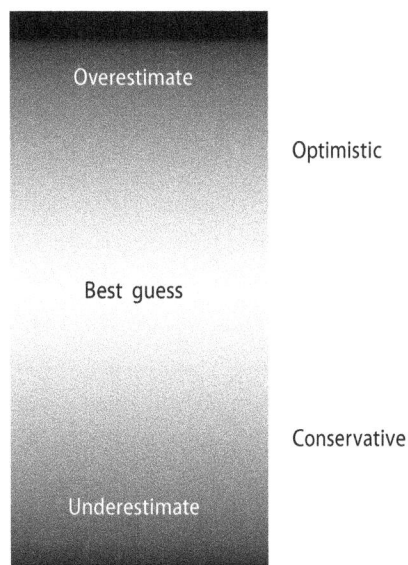

1. Chapter 159, Article 13 of the North Carolina General Statutes (hereinafter G.S.).

An important foundation in preparing to forecast is having a clear understanding of where one is aiming. If our forecast is exactly right, balancing the budget should be easy. However, as Figure 6.1 illustrates, there are consequences of being too high or too low with our estimates. If we overestimate revenues that are eventually collected, we will be short on money for operations. This can be a significant and disruptive problem requiring midyear cutbacks or tapping into unreserved fund balance. Choosing to be conservative and underestimate revenues may seem to be the safer strategy. But if revenues come in higher than the forecast, a local government may have unnecessarily raised tax rates higher than needed, made unneeded budget cuts, or put limits on services. In general, most local governments appear to aim to be slightly on the conservative side of the middle line (in Figure 6.1), as this appears to have less critical consequences. If you intentionally aim to be conservative, this should mean that you generally have more surplus revenue results than lows. If you seek to be exactly right, forecast results should appear on both sides of the target: surpluses and shortfalls. The key here is to have an awareness of where you are aiming so you can judge your accuracy and know what should be expected when monitoring revenue results during the budget year. In any case, you want to be sure you are not hitting very wide of the target because of the costs of being too optimistic or too conservative.

Have a Model for How Revenue Is Generated

When it comes time to prepare to make a revenue forecast, we ought to have an idea of what drives revenue collected. Even a simple model for the factors we expect to drive a particular revenue can help us improve our forecasting. Figure 6.2 provides a generic model for what may drive collected revenues. Typically, population or economic activities are key factors. But another key insight of the model is that while we wish to forecast the final box of collected revenues, the amount we collect from year to year is also being determined by the tax rate (or fee rate) and collection efficiency, which are variable. Because these factors can vary from year to year and represent policy choices or administrative capabilities, we should really seek to forecast the tax or fee base rather than the final collected revenues and then apply the relevant tax rates or collection efficiency for the coming year. For example, if we have data on collected property tax revenues over a decade, the variation in the final revenue collected is being driven by changes in the tax base, but it is also being determined by changes in the tax rate or the collection efficiency over time. Collected revenues over time may not have risen because of a higher tax base but rather higher tax rates.

Figure 6.2. Generic Revenue Model

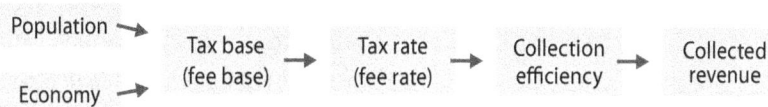

When we seek to forecast next year's revenue, we should be making the forecast on the base and then applying whatever new tax rate we want to use. If the rates or collection efficiency have not changed notably over time, this step could be skipped. But whenever possible, one should forecast the base and then apply the tax rate and the collection efficiency to estimate expected revenues with more accuracy.

Part of the challenge for a local government is that there is not a single revenue source but many, and each is likely to have differences that may affect how to forecast them. This will vary by jurisdiction, but a typical local government may have thirty to sixty different revenue sources. Some may be quite small relative to the entire budget, but all must be forecast. To make sure this is done well, the revenue forecaster should have a good understanding of the jurisdiction's revenue sources.

Create a Revenue Manual

Because of the varying details and the other competing tasks of the budget process, a best practice is to create a revenue manual that gathers the essential background information into a single simple document. The revenue manual is meant to be a depository of key knowledge that can be pulled out as a resource each year when it comes time to produce a revenue forecast.

A revenue manual does not have to be a large or complicated document. Typically, jurisdictions set up a single page or sometimes two per revenue source, which contain a small set of items. Possible items that might be included are as follows:

- description of the revenue source,
- authority for levying the tax or fee (e.g., statutes or ordinances),
- use and restrictions,
- rates (current and changes over time),
- possible exemptions,
- special events in the local history of the revenue,
- drivers of the revenue,
- forecasting method and assumptions used,
- multiple years of the data in tabular format, and
- a graph showing multiple years.

Creating a revenue manual the first time may take more effort than is available to do it all in one year. Consider creating the pages for just five to ten revenue sources in the first year and gradually adding to the document until it is complete. Over time the revenue manual should be updated each year with new data for the tax rates, data table, and graph, along with any changes to other items that should mostly be consistent. With a good command of details for the revenues to be forecast, the revenue forecaster can move on to the next step of making the actual forecast.

Best Practice 1: Know Your Revenues; Create a Revenue Manual

A revenue manual is a simple document describing the revenues that a local government collects. It is meant to be a background document to inform elected officials, citizens, and staff.

See Appendices A, B, C, and D at the end of this chapter for example pages from local government revenue manuals.

Making the Forecast

There are a variety of methods used to make revenue forecasts in local government. There are tradeoffs typically in accuracy, level of effort required, and the transparency behind the method. The objective should be to use the most appropriate method. Best practice 2 is to select a method or methods that fit the abilities and needs of the organization. But which method? There are a variety of ways to categorize forecasting techniques. Here, we will divide these techniques into two broad categories: qualitative and quantitative. The best method for estimation should probably be a blend of different techniques/approaches that depends on the situation in both time and place.

> **Best Practice 2: Select an Appropriate Method to Make a Forecast**
>
> Selecting the right method or combination of methods to make a forecast depends heavily on the availability of data, staff time, and technical skills. The right approach may vary by revenue source, as not all revenues will be the same. Estimation is probably strongest when using a combination of quantitative data with qualitative judgment to sharpen the forecast. Blending methods should be done to best fit needs and capabilities.

Qualitative Techniques

Qualitative forecasting techniques include expert judgment, consensus forecasting, and more elaborate approaches, such as the Delphi method.[2] Expert judgment by far is the most common and appropriate qualitative method for a local government, particularly smaller jurisdictions. Expert judgment for forecasting relies on some identified expert to make a reliable forecast. This method is particularly valuable when there are little or no historical data available or when major changes are anticipated in what is driving local revenues, such as economic downturns or demographic shifts. Critically, this approach depends on having an expert with some track record that demonstrates the expertise rather than just a person who by position would be thought to have expertise. Although many experts will not have kept such a track record, it may be useful to ask about their specific experience with making forecasts, in order to validate whether you should rely on their expert judgment.

Expert judgment may come through a variety of routes that are connected to different revenue streams. Typically, someone in the budget, finance, or manager's office may have had this responsibility for overall forecasting. For someone with prior experience and knowledge who has a feel for the local jurisdiction, this expertise may be very accurate and should be counted as a boon if it is the case. But if possible, seek to verify that expertise is evident when it comes to forecasting. In other cases, local expertise may be found with specific service professionals. For example, staff in the parks department may be in tune with fee revenue associated with recreational fees and likely changes in the future. Staff in planning or building inspections will probably have a good feel for future building activity that might influence property tax base growth. A utilities director should have a handle on the future direction

---

2. Although not as common anymore, the Delphi method is still used, but not at the local level, as far as is known. For more detail, see *Wikipedia*, s.v. "Delphi method," last modified June 4, 2021, https://en.wikipedia.org/wiki/Delphi_method.

of utilities revenues. Beyond local expertise, a local government forecaster may find experts in finance in state or regional organizations. For example, in North Carolina, the League of Municipalities (NCLM) provides advice on several revenue trends and can bring expertise to bear that a local government may not have.[3] There are economic forecasters who work in state universities whose work can be helpful. Finally, there are other economic forecasters in regional organizations or working for private banks who circulate economic forecasts that might provide guidance.

Surveys suggest that expert judgment is one of the most common methods local governments use in some way. If the expert judgment is good, this forecasting may be reasonably accurate. It is especially helpful when data are lacking, or the circumstances appear to be changing. The cost of using expert judgment is typically low (usually free beyond the search effort) and requires few resources from the local government. However, it is important to recognize that experts can have limits that may not always be obvious, such as biases, selective perceptions, wishful thinking, and inconsistency; it is also not possible for expert judgment to be replicated by others. This expert judgment is typically easy to present, but we may not be able to understand the basis for the judgment. Very limited evidence suggests expert judgment may be somewhat less accurate than other estimation methods when trends are in place but may be needed at inflection points in trends.[4]

Quantitative Techniques

Quantitative techniques, as the name suggests, rely on numbers to make forecasts. As a rule, these techniques use historical data and assume past trends will continue. Where trends are in place, the limited research in local government forecasting suggests these methods are more accurate. Broadly, quantitative methods can be broken into several categories:

- Trend Models
  - Naive
  - Incremental
  - Moving Average
  - Time Series
    - Simple Regression
    - Additive Regression
- Causal or Econometric Models

Trend Models

Trend models all use historical data to make forecasts. The simplest model is known as the *naïve forecast*. The naïve forecast simply takes the last number from a data series and uses that as the estimate for the next period. So if last year's revenue was

---

3. For more information, see the "Revenue Forecasting" page on the NCLM's website at https://www.nclm.org/financial-consulting/revenue-forecasts.

4. Dongsung Kong, "Local Government Revenue Forecasting: The California County Experience," *Journal of Public Budgeting, Accounting & Financial Management* 19, no. 2 (2007): 178–99.

$1 million, that becomes the forecast for the next year. The method is very simple and consequently easy to implement in terms of time required and not needing technical skills. The term *naïve* should not be taken to be disparaging in this context but rather refers to a situation when you lack historical data or do not have a good model for what drives a given revenue. Starting with the last value arguably makes sense in this situation. However, once you have more historical data, other simple methods are not significantly more difficult and will almost certainly provide more accuracy. The last value forecast may nevertheless make sense in some cases, where the amount of the revenue is relatively small or volatile and creating more complex analysis will only be of marginal utility.

Incremental

Incremental models simply take the last actual revenue and add (or subtract) some increment to get the forecast. This increment might be expressed as dollars or in percentage terms. The increment selected may be tied to a single point or use multiple points in the history. The method can rely solely on historical data to determine the increment, or it might be "fine-tuned" with expert judgment. The method is easy to explain. Only modest amounts of historical data are needed, and the technique is easy to implement. The important limitation of this forecasting method, like all trend models, is that accuracy may suffer during times of significant change, such as an economic downturn, if the past trend is being broken.

There are several different ways to select the increment to be used. The simplest would be to look at the last change in dollar terms or percentages and use that. For example, if the current year showed a 3 percent increase over the prior year, we would forecast a growth of 3 percent for next year. A more sophisticated approach would be to look at a period of several years of past data and determine the average increment over this period and use that as a forecast. This calculation is less likely to be influenced by exceptional years (high or low increments). A third approach would be to look at a historical set of data and select the largest or smallest increment or perhaps the second largest or smallest increment. Assuming there has been growth, selecting the smallest or second smallest increment would be a conservative strategy that still reflects the available recent experience of the jurisdiction. Selecting the highest increment (or second highest) is probably not warranted, as it is more likely to be optimistic and lead to overestimating revenue. Here again, expert judgment might be brought in to examine the increments to decide which is most appropriate. If the revenue has been increasing but at a slower rate, selecting one of the lower numbers rather than an average might be better. Conversely, if the history of revenue changes indicates higher rates of growth in more recent years, then an increment above average might be more appropriate. For incremental models using the average or the largest or smallest increment, you should try to look at five or more years of historical data if possible. The analysis can still be done with fewer years but runs the risk that the most recent years are not fully representative.

Figure 6.3 shows how an analysis might be done starting with the percentage changes in property taxes collected over the prior six years. On average, property tax

Figure 6.3. Percentage Changes in d Valorem Revenue

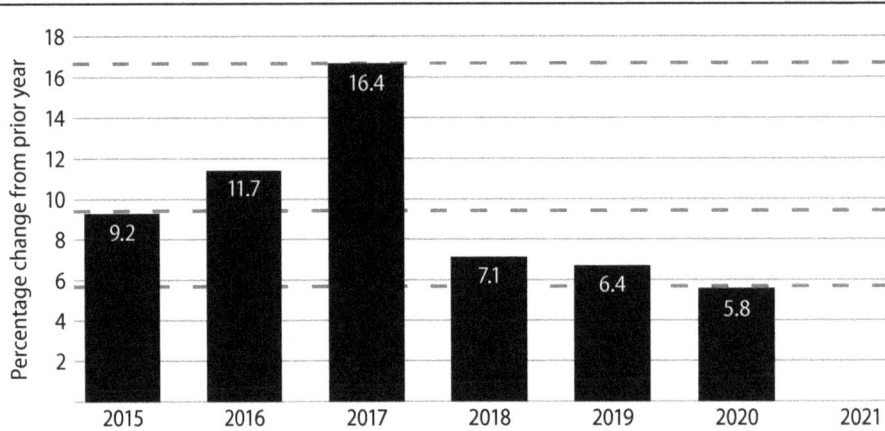

revenues increased by 9.4 percent each year. The lowest year, which was the prior year, saw a growth of only 5.6 percent, while the largest year, 2017, saw a growth of 16.4 percent. For next year's increment, one might use the average increment. However, the last three years were all below average, suggesting that growth is slowing, and a lower estimate is warranted. Using the last increment of 5.6 percent may be the best option. This would ideally be supplemented by expert judgment as to why growth has slowed and what increment seems most appropriate for the coming budget year. It could even be the case that if the considered view is that growth will continue to slow, an expected increment of something lower than 5.6 percent would be the best choice.

Moving Average

Moving average trend models also depend on having historical data. The technique simply takes the last x years, calculates the average, and uses this as the forecast. They are easy to calculate and easy to explain. Microsoft Excel (hereinafter Excel) spreadsheet software will even calculate the moving average on a line chart without having to make the calculations in the spreadsheet. Typically, the average is done for a period of three to ten years. Table 6.1 shows how you might take a set of data and calculate an average for the first three years, as shown in the right-hand column. The

Table 6.1. Sales Tax and Moving Average Calculation

Year	Local option sales tax	Three-year moving average
2014	$1,900,287	
2015	$1,992,311	
2016	$2,108,683	$2,000,427
2017	$2,102,576	$2,067,857
2018	$2,278,779	$2,163,346
2019	$2,705,076	$2,362,144
2020	$2,874,741	$2,619,532

Figure 6.4. Moving Average Forecast for Local Option Sales Tax

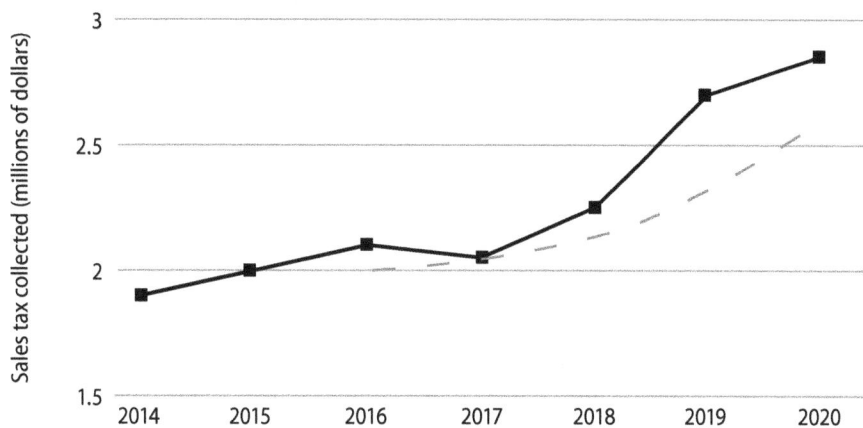

average is then copied down, or "moves," creating a moving average that is always three years in this example but constantly moving to the next year each time. The shorter the period selected, the more responsive the moving average line will be to changes. The biggest drawback of moving average forecasts is they will lag data that are strongly trending. For a data series that is rising, this means the moving average forecast will generally be too low. This has the advantage of being conservative, but it may be too conservative. If the historical data are trending down, the moving average forecast will always be too high or overestimate the likely revenues. This problem of lag with moving averages can partly be reduced by using shorter time lengths or by using more sophisticated types of moving averages, such as exponential moving averages. Another technique that is sometimes used is to create a moving average and then apply a second technique of regression on the smoothed average line to project the revenues. Usually however, simply using regression on the untransformed data will produce results that are as good. The moving average technique for forecasting local government revenues is less commonly used, but some jurisdictions do use it.[5]

Figure 6.4 shows a simple three-year moving average for sales tax. In the early years, the sales tax revenues were growing only slowly, so the moving average stayed close to the actuals, though always below or lagging. In the latter years of the sales tax data, revenues increased significantly, and the lagging gap got larger. Excel spreadsheets can create this chart easily. Simply first create the line chart for the revenue of interest. Then right click with a mouse while pointing at the selected graph line, choose Add Trendline in the pop-up menu, and then select Moving Average in the format trendline box. In this case, the average period of three years was selected, but other lengths can be chosen.

---

5. For further discussion of methods, see Kong, "Local Government Revenue Forecasting"; Carmen Cirincione, Gustavo A. Gurrieri, and Bart van de Sande, "Municipal Government Revenue Forecasting: Issues of Method and Data," *Public Budgeting and Finance* 19, no. 1 (1999): 26–46; Howard A. Frank and Yongfeng Zhao, "Determinants of Local Government Revenue Forecasting Practice: Empirical Evidence from Florida," *Journal of Public Budgeting, Accounting & Financial Management* 21, no. 1 (2009): 17–35.

Figure 6.5. Time Series Simple Regression

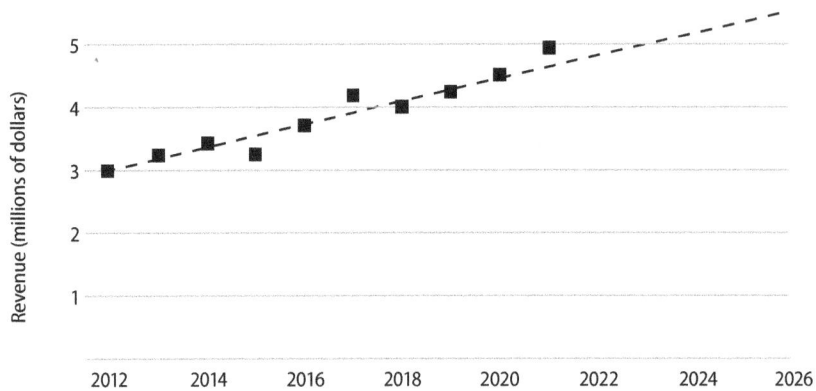

Figure 6.6. Time Series Simple Regression with Volatile Data

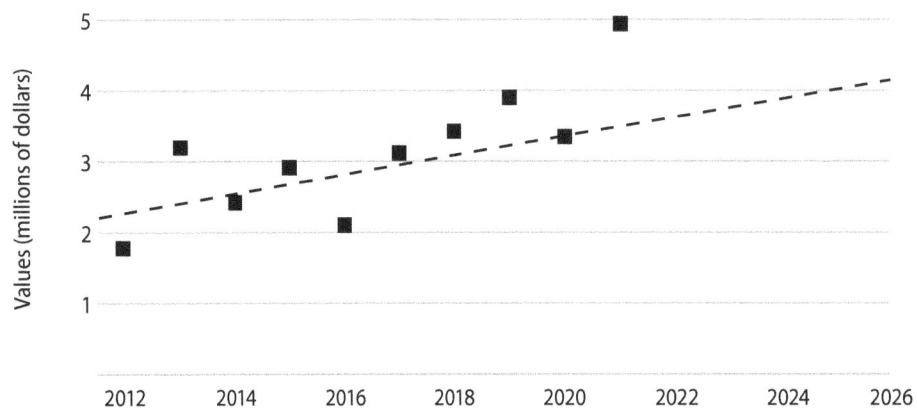

Time Series—Simple Regression

Although the term *regression* may be intimidating for those who have not had much statistical experience, the method is quite straightforward and easy to implement using tools that are available in Excel spreadsheet software. Linear regression in this context simply takes historical data and seeks to draw the best fitting line through the data. Figure 6.5 shows a set of historical revenues from 2012 to 2021. The dotted regression line simply represents a trend line through this data. This line could have been drawn by hand, but the regression fit is designed to statistically best fit the pattern with a straight line. The regression line can then be extended into the future to project future revenues. As with all trend models, this assumes the underlying trend from 2012 to 2021 will continue. In this case the regression line represents a good fitting of the data and would be a useful forecast if something does not notably alter the trend. To create this chart in Excel, simply create the desired line or scatterplot chart, right click with a mouse, and select Add Trendline in the pop-up menu. Then, select Linear under the Format Trendline box that shows up. Linear in this case is the default and is simply a regression line. If you wish to create the calculated data with the estimated numbers in Excel, you should use the Trend function to create the line fitting the actual data, but this function can also be used to create a forecast for future years.

In other situations, regression lines may not fit the data as closely but still represent a reasonable forecast. Figure 6.6 shows a different set of historical revenues that are rising over time but change more dramatically from year to year. The regression line still represents the best fit for this data, but the level of deviation from the trend line is clearly higher. The accuracy of any forecast, whatever the trend method, is going to be lower with this data than the revenue series depicted in Figure 6.5. If some analysis could be brought to bear to determine what might be causing this volatility, a more complex model might be able to improve the accuracy but will depend on a more sophisticated analysis.

Time Series—Additive Regression

Simple regression works well for many data series, but a more advanced version is additive or exponential smoothing regression. Previously this required expertise that was beyond what might be reasonable to expect in most local governments. However, starting with Excel 2016, this type of analysis has become very easy, and this method is worth consideration. Excel uses a version of additive regression known as the AAA algorithm. This stands for additive error, additive trend, and additive seasonality. This model in Excel will automatically detect if there are trends and if there is seasonality in the data. This addition of seasonality can be very helpful if you are forecasting monthly data with sales tax or other revenues that regularly vary over the course of a year. The AAA model is a sophisticated form of forecasting and will generally be more accurate with data that is trending. Additionally, the implementation within Excel will not only calculate the forecast but also show confidence intervals around the forecast and include seasonal patterns, if present. To perform this analysis in Excel, go to the Data tab on the menu and select Forecast Sheet after highlighting your data. Excel will automatically create a new worksheet, which includes the new Forecast function in Excel, and create a graph. The Forecast tool will let you force a seasonal pattern (e.g., twelve periods reflecting months) if you choose and let you set several other options that may be helpful, including the width of the confidence interval around the forecast estimate.

Figure 6.7 shows data for sales tax for a North Carolina county. This forecast was based on the first five years of actual monthly data. Seasonality was detected as expected, along with a clear upward trend. The model then forecasted its prediction, along with low and high confidence interval bands set at the 95 percent confidence level. This was then compared against the actual data extended through the forecast period. One can see that while the monthly forecast frequently missed the exact mark, the predicted confidence interval nearly always included the actual data

Figure 6.7. Time Series Additive Regression Forecast for Sales with Seasonality

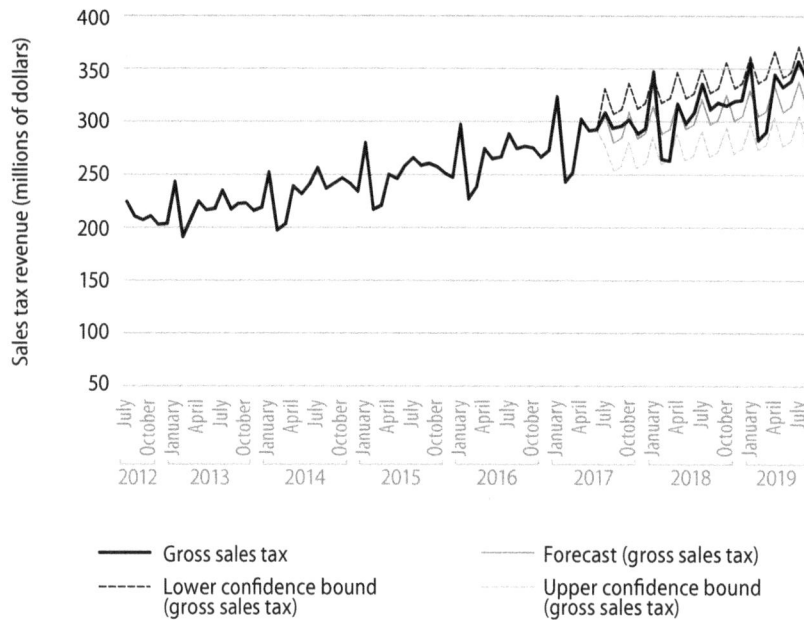

for the forecast months. The error rate by month was usually less than ten percent and on average only low by 1.9 percent. Because the additive regression technique is now easily implemented using the forecast tool in Excel 2016 or later versions, this technique can easily be added to the local government forecaster's toolbox. The important caveat is that this model, as with all the other trend models, will not work well when conditions dramatically change, as with an economic downturn. But the greater accuracy in terms of smaller forecasting errors and the automatic calculation of error bands make it worth using.

The example in Figure 6.7 used monthly data. If this forecasting tool were instead applied to annual data where we would not expect to see seasonality, the results should be the same as those of simple regression forecasts. However, this forecasting tool would also add the confidence bounds automatically, which would probably make it the better tool to use. Figure 6.8 shows the earlier revenue forecasts for Figures 6.5 and 6.6 but using the Excel forecast tool. Because seasonality was not used, the projected forecasts are straight lines. The variation in the data from Figure 6.5 was smaller, and consequently the confidence interval around the projection is narrower. The data from Figure 6.6 showed more volatility, and as a result the confidence interval is noticeably wider. The Excel forecasting tool simply makes the task of projecting the forecast much easier, adds the confidence intervals, and includes seasonality if desired.

Causal or Econometric Models

A final category of quantitative models is causal or econometric models. These models use statistical techniques, as with the simple regression techniques, but rather than relying on just the historical data, these models use gathered data that are thought to

Figure 6.8. Showing Earlier Data Using Excel Forecast Tool

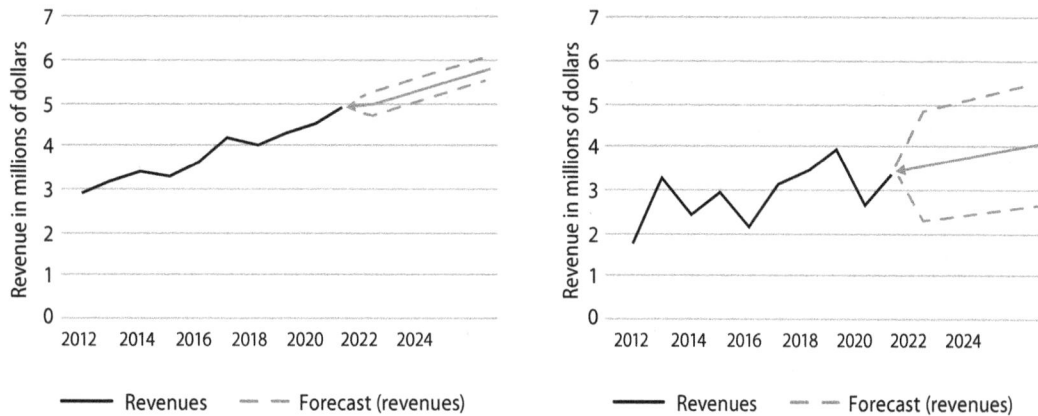

Table 6.2. Variables Used in California Econometric Model

Personal income	County personal income
	State personal income
	County income growth rate
	County per capita personal income
Employment	County total employment
	County total unemployment
	County total labor force
	County unemployment rate
	State unemployment rate
Population	County total population
	County population growth
Inflation	National prime interest rate
	National mortgage interest rate
	California Consumer Price Index (CPI)
	California CPI growth rate

drive revenues. Evidence suggests these models may be the most accurate. However, these models do not represent a technique that would be easily implemented in a local government due to the technical expertise required and the resources needed. The State of California uses a complex econometric model to predict sales tax forecasting to assist counties in their revenue projections. Table 2 shows the variables the state collects for each county before using statistical techniques to create their forecast. Its analysis showed that this econometric model was the most accurate in forty-five of fifty-eight counties studied, with an average error of 3.06 percent. Incremental models were the next best, with an average of 4.58 percent. While the improved accuracy is notable, only the state was able to make this forecasting effort. The amount of time and level of technical skills needed to use a causal/econometric model for forecasting simply make this method outside the reach of what most local governments could even consider doing. As a result, this type of model should be understood to be out there but cannot be recommended as a realistic option for local government. Many economic experts who make forecasts will use various econometric models to come to their judgments.[6]

Selecting a Method

Best practice 2 is to select an appropriate method to use for estimation. Table 6.3 provides some of the key comparisons to keep in mind with regards to the methods described. Although a jurisdiction may choose to rely on a single method, blending methods may be the best approach. Use of trend models tempered with expert judgment may be the right approach for local government in most situations. The best practice of selecting the right method should depend on accuracy, effort, and transparency (see Table 6.3).

Table 6.3. Comparing Forecasting Methods

Method	Accuracy	Effort	Transparency
Judgmental	Low to moderate (may be reasonably high if expert is good)	Low	Low to moderate, as it depends on the expert
Trend	Moderate to high when trend is stable	Low to moderate	Moderate to high
Causal	Best if good model	High	Moderate to high, as it depends on complexity

Testing Assumptions

Techniques used to make forecasts typically require assumptions, which might be about population growth rates in the community or sales estimates. These assumptions should be made on the best evidence or judgment available. To make the calculations, these assumptions must be treated as a singular number, such as a 3 percent growth rate. However, because of the uncertainty, a more honest statement would be that the best estimate is that the growth rate is going to be a certain level, such as 3 percent, but it would be plausible to see it range from 1 percent to 5 percent. The uncertainty range here may simply be noted or not, but the responsible forecaster should go the extra mile and test out this uncertainty with sensitivity analysis. Rather than make a single calculation, a forecaster should try different values for key assumptions to determine the effect on the outcome of interest. In some cases, this range of assumptions would not lead to different decisions. In these cases, we conclude the decision is insensitive to the

> **Best Practice 3: Test Assumptions for Forecasts**
>
> As part of the forecasting process, alternative assumptions should be tested to understand the range of possibilities and the sensitivity of results to key assumptions. Assumptions causing wider variation may warrant additional analysis and discussion among decision makers. Consider best- and worst-case scenarios.

---

6. Kong, "Local Government Revenue Forecasting."

uncertainty. In other cases, changes in the assumption may lead to different choices, as the decision is sensitive to the assumptions made.

Fortunately, spreadsheets make it easy to test out different assumptions. Moreover, Excel has in place three tools labeled "What-If Analysis" that can boost this testing of assumptions. These three tools make it easy for a forecaster to quickly and efficiently run a given forecast estimation and try out different assumptions to better understand the impact. The three What-If tools in Excel are Data Table, Scenario Manager, and Goal Seek and can be found on the Excel Data menu ribbon under Forecasts. Data Table allows the forecaster to test one or two assumptions at a time by specifying a range of values to substitute in the original estimation model and then quickly see the result. This is the preferable alternative to creating multiple copies of the spreadsheet and changing the values. The Data Table alternative allows the combination of assumptions to be in a single table, and it avoids the real risk that multiple copies of the spreadsheet may begin to have modifications, which means you no longer are using the same model to make your forecast. The Scenario Manager tool allows a forecaster to take a given estimation model and save it with many variables changing between different scenarios. Then, it is easy to navigate between the scenarios, and key outcome variables can be selected to produce a single table output of the various scenarios side by side. One way to use the Scenario Manager might be to create best- and worst-case forecasts, along with a best estimate, and see how the results compare. Finally, the Goal seek tool simply allows a forecaster to set a desired outcome level for some variable and let Excel figure out how to change another connected variable to produce the desired outcome. For example, you might want to figure out what the property tax rate would need to be set at to produce a given amount of revenues. You could guess manually and keep correcting until you reached the right number, but Goal Seek will do it faster and more accurately with just a few clicks. Forecasters interested in learning more about these three tools can find many videos and written content on the Internet.

Make Forecasts for Additional Years

For the purposes of the annual budget, forecasting need only be done for the coming budget year. But extending forecasting out for additional years can be worthwhile. Imagine a jurisdiction in the year 2021 forecasting for next year. Based on their examination of all revenues and expenses, their estimate is that in 2022 revenues will exceed expenses, so they expect to see a $0.1 million surplus. So their forecast is complete and conservative, and the work is done. However, as seen in Figure 6.9, if they had extended their forecast out for five years rather than a single year, the projections suggest that while the first year looks fine, expenditures are projected to rise faster than revenues, leading to growing deficits. One approach might be simply leaving this problem for next year's budget

> **Best Practice 4: Forecast Finances for Multiple Years**
>
> To provide an understanding of longer-term concerns, financial forecasting (both revenues and expenditures) should be extended for multiple years into the future. Three to five years may be enough for operational finances. A longer window of ten to twenty years might be needed for capital finances. The key is to see if projected trends in revenues and expenditures raise concerns beyond just the need to budget for the next year.

Figure 6.9. Forecast for Five Years

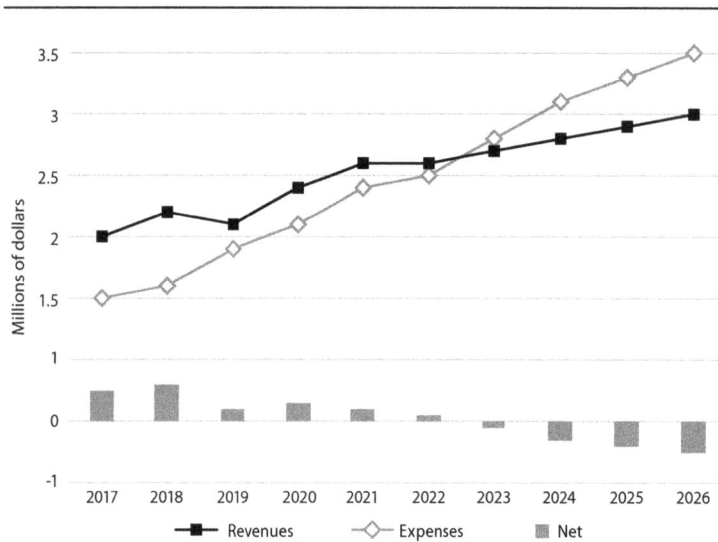

staff. However, by recognizing the looming problem early, it becomes possible for the jurisdiction to begin to look at adjustments that might be made before the crisis hits and changes become more burdensome. Additionally, even if no changes were made immediately, knowing the problems that might arise several years in the future allows time for political consensus to be built on the desired strategy to address the future projected shortfalls.

The fourth best practice recommended in this chapter is to forecast beyond the immediate budget cycle. This type of longer-term forecasting might need to be done only at the total line of all revenues and expenditures, but having detail by major categories may help clarify where the trends are moving by expense or revenue categories. The appropriate period to forecast for is probably five to at most ten years for operational budgets. However, for capital budgeting it may be helpful to extend the forecast out as much as twenty years. There clearly is more uncertainty as you extend the forecast beyond the immediate budget year. But making these projections further out can help to shape the conversations around budget and finance in ways that make a jurisdiction more prepared to make longer-term plans and choices.

Best Practice 5: Monitor Actual Revenues against Forecast

As the budgeted year unfolds, actual revenues should be tracked compared to projections. The tracking should consider seasonality for revenues that are received monthly or when other revenues are collected during the year. As the year progresses, when actuals are out of line with the forecast, appropriate steps should be taken to make changes as early as possible, such as adjusting spending or using fund balance.

After the Forecast Is Made

Too often, people assume the job of forecasting is complete once the forecast is made and the budget adopted. But in truth, what happens after the forecast is done is as important if not more important to the process of good revenue forecasting. Critically, we need learning feedback loops for the short and long term that can guide us in making better financial decisions.

Monitor Forecasts in the Budget Year

For the short term, defined as the budgeted fiscal year, we need to monitor and update our forecasts throughout the year. If our forecasts are coming in low or high, adjustments to the budget may be needed. Forecasts are just estimates; they are not guarantees. If monitoring is not done, the need to take action may come too late, forcing more drastic budget changes with serious consequences. The critical task is that finance or budget staff should be systematically gathering the data on what is being collected and comparing that to the financial forecast. This needs to be done for all revenue sources but is more critical for the largest revenue sources, such as property or sales tax. This type of monitoring should be done at least quarterly. Monthly monitoring may be useful if time and resources permit. A compromise might be to do monthly monitoring just for large revenue sources that are spread throughout the year, such as sales tax, rather than wait for a quarterly update. An additional consideration is to recognize that most revenues probably do not come in evenly across the fiscal year. Using past data, it should be possible to estimate on average what percentage of a given revenue source might come in by quarter and use this as the target expectation against which to judge whether this year's forecast is ahead or behind.

Figure 6.10 shows an example of a possible report that might be done quarterly. Note that if budget amendments are done during the year, these amendments should be reflected in the data monitoring. In this example, the fictional Town of Blue Heaven is roughly on target with potential concerns around unrestricted intergovernmental revenues and on permits and fees that should be investigated. These shortfalls were partially offset by higher collections than expected in restricted intergovernmental revenues, taxes and licenses, and investment earnings. By keeping track of actual revenues as compared to forecasts, the proactive forecaster can improve a jurisdiction's ability to make better financial decisions in a timely manner.

Figure 6.10. Revenue Monitoring Report

Town of Blue Heaven Third-Quarter General Fund Revenues
Overall revenues are on target through the end of March.

Total general fund revenues collected are within historical expectations, only 1.6% lower than average.

General fund revenues	Amended FY budget	YTD collections	YTD collected	Expected (avg. of last five years)	Status compared to target zone	Variance collected vs. expected
Ad valorem taxes	$9,385,980	$9,495,059	101.2%	96.5%	OK	5%
Local sales taxes	$3,159,428	$1,593,415	50.4%	51.0%	OK	-1%
Permits and fees	$932,828	$748,656	80.3%	85.6%	Low	-5%
Restricted intergovernmental	$712,136	$654,588	91.9%	80.0%	High	12%
Unrestricted intergovernmental	$575,853	$321,306	55.8%	73.2%	Low	-17%
Other taxes/licenses	$449,199	$352,219	78.4%	68.3%	High	10%
Sales and services	$277,400	$222,907	80.4%	84.1%	OK	-4%
Investment earnings	$75,000	$296,996	396.0%	114.9%	High	281%
Other revenues	$46,203	$60,456	130.8%	121.3%	High	10%
Other financing services	$3,786,939	0	0	3.8%	OK	-4%
Total revenues	$19,400,966	$13,745,603	70.9%	72.5%	OK	1.6%

Monitor Forecast Accuracy

Beyond the short term or budget forecast year, there is also a need for a longer-term feedback learning loop. After making the effort to create a forecast, it is essential that tracking be done that compares the forecasts by year against what revenues were actually realized, which is Best practice 6.

The goal is to create a learning loop that informs us how good our forecasts were. This step is easy to ignore. By the time you can close the books on the last fiscal year, the revenue forecaster has already had to forecast a new budget year and would be monitoring the next budget year. Going back to look at past forecasts may get pushed to a low priority against other pressing work. But without this retrospective examination, there is no way to have a considered determination of the accuracy of forecasting efforts. This assessment needs to be made for overall revenues but also by each revenue source or at least the largest critical revenues. The important matters are to determine deviations by year, average deviations, whether deviations are spread evenly or vary notably, whether deviations are always above or below the actuals, and finally whether there is any trend with reduced or increasing deviations over time. The insight being sought is how accurate forecasts have been so that you might apply this confidence range going forward and possibly even learn how to improve accuracy. Additionally, it would be worthwhile if this assessment of deviations were made looking at forecasts by the methods used. It may be that certain methods have produced better forecasts, and, if so, perhaps more forecasting should be shifted to those forecasting techniques.

> **Best Practice 6: Verify Accuracy of Forecasts against Actual Revenues Received for the Past**
>
> To know what level of accuracy to expect, staff need to track actual revenues collected against the original forecasts for each past fiscal year. This tracking should be done for all or at least the major revenue sources. Over time, knowledge about the track record for past forecasting accuracy can be used to determine confidence bands for estimates. The results can also help determine if there is too much conservatism or optimism in the forecasts. This tracking can also help determine which forecasting methods or revenue sources may require more effort to improve forecast accuracy.

Figure 6.11 shows a simple example graph of how forecast deviations might look. In this case, deviations have gotten smaller over time, indicating improved forecasting. The experience suggests this jurisdiction might expect actual revenues to be within 3 to 6 percent of the forecast, providing a rough confidence interval based on the last eight years and possibly a better confidence interval based on the last three years. Finally, with one exception the forecasts were always conservative or low compared to the actuals.

Calculating Forecast Error

To help assess forecast deviations or errors, two common measures are used to assess forecasting accuracy. The simplest measure is known as *mean absolute deviation* (MAD). The measure simply adds up the absolute value of the deviations from the forecast and then takes the average. Large forecasting errors create larger problems, so a second measure, known as *mean square error* (MSE), can be used instead. MSE takes the forecast errors and squares each of them before dividing by the number of

Figure 6.11. Comparison of Actual Revenues as a Percentage of Budgeted Revenues

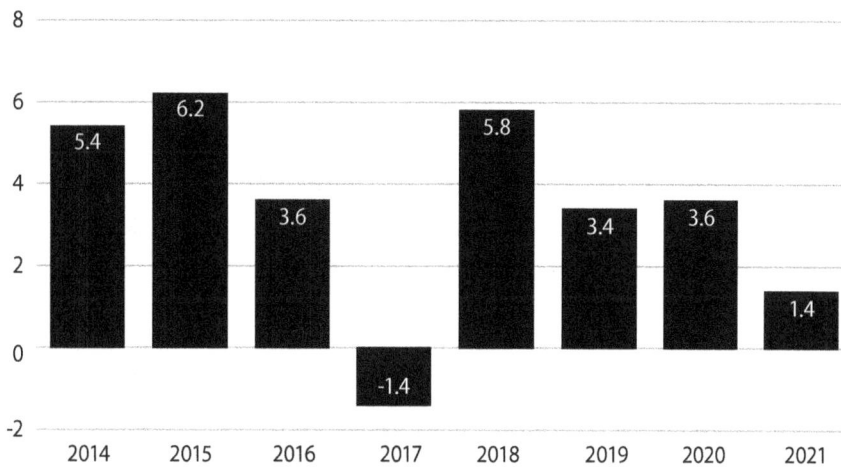

Table 6.4. Calculation of Forecasting Error Using MAD and MSE

Year	Forecasting Deviations	Absolute Deviation	Squared Deviation
2014	5.4	5.4	29.16
2015	6.2	6.2	38.44
2016	3.6	3.6	12.96
2017	-1.4	1.4	1.96
2018	5.8	5.8	33.64
2019	3.4	3.4	11.56
2020	3.6	3.6	12.96
2021	1.4	1.4	1.96

Mean absolute deviation = 3.85
Mean square error = 17.83
Square root of mean square error = 4.22

errors to create an average of the squared errors. MSE effectively gives more weight to the largest errors and is therefore more sensitive to forecasting errors when the data vary more widely from year to year. If you take the square root of the MSE, its relative scale is back to the magnitude of the original data. Using the MAD or the square root of the MSE gives you an approximate confidence interval for the forecasting data roughly two-thirds of the time. Doubling these errors should give you a confidence interval that works nearly all the time. Table 6.4 shows the data from Figure 6.11 with the calculated MAD, MSE, and square root of the MSE. The square root of the MSE is larger than the MAD, reflecting the volatility of the forecasting deviations. The MSE is a more conservative estimate of the amount of variation one might expect on average, and hence a wider confidence level is being calculated.

These measures of forecasting error can also be used to make comparisons across different forecasting techniques or assessing forecasting deviations between different revenue sources. One can calculate the MAD and MSE for two different forecasting methods side by side for a given revenue source. Those methods with lower MADs or MSEs exhibit lower forecast error and should be better techniques to use for future forecasting. By comparing MADs and MSEs between different revenue sources, the forecaster can also gain a more objective understanding of which revenue sources have more volatility and therefore deserve closer consideration when making forecasts and when monitoring forecasts in the budget year.

Financial Forecasting: Art and Science

Good financial forecasting is not a simple science where the numbers add up and the forecasts are always right. Uncertainty and variability cannot be eliminated. Actual results will almost never match the forecasts. But good forecasting can still hold important value. With a reasonable level of accuracy, the forecast can help us understand when results are on target but also when changes might need to be made as early as possible to avoid significant problems later. Good forecasting can also help alert us to problems in future years so that we have longer to determine the needed adjustments and are able to make them in more moderate steps. Good forecasting supports timely and appropriate financial management decision-making.

There is science that can be used to make forecasting more rigorous and not just throwing darts at the wall. But forecasting is also an art, in consulting good judgment, following a process, and using best practices. The proactive forecaster can take steps to improve what is done. Follow the three parts of the framework suggested in this chapter: prepare for the forecast, make the forecast, and follow up on the forecast. Adopt the six best practices as you are able. Starting from where you are, see how you can move to adopt best practices that you currently do not use. Good forecasting should be based on a considered approach. When making forecasts, a degree of conservatism is probably warranted, particularly for more volatile revenue sources. A good forecaster will appreciate how healthy fund reserves can help with the inevitable misses with forecasting. Uncertainty will still reign, but with work forecasting can become a manageable and helpful activity to support a local government's efforts to serve its citizens and residents by budgeting responsibly and sustainably.

Revenue Forecasting Best Practices

Best practice 1: know your revenues; create a revenue manual

Best practice 2: select an appropriate method to make a forecast

Best practice 3: test assumptions for forecasts

Best practice 4: forecast finances for multiple years

Best practice 5: monitor actual revenues against forecast

Best practice 6: verify accuracy of forecasts against actual revenues received for the past

Additional Resources

Books and Web Pages

Garrett, Thomas A., and John C. Leatherman. "Revenue Forecasting." In *An Introduction to State and Local Public Finance*, edited by Scott Loveridge and Randall Jackson. Morgantown, W.V.:WVU Research Repository, 2020. https://researchrepository.wvu.edu /cgi/viewcontent.cgi?article=1021&context=rri-web-book. First published 2000 by Regional Research Institute, West Virginia University.

Government Finance Officers Association. "Best Practices, Financial Forecasting in the Budget Preparation Process." https://www.gfoa.org/materials /financial-forecasting-in-the-budget-preparation-process.

———. "Local Government Revenue Sources—Cities." https://www.gfoa.org /revenue-dashboard-cities.

———. "Local Government Revenue Sources—Counties." https://www.gfoa.org /revenue-dashboard-counties.

North Carolina League of Municipalities. "Revenue Forecasts." https://www.nclm.org /financial-consulting/revenue-forecasts.

Listservs

Listserv of the North Carolina Local Government Budget Association: https://www .sog.unc.edu/resources/listservs/local-government-budget-association-nclgba.

Listserv of North Carolina Finance Connect: https://www.sog.unc.edu/resources /tools/nc-finance-connect.

Listserv of the North Carolina Government Finance Officers Association: https:// www.ncgfoa.org/listserv.

Appendix A. Revenue Manual Page for
Whispering Pines, North Carolina

LOCAL SALES AND USE TAX

Description:

Currently, Moore County levies 2% in local sales tax which is composed of three different taxes – the Article 39 one cent tax, the Article 40 one-half cent tax, and the Article 42 one-half cent tax. This sales tax is added to the state sales and use tax of 4.75% for a combined rate of 6.75%. Proceeds of the sales tax component of the local sales tax are collected by retailers and remitted to the North Carolina Department of Revenue (DOR). NCDOR distributes sales tax to the counties who must share the tax proceeds with municipalities within its territorial jurisdiction. The Village of Whispering Pines receives funds under the per capita method; the funds are distributed based on relative population.

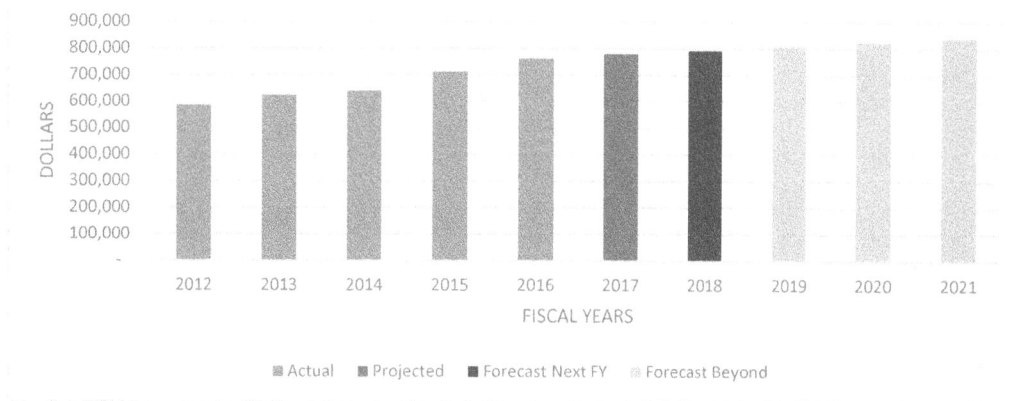

Legal Authority:

North Carolina General Statute Articles 39, 40, 42, & 44

Fiscal Capacity:

In order to calculate the municipal sales tax collection factor, it is first necessary to allocate a share of the sales tax collected within a county to each of its respective municipalities. This allocation is derived based on population.

Forecast Assumption(s):

The forecast is adjusted annually by projected sales tax estimates provided by the North Carolina League of Municipalities. The projections are statewide and therefore prudence must be exercised to the local conditions that may affect to what extent an adjustment is made for the Village's particular jurisdiction.

Source: Village of Whispering Pines, N.C, *Revenue Manual* (June 2017), https://whisperingpinesnc.net/files/documents/RevenueManual1316100929032818AM.pdf.

Appendix B. Revenue Manual Page for King, North Carolina

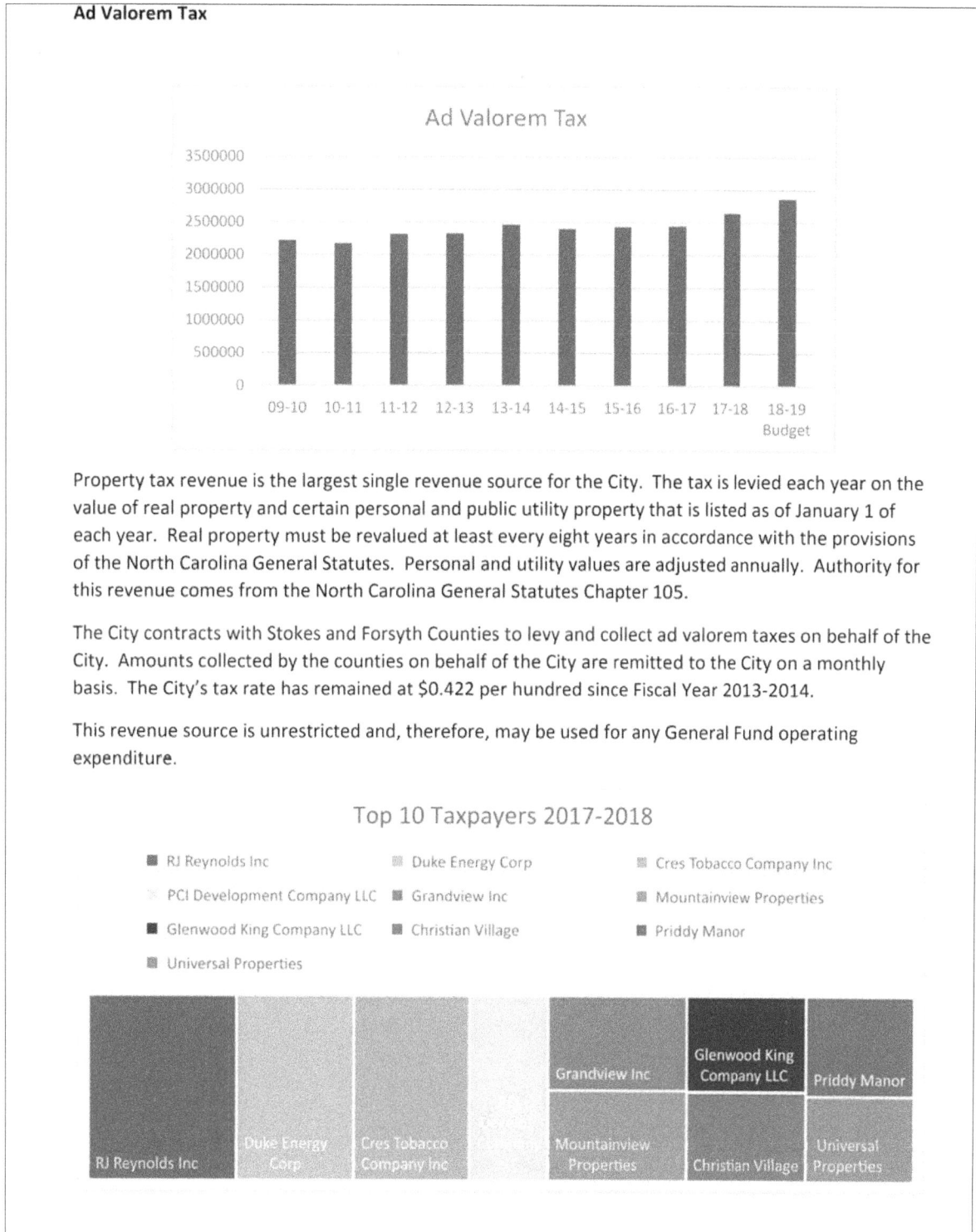

Ad Valorem Tax

Ad Valorem Tax

Property tax revenue is the largest single revenue source for the City. The tax is levied each year on the value of real property and certain personal and public utility property that is listed as of January 1 of each year. Real property must be revalued at least every eight years in accordance with the provisions of the North Carolina General Statutes. Personal and utility values are adjusted annually. Authority for this revenue comes from the North Carolina General Statutes Chapter 105.

The City contracts with Stokes and Forsyth Counties to levy and collect ad valorem taxes on behalf of the City. Amounts collected by the counties on behalf of the City are remitted to the City on a monthly basis. The City's tax rate has remained at $0.422 per hundred since Fiscal Year 2013-2014.

This revenue source is unrestricted and, therefore, may be used for any General Fund operating expenditure.

Top 10 Taxpayers 2017-2018

- RJ Reynolds Inc
- Duke Energy Corp
- Cres Tobacco Company Inc
- PCI Development Company LLC
- Grandview Inc
- Mountainview Properties
- Glenwood King Company LLC
- Christian Village
- Priddy Manor
- Universal Properties

Source: King, N.C. Shared on the N.C. Local Government Budget Association listserv.

Appendix C. Revenue Manual Page for Orange County, North Carolina

---

Interest on Delinquent Taxes

Department:	Tax Administration
Revenue Description:	Interest portions of tax payments made on tax accounts in delinquent status.
Legal Authorization:	G.S. 105-360
Fund & Account:	General Fund 10-1000-01-400025

Source:	Orange County tax payers with delinquent tax payments.
Authorized Use:	All General Fund expenditures.
Method of Collection:	Property tax bills are due September 1 and enter delinquent status if the amount billed remains unpaid after January 5 following the tax year. Registered classified motor vehicle taxes are due with vehicle registration and enter delinquent status if unpaid 30 days after the due date. Enforced collection of delinquent taxes and applicable fees, interest, and penalties begin immediately upon the account reaching the delinquent status. Legal actions to collect delinquent taxes may include, but are not limited to, garnishment of wages, attachment of bank accounts and rents, seizure and sale of personal property, and foreclosure and sale of real property.
Rate:	For real and personal property, interest accrues at the rate of two percent (2%) for the first calendar month and three-fourths percent (3/4%) for each subsequent month until paid. Interest for Registered Motor Vehicles begins accumulating at the rate of five percent (5%) the first month and three-fourths percent (3/4%) for each subsequent month until paid. Interest is not compounded.
Frequency:	For real and personal property, interest accrues on tax bills not paid on or before January 5 of the following year. Interest begins accruing at the time stated on the tax bill for registered classified motor vehicles.
Exemptions:	The taxpayer may raise any defenses in writing under oath. If approved by the tax collector, the garnishment shall thereupon be discharged to the amount required by the defense.
Restrictions:	A County may not spend property tax proceeds for any function without the approval of the unit's voters unless the General Assembly has authorized it to do so.

Revenue History

Fiscal Year	FY 2013-14	FY 2014-15	FY 2015-16	FY 2016-17	FY 2017-18
Amount	$587,842	$502,501	$439,256	$429,337	$489,836

Source: Orange County, North Carolina, Department of Finance and Administrative Services, *Revenue Manual* (December 2018), https://www.orangecountync.gov/DocumentCenter/View/6027/Revenue-Manual.

BUSINESS TAX

Description:

The Local Business Tax, formerly known as Occupational License Tax, is a tax for the privilege of engaging in or managing any business, profession, or occupation within the City limits.

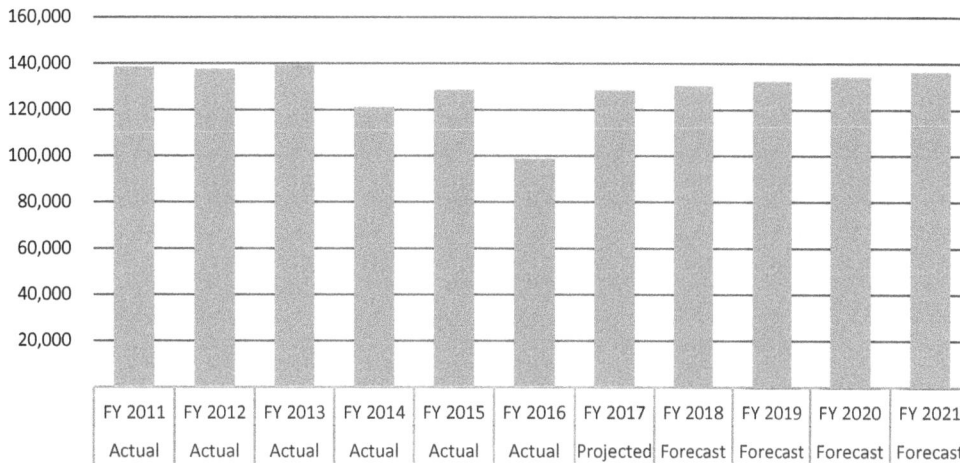

	FY 2011 Actual	FY 2012 Actual	FY 2013 Actual	FY 2014 Actual	FY 2015 Actual	FY 2016 Actual	FY 2017 Projected	FY 2018 Forecast	FY 2019 Forecast	FY 2020 Forecast	FY 2021 Forecast
Value	~138,000	~137,000	~140,000	~120,000	~127,000	~99,000	~127,000	~129,000	~131,000	~133,000	~135,000

Legal Authority:

City of St. Augustine Code, Chapter 17, Article III, Sec. 17-61 through 17-95
Florida Statute 205.043(1)
Florida Statute chapters 205.0535, 205.0536

Fiscal Capacity:

A business tax rate increase would require St. Augustine City Commission approval and adherence to the guidelines of Florida State Statutes. The business tax rate can increase 5% every other year by June 30. The expectation is for business tax receipts to remain stable because there is no significant change anticipated in the number of new businesses in the next fiscal year. The Florida Legislature has proposed changes to this tax; however, no changes have occurred to date.

Chapter 7

The Property Tax and the Revenue-Neutral Tax Rate[*]

Chris McLaughlin

In theory, the revenue-neutral property tax rate (RNTR) exists to educate the public and make the process of setting property tax rates more transparent. In practice, the RNTR is widely misunderstood by the public and policy makers alike. Some of this confusion is caused by the complicated, statutorily mandated process used to calculate the RNTR, some by the inability of local government officials to accurately explain what the RNTR is and how it is best used.

The goal of this chapter is to provide a detailed analysis of the RNTR so that local government budget officials can better calculate, employ, and explain the RNTR to their colleagues, their elected officials, and their constituents. Before jumping into details about the RNTR, this chapter will provide a quick overview of the property tax

---

[*]This chapter includes material from two previous School of Government publications: Shea Riggsbee Denning and William C. Rivenbark, *Statement of Revenue-Neutral Tax Rate and Provision for Mid-Year Property Tax Rate Change*, Local Finance Bulletin 32 (UNC School of Government, November 2004); Christopher B. McLaughlin and William C. Rivenbark, *Statement of Revenue-Neutral Tax Rate: Questions and Answers*, Local Finance Bulletin 39 (UNC School of Government, August 2009), https://www.sog.unc.edu/sites/www.sog.unc.edu/files/reports/lfb39.pdf. Used by permission.

system in North Carolina. The discussion will then turn to illustrating how the RNTR is calculated and provide answers to common questions about its implementation.

I. Overview of Property Taxes

Property taxes represent the single largest source of unrestricted revenue for both counties and municipalities. According to the most recent fiscal data available from the North Carolina Department of State Treasurer, property taxes represent more than one-half of county revenues and nearly one-quarter of municipal revenues.[1] Figures 7.1 and 7.2, below, illustrate the relative importance of property taxes as compared to other revenue sources. Note that both tables exclude debt proceeds, which must be paid back in the future using other revenue sources and are, therefore, not truly revenue sources themselves.

Figure 7.1. County Revenues, Excluding Debt

2017–2018 County Revenues
$12.6 Billion Total

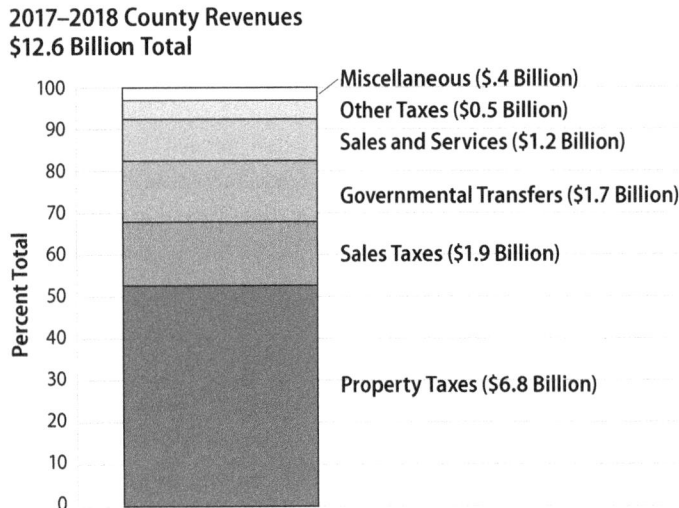

Miscellaneous ($.4 Billion)
Other Taxes ($0.5 Billion)
Sales and Services ($1.2 Billion)
Governmental Transfers ($1.7 Billion)
Sales Taxes ($1.9 Billion)
Property Taxes ($6.8 Billion)

---

1. Searchable statistics are available on the "North Carolina County and Municipal Financial Information" page of the State Treasurer's website: https://www.nctreasurer.com/slg/lfm/financial-analysis/Pages/Analysis-by-Population.aspx.

Figure 7.2. Municipal Revenues, Excluding Debt

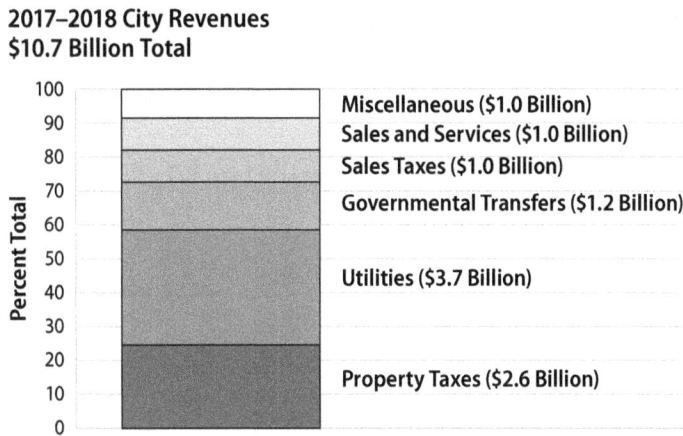

**2017–2018 City Revenues
$10.7 Billion Total**

Miscellaneous ($1.0 Billion)
Sales and Services ($1.0 Billion)
Sales Taxes ($1.0 Billion)
Governmental Transfers ($1.2 Billion)

Utilities ($3.7 Billion)

Property Taxes ($2.6 Billion)

Although utility fees represent a larger percentage of municipal revenues than do property taxes, those funds are not *unrestricted* revenues because they generally must be used to cover the cost of providing utility services. If utility fees and charges were excluded from the calculation, property taxes would represent more than one-third of municipal revenues.

In recent years, North Carolina local governments' reliance on property taxes has grown as other revenue sources have suffered. Consider the sales tax: economic woes in place since the Great Recession of 2008, combined with the loss of a portion of counties' local sales tax authority as part of the 2007 state Medicaid funding reform legislation, have reduced county sales- and use-tax revenues by more than one-third since their peak in fiscal year 2007–2008. As Figure 7.3, below, illustrates, county and municipal sales- and use-tax revenues have yet to return to pre-recession levels, while property tax revenues sustained slow but steady growth during and after the highlighted recession period.

Figure 7.3. Comparison: Combined County and Municipal Sales- and Use-Tax Revenues vs. Combined County and Municipal Property Tax Revenues

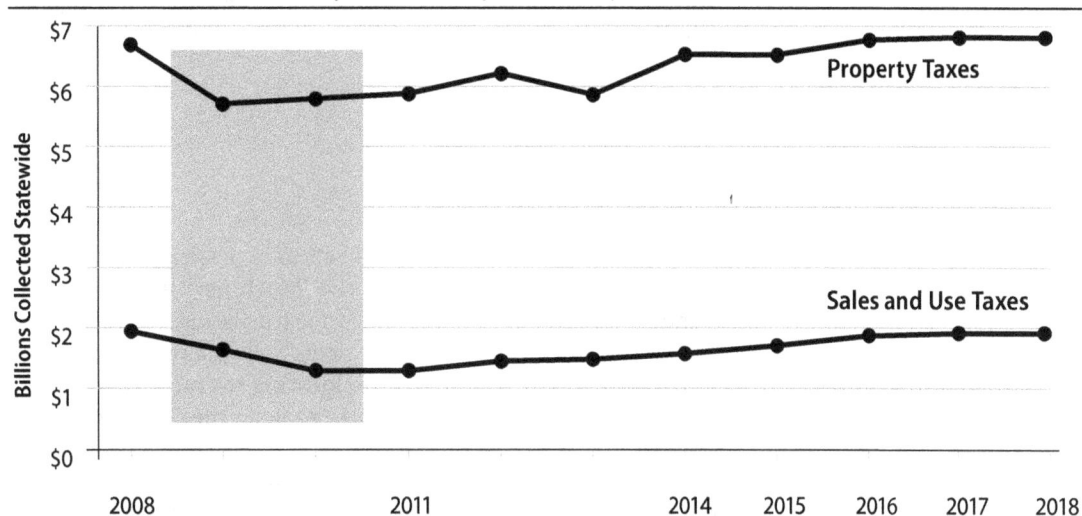

Note: The shaded rectangle represents the duration of the Great Recession of 2008.

A. The Governing Law and the Cast of Characters

The North Carolina Constitution, Article V (Finance), Section 2 (State and local taxation) sets the basic ground rules for property taxes, while Chapter 105, Subchapter II, of the North Carolina General Statutes (hereinafter G.S.), commonly known as the Machinery Act, provides the details.[2]

Actors at both the state and local levels play major roles in the property tax process.

Table 7.1. Property Tax Cast of Characters

Governmental Level	Actor Involved in Tax Process
State	General Assembly
	Department of Revenue, Local Government Division
	Property Tax Commission
	Court of Appeals
	Supreme Court
Local	Governing board
	Assessor (county)
	Tax collector
	Board of Equalization and Review (county)

As mentioned above, the property tax process is governed by statutes enacted by the North Carolina General Assembly as part of the Machinery Act. The Local Government Division of the state Department of Revenue is charged with ensuring that local governments adhere to the Machinery Act's requirements. This division also provides education, training, and guidance to local government tax officials and assesses and allocates public service company property to counties so it can be subject to local property taxes.

Note that the Department of Revenue's Local Government Division is distinct from the Local Government Commission (LGC), which operates out of the N.C. Department of State Treasurer.[3] The LGC monitors the fiscal and accounting practices of the state's local governments but does not play a direct role in property tax administration.

---

2. G.S. 105-271 and -272, respectively, state that the collection of property tax statutes in Subchapter II of Chapter 105 can be referred to as the "Machinery Act" because "the purpose of this Subchapter is to provide the *machinery* for the listing, appraisal, and assessment of property and the levy and collection of taxes on property by counties and municipalities." (Emphasis added.) The best source for locating the most up-to-date Machinery Act provisions is the searchable General Statutes page on the General Assembly's website: https://www.ncleg.net/Laws/GeneralStatutes.

3. *See* North Carolina Department of State Treasurer, "State and Local Government: Local Government Commission," https://www.nctreasurer.com/slg/Pages/Local -Government-Commission.aspx.

County boards of equalization and review, the state Property Tax Commission, the state Court of Appeals, and the state Supreme Court are all involved with the resolution of appeals concerning property tax values and property tax exemptions and exclusions.

The county assessor is responsible for listing and assessing all taxable property in the county for purposes of property taxes.[4] In other words, the assessor must determine the what, the where, the who, and the how much for all property that will be taxed for the coming fiscal year. The tax collector must collect the taxes levied on that property, if necessary by use of the enforced collection remedies available under the Machinery Act and other statutes.[5] In many counties, the county commissioners have chosen to appoint a single individual as both assessor and tax collector under the title of "tax administrator."

The role of the local government governing board in the property tax process is summarized in Table 7.2, below. Table 7.3, also below, lists the important dates in the property tax calendar. More details on all of these issues are provided in subsequent chapters.

Table 7.2. Rights and Duties of Local Government Governing Boards

Local Board	Rights/Duties
Boards of county commissioners	• Adopt property tax rate annually
	• Appoint assessor and tax collector
	• Review performance of assessor and tax collector
	• Accept settlement of prior year's taxes from tax collector and charge tax collector with responsibility for current year's taxes
	• Decide when to conduct countywide reappraisals of real property (at least once every eight years)
	• Appoint Board of Equalization and Review (county commissioners may serve as this board)
	• Rule on taxpayer requests for refunds and releases
Town/city councils	• Adopt property tax rate annually
	• Appoint tax collector OR contract with county for tax collection
	• Review performance of tax collector
	• Accept settlement of prior year's taxes from tax collector and charge tax collector with responsibility for current year's taxes
	• Rule on taxpayer requests for refunds and releases

---

4. G.S. 105-296.
5. G.S. 105-350.

Table 7.3. Important Dates on the Property Tax Calendar

Date	Action/Event
January 1	• Listing date (ownership, situs, value, and taxability determined)[a] • Tax liens attach to real property[b]
July 1	• Fiscal year begins[c] • Deadline for adoption of new budget and tax rate[d]
September 1	• Discounts end (if offered)[e] • Taxes due[f]
January 6 (following year)	• Taxes become delinquent, interest accrues, and enforced collections may begin[g]
June 30 (following year)	• Fiscal year ends[h]

a. G.S. 105-285.
b. G.S. 105-355.
c. G.S. 159-8(b).
d. G.S. 159-11(b), -13(a).
e. G.S. 105-360(c).
f. G.S. 105-360(a).
g. G.S. 105-365.1.
h. G.S. 159-8(b).

B. Real Property versus Personal Property

Collection remedies under the Machinery Act differ depending on whether the property being taxed is *real* or *personal*. Real property is essentially land, buildings, and things that are permanently affixed to those buildings—think of light fixtures or kitchen cabinets. Personal property is everything else: vehicles, boats, planes, business equipment, etc.[6] With the exception of some software, personal property is taxable only if it is tangible.[7] Intangible personal property such as cash, stocks, bank deposits, patents, and franchise rights are not taxable.

C. Why Cars Are Different

Cars, trucks, vans, motorcycles, and trailers with valid registrations and license plates are called "registered motor vehicles" (RMVs) by the Machinery Act. In 2013, the obligation and authority to collect property taxes on RMVs shifted from the counties to the state Division of Motor Vehicles (NCDMV).[8] Under this "Tag & Tax Together" system, taxes on RMVs are collected by the NCDMV at the time of initial registration or renewal of an existing registration. If the owner refuses to pay the taxes, the

---

6. The term "real property" is defined in G.S. 105-273(13). The term "personal property" is not defined by the Machinery Act and, therefore, encompasses all property not expressly designated as real property by the Machinery Act.

7. G.S. 105-275(31) excludes from taxation all intangible property other than certain software.

8. For more details on the taxation of RMVs, see Christopher B. McLaughlin, *The Collection of Property Taxes on Motor Vehicles*, Property Tax Bulletin 172 (UNC School of Government, December 2016), https://www.sog.unc.edu/publications/bulletins/collection-property-taxes-motor-vehicles.

NCDMV will refuse to register the motor vehicle. RMV property tax revenue and collection percentages have risen dramatically as a result of the new system.[9] Although the collection process for property taxes on RMVs is different, they are subject to the same city and county property tax rates that apply to all other types of property.

How Do I Use the Tax Rate to Calculate a Tax Bill?

Tax rates are expressed as "$ of tax per $100 dollars of taxable value." For example, if a home is valued for tax purposes at $200,000 and the county tax rate is 0.25 percent, the county property taxes on that home will be $500. You arrive at this amount by first dividing the taxable value of the property by 100 ($200,000/100 = $2,000), then multiplying the result by the tax rate ($2,000 x 0.25 = $500).

II. The Property Tax Rate

Although local governments are not required to levy property taxes, nearly all do. The rates at which they levy those taxes vary greatly, however.

Traditionally, the lowest county rates were found along the coast and in the mountains, in counties where expensive vacation homes abound. But the post-recession national real estate slump hit the North Carolina vacation home market harder than it hit the state's primary home market. Some counties with lots of vacation homes experienced dramatic drops in their real property tax bases and, as a result, were forced to raise their tax rates substantially. For example, Brunswick County raised its tax rate by 45 percent following its 2011 revaluation.[10]

Property tax rates for a particular local government are generally capped at $1.50 (per $100 of taxable value; see sidebar on page 160), but that cap is subject to many exceptions.[11] For example, there is no statutory limit on the rate for property taxes that are used to fund schools or jails. (See Section II.B, below, for a discussion about "use-specific" property taxes.) For uses that are subject to the statutory cap, a local government may obtain voter approval to exceed the $1.50 maximum tax rate.

As Table 7.4 demonstrates, no local government comes even close to the maximum tax rate. This "tax gap"—the difference between actual property tax rates and the statutory maximum for those rates—is often a point of contention when local governments seek additional revenue from the General Assembly. From the state legislature's perspective, local governments have ample opportunities to generate more

---

9. After the first full year of Tag & Tax Together, registered motor vehicle property tax revenues were up by more than 40 percent and collection percentages rose from 86 to 99 percent. See Chris McLaughlin, " 'Tag and Tax Together' One Year Later," *Coates' Canons: NC Local Government Law* (blog), UNC School of Government, August 29, 2014, https://canons.sog.unc.edu/tag-and-tax-together-one-year-later/.

10. See the Tax Office page of Brunswick County's website: http://www.brunswickcountync.gov/tax-office/rates/.

11. G.S. 153A-149 (counties); 160A-209 (municipalities).

revenue from local property taxes and, therefore, do not need additional revenue from state coffers. Local governments obviously have a different perspective on this issue.

The $1.50 cap applies to individual taxing jurisdictions, not to individual taxpayers. A taxpayer who lives in a municipality could very well wind up paying a total property tax rate of greater than $1.50 because that taxpayer's property is subject to both county and municipal taxes. As a result, a municipality need not worry about the county's property tax when setting its own rate, or vice versa.

Table 7.4. County and Municipal Property Tax Rates (in $), 2017–2018

	Lowest Rate	Highest Rate	Average Rate
Counties	0.31 (Carteret)	1.01 (Scotland)	0.66
Municipalities	0.0165 (Wesley Chapel)	0.82 (Roper)	0.46

Source: N.C. Department of Revenue; N.C. Department of State Treasurer.

Note: See the sidebar below for more on the factors used, including tax rate, to calculate a property owner's tax bill.

A. Tax Rate Uniformity and Tax Districts

Article V, Section 2 of the North Carolina Constitution requires that all property within a specific taxing jurisdiction be subject to the same tax rate. This uniformity requirement prohibits local governments from adopting different tax rates for different property or for different areas of that jurisdiction. For example, a county could not adopt one tax rate for real property and a different tax rate for motor vehicles. Nor could a county choose to adopt one tax rate for its incorporated areas and a different tax rate for its unincorporated areas.

The only exception to the uniformity requirement is the constitutional provision that permits special tax districts. Often called "service districts," these tax districts are authorized by Article V, Section 2(4) of the N.C. Constitution to fund additional services in their geographic areas. Multiple tax districts are permitted in the same local government, so long as each tax district is created for a permissible purpose.

Counties most often use special tax districts to fund fire protection in unincorporated areas, but they can also use them to fund services such as trash collection, sewer and water systems, and beach erosion control.[12] Cities can use municipal tax districts to fund many of those same services, but they more often use them to create districts for "downtown revitalization projects."[13] This category is broadly defined to cover a variety of expenditures, including new parking facilities, improved lighting, additional police protection, and tourism promotion within the downtown city core.[14]

Another type of special tax district tax is a special supplemental school district tax. This tax must be approved by voters before it can be levied and must be used

---

12. G.S. 69-25.4 (rural fire tax districts); 153A-301 (special service districts).
13. G.S. 160A-536.
14. Ibid.

only to fund the public schools in that district. Once adopted, a supplemental school tax applies to all property within that particular school district.

The taxes levied in a special tax district count toward the $1.50 cap on general property tax rates. This fact means that the total of "regular" property taxes and special district taxes in a particular tax district cannot exceed $1.50 for certain uses, unless the local government obtains voter approval to exceed that cap.

B. Use-Specific Taxes

A local government may adopt a single property tax rate to satisfy all of its budgetary needs, or it may adopt multiple tax rates with the revenue from each earmarked for a specific use. For example, instead of funding police and fire protection services out of its general property tax revenue, a city could choose to adopt two property tax rates: one for general fund revenue and one to fund police and fire services.

There is no limit on the number of different use-specific property tax rates that may be adopted, so long as each such tax applies uniformly to all taxable property within the jurisdiction. Use-specific taxes may be adopted as part of the local government's annual budget and do not require voter approval.[15]

A key difference between use-specific property taxes and special tax district taxes is that use-specific taxes must apply to the entire jurisdiction. Special tax district taxes may be levied on portions of a jurisdiction to fund specific services in that district.

Surprisingly, the North Carolina Supreme Court has ruled that a local government may change its spending for a particular use regardless of what it promised to spend on that use in its budget through a use-specific tax rate.

For example, assume that Carolina County adopts a 50-cent general tax rate, a 12-cent tax rate for law enforcement, and a 2-cent tax rate for libraries. Based on its budgeted tax base, the 12-cent tax would raise $1,200,000 for county law enforcement and the 2-cent tax would raise $200,000 for county libraries. Despite the adoption of the use-specific taxes, the county could choose to spend more or less than these amounts on law enforcement and libraries in the coming fiscal year. Voters may not take kindly to such variations from the budget, but they are legal.

C. Setting the Tax Rate

Property taxes are levied on a fiscal year basis, despite the fact that many of the important dates on the property tax schedule seem to be configured around the calendar year. A local government that levies property taxes must set its property tax rate(s) in its annual budget, which should be adopted by July 1, the beginning of the fiscal year.[16]

---

15. For more on this issue, see Kara Millonzi, "Levying the Property Tax: Earmarking Tax Revenue for Specific Purposes," *Coates' Canons: NC Local Government Law* (blog), UNC School of Government, January 21, 2010, https://canons.sog.unc.edu/levying-the -property-tax-earmarking-tax-revenue-for-specific-purposes/.

16. G.S. 159-13.

Calculating the Tax Rate

Assume that Carolina County needs to generate $50,000,000 in property tax revenue to balance its budget for the coming fiscal year. The basic property tax calculation is as follows:

$$(Tax\ Base\ /\ 100) \times Tax\ Rate = Tax\ Revenue.$$

The first thing the county should do is get from the tax collector the estimated property tax collection percentage for the current fiscal year. This percentage will be an estimate because the current fiscal year will not have ended at the time Carolina County creates the budget for the next fiscal year. Assume that the estimated collection percentage for the current fiscal year is 97 percent.

The county should then divide the revenue target by this percentage to account for the fact that not every penny of the property tax levy will be collected. Result:

$$\$50,000,000 / 0.97 = \$51,550,000.$$

This result is the adjusted revenue target for the next fiscal year. In other words, if the county wishes to produce $50,000,000 in property tax revenue next year, it must levy $51,550,000 in property taxes.

The second thing the county should do is get from the assessor the estimated tax base for the next fiscal year. It will be an estimate because subsequent tax appeals, discoveries, and motor vehicle registrations will affect the final figure.

Assume that the estimated tax base is $10,000,000,000. The county should divide the estimated tax base by 100, to reflect the fact that the tax rate is "per $100 in value." Result:

$$\$10,000,000,000 / 100 = \$100,000,000.$$

Finally, the county should divide the adjusted revenue target by the result set out immediately above to determine the rate. Final result:

$$\$51,550,000 / \$100,000,000 = \$0.516.$$

Carolina County must levy a property tax of $0.516, or 51.6 cents per $100 of value, to meet its budgetary needs for the coming fiscal year.

When budgeting, many local governments start with a tax rate target rather than a revenue target. Regardless of the approach used, the local government must account for the current year's tax collection percentage when budgeting for next year.

For example, assume that Carolina County wished to keep its tax rate at $.51 per $100 of value for the coming year. If next year's tax base is estimated to be $10,000,000,000, a tax rate of $.51 would produce tax revenue of $51,000,000. However, this estimated revenue must be reduced by this year's collection percentage:

$$\$51,000,000 \times 0.97 = \$49,470,000.$$

As a result, if Carolina County wishes to keep its tax rate at $0.51 for the coming year, it should budget for no more than $49,470,000 in property tax revenue.

Until a budget is adopted, there can be no property tax levy. Although interim budgets are permitted, they authorize only continued spending by local governments and not the levying of taxes.[17] A delay in the adoption of the budget can delay property tax collections and do serious harm to a local government's revenues.

The property tax rate should be based on the amount of revenue the local government needs to balance its budget after all other revenue sources are accounted for, given the expected tax base for the coming year. Obviously, this amount will be driven by important decisions regarding what services the local government can and should provide.

When balancing the budget with property taxes, a local government must be realistic about how much of its tax levy it will actually collect. While property tax collection percentages are generally very good—almost 99 percent on average[18]—no local government collects every penny of its property taxes. For budget purposes, state law prohibits local governments from assuming a higher collection rate for the coming year than it experienced in the current year.[19]

D. Changing the Tax Rate

Once the total tax rate is set in the budget, the governing board is generally prohibited from changing it.[20] Absent an order from a judge or from the Local Government Commission, the only justification for adjusting a tax rate after adoption of the budget is when the local government receives revenues that are "substantially" different than expected. And even then, the change must occur before January 1 following the start of the fiscal year.[21] For example, if a governing board wished to change its 2018–2019 tax rate due to a substantial change in revenues, it would need to act before January 1, 2019.

What type of events could justify a change in the total tax rate under this standard? The relevant statutes do not provide additional details but, presumably, changes could occur after a misfortune such as a bankruptcy filing by a large industrial taxpayer that will prevent collection of a substantial portion of the local government's property tax levy or the elimination of an important revenue source due to new legislation enacted by the General Assembly. Good news, such as the creation of a major new revenue source for the local government, could also justify a mid-year change in the tax rate, but sadly such occurrences seem quite rare.

As mentioned above, local governments may adopt multiple tax rates for different uses. These use-specific rates may be changed during a fiscal year without regard for statutory restrictions, so long as the total tax rate levied by the local government does not change.

---

17. G.S. 159-16.

18. As per the N.C. Department of State Treasurer.

19. G.S. 159-13(b)(6). For more on the collection percentage and budgeting, see Chris McLaughlin, "Budgets and the Tax Collection Percentage," *Coates' Canons: NC Local Government Law* (blog), UNC School of Government, March 23, 2012, https://canons.sog.unc.edu/budgets-and-the-tax-collection-percentage/.

20. G.S. 159-15.

21. Ibid.

Consider again the example of Carolina County adopting a general tax rate of 50 cents, a law enforcement tax of 12 cents, and a library tax of 2 cents, for a total combined rate of 64 cents. The county would be free to alter any or all of its three different tax rates, so long as the total combined rate still equaled 64 cents.

III. The Revenue-Neutral Tax Rate (RNTR)

To help taxpayers compare tax rates before and after countywide reappraisals of real property, G.S. 159-11(e) requires that all local governments (both counties and municipalities) calculate and publish RNTRs following their reappraisals.

The RNTR is the tax rate that would produce the same amount of tax revenue from the new revaluation-year tax base as was produced this year from the current tax rate and tax base. If the new tax rate adopted by the governing board is higher than the RNTR, then the local government has increased its total property tax levy. If the new rate is lower than the RNTR, then the local government has decreased its total property tax levy.

In normal economic times, tax bases increase after reappraisals. When the tax base increases, the tax rate can be lowered without decreasing tax revenue. As a result, the RNTR is normally lower than the existing tax rate.

But when market prices are dropping—as they did in many areas of the state following the 2008 recession[22]—a local government's tax base can decrease after a reappraisal. In these circumstances, if the governing board wishes to keep revenues constant, it must raise the tax rate. As a result, the RNTR will be higher than the existing tax rate.

Local governments are not required to adopt the RNTR, but they must publish it as part of their annual budget process. Even if the RNTR is adopted, individual taxpayers may see their tax bills increase or decrease because their individual property appreciated or depreciated more than did the tax base in the aggregate. Much confusion surrounds the RNTR, in large part because, despite its name, it does not guarantee that taxpayers' bills will remain constant.

For example, assume that Carolina County's tax base increased by 10 percent following its 2018 reappraisal. The RNTR is calculated to be 50 cents per $100 of value, a bit lower than the county's 2017–2018 tax rate of 55 cents per $100 of value. The county commissioners decide to adopt the RNTR as the tax rate for 2018–2019 and proudly announce that they have avoided a tax increase. However, when the 2018

---

22. This blog post lists numerous counties that suffered reductions to their property tax bases as a result of their first reappraisals after the recession: Chris McLaughlin, "N.C. Housing Market Improves but Local Tax Bases Continue to Suffer," *Coates' Canons: NC Local Government Law* (blog), UNC School of Government, April 26, 2013, https://canons.sog.unc.edu/n-c-housing-market-improves-but-local-tax-bases-continue -to-suffer/.

tax bills are mailed in August, Tommy TarHeel is furious because his new tax bill is higher than last year's tax bill.

How can this be? The likely answer is that Tommy's real property appreciated more than 10 percent, which was the average increase in value for all real property in the county. Assume that Tommy's real property tax appraisal increased from $100,000 to $150,000 as a result of the 2018 reappraisal. For 2017–2018, Tommy's tax bill was $550 ($100,000/100 × $0.55). For 2018–2019, his tax bill is $750 ($150,000/100 × $.50). The drop in the tax rate was not enough to offset the increase in Tommy's tax appraisal, meaning that Tommy's tax bill increased $200 despite the county's adoption of the RNTR.

By adopting the RNTR, a local government may keep its aggregate property tax revenue constant. But individual taxpayers' bills are not guaranteed to remain constant because individual properties are likely to have appreciated or depreciated differently than did the county-wide tax base.

A. The RNTR and the Growth Rate

The revenue-neutral rate is the rate for the fiscal year after revaluation that, taking into account expected rates of growth in the tax base and excluding increases in market value recognized by the revaluation, would produce revenue that equals the current year's tax levy. The expected rate of growth in the revaluation year is based upon an average of increases or decreases to the assessed value since the last revaluation. This growth or decline is based upon additions to or reductions in a taxing unit's base of taxable property rather than the increases and decreases in market value that are accounted for by the effective tax rate but are not recouped by the taxing unit in non-revaluation years.

Changes to the real property tax base in non-revaluation years result from the construction of new homes and businesses, improvements to existing structures, divisions and conveyances of land, rezoning, and other occurrences unrelated to economic conditions affecting the taxing unit in general. Changes in the personal property tax base occur each year because personal property is valued on an annual basis and because many taxpayers move personal property in and out of the county each year.

G.S. 159-11(e) provides that the growth rate used in calculating the revenue-neutral rate is based upon the average increase in the tax base "due to improvements since the last general reappraisal." The term "improvements" presumably was intended to include real property improvements (new construction, renovations, additions, etc.) as well as all additions and reductions in the tax base recognized in non-revaluation years. This is because the revenue-neutral rate is the rate necessary to provide the same amount of revenue received by the taxing unit in the current fiscal year. Current-year revenue is based upon real and personal property taxes. Basing the tax levy calculation in a revaluation year upon the rate of growth associated only with real property improvements and ignoring the growth rate of personal property would result in an estimated tax levy noncomparable to prior year levies that included all property types.

B. How Many Decimal Places?

The General Statutes do not mandate a certain number of decimal places for property tax rates, including the RNTR. This means that local governments are free to truncate or round off their tax rates as they wish. Most local governments report tax rates to the fourth decimal place ("$0.5482" or 54.82 cents), but that is not a requirement.

C. Calculating an RNTR

To arrive at the RNTR, G.S. 159-11(e) requires the following calculation process:

1. Determine the tax levy for the current fiscal year.
2. Using the **new** tax base, determine the tax rate that would produce a tax levy equal to the tax levy for the current fiscal year.
3. Determine the "growth rate," which is the average annual percentage increase in the tax base due to improvements since the last general reappraisal. When calculating this growth rate, adjust for annexations, mergers, or other "similar events."
4. Increase the rate calculated in step 2, above, by the growth rate.

To some degree, the revenue-neutral rate must be based upon estimations of the revaluation year tax base in a revaluation year because all assessment appeals will not be resolved at the time the rate is calculated. (Successful taxpayer appeals lower the tax base.) Additional estimations are required for the unit's registered motor vehicle (RMV) tax base, which is the sum of monthly registrations and renewals throughout the twelve-month fiscal year. At the time the RNTR is calculated, budget officials will need to estimate several months of RMV renewals and registrations yet to occur in the current, non-revaluation year and a full twelve months of renewals and registrations in the coming revaluation year. Close cooperation with the assessor will be required to ensure that these estimations are as accurate as possible.

D. Sample RNTR Calculations

1. Municipal RNTR Example: Four-Year Revaluation Cycle Including Annexation

Blue Devil City lies in Carolina County, which conducts a reappraisal of its real property in 2019. The county's last reappraisal occurred in 2015.

Effective June 30, 2017, Blue Devil City completed an annexation that added $100 million to the city's tax base for the 2017–2018 tax year. In 2018, Widgets, Inc. opened a new production facility that added $50 million to the city tax base for 2019.

Blue Devil City Tax Bases:

2015–2016*	$850 million
2016–2017	$862 million
2017–2018	$975 million
2018–2019	$990 million
2019–2020*	$1,200 million

*Revaluation year

Blue Devil City 2018–2019 Tax Rate: $0.50

Calculating the RNTR

Step 1: Tax Levy for Current Year

The current fiscal year in this example is 2018–2019. (Remember that budget officials would be completing these calculations before the new revaluation fiscal year begins). Note that the calculation involves the tax levy (rate times base), not actual tax collections.

Keeping in mind the fact that the tax rate is expressed as "tax per $100 of property value," the formula for calculating the current year's tax levy is as follows:

$$(\text{Current Tax Base}/100) \times \text{Current Tax Rate} = \text{Current Tax Levy}$$

Inserting the correct figures for Blue Devil City produces this result:

$$(\$990,000,000/100) \times 0.5 = \$4,950,000$$

Step 2: New Tax Rate

The second step is to determine the tax rate that, using next year's new revaluation tax base, would produce a tax levy equal to the current year's tax levy. This calculation is as follows:

$$\text{New Tax Base} \times \text{New Tax Rate} = \text{Current Tax Levy OR}$$
$$\text{New Tax Rate} = \text{Current Tax Levy}/\text{New Tax Base}$$

Plugging in the appropriate Blue Devil City figures produces this result:

$$\text{New Tax Rate} = \$4,950,000/\$1,200,000,000 = 0.004125$$

Change that result to be expressed as "rate per $100 of property value," and it produces a new tax rate of $0.4125. (Note that we do not adjust the revaluation year's tax base for unusual events such as the new production facility described above. Those adjustments are made only for purposes of calculating the growth rate for non-revaluation years, as demonstrated below.)

The new tax rate is lower than the current year's tax rate, which make sense because the tax base will increase next year due to the revaluation. A larger tax base next year means that the city can drop its tax rate and still produce the same tax levy as this year.

But before this new tax rate can be called the official RNTR, it must adjusted by the city's "natural" growth rate during the three previous non-revaluation years. G.S. 159-11(e) requires this adjustment to account for the fact that the city's tax base (and, therefore, tax levy) would have changed even without a revaluation.

Step 3: Growth Rate

To calculate the growth rate since the last revaluation, the city must determine the percentage change between tax bases for each of the three non-revaluation years and then calculate the average of those three rates.[23] Table 7.5, below, illustrates this

---

23. No growth rate is calculated for the change between the tax bases in the last non-revaluation year and in the revaluation year because that change reflects the effect of the revaluation and not "natural" growth. As a result, the number of growth rates calculated should always be one fewer than the number of years in the revaluation cycle. The

process. This calculation compares tax bases, not tax levies or tax collections, and adjusts those bases to account for unusual events such as the annexation in 2017.

Table 7.5. Growth Rate—City

Fiscal Year	Assessed Value ($)	Growth Rate (%)	Notes
2015–2016	850,000,000		a
2016–2017	862,000,000	1.41	
2016–2017	862,000,000		
2017–2018	875,000,000	1.51	b
2017–2018	975,000,000		c
2018–2019	990,000,000	1.53	d

a. Previous revaluation year.
b. The 2017–2018 tax base is reduced by $100 million to account for the annexation that first took effect for that tax year. Because this event is unusual and not likely to occur regularly, it should be removed from the tax base for this calculation so that the growth rate is not artificially inflated.
c. The $100 million annexation value is added back into the 2017–2018 tax base when it is compared to the 2018–2019 tax base to calculate the growth rate between those two years.
d. There are only three individual growth rates to calculate, not four, because the change in the tax base between 2018–2019 and 2019–2020 reflects the revaluation and not "natural" growth.

The city's average non-revaluation growth rate is as follows:

$$(1.41 + 1.51 + 1.53)/3 = 1.48 \text{ percent.}$$

Step 4: Adjust New Tax Rate by Average Growth Rate

The final step adjusts the new tax rate to reflect the change in the tax levy that would have been expected if no revaluation had occurred.

$$\text{New Tax Rate} \times \text{Average Growth Rate} = \text{RNTR}$$

While this step normally increases the final RNTR, it could decrease that rate if the government's average growth was negative in the previous non-revaluation years, as was the case for many counties and municipalities in the years immediately following the 2008 recession.

For Blue Devil City, the adjustment would be as follows:

$$\$0.4125 \times 1.0148 = \$0.4186$$

The city's RNTR for the 2019 revaluation is $0.4186. This is the tax rate that is estimated to produce the same tax levy as the city would have experienced in 2019 had the city not had a revaluation for that year.

Blue Devil City example involves a four-year revaluation cycle, meaning that the budget office must calculate three growth rates and then average them. The Tar Heel County example below involves an eight-year revaluation cycle, which requires the calculation and averaging of seven growth rates.

2. County RNTR Example: Eight-Year Revaluation Cycle Including Public Service Company Property Value Adjustment

Assume that Tar Heel County revalues its property in 2019, with its last revaluation occurring in 2011. The tax base for 2015–2016 reflects a $9,000,000 reduction in public service company property resulting from the N.C. Department of Revenue's mandatory equalization[24] when the county's sales assessment ratio fell to 0.85. Similarly, the tax base for 2018–2019 reflects a $6,000,000 reduction in public service company property resulting from the Department of Revenue's mandatory equalization when the county's sales assessment ratio fell again to 0.75.[25]

Tar Heel County Tax Bases:

2011–2012*	1,100 million
2012–2013	1,200 million
2013–2014	1,300 million
2014–2015	1,400 million
2015–2016	1,491 million
2016–2017	1,591 million
2017–2018	1,691 million
2018–2019	1,785 million
2019–2020*	2,300 million

*Revaluation year

Tar Heel County 2018–2019 Tax Rate: $0.50

Calculating the RNTR

See the text set out in the four steps listed in Section III.D.1, above, for particulars about the calculation process.

Step 1: Tax Levy for Current Year

(Current Tax Base/100) × Current Tax Rate = Current Tax Levy

($1,785,000,000/100) × 0.50 = $8,925,000

Note that this calculation uses the actual 2018–2019 tax base, which reflects the public service company property reduction. That reduction is added back to the tax only for the growth-rate calculation, as demonstrated below in step 4.

Step 2: New Tax Rate

The second step is to determine the tax rate that, using next year's new revaluation tax base, would produce a tax levy equal to the current year's tax levy. This calculation is as follows:

New Tax Base × New Tax Rate = Current Tax Levy **OR**

New Tax Rate = Current Tax Levy/New Tax Base

New Tax Rate = $8,925,000/$2,300,000,000 = 0.00388

---

24. See Question 8 in Section III.H, below, for a more detailed discussion of equalization.

25. See a detailed discussion of these issues in Section III.H, below.

Table 7.6. Growth Rate—County

Fiscal Year	Assessed Value ($)	Growth Rate (%)	Notes
2011–2012	1,100,000,000		a
2012–2013	1,200,000,000	9.1	
2012–2013	1,200,000,000		
2013–2014	1,300,000,000	8.3	
2013–2014	1,300,000,000		
2014–2015	1,400,000,000	7.7	
2014–2015	1,400,000,000		
2015–2016	1,500,000,000	7.1	b
2015–2016	1,491,000,000		c
2016–2017	1,591,000,000	6.7	
2016–2017	1,591,000,000		
2017–2018	1,691,000,000	6.3	
2017–2018	1,691,000,000		
2018–2019	1,791,000,000	5.9	d

a. Revaluation year.
b. For purposes of calculating the tax base growth rate between 2014–2015 and 2015–2016, the assessed value for 2015–2016 ignores the $9,000,000 reduction in public service company property mandated by the Department of Revenue.
c. The $9,000,000 public service company reduction is applied to the tax base for purposes of calculating growth rates for 2016–2017 and future years.
d. For purposes of calculating the tax base growth rate between 2017–2018 and 2018–2019, the assessed value for 2018–2019 ignores an additional $6,000,000 reduction in public service company property resulting from the mandatory equalization when the county's sales assessment ratio fell to 0.75.

Adjust that rate to reflect "rate per $100 of property value" and it produces a new tax rate of $0.388.

But before this new tax rate can be called the official RNTR, it must adjusted by the county's growth rate during the seven previous non-revaluation years. G.S. 159-11(e) requires this adjustment to account for the fact that the county's tax base would have changed even without a revaluation.

Step 3: Growth Rate

To calculate the growth rate since the last revaluation, the county must determine the percentage change between tax bases for each of the previous seven non-revaluation years and then calculate the average of those seven rates. Table 7.6 illustrates this process. Note that the calculation compares tax bases, not tax levies or tax collections, and adjusts those bases to account for unusual events such as the public service company property reductions in 2015 and 2016.

The average of the seven growth rates displayed in Table 7.6 is as follows:

$$(9.1 + 8.3 + 7.7 + 7.1 + 6.7 + 6.3 + 5.9) / 7 = 7.3 \text{ percent}$$

Step 4: Adjust New Tax Rate by Average Growth Rate

The final step adjusts the new tax rate to reflect the change in the tax levy that would have been expected if no revaluation had occurred. As was the case in the Blue Devil City example, this adjustment increases the resulting RNTR because the county experienced positive growth in the previous seven non-revaluation years. The calculation is as follows:

$$\text{New Tax Rate} \times \text{Average Growth Rate} = \text{RNTR}$$
$$\$0.388 \times 1.073 = \$0.4163$$

The county's RNTR for 2019 is $0.4163. This is the tax rate that is estimated to produce the same tax levy as the county would have experienced had the county not conducted a revaluation for 2019.

E. Publishing the RNTR

G.S. 159-11(e) requires that the budget officer, in the year in which a general reappraisal of real property has been conducted, include a statement of the RNTR in the budget for comparison purposes. In other words, a statement of the RNTR must be included in the budget document for the fiscal year following the January 1 on which the reappraisal became effective. Although G.S. 159-11(e) contains the formula for calculating the RNTR, it does not provide details about the location of an RNTR statement within the budget or provide recommended language for such a statement.

F. Recommended Placement

There are several places within the budget document that could be used by the budget officer to address the RNTR, including the budget message, the budget summary, the revenue section, or the budget ordinance. The best course of action is for budget officers to use the budget message for providing a statement of the RNTR. One reason for using the budget message is found in G.S. 159-11(b), which requires that the budget, together with a budget message, be submitted to the governing board not later than June 1. The Local Government Budget and Fiscal Control Act does not require the submission of other sections commonly found in budget documents.

G.S. 159-11(b) also recommends that the budget message address any major changes in fiscal policy and in appropriation levels. A difference between the actual tax rate for the forthcoming fiscal year and the RNTR represents a change in fiscal policy, resulting in an effective tax increase or decrease for taxpayers. Because the RNTR may represent such a shift in fiscal policy, it is not recommended that such a statement be incorporated into the budget ordinance. The budget ordinance is not the preferred place for communicating changes in fiscal policy and does not always accompany the proposed budget submitted to elected officials for consideration by the budget officer.

Another reason for using the budget message to address the RNTR is found in the recommended budget practices promulgated by the Government Finance Officers Association (GFOA). The GFOA recommends that the budget contain a budget message that summarizes the major factors and trends affecting the preparation and adoption of the annual operating budget.[26] Such factors and trends include revenue collections, tax rates, debt obligations, and changes in fund balance. Placing a statement of the RNTR in the budget message highlights the significance of the reappraisal process, gives readers a benchmark for an increase or decrease in the property tax rate, and represents professional financial management.

G. Recommended Language

The main variables needed to calculate the RNTR are the reassessed value of real property, the tax levy from the current fiscal year, and the average growth rate of the tax base. A statement of the RNTR in the budget message should at a minimum reference these variables when communicating about the RNTR. While local governments may choose to provide more detail or links to additional materials to help explain the RNTR,[27] the language set out below would satisfy the statutory publication requirement for the RNTR.

Sample Revenue-Neutral Tax Rate Explanation

The general reappraisal of real property for Carolina City occurs once every XX years. State law requires that units of local government, including public authorities, publish a revenue-neutral tax rate in the budget immediately following the completion of the general reappraisal of real property. The purpose of the revenue-neutral tax rate is to provide citizens with comparative information.

The FY 20XX operating budget follows the general reappraisal of real property for Carolina City. The revenue-neutral tax rate, as defined by G.S. 159-11(e), is the rate that is estimated to produce revenue for the next fiscal year equal to the revenue for the current fiscal year if no reappraisal had occurred. The rate is then adjusted by a growth rate equal to the average annual percentage increase in the tax base due to improvements since the last general reappraisal.

The reappraisal produced a tax base of $XX for Carolina City. The tax levy for the current fiscal year is $XX, and the growth rate since the last general reappraisal is XX percent. Using the formula mandated by state

---

26. See the following resources on the GFOA's website: "Recommended Budget Practices from the National Advisory Council on State and Local Budgeting," http://www.gfoa.org/recommended-budget-practices-national-advisory-council -state-and-local-budgeting; "Presenting the Capital Budget," http://www.gfoa.org /presenting-capital-budget.

27. This additional information could include the following School of Government resource: Chris McLaughlin, "The Revenue-Neutral Tax Rate," *Coates' Canons: NC Local Government Law* (blog), UNC School of Government, June 30, 2011, https:// canons.sog.unc.edu/the-revenue-neutral-tax-rate/.

law, the revenue-neutral tax rate for Carolina City is XX cents. The proposed property tax rate for FY 20XX is XX cents, which represents an/a [increase/decrease] from the property tax rate of XX cents for the current fiscal year.

H. Frequently Asked RNTR Questions and Answers

Since its debut in 2003, the RNTR requirement has proven to be confusing and occasionally ambiguous. The question-and-answer section below addresses many of these areas of concern about the RNTR raised by local government budget officials and reiterates some of the important points made above.

1. For what taxes must a local government calculate an RNTR?

A local government must calculate a revenue-neutral rate for each separate levy included in its budget ordinance.[28] For example, a county would publish revenue-neutral rates for its general property tax levy, for all service districts and rural fire districts, and for school supplemental taxes, while a municipality would publish revenue-neutral rates for its general property tax levy and for all service districts. One reason for this interpretation is to provide transparency for all taxes paid by a particular resident. A citizen who lives in a rural fire district, for example, would benefit from two revenue-neutral rates, one to analyze the impact of the revaluation on the county's general property taxes and one to analyze the impact of the revaluation on the fire district taxes.

2. Does the RNTR calculation include only real property?

No. It includes all taxable property in the taxing jurisdiction. Although it is the revaluation of *real* property that triggers the obligation to publish a revenue-neutral rate, this calculation is based on *all* property: real property, personal property, registered motor vehicles, and public service company property. This is because a local government must determine a rate that would produce revenues equal to those produced for the current fiscal year. Revenues produced for the current fiscal year result from applying the tax rate against all property subject to the ad valorem tax, not just real property. A revenue-neutral rate calculated on real property alone would not be comparable to the actual property tax rate that is based on the total tax base.

3. When calculating the average growth rate in the tax base due to improvements since the last general revaluation, should a local government use the budgeted assessed value for each fiscal year?

No. The assessed value used for budgetary purposes represents an estimate, which is used for estimating property tax revenue for the coming fiscal year. Local officials should use the final assessed value at fiscal year's end, giving them the ability to calculate a growth rate based on actual figures rather than on budgeted figures. For local

---

28. A. Fleming Bell, II, and David M. Lawrence, "Local Government and Local Finance," in *North Carolina Legislation 2003: A Summary of Legislation in the 2003 General Assembly of Interest to North Carolina Public Officials*, ed. William A. Campbell (UNC School of Government, 2004).

governments that publish a comprehensive annual financial report, this information can be found in the statistical section. Other local governments will need to contact their tax assessor for final figures. Of course, given that a revenue-neutral rate will need to be calculated before the end of the current fiscal year, the final assessed value for this year will not yet be available. As discussed above, the revenue-neutral rate calculation will require an estimate of the final assessed value for the current fiscal year and for the coming revaluation year.

4. Should the RNTR be adjusted by a local government's tax collection rate?

No. The revenue-neutral rate calculation focuses on the tax rate needed to produce the current fiscal year's tax levy from the newly revalued tax base, without regard for whether this levy was sufficient to satisfy budget needs for the current fiscal year. As discussed in the previous question, the current fiscal year's tax levy is the product of the current fiscal year's estimated final assessed value multiplied by the current tax rate. However, one reaches the same result if the revenue-neutral calculation begins with the current fiscal year's actual revenues instead of the actual tax levy. When the current fiscal year's actual revenues are divided by the actual collection rate, the resulting figure is the current fiscal year's actual tax levy. G.S. 159-13(b)(6) requires that the estimated percentage of property tax collections not be greater than the percentage of the levy actually realized in cash as of the June 30 during the preceding fiscal year. Therefore, one would return to a revenue-neutral rate that will produce the current fiscal year's tax levy when applied to the tax base after revaluation.

5. Why is the average annual tax base growth rate part of the RNTR calculation?

Even in non-revaluation years, most tax bases increase due to new construction and the accumulation of personal property by taxpayers. Absent a revaluation, the current tax base can be expected to increase by the average growth rate over the past several years. This means that even if the tax rate were kept constant, next year's tax levy would be larger than this year's tax levy. A revenue-neutral rate must be increased by an average annual growth rate to account for this expected natural growth in the tax base and tax levy. Remember that the revenue-neutral rate represents the tax rate that, when applied to the newly revalued tax base, is estimated to produce the same tax levy as would have been produced next year using the current year's tax rate if a revaluation had not occurred. If a revenue-neutral rate were not increased by an average annual growth rate of the tax base, the calculation would understate the tax levy that would be produced without the revaluation in the coming fiscal year.

6. How should a local government account for any annexations since the last revaluation?

G.S. 159-11(e) requires a budget officer to adjust the growth rate to account for any annexation, de-annexation, merger, or similar event. The most common adjustment occurs when a municipality annexes property. The reason for this requirement is to prevent the act of annexation from skewing the tax base growth rate from one fiscal year to another. Therefore, the value of the annexed property is backed out of the assessed value for the fiscal year when calculating the annual growth rate from the previous fiscal year. However, it is put back in the assessed value for the fiscal year when calculating the annual growth rate for the next fiscal year. Although the annexation itself should not be permitted to skew the annual growth rate, the annual growth rate should reflect growth within the annexed area once the property is annexed.[29]

7. How should a local government account for the discovery of substantial taxable property since the last revaluation?

Discovery is the term used to describe the process by which the county assessor identifies, appraises, and taxes property that previously avoided taxation. Discoveries increase both the tax base and the current-year tax levy. The former increase does not skew the revenue-neutral rate calculation; the latter increase may need to be taken into account so that the current-year tax levy is not overstated. When calculating the average annual growth rate of the tax base since the last revaluation, adjustments must be made to account for any annexation, de-annexation, merger, or similar event. Routine changes to the tax base, such as discoveries and assessment appeals, are part of the normal tax base growth process and should be included in the growth-rate calculation regardless of their magnitude. Although a discovery bill can include up to six years of property taxes, the assessed value of the discovery is added to the tax base only once. No adjustments are required for the revenue-neutral rate calculation regardless of the scope of the discoveries involved.

This is not necessarily the case for the current-year tax levy. If a budget officer calculates the current tax levy by multiplying the current tax rate by the current tax base, discoveries will not skew the calculation. However, if the budget officer obtains the current year's tax levy from the tax office, adjustments may be required. From a tax collector's perspective, the current-year tax levy is the total billed and payable in the current fiscal year. This amount will include not only the current year's taxes but also past taxes and penalties included on discovery bills. Because these amounts are one-time increases in the current-year levy that will not be repeated in future years, they need to be removed from the levy figure obtained from the tax assessor before beginning a revenue-neutral rate calculation. Otherwise, both the target levy for the coming fiscal year and the revenue-neutral rate will be overstated.

8. What happens if the value of public service company property is reduced because a county's sales assessment ratio falls below 90 percent?

This reduction must be accounted for in the growth-rate calculation. In a process known as *equalization*, G.S. 105-284(b) requires that if the sales assessment ratio for real property in a county falls below 90 percent in the fourth and seventh years following a revaluation of real property, the value of public service company property allocated to that county is reduced according to that percentage. This causes a reduction in the county's tax base, but one that has nothing to do with the "normal"

---

29. See the Blue Devil City RNTR sample calculation in Section III.D.1, above, for a demonstration of how to account for annexations when calculating the average growth rate.

growth or contraction in the county's property value. Accordingly, this reduction in public service company property value must be backed out of the growth-rate calculation in the same manner as an increase in property value caused by an annexation.[30]

Counties on four-year revaluation cycles should escape equalization because they will revalue their property in the fourth year after revaluation—the first year that a sales assessment study can trigger equalization. Counties on five-, six-, or seven-year revaluation cycles may be subject to equalization once, in the fourth year after revaluation. Counties on eight-year cycles could be subject to equalization twice, once in the fourth year after revaluation and again in the seventh year. If equalization occurs, a local government must add the lost value back to the tax base when calculating the annual growth rate between the fiscal year preceding the reduction and the fiscal year of the reduction. Doing so will prevent the equalization from skewing the annual growth rate.

9. If a municipality is located in more than one county, must it calculate an RNTR whenever any one of those counties conducts a revaluation?

Yes. G.S. 159-11(e) does not explicitly answer this question; instead, it states simply that a revenue-neutral rate must be calculated "in each year in which a general revaluation of real property has been conducted." It seems appropriate to interpret this requirement as being triggered when *any* portion of a municipality's property is subject to a general revaluation, even if the reappraised property represents only a small percentage of the municipality's total taxable property.

This requirement could become burdensome for municipalities in multiple counties. Consider the city of High Point, unique among North Carolina municipalities because it sits in four counties: Davie, Forsyth, Guilford, and Randolph. If all four of those counties were on different four-year revaluation cycles, High Point would be required to calculate a revenue-neutral rate each time one of those counties conducted a revaluation of real property—in other words, every year.

When a multicounty municipality calculates a revenue-neutral rate because one of the counties in which it is located has conducted a revaluation, it should calculate the average growth rate for its tax base back to the most recent revaluation by *any* of the counties in which it is located, not back to the last revaluation by the county whose current revaluation triggered the calculation. Otherwise, the average annual growth rate would capture increases due to revaluations rather than only improvements and additions as intended by the statute.

10. Must the local government adopt the RNTR?

No. As is true every budgeting season, the governing board is free to adopt any tax rate it wishes for the new fiscal year.[31]

---

30. See the Tar Heel County RNTR sample calculation in Section III.D.2, above, for a demonstration of how to account for public service company property equalizations when calculating the average growth rate.

31. Subject only to the $1.50 cap on county and municipal tax rates discussed in Section II, above.

11. Why will some taxpayers still face a tax increase if their local government adopts the RNTR?

A revenue-neutral tax rate is intended to be revenue-neutral for the county as a whole, not for individual property owners. Therefore, some taxpayers may receive a higher tax bill (for real and personal property) even if the taxing unit adopts a revenue-neutral rate.

One reason that individual property owners may pay a higher tax bill (real and personal) is because the statute requires a taxing unit to increase its revenue-neutral rate by a growth rate equal to the average annual percentage increase in the tax base due to improvements since the last general revaluation.

Another reason is that a taxing unit's tax burden generally shifts toward real property and away from personal property in a revaluation year. Real property is valued at market value only in revaluation years, which in most counties occurs every four or eight years. When property values are rising, real property is assessed below its market value in the years following a revaluation. In contrast, personal property is valued at market value annually. As a result, personal property bears a greater proportion of the tax burden than does real property relative to market value. This imbalance is corrected in a revaluation year, when the tax value of real property is increased to market value. Because real property will now bear more of the tax burden, most real property owners will see a tax increase even if the county adopts a revenue-neutral rate. Personal property tax bills, however, will generally drop.

Consider this example. In the year prior to revaluation, Carolina County's tax base—that is, the total assessed value of its taxable property—is $100 million. (Of that amount, 75 percent, or $75 million, is real property; 20 percent, or $20 million, is personal property; and the remaining 5 percent, or $5 million, is public service company property.) After revaluation, the total assessed value of Carolina County's real property increases by 20 percent, from $75 million to $90 million. But, as is often the case, the value of the county's personal property and public service company property remains basically flat. Thus, after revaluation, the county's tax base is now $115 million. (Of this amount, 78 percent is real property, 18 percent is personal property, and 4 percent is public service company property.) Real property now represents 78 percent of the county's tax base, up from 75 percent prior to the revaluation. Because real property now bears a greater share of the tax burden, a Carolina County real property owner will see a tax increase even if the revenue-neutral rate is adopted, unless the owner's real property increased in value substantially less than the 20 percent average countywide increase.

I. Guidance from the Local Government Commission

The N.C. Local Government Commission (LGC) has created an Excel worksheet to help with the RNTR calculation process. The worksheet can be downloaded from the LGC's website at https://www.nctreasurer.com/lgc-worksheets-revenue-neutral -property-tax. This electronic template gives examples and calculates revenue-neutral rates for four-, six-, and eight-year revaluation cycles and demonstrates how annexations and other unusual events should be removed from the growth-rate calculation.

PART III

FINANCIAL MANAGEMENT AND PLANNING

Chapter 8

Fund Balance and Budgeting for Local Governments

Sharon G. Edmundson

Introduction

Fund balance is an element of financial reporting that is unique to government. In its simplest terms, fund balance is the equity in a fund, reported on the modified accrual basis of accounting. The basic accounting equation that underpins all forms of double entry bookkeeping applies to fund balance: assets equal liabilities plus equity. Most of the time, we refer to fund balance as it exists in the General Fund, but all funds have fund balance, and it plays a part in the budgeting process.

This chapter will focus on further defining fund balance as well as discussing why it is important to maintain certain levels of fund balance, how we determine when and why it may be appropriate to use fund balance to fund budgetary appropriations, and how we report fund balance on government financial statements.

Why Does a Government Need to Maintain Fund Balance?

Why is it important to maintain some level of fund balance? What purpose does it serve? Why is it more important in some funds than others within the same government? Why is it more important for some types of government than for others? Anyone that has spent much time in local government finance or management is likely familiar with these questions and probably many others!

Fund Balance as a Savings Account

The most common understanding of fund balance is that it serves as a government's savings account. Fund balance, at least the spendable portion, is a source of cash flow that governments can tap for a number of reasons. If a government has an unexpected drop in revenues, its governing board and management may decide to use fund balance to fill the gap created by that drop, rather than reduce appropriations. They may decide to only partially fund the gap with fund balance and make up the remaining difference by reducing some appropriations. Similarly, if an unexpected need arises, and a government therefore needs to expend funds it did not anticipate spending, it can use fund balance to cover those expenditures. The COVID-19 pandemic required many instances of this type of use of fund balance. Governments were faced with unexpected drops in revenue in utility funds and faced additional expenditures in providing for the public's safety. Some opted to amend their budgets to use fund balance to cover the drop in revenues and to provide funds for the unexpected expenditures.

In a more positive context, a government may find itself with an unexpected opportunity; fund balance can allow that government to take advantage of that opportunity. During the Great Recession, governments that had sufficient amounts of fund balance on hand were able to take advantage of depressed real estate prices to acquire needed land and facilities. These governments amended their budgets to use fund balance as the source of funding for these acquisitions.

Fund balance also can provide needed cash flow during months when inflows are reduced. Tax-levying units of government in North Carolina operate on a July 1 to June 30 fiscal year. Property taxes, one of the primary sources of revenue for these governments, are paid starting in August, and typically reach their peak in December each year. From January through July, the amount of property tax paid declines. Governments can use fund balance to even out that cyclical cash flow if needed. Although there are extremely limited options for North Carolina local governments to borrow for short-term operations, having a sufficient fund balance on hand eliminates the need to consider these very limited sources of cash flow.

Fund Balance as an Indication of Fiscal Health

Governments in North Carolina and across the country can count on receiving positive feedback from rating agencies if they consistently maintain appropriate levels of fund balance. Strong credit ratings lead to lower interest costs on bonds and other debt. For smaller units that do not have rated debt, a strong fund balance can lead to lower interest rates and therefore lower interest costs on bank financings. Lenders to governments want to see that those governments can maintain sufficient savings similar to what lenders expect from individuals seeking financing for a car or a home.

In North Carolina, local governments must get approval from the Local Government Commission (LGC) for most debt issuances.[1] In addition, local governments must submit their annual audits to the LGC staff for review, including an assessment of each unit's fiscal health. One of the key components of that review is an analysis of the unit's fund balance and fund balance available in the General Fund. Staff also look at fund balance in a utility fund if there are signs of distress. A unit that does not maintain sufficient levels of fund balance available will be expected to provide a corrective action plan explaining how it intends to rebuild its fund balance available to an acceptable level. This plan and its implementation will be considered if the unit submits a debt application to the LGC. Units that routinely fail to maintain acceptable levels of fund balance available may appear on the LGC's unit assistance list (UAL). This list is compiled annually and consists of the local governments in the state that the LGC staff feels are at risk for financial distress. Units on the UAL may find it difficult to get debt approved by the LGC unless they have strong corrective action plans in place that will build fund balance available to acceptable levels.

Fund Balance versus Fund Balance Available for Appropriation

Fund balance, as stated earlier, is the "equity" in a fund, and is calculated using the modified accrual basis of accounting. Fund balance *available for appropriation* is a concept that is unique to North Carolina and is defined by the state's statutes. The Local Government Budget and Fiscal Control Act (LGBFCA) defines the maximum amount of fund balance that is available for a local government to legally appropriate in its budget each year, hence the term *fund balance available for appropriation* (often shortened to *fund balance available*).[2] The fact that North Carolina has this concept spelled out in statute is indicative of the conservative approach to local government finance for which the state has long been known: "Appropriated fund balance in any fund shall not exceed the sum of cash and investments minus the sum of liabilities, encumbrances, and deferred revenues arising from cash receipts, as those figures stand at the close of the fiscal year next preceding the budget year."[3]

Fund balance available represents the amount of fund balance that is on hand in cash form, less any amount that is already owed to another fund, vendor, or creditor in the short term. The actual formula for determining fund balance available is shown in Figure 8.1.

---

1. *See* Chapter 159, Sections 51, 85, 100, 105, 149, 161, 169, 170, and 171 of the North Carolina General Statutes (hereinafter G.S.).

2. G.S. Ch. 159, Art. 3.

3. G.S. 159-8a.

Figure 8.1. Formula for Determining Fund Balance Available

For any given fund (except internal service or fiduciary funds):

Cash and investments (including restricted cash and investments)

Less:

- Fund liabilities

- Fund encumbrances outstanding

- Deferred revenues arising from cash receipts [a]

Equals: Fund balance available for appropriation

a. These are usually prepaid taxes or other items and are normally captioned as "Deferred Inflows of Resources" in financial statements, or cash on hand that has not yet been earned.

Calculating Fund Balance Available and Fund Balance Restricted by State Statute—Carolina County

Step 1	Calculate Fund Balance Available	
Cash and investments	$11,394,762	(10,642,875 + 751,887)
Subtract:		
Fund liabilities	3,901,064	(3,561,492 + 226,142 + 50,551 + 62,879)
Encumbrances	20,890	Found in the notes to the financials
Deferred revenues arising from cash receipts	329,403	Details found in the notes to the financials
Fund balance available for appropriation	**$7,143,405**	

Step 2	Calculate Restricted by State Statute	
Total fund balance	$13,850,333	
Subtract:		
Fund balance available	7,143,405	
Non-spendable fund balance	2,551,800	Inventory and prepaid expenditures
Restricted by state statute	**$4,155,128**	

Step 3	Calculate Fund Balance Available as a Percentage of Expenditures
Total General Fund expenditures	$86,039,391
Add	
Transfers out	+370,000
Subtract	
Capital leases and installment purchases	-100,000
Adjusted total expenditures	$86,309,391
Divided by fund balance available	$7,143,405

FBA as a % of General Fund expenditures	**8.28%**

Source: Data from *Carolina County, North Carolina, Balance Sheet, Governmental Funds, June 30, 2020*. (See Appendix A at the end of this chapter for the full document).

Fund balance available (FBA) always starts out with the amount of cash and investments held by the fund for which the calculation is being made. A quick check on the calculation of FBA is that if the amount exceeds the amount of cash and investments in the fund, there is an error in the FBA calculation.

Fund balance available is calculated each year based on final fiscal year-end financial statements and is applicable to the succeeding fiscal year. The FBA calculation that is applicable to the 2022–2023 fiscal year and budget is calculated using the fund financial statements as of fiscal year-end 2022. The calculation is applicable to the entire 2023 fiscal year; a unit cannot recalculate FBA using interim financial statements or results. The calculation represents the **maximum** amount of fund balance that is available for appropriation; it is not required that a unit appropriate any amount of fund balance—only that the cumulative amount of appropriations made during the budgetary process or through an amendment cannot exceed that amount. The number is recalculated each year for the next fiscal year.

The converse of fund balance available is the concept of restricted by state statute, which is unique to North Carolina. It stands to reason that if only a portion of a unit's total fund balance is available for appropriation, there is another portion that is not available. This is known as fund balance that is restricted by state statute. It represents the amount of fund balance that is not available for appropriation because it does not yet exist in cash form, or is cash received that is applicable to a future period. A third category of fund balance is non-spendable; that is, it does not exist and will not exist in a spendable form.

Fund balance available is expressed as a percentage of fund expenditures so that units can compare their results to those of other entities. Comparing dollars to dollars does not take into account the differences across governments in the sizes of their budgets. The amount of expenditures is adjusted to include transfers out, as that is an outflow of resources. It also is adjusted to remove the amount of resources provided by financings, as an offsetting amount should be included in the total expenditure number and is not considered to be a recurring operating cost.

Local Government Commission Policies on Fund Balance Available

Many local government officials are surprised to learn that there is no statutory minimum percentage for fund balance available. Many believe that the oft-quoted 8 percent minimum is dictated in statute or in administrative code. This is not the case. The 8 percent of fund balance available as a percentage of expenditures is an established "bare-bones" minimum for tax-levying units of government.[4] Most, if

---

4. *See* N.C. Department of State Treasurer, State and Local Government Finance Division, *Management of Cash and Taxes and Fund Balance Available—Counties—for the Fiscal Year Ended June 30, 2020* (May 26, 2020), https://files.nc.gov/nctreasurer /documents/files/SLGFD/Memos/2020-08.pdf; *See* N.C. Department of State Treasurer, State and Local Government Finance Division, *Management of Cash and Taxes and*

not all, governments find that 8 percent does not meet their needs; many determine that they need much more than 8 percent to operate effectively. To help put this in perspective, an 8 percent FBA represents approximately one month of expenditures. Most units are more comfortable with at least three to six months of savings. The Government Finance Officers Association (GFOA) recommends that governments maintain at least two months of savings and that each government should adjust that target to meet its needs.[5] The staff of the LGC publishes annual reports of county and municipal fund balance available, grouped by population. Municipalities are further segregated by those with and those without electric funds. Units can see how their FBA percentages stack up against those of their peers. The reports are published in the spring each year and are available on the N.C. Department of State Treasurer State and Local Government Finance Division's (SLGFD) website.[6]

In these reports, it is clear that the larger the government, the smaller the FBA percentage, generally speaking. There are, of course, outliers. Keep in mind that these reports are on FBA in the General Fund. Larger governments are more likely to have resources available in other funds. Smaller governments typically do not have as many alternative resources and therefore need to maintain higher amounts of fund balance available.

A tax-levying unit of government that has less than 8 percent fund balance available in its General Fund can expect to be contacted by LGC staff to determine how the unit plans to address its deficiency. In most cases, a unit with such a low FBA percentage will not be approved for a debt issuance until the FBA percentage is increased. Similarly, a unit whose fund balance available consists primarily of restricted funds (usually a municipality whose fund balance available consists primarily of Powell Bill funds that are restricted to certain transportation expenditures) also will be expected to improve its financial position and, until it does so, will face limitations on its ability to obtain debt.

Any government that has a deficit (calculated on the modified accrual basis of accounting) at fiscal year-end is required by statute to fund that deficit in the next budget.[7] It is important to note that this requirement applies to **total fund balance** in governmental and proprietary funds, **not to net assets and not to fund balance available**. Again, the concept of fund balance is based on the modified accrual basis of accounting and the current financial resources measurement focus.

The concept of fund balance available was developed and implemented to prevent a unit of government from appropriating fund balance in the coming year's budget that exceeds more than a unit has on hand in cash form and not owed at the end of the current fiscal year. The amount of fund balance available that has been appropriated in the next year's budget is disclosed in the annual financial report of each unit. That

Fund Balance Available—Municipalities—for the Fiscal Year Ended June 30, 2020 (June 10, 2020), https://files.nc.gov/nctreasurer/documents/files/SLGFD/Memos/2020-09.pdf.

5. "Fund Balance Guidelines for the General Fund," Government Finance Officers Association, https://www.gfoa.org/materials/fund-balance-guidelines-for-the-general-fund.

6. *See* https://www.nctreasurer.com/links/state-and-local-government-finance-division.

7. *See* G.S. 159-13(b)(2).

amount by law cannot exceed the fund balance available amount that was calculated at the current year-end.[8] If during the subsequent fiscal year a unit later determines it over-appropriated fund balance, it must take immediate action to amend its budget and reduce the appropriation below the legal limit.

Interfund Loans and Fund Balance Available

Sometimes units consider loaning funds from one fund to another within the government. Discussing whether or not that is a good idea is beyond the scope of this chapter, but units considering this action should be sure they understand the effect of such a transaction on fund balance available. The lending fund will see its fund balance available drop by the amount of the loan. Even though the lending fund is exchanging one asset, cash, for another, a receivable, it also is reducing cash, which is the starting number to calculate fund balance available. In the receiving fund, there is no effect on fund balance available. While cash is increasing by the amount of the loan, so are liabilities, so the net effect on fund balance is zero. Regardless of the terms, the unit's board should approve such a loan before it occurs, along with plans and a timetable for repayment.

Trends in Fund Balance Available

Reporting changes resulting from the Governmental Accounting Standards Board's (GASB) changing standards have resulted in fund balance available numbers trending higher in recent years. Units that maintain savings to cover pension or retiree health care costs but do not have those funds in a legally separate trust now record those amounts in the General Fund. While those funds are to be spent only on pension or health care benefits, they are, in fact, spendable and are included in the total cash figure that is used to calculate fund balance available. In addition, most counties now report their revaluation funds in the General Fund for financial statement purposes, again pushing fund balance available numbers higher.

Fund Balance Policies Adopted by Local Governments

Each government needs to determine an appropriate amount of fund balance available that is wants to hold. There is no one-size-fits-all approach. The development and adoption of a fund balance policy is an excellent means by which to evaluate a

---

8. *See* G.S. 159-8(a).

unit's needs. The exercise of determining policy parameters can be helpful in educating elected leaders and citizens on the components and allowable uses of fund balance. There are multiple approaches to establishing a targeted fund balance available amount for a unit. Targets can be set as a percentage of revenues, expenditures, or budgeted amounts. Targets may be set as a range of percentages or as one targeted percentage. Some units set a targeted dollar amount as their policy. However targets are crafted, elected leaders and management need to make sure their policies are realistic and not unattainable over time. Units that have low or declining fund balances available should not expect to restore them immediately.

Units also need to consider the makeup of their fund balance available amounts. Remember that restricted funds are included in fund balance available because they can be spent. However, if, for example, the target FBA is 40 percent, and 35 percent of that is restricted to a particular purpose, the unit does not have much in the way of unrestricted funds to use as its board and management see fit. Units that maintain large amounts of restricted funds on a regular basis may want to differentiate between restricted and unrestricted fund balances in their policies.

In addition to addressing a target fund balance available amount or percentage, a fund balance policy also should address what the unit will do if its fund balance available exceeds the target. It is a nice problem to have, and it is important for elected leaders and management to have a plan for these funds. One option is to simply let the FBA grow. This provides the unit with the most flexibility (unless the funds are restricted, as discussed previously). However, some taxpayers may question the need for the unit to continue to grow its savings without a plan for their use. Another option is for the board to commit the funds to a particular purpose. This action must be taken with a resolution of the board and can only be undone by another resolution of the board. A third option is to transfer the funds to a formally established capital reserve fund. Once funds are moved to a capital reserve fund, they can only be used for capital needs or for debt service on a capital project.[9] Some units may find this arrangement too restrictive, while others find it appealing. The specified project can change, but the overall restriction to capital expenditures or debt service is permanent.

Adopting a policy is seen as a positive step by rating agencies and can help hold elected officials and management accountable regarding their use of fund balance available as a source of funds. Units of government that choose to adopt a fund balance policy should disclose this policy in the notes to the annual financial statements.

---

9. *See* G.S. 159-18.

Fund Balance Available in Non-Tax-Levying Units of Government

Units of government that do not have the ability to levy taxes are not expected to maintain fund balances like those of their county and municipal neighbors. Non-tax-levying units should keep some level of savings on hand to provide cash flow and allow for unexpected needs and opportunities. However, most non-tax-levying units rely on some other entity for funding and should come to an agreement with each of their funders on how much savings is appropriate.

Fund Balance in Funds Other Than the General Fund

Typically any references to fund balance or fund balance available are made in the context of the General Fund—the main operating fund of most units of government. However, most funds have fund balance, including proprietary funds. For a governmental fund, fund balance is reported on a balance sheet for governmental funds. For all funds but the General Fund, fund balance is not unrestricted, which makes sense in terms of why other governmental funds exist. Fund balance in a proprietary fund is not reported anywhere in a generally accepted accounting principles (GAAP) financial statement and must be derived based on what is known about the current financial inflows and outflows in a proprietary fund. Most of the time, an approximation of fund balance available can be calculated using the same components of the calculation made for the General Fund: cash and investments, less current payables (not including debt service) and deferred inflows from cash receipts. This approximation is necessary as part of the budget preparation process if a unit is intending to appropriate fund balance in a proprietary fund to support appropriations.

Calculating Fund Balance Available (Estimated) for the City of Dogwood's Water and Sewer Fund

Total cash and investments	$1,773,751	($98,696 + $1,675,055)
Subtract:		
Accounts payable due from current resources	65,250	(62,010 + 3,240)
Outstanding encumbrances	22,437	See note
Deferred revenues arising from cash receipts	0	
Fund balance available for appropriation		
City of Dogwood Water and Sewer Fund	$1,686,064	

Note: Encumbrances included for illustrative purposes; data is not available in City of Dogwood financials. May be excluded from the calculation if not material.

Source: Data from *City of Dogwood, Statement of Fund Net Position, Proprietary Funds, June 30, 2020*. (See Appendix B at the end of this chapter for the full statement).

Using Fund Balance Available to Balance the Budget

When is it appropriate to use fund balance available as a planned funding source for an appropriation? It might be easier to explain when it is **not** appropriate! Using fund balance available to fund recurring operational costs is not an acceptable practice. Why? If recurring operating appropriations exceed estimated revenues, the budget is structurally deficient. Fund balance can be used to fund those appropriations initially, but what happens if the revenue shortage is not addressed? Eventually, fund balance is depleted. Rating analysts and creditors do not look favorably on this practice. Fund balance available may be used to provide initial funding to kick off a new program, but using it as a long-term source of funds is not feasible. Fund balance available also may be used to fund one-time appropriations, such as a capital project or capital purchase, if there is enough fund balance available to appropriate. Elected leaders and management must always consider the impact of using fund balance available as a funding source on the unit's long-term financial goals and fiscal health.

Categories of Fund Balance as Reported on a Governmental Balance Sheet

With the implementation of GASB Statement 54, units of government changed the manner by which fund balance is reported on their GAAP financial statements. Fund balance is now broken down into a maximum of five categories.[10] Not all entities will have an amount reported in each category, but in the General Fund there will almost always be an amount indicated as unassigned; that amount may be negative.

The five categories of fund balance are

- non-spendable,
- restricted,
- committed,
- assigned, and
- unassigned.

These four categories are all considered spendable, with each category being less restrictive as one moves down the list.

What does each category indicate in terms of how a unit can spend these funds? It differs by category. Table 8.1 explains the distinct differences among the categories as well as provides some common examples of the types of funds that may fall into each.

---

10. Governmental Accounting Standards Board of the Financial Accounting Foundation, *Statement No. 54 of the Governmental Accounting Standards Board, Fund Balance Reporting and Governmental Fund Type Definitions* (February 2009), https://gasb.org /resources/ccurl/313/494/GASBS%2054.pdf.

Table 8.1. Categories of Fund Balance

Category	Spendability	Description	Examples	More Info	Applicability to Funds
Non-spendable	Does not exist in a spendable form	Created by non-cash or otherwise non-spendable governmental assets	Prepaid expenditures, inventories, principal in a permanent fund		Can exist in any governmental fund
Restricted	Spendable but only as dictated by funding source	Restricted by an external source, such as a grantor	Restricted by state statute; Powell Bill funds held by a North Carolina municipality	Can only result from restrictions from an outside source, such as enabling legislation	Can exist in any governmental fund
Committed	Spendable but set aside for a specific purpose by board action	Board must take action to undo a commitment	Board passes a resolution to set aside funds for a new accounting system; must adopt another resolution to undo the commitment	Action must be taken before the end of the fiscal year to report as committed in that year's financials.	
Assigned	Spendable but designated for some purpose and is neither restricted nor committed.	Does **not** take board action to undo the assignment; board can delegate responsibility for making assignments.	Fund balance available appropriated in an annual budget ordinance is presented as assigned because it does not take a board action to undo the appropriation. It expires when the budget ordinance expires.	Action can be taken any time before financials are finalized.	All remaining **positive** spendable amounts in governmental funds other than the General Fund
Unassigned	Spendable on any item that is an appropriate expenditure of the unit	Once the other four categories are calculated, unassigned is what is left of total fund balance.			The residual category for the General Fund. May be negative. For all other governmental funds, negative residual amounts are reported as unassigned.

Funds Set Aside as Rainy-Day or Stabilization Funds

Stabilization funds are those specifically and formally set aside by a board for future use in certain circumstances, sometimes referred to as "rainy-day" funds. If local governments want to establish a stabilization fund, it can do so, but it must be very specific as to the acceptable circumstances for use of the funds. Stabilization funds are normally reported as restricted or committed (most likely as committed in North Carolina), depending on the availability of the funds and the flexibility of acceptable use. If there is no justification for reporting as restricted or committed, these funds should be reported as unrestricted.

How Does Fund Balance Available for Appropriation Fit with GASB 54 Fund Balance Classifications?

The North Carolina General Statutes that give us the available fund balance concept and calculation were adopted long before the GASB issued Statement 54 on fund balance reporting.[11] However, with a little information and some simple math, fund balance available can be teased out of the Statement 54 classifications. It is important to note that many units and their auditors have moved to focusing on unassigned fund balance rather than on fund balance available. Because of the legal requirement to not appropriate more fund balance than the statutes allow, governments should still be aware of the amount of fund balance available that is on hand.

Generally speaking, the amount of fund balance available should equal the total of all spendable categories of fund balance less the restricted by state statute amount that is part of the restricted fund balance number on the face of the balance sheet. For Carolina County, the total of all spendable categories of fund balance (restricted, committed, assigned, and unassigned) equals $11,298,533. Reduce that total by the restricted by state statute amount of $4,155,128 to equal $7,143,405. This matches the fund balance available appropriation that is calculated in the example provided earlier ("Calculating Fund Balance Available and Fund Balance Restricted by State Statute—Carolina County").

Conclusion

Fund balance available is an important indicator of a local government's fiscal health. How and when the funds are spent and how much importance a unit's elected leaders and management place on properly maintaining fund balance available offer great insight into a unit's fiscal future. There are times when it is appropriate to spend these funds, just as there are times when it is not appropriate to tap this source. Understanding the components of fund balance and those of fund balance available are equally important. Managers and elected leaders need to fully understand this piece of the financial picture, especially when they are developing the annual budget.

---

11. Ibid.

Appendix A. Balance Sheet, Governmental Funds, June 30, 2020, Carolina County, N.C.

Exhibit 3

Carolina County, North Carolina
Balance Sheet
Governmental Funds
June 30, 2020

	Major	Non-Major	Total
	General	Other Governmental Funds	Total
ASSETS			
Cash and cash equivalents	$ 10,642,875	$ 50,757	$ 10,693,632
Restricted cash and cash equivalents	751,887	560,270	1,312,157
Receivables, net	3,525,337	14,916	3,540,253
Due from other governments	3,200,000	54,800	3,254,800
Due from component unit	36,100	-	36,100
Inventories	2,551,800	-	2,551,800
Total assets	$ 20,707,999	$ 680,743	$ 21,388,742
LIABILITIES AND FUND BALANCES			
Liabilities:			
Accounts payable and accrued liabilities	$ 3,561,492	$ 13,346	$ 3,574,838
Miscellaneous liabilities	226,142	-	226,142
Due to other governments	50,551	-	50,551
Contract retainage	-	85,030	85,030
Liabilities to be paid from restricted assets	62,879	-	62,879
Total liabilities	3,901,064	98,376	3,999,440
DEFERRED INFLOWS OF RESOURCES	2,956,602	1,345	2,957,947
Fund balances:			
Nonspendable:			
Inventories	2,551,800	-	2,551,800
Restricted:			
Stabilization by State Statute	4,155,128	4,478	4,159,606
Register of Deeds	17,285	-	17,285
Fire Protection	-	1,783	1,783
School Capital	-	558,550	558,550
Committed:			
Tax Revaluation	471,723	-	471,723
LEO Special Separation Allowance	1,028,267	-	1,028,267
Assigned:			
Recreation Capital	-	7,969	7,969
Future School Capital	-	10,270	10,270
Subsequent year's expenditures	255,000	-	255,000
Unassigned:	5,371,130	(2,028)	5,369,102
Total fund balances	13,850,333	581,022	14,431,355
Total liabilities, deferred inflows of resources, and fund balances	$ 20,707,999	$ 680,743	

(cont.)

Carolina County Balance Sheet *(continued)*

Exhibit 4

Carolina County, North Carolina
Statement of Revenues, Expenditures, and Changes in Fund Balance
Governmental Funds
For the Year Ended June 30, 2020

| | Major | Non-Major Other Governmental | |
	General Fund	Funds	Total
REVENUES			
Ad valorem taxes	$ 55,132,894	$ 20,861	$ 55,153,755
Local option sales taxes	12,849,824	376,400	13,226,224
Other taxes and licenses	230,360	-	230,360
Unrestricted intergovernmental	145,522	-	145,522
Restricted intergovernmental	14,057,550	756,797	14,814,347
Permits and fees	445,049	-	445,049
Sales and services	1,144,821	-	1,144,821
Investment earnings	1,614,828	51,949	1,666,777
Miscellaneous	616,284	70,000	686,284
Total revenues	86,237,132	1,276,007	87,513,139
EXPENDITURES			
Current:			
General government	9,046,771		9,046,771
Public safety	6,999,965	96,663	7,096,628
Transportation	1,138,578	-	1,138,578
Economic and physical development	1,316,929	-	1,316,929
Human services	22,419,822	-	22,419,822
Cultural and recreational	2,308,240	-	2,308,240
Intergovernmental:			
Education	41,418,016	-	41,418,016
Capital outlay	-	1,826,519	1,826,519
Debt service:			
Principal	618,166	-	618,166
Interest	692,904	-	692,904
Bond issuance costs	65,000	-	65,000
Advance refunding escrow	15,000	-	15,000
Total expenditures	86,039,391	1,923,182	87,962,573
Excess (deficiency) of revenues over expenditures	197,741	(647,175)	(449,434)
OTHER FINANCING SOURCES (USES)			
Transfers from other funds	619,059	280,000	899,059
Transfers to other funds	(370,000)	(629,059)	(999,059)
Capital lease obligations issued	100,000	-	100,000
Refunding bonds issued	3,365,000	-	3,365,000
Installment purchase obligations issued	-	1,200,000	1,200,000
Payment to refunded bond escrow agent	(3,300,000)	-	(3,300,000)
Sale of capital assets	28,482	-	28,482
Total other financing sources and uses	442,541	850,941	1,293,482
Net change in fund balance	640,282	203,766	844,048
Fund balances, beginning	13,087,077	377,256	13,464,333
Increase in inventory	122,974	-	122,974
Fund balances, ending	$ 13,850,333	$ 581,022	$ 14,431,355

The notes to the financial statements are an integral part of this statement.

Carolina County, North Carolina

3. Deferred Outflows and Inflows of Resources

	Deferred Outflows of Resources	Deferred Inflows of Resources
Charge on refunding of debt	$ 303,063	$ -
(Pensions, OPEB) - difference between expected and actual experience	965,818	172,917
(Pensions,OPEB) - Net difference between projected and actual investment earnings	862,888	548
(Pensions) - change in proportion and difference between employer contributions and proportionate share of contributions	85,138	111,623
(Pensions, OPEB) - change in assumptions	1,666,955	411,492
Contributions to pension plan subsequent to measurement date (LGERS, ROD)	1,289,342	-
Benefit payments for the OPEB plan paid subsequent to measurement date	43,000	
Benefit payments and admin costs paid subsequent to the measurement date (LEOSSA)	17,279	-
Prepaid taxes not yet earned (General)	-	329,403
Taxes receivable, net, less penalties (General)	-	2,556,406
Taxes receivable, net, less penalties (Special Revenue)	-	1,345
Special assessments receivable, net (General)	-	70,793
Total	$ 5,233,483	$ 3,654,527

Note to preparer: The deferred inflows of financial resources resulting from the taxes receivable amount does not include the portion related to penalties levied on the ad valorem taxes. As a reminder, penalties should be turned over to the local educational agency (LEA). In addition, these penalties will not be due to the LEA until received. Therefore, they should not be included in deferred inflows of resources. When cash is finally received for these penalties, it will immediately be set aside for the LEA in the Fines and Forfeitures Agency Fund. Please refer to Memorandum #1060 for more background.

4. Closure and Postclosure Care Costs - Wingate Drive Landfill Facility

State and federal laws and regulations require the County to place a final cover on its Wingate Drive Landfill Facility when it stops accepting waste and to perform certain maintenance and monitoring functions at the site for thirty years after closure. Although closure and postclosure care costs will be paid only near or after the date the landfill stops accepting waste, the County reports a portion of these closure and postclosure care costs as an operating expense in each period based on landfill capacity used as of each balance

Governmental Funds, Carolina County *(continued)*

Carolina County, North Carolina

Note to Preparer: The above schedule is prepared from the General Fund Balance Sheet as presented in the basic financial statements. Each restriction, commitment, and assignment of fund balance should be included in the calculation above.

The unit should also include any other items that the board authorized even if it is included in unassigned on the Balance Sheet. This is where the unit can disclose any fund balance policies and reduce it from the remaining amount. In this example, the fund balance policy is included in unassigned fund balance. In unusual circumstances fund balance policies can be included in Committed Fund Balance. For more information on GASB 54 components of fund balance please review Memorandum #2010-35 on our website.

The unit is also required to disclose the dollar amount of outstanding encumbrances for all major funds and non-major funds in the aggregate. Outstanding encumbrances are not shown on the face of the statement but are included in Restricted for Stabilization by State Statute (RSS); however, in funds other than the General Fund they might be shown as some other restricted amount. In either case the amount of significant outstanding encumbrances must be disclosed for **each major fund** and in the **aggregate for non-major funds**. Below is example of such disclosure.

The outstanding encumbrances are amounts needed to pay any commitments related to purchase orders and contracts that remain unperformed at year-end.

Encumbrances	*General Fund*	*Non-Major Funds*
	$20,890	$0

Note to preparer: General Fund encumbrances should include those for the legally adopted general fund as well as any funds consolidated into the general fund for a GAAP presentation in accordance with GASB Statement No. 54.

IV.   Segment Information

Note to preparer: Be alert if a non-major proprietary fund has revenue-backed debt. Segment information is only required for enterprise funds with outstanding revenue-backed debt if the fund is not presented as major or when the segment does not encompass the entire fund. In disclosing segment information, present the type of goods or services; a condensed statement of net position; condensed statement of revenues, expenses, and changes in net position; and a condensed statement of cash flows. See paragraph 122 of GASB Statement No. 34 for more details.

Appendix B. Statement of Fund Net Position, Proprietary Funds, June 30, 2020, City of Dogwood, N.C.

Exhibit 6

City of Dogwood
Statement of Fund Net Position
Proprietary Funds
June 30, 2020

| | Major Enterprise Funds | | | Internal Service |
	Electric Fund	Water and Sewer Fund	Total	Fund
ASSETS				
Current assets:				
Cash and cash equivalents	$ 41,843	$ 98,696	$ 140,539	$ 22,874
Accounts receivable (net) - billed	160,909	78,336	239,245	-
Accounts receivable (net) - unbilled	54,262	21,472	75,734	-
Due from other funds	-	-	-	2,600
Inventories	95,378	110,281	205,659	2,700
Prepaid items	4,630	2,565	7,195	-
Restricted cash and cash equivalents	56,105	1,675,055	1,731,160	-
Total current assets	413,127	1,986,405	2,399,532	28,174
Noncurrent assets:				
Capital assets:				
Land and construction in progress	289,400	2,778,549	3,067,949	-
Other capital assets, net of depreciation	708,272	9,781,456	10,489,728	24,670
Capital assets	997,672	12,560,005	13,557,677	24,670
Total noncurrent assets	997,672	12,560,005	13,557,677	24,670
Total assets	1,410,799	14,546,410	15,957,209	52,844
DEFERRED OUTFLOWS OF RESOURCES				
Pension deferrals	45,132	180,529	225,661	6,914
OPEB deferrals	5,106	20,426	25,532	776
Deferred charge on refunding	-	157,614	157,614	-
Total deferred outflows of resources	50,239	358,569	408,807	7,689
LIABILITIES				
Current liabilities:				
Accounts payable and accrued liabilities	202,957	62,010	264,967	2,900
Due to other funds	160	3,240	3,400	-
Compensated absences - current	12,000	9,000	21,000	-
General obligation bonds payable- current	-	449,022	449,022	-
Revenue bond payable - current	-	34,339	34,339	-
Bond anticipation notes payable	-	675,000	675,000	-
Liabilities payable from restricted assets:				
Accounts payable	-	115,557	115,557	-
Customer deposits	56,105	16,930	73,035	-
Total current liabilities	271,222	1,365,098	1,030,320	2,000
Noncurrent liabilities:				
Advance from other funds	-	27,000	27,000	-
Compensated absences	26,200	41,900	68,100	2,400
Net pension liability	51,727	206,907	258,634	7,923
Total OPEB liability	94,588	378,353	472,942	14,368
General obligation bonds payable-noncurrent	-	2,509,592	2,509,592	-
Revenue bond payable - noncurrent	-	872,584	872,584	-
Total noncurrent liabilities	172,515	4,036,336	4,181,852	24,691
Total liabilities	443,737	5,401,434	5,818,172	27,591
DEFERRED INFLOWS OF RESOURCES				
Pension deferrals	1,083	4,332	5,415	166
OPEB deferrals	479	1,916	2,395	73
NET POSITION				
Net investment in capital assets	997,672	9,677,593	10,675,265	-
Restricted pursuant to loan requirements	-	109,725	109,725	-
Unrestricted	18,066	(290,022)	(271,956)	32,704
Total net position	$ 1,015,738	$ 9,497,296	10,513,034	$ 32,704

Adjustment to reflect the consolidation of internal service fund activities related to enterprise funds.		300
Net position of business-type activities	$	10,513,334

> **NOTE TO PREPARER:** The consolidation of the internal service fund activities related to the enterprise fund is shown for illustrative purposes only. The amount shown here is clearly immaterial and should be allocated back to the primary user of the internal service fund (in Dogwood, the General Fund) instead of consolidated with the enterprise fund. However, we chose to leave the allocation here for illustrative purposes so that the user could see how this consolidation, if material, should be treated.

The notes to the financial statements are an integral part of this statement.

Source: City of Dogwood, N.C. Revised July 2020.

Chapter 9

Capital Planning

Renee Fuller Paschal

Introduction

North Carolina law, particularly the Local Government Budget and Fiscal Control Act,[1] has a great deal to say about how local governments should develop their operating budgets, but surprisingly little about capital planning. While the act requires all local jurisdictions to approve an annual operating budget, there is no requirement for jurisdictions to develop and adopt a capital plan. Perhaps, as a result, capital planning practices vary widely among towns, cities, and counties in the state.

Because having a capital plan is voluntary, many smaller jurisdictions simply do not engage in formal capital planning. Rather, decisions about capital projects and how they are funded are made one by one as needs or opportunities arise. Conversely, some North Carolina jurisdictions adopt policies that require all capital projects to be requested through a capital planning process.

If capital planning is not required in North Carolina, why do many jurisdictions engage in it? The concerns around capital planning are as follows: First, producing a plan that spans a number of years can require a lot of work and calls for expertise that existing staff may not have. Second, unless elected officials buy into the need for a capital process, plans may be relegated to the proverbial shelf, and projects may

---

1. Chapter 159, Article 3 of the North Carolina General Statutes (hereinafter G.S.).

not be funded. Third, plans that are produced without careful financial analysis may result in "wish lists" that jurisdictions cannot afford. In spite of these concerns, capital planning is a powerful tool that many jurisdictions use, even when it is not mandatory, and most jurisdictions should consider. The concerns acknowledged above can usually be mitigated through best practices already in use across the state, many of which this chapter will address.

Capital planning can provide the following benefits to local governments:

- It provides the ability to identify all possible projects and prioritize the ones that help the jurisdiction best meet its goals. Some jurisdictions use a formal system, assign points, and develop a ranking of proposed projects. Even informal or "gut-based" prioritization work better when all possible projects are viewed simultaneously.

- It allows local governments to achieve long-term goals and adopted plans through capital projects. A capital plan offers the opportunity to complete projects identified in long-term plans, such as parks and recreation master plans or downtown development plans. If these plans have been developed without coordination between the planning parties, the capital planning process can reveal inconsistencies and help a jurisdiction choose among competing priorities. Perhaps more importantly, a capital planning process linked to long-term goals offers the opportunity to view proposed capital projects through the lens of these goals. For example, a county comprehensive plan that calls for development concentrated in municipalities and preservation of rural areas offers important context for a proposed project to run water and sewer lines outside municipalities.

- It helps local governments to determine the cumulative fiscal impact of all capital projects. A jurisdiction can use this information to decide what projects it can afford, when is the best time to move forward with projects, and how best to pay for them. Some jurisdictions go beyond project costs and include operating costs as part of their project affordability analyses. Debt affordability is another key component of capital planning and is addressed in this chapter.

- It allows local governments to understand how projects relate to each other. Sometimes the overlap between projects is not obvious, but a capital planning process can reveal relationships between those projects as well as opportunities for grants and partnerships, especially if a formal vetting process that involves multiple stakeholders is used.

What Is a Capital Project?

Capital plans are made up of capital projects. The types of capital projects included in capital plans vary among jurisdictions. While rules from the Government Accounting Standards Board (GASB) govern how capital assets are recorded and depreciated, practice shows that no hard-and-fast rules define what constitutes a "capital project" for capital planning purposes; rather, the definition should fit the needs of the jurisdiction. Generally, capital projects feature the following characteristics:

- A capital project results in a capital asset being purchased, constructed, renovated, or otherwise acquired. The asset typically has a long useful life, often beyond the time frame of the capital plan, though some jurisdictions include items with shorter useful lives, such as vehicles, in their plans. Again, the jurisdiction's particular needs should be considered in the decision of whether to include replacement capital in the capital plan.

- The cost of the project is considered substantial by the jurisdiction and is usually much more than the threshold set for capital outlay. Thresholds vary widely; typically, higher thresholds are found in jurisdictions with larger budgets. The jurisdiction should include projects that cost more than what is routine for operating budgets and require planning to fund. In setting an initial threshold, some trial and error may be needed to find the right amount. Although not absolutely necessary, setting a particular cost threshold amount does help communicate to the governing board, the public, and requesting agencies what projects are appropriate for the capital plan.

- The project includes all elements necessary to bring it to fruition. For a building project, these might include architectural design, construction, land purchase, and furnishings. For a software project, these could include data conversion and staff training in addition to software licenses and required hardware. The rule is that costs are considered part of the project if they are necessary to ready the project for first use. Operating costs, such as utilities or ongoing maintenance, are not considered part of the project cost but may be important to identify in order to determine the overall affordability of the project. The jurisdiction's finance officer should weigh in on what costs may or may not be appropriate for capitalization and inclusion in the project.

- Capital projects, particularly those involving construction, often take more than a year to complete. Some projects, like constructing a new wastewater treatment plan, can take many years for permitting, design, and construction to occur. In particular, this characteristic makes the annual operating budget an unsuitable mechanism for budgeting capital projects.

- Debt financing may be used and, if so, should be carefully considered. Though capital projects may be financed by other means, if financed by debt, the project should be included in the capital plan so that all debt obligations, existing and proposed, can be known and understood.

Example of a Capital Project: Building or Purchasing a House

For most people, building or purchasing a house is a personal capital project that offers an easy-to-understand example for describing the nature of capital projects to staff and elected officials. Purchasing or building a house

- results in an important asset with a long useful life;
- is a substantial cost for most people and requires planning to achieve;
- includes all the necessary elements, such as land, architectural drawings, kitchen appliances, and connection to water and sewer systems to get the house ready for occupancy; and
- may take a year or longer for design, land purchase, and construction.

Moreover, most people use debt to finance a house, and the approval process can be cumbersome. Homebuyers must consider all of their financial commitments, in addition to the operating costs of the house (such as utilities and insurance), to determine whether they can afford it.

Chatham County's (North Carolina) experience offers an example of how failing to include all necessary project elements up front can create financial problems for the project. In the mid-1990s, before Chatham County developed a capital plan, a new school was built using proceeds from general obligation bonds. Unfortunately, after the bonds were sold, the school system requested funding for furnishing and computer equipment. Only then did the county realize these costs were not included in the bond, and the county had to appropriate nearly $1 million from its operating budget, which was a substantial hit at the time. Since then, the county has refined its capital planning process to identify and include all costs and communicate effectively with partner organizations, but this example serves as a good lesson for why identifying all categories of costs early on is important. Often when projects are first discussed, only the acquisition and/or construction costs are mentioned. Other costs can be substantial to the project and include generally in the order incurred:

- Feasibility study: To budget projects accurately, the services of an architect or engineer may be necessary to develop a proposed scope and cost estimate (called a preliminary engineering report for utility projects). This cost estimate may be capitalized and considered part of the project cost or may be paid for from the operating budget.
- Cost escalation: The time frame for the initial cost estimate should be understood. If the project is budgeted beyond this time frame, additional amounts for cost escalation should be included.
- Permitting costs: Environmental, zoning, and building permits may be needed from federal, state, and/or local authorities, depending on the nature of the project. Jurisdictions should meet with authorities and understand these costs up front. The architect or engineer can also assist in identifying needed permits.
- Land costs: Land and rights-of-way acquisition costs, realtor fees, surveys, and attorney fees should be included if land is being purchased. In addition,

the North Carolina Local Government Commission requires that a Phase 1 Environmental Assessment be completed for most debt-financed projects.[2]

- Architectural or engineering design: Typically, design services include pre-design, design development, construction drawings, project administration, and project closeout. If a Leadership in Energy and Environmental Design (LEED) certification or other energy-efficiency designation is desired, the designer's fee may be higher and additional consultants may be needed for commissioning building systems.
- Grant writing and administration: This expense may be necessary if grant funds are sought to cover all or part of the project cost.
- Construction or acquisition costs: Often these costs are obtained through bidding or other mandated procurement processes. Attorney fees should also be included for contract review. Professional assistance may also be needed to write bid specifications and evaluate bid responses for projects that do not require an architect or engineer.
- Hazardous material surveys, geotechnical work, and materials testing: These services require specialized consultants. The need for outside consultants should be discussed with the architect or engineer to make sure these costs are included.
- Furnishing and equipment: For building projects, the furniture and equipment attached to the building are typically included in the project cost. If they are not included, it is important to understand how these costs will be covered. Professional assistance may be needed to develop bid specifications and evaluate bids.
- Implementation costs: For technology projects in particular, funding for staff training and data conversion should be included.
- Financing costs: If the project is debt financed, services from a number of outside professionals and organizations are required, including the Local Government Commission (LGC), rating agencies, financial advisor, underwriter, and bond counsel. These roles are discussed in more detail in the "Actors in the Debt Issuance Process" section of this chapter.
- Contingency: This is a percentage of the project cost beyond the other elements listed above. The amount may be a factor of the main contract or a factor of the total project. The Local Government Commission typically requires at least 5 percent for debt-financed projects. Higher contingency amounts for projects with more unknown factors, such as building renovations or utility line construction in rocky areas, should be considered.
- Unique expenses: Some jurisdictions require additional costs. For example, Mecklenburg County requires 1 percent of the building project cost to be used for public art. Other jurisdictions hire project managers to oversee construction projects, and this expense is treated as part of the project cost. The expectation for these costs should be communicated early on.

---

2. *See* N.C. Department of State Treasurer, State and Local Government Finance Division, *Guidelines on Debt Issuance (Revised)* (September 4, 2019), https://files.nc.gov/nctreasurer/documents/files/SLGFD/LGC/LocalGovDebtMngmt/guidelinesfordebtissu-ancefinal2.pdf (discussing the Local Government Commission (LGC) requirement).

What Is a Capital Plan?

Simply stated, a capital plan puts together into one document all of the capital projects a jurisdiction plans to undertake over a particular time period. A capital plan is frequently referred to as a capital improvements program/plan (CIP). The following characteristics of CIPs are explored in greater detail in this chapter:

- CIPs include all capital projects a jurisdiction is planning to undertake. Some jurisdictions have separate capital plans for different funds.
- CIPs are multiyear and typically range from five to ten years. Though they span a number of years, CIPs are typically updated annually.
- Projects are often multiphased: As discussed above, most projects have multiple components, and these costs can be spread over several years in a CIP.
- CIPs should identify funding sources for each included project that equal the project costs. Best practices would call for these sources to be identified (and, if necessary, set aside) before a project is scheduled in the CIP.
- In addition to project costs and funding sources, many CIP documents contain narrative descriptions of each project that explain need, provide justification, and discuss alternatives. The level of detail in CIP documents varies widely among jurisdictions.
- CIP documents often include a transmittal letter from the manager outlining how the CIP furthers the jurisdiction's goals. Important considerations, such as impact on debt capacity and operating budget, may also be addressed. Rating agencies and grant funders often review the jurisdiction's CIP, so it is important for CIP documents to set the context and explain the decision-making process behind the CIP.
- CIPs may be included in the operating budget or may be stand-alone documents and processes.
- CIPs typically summarize the resource implications and appropriations for all projects.

A capital plan is not a "budget," in that a separate action is needed to appropriate funds for capital projects. Some jurisdictions combine the "plan" and the "budget," but there are differences. A plan is most commonly and appropriately adopted by resolution. A plan estimates expenses and revenues associated with projects over the plan's time horizon, which is typically five to ten years beyond the current fiscal year. It is envisioned that most projects will enter the plan in one of the last years the plan covers (whether in practice that is true warrants another discussion). As the project scope is refined and better cost estimates are obtained, projected project costs often change. When it is time to "budget" the project, specific costs and financing sources must be known, and funds are appropriated through an ordinance, either the annual budget ordinance or a stand-alone project ordinance. In discussing the plan with requesting agencies and elected officials, it is important to note that project costs can change; in theory, the jurisdiction is not fully committed to carrying out the project until an ordinance is adopted.

Legal Framework in North Carolina

State General Statutes provide few requirements for the CIP process. Debt financing, governed by the Local Government Bond Act,[3] is the exception and should be reviewed in detail before a jurisdiction decides to issue debt. Though this chapter discusses debt issuing, it is not intended to be an exhaustive resource on the legal requirements of issuing debt.

If a capital plan is developed by a jurisdiction and that jurisdiction has a professional manager, the statutes charge the manager with preparing the plan for consideration.[4] That responsibility is often delegated in larger jurisdictions. If the town does not have a manager (all North Carolina counties do at this point), the mayor or a committee of the governing body may be responsible for developing the plan in conjunction with certain staff.

Statutes also set out the requirements for project budgets. G.S. 159-13.2 sets the process for adopting and amending project ordinances. While some projects may be budgeted in the annual operating budget, a project ordinance is not tied to a specific fiscal year and is more appropriate for complex capital projects that will have spending over multiple years. The statute states that the project ordinance must be adopted before spending can occur. In addition, it requires that revenues and expenditures be set out in the ordinance and be equal. Finally, the statute states that the project ordinance should "clearly identify the project and authorize its undertaking."[5]

The procedures for establishing a capital reserve fund, which is typically set up as a funding mechanism for pay-as-you-go projects, are outlined in G.S. 159-18 through -22. The main requirements for using capital reserve funds as funding methods for capital projects are as follows:

- Capital reserve funds may be established for any purpose for which a jurisdiction may issue bonds.
- The fund must be set up by the governing board through adoption of an ordinance or resolution that states the purposes for which the fund may be used, how much is to be accumulated for each purpose and for what time period, and the source of funding for each purpose.
- The resolution or ordinance that created the fund may be amended in the same way it was adopted. Amendments can change the purposes for which the fund was created.
- Capital reserves can be funded from appropriations from other funds, as long as the restrictions imposed in G.S. 159-13(b) are met. If these funds have legal restrictions, those remain in force within the capital reserve fund and must be tracked and reported as those restrictions require.
- Funds may be withdrawn from the capital reserve through an ordinance or resolution adopted by the governing board. The purpose for which the withdrawal is being made must match the purpose for which the capital reserve fund was established or has subsequently been amended.

---

3. G.S. 159-43 through -100.
4. G.S. 160A-148(5) (cities), 153A-82(5) (counties).
5. G.S. 159-13.2(c).

Capital Improvements Program/Plan (CIP) Process

A quick review of the legal requirements of CIPs demonstrates that North Carolina jurisdictions have a great deal of flexibility in how a CIP is prepared. Who prepares the CIP, when it is prepared, what projects it includes, how projects are selected for funding, how the public is involved, what time frame it covers, and what plans and policies guide its preparation are all issues for consideration and discussion.

Who Manages the Process?

The staff member or department assigned to manage the process and prepare the CIP document for governing board consideration is critical to a successful plan. While statutes charge the city/county manager with that responsibility, in many jurisdictions it is delegated to other departments, including finance and budget departments, and, less frequently, to planning and public works departments. Whether these departments actually manage the process, they all should be involved to ensure the best possible outcome. The skills needed to manage the process include the following:

- an understanding of the various types of capital projects and the costs and activities associated with carrying them out, including the role of professional consultants (familiarity with building and infrastructure construction as well as other project management experience is also helpful);
- substantial knowledge of how projects are financed (expertise in debt financing and knowledge of available grants are particularly important);
- an understanding of the time value of money and how to apply inflation to cost estimates;
- an understanding of mandated and recommended procurement processes and how they affect project timing;
- an understanding of how projects impact the organization and vice versa, as well as the ability to identify potential project partners;
- an understanding of the organization's long-term plans and goals and how the CIP relates to or achieves those goals;
- the ability to communicate with key stakeholders, including elected officials, professional staff, outside agencies, and the public; and
- the technical ability to evaluate project requests, assemble project budgets, and present project justifications effectively.

When a jurisdiction begins a capital planning process or experiences a change in staffing, it is important to assess the knowledge and skills of assigned staff and seek training and assistance from other departments or outside professionals as needed. On-the-job training alone, without proper oversight, is not appropriate for the costly, critical, and long-lasting decisions made in the CIP process. The School of Government at the University of North Carolina at Chapel Hill and jurisdictions with known track records in capital planning are obvious resources for jurisdictions to use when engaging in the capital planning process.

Summary of Steps for Preparing a CIP

1. Develop a calendar of key deadlines and distribute to requesting agencies
2. Distribute forms and instructions to requesting agencies, conduct training, and provide technical assistance
3. Hold concept meetings (if used)
4. Receive CIP requests
5. Evaluate CIP projects using cost/benefit analysis
6. Prioritize CIP projects
7. Identify project funding for desired projects
8. Develop recommended CIP document, including project description/justification and a schedule of expenses and revenues for each recommended project
9. Present recommendation to governing board
10. Hold public hearing (optional)

When Is the CIP Prepared?

The first step in preparing a CIP is identifying the key deadlines for forms and instructions to be provided, departments to submit requests, and the recommended CIP to be presented to the governing board. Most jurisdictions adopt a calendar of key dates for preparation that is shared with potential submitters before the process begins. The time it takes to prepare the CIP should match the available staffing. Departments' technical ability to prepare requests also impacts the time frame of CIP preparation. Systematically reviewing the process after the fact each year can help the jurisdiction make changes to its time frames and achieve a more effective process overall.

In addition to establishing time frames, the jurisdiction must decide whether to run the CIP process concurrently with the operating budget process. This practice occurs frequently in larger jurisdictions with greater available staffing. The benefit of this approach is that staff and departments are engaged in budget work during a more limited time frame and can focus on other responsibilities during other times of the year. Capital needs are considered in the context of the operating budget, when revenues and other obligations are better known.

One risk in a concurrent process is that the capital plan will not receive the attention it warrants. Recently, Harnett County, N.C., with limited staffing, moved its CIP process to the fall and made it entirely separate from the operating process. County Manager Paula Stewart describes the benefit of this approach:

> When I became Deputy County Manager in February 2015, I quickly realized during budget preparation that Harnett County did not have a defined process in place for prioritizing or funding capital needs. We started with a very basic CIP in fiscal years 2017 through 2019. I became County Manager in 2018 and made the decision to hire a part-time Budget Director whose sole focus was the budget. With the help of that position, we finally formalized the CIP process and moved it from the typical spring timeframe to the fall. By doing this, department heads are able to devote more time to

evaluating their needs and planning for them instead of having to work on both operating and capital at the same time. We have seen many positive impacts of the new CIP process. We are finally able to proactively plan for and carry out costly maintenance items such as new roofs and HVAC units, adequately plan for technology upgrades or replacements, and ensure that funds are available annually for the purchase of public safety vehicles and equipment. Capital needs are no longer pushed out to future years or ignored altogether. The new process and timeframe have resulted in a CIP that better meets the needs of Harnett County.[6]

If a jurisdiction chooses this approach to preparing a CIP, it is important to revisit key assumptions during the operating budget process and ensure funding obligations can be met. Wake County combines the advantages of both approaches, with departments submitting capital requests ahead of the operating budget, but preparation of the recommended CIP is concurrent with the operating budget.

What Types of Projects Does the CIP Include?

Some characteristics of projects that can be included in a CIP were discussed in the section above entitled "What Is a Capital Project?", namely the cost threshold for projects to be included. In addition, the jurisdiction should consider if it wants to set a threshold for the useful life of the asset being acquired. Other considerations include

- whether large one-time maintenance projects are included (including these in the CIP helps plan funding over several years to even out the impact on the operating budget, and less costly routine maintenance items are appropriately included in the operating budget);
- whether large expenses not resulting in capital assets, such as funding long-term plans, are included; the rationale for budgeting large maintenance projects in the capital plan applies here as well;
- whether revolving funds to replace less costly capital items, such as vehicles and IT equipment, are included (in the aggregate, these expenses can be quite large and not consistent from year to year, and a revolving fund allows the jurisdiction to make equal contributions each year for expenses that vary from year to year); and
- whether projects with unknown costs or cost "guesstimates" are included. One risk in doing this is that the project may gain traction with the governing board, department, and the public only to be found too costly to carry out. Reliable cost estimates are important in maintaining credibility with the governing board and public. Harnett County has adopted the practice of only including projects with known costs estimated by a vendor, architect, or engineer. Large jurisdictions may have professionals on staff who can provide reliable cost estimates, but often smaller jurisdictions must engage outside consultants for this work.

---

6. Paula Stewart (Harnett County Manager), email message to author, June 24, 2020.

What Time Frame Does the CIP Cover?

At first it may seem that a longer time frame is better for a CIP than a shorter one. If the time horizon is too long, departments may have a difficult time planning that far ahead. Few projects may be initially scheduled in the later years of the CIP, or if scheduled in the later years, cost estimates and project scopes could change substantially before they are undertaken. Of course, if the time horizon is too short, the CIP loses its utility as a planning tool. What is important in establishing a time horizon is weighing the needs of requesting agencies against the jurisdiction's need for long-term planning.

The requests made in a shorter time frame are easier to comprehend, and projects tend to be better defined at the point they are initially requested. In rapidly changing environments, such as information technology, a longer time frame may not be practical, and projects scheduled later in the CIP may become obsolete. A longer time frame is appropriate for projects that take a number of years to realize, such as large utility treatment facilities. A time frame that is too short for these projects may mean that key parts of the project are already underway before the project is officially approved as part of the CIP.

Jurisdictions in North Carolina typically use a five- to ten-year time frame. Moore County has a fifteen-year CIP for utility projects, in contrast to a ten-year time frame for general county projects. Chatham County began its CIP with a five-year time frame and later changed it to seven years. Generally, the additional two years made no difference in when projects were initially requested by departments. Departments and requesting agencies may request their projects be scheduled earlier in the CIP than the later years. The jurisdiction will need to decide how to handle such requests. Both Chatham and Harnett counties require an additional layer of justification for requested projects to begin before the later years of the CIP.

What Entities May Submit Projects?

Many towns and cities limit the entities making requests to their own departments. This practice is more straightforward and easier to manage than allowing outside entities to submit requests. North Carolina counties do not have that option; they are mandated to provide funding for public school and community college facilities. Because these facilities often constitute the majority of a county's capital needs, it is critical that these agencies be invited to submit requests. Some cities have neighborhood planning initiatives that result in capital projects, which require a method for these requests to be considered. Finally, depending on the relationships, some jurisdictions may invite particular nonprofit agencies to submit requests.

A critical part of the invitation to submit projects is managing expectations of requesting departments and, in particular, outside agencies. If a jurisdiction has limited debt capacity or revenue for pay-as-you-go projects, those constraints should be communicated up front. Board funding priorities, expectations for the information to include in the requests, and key deadlines are important to share early on. One of the best practices in this process is ongoing communication between the jurisdiction and these partners to communicate needs and funding constraints.

In Chatham County, new projects are often requested as "future projects." This satisfies the political need to acknowledge a project, but does not commit the county to funding or a particular time frame for carrying out the project. Future projects are often discussed for several years. When and if the need becomes clearer and a funding source is identified, the county moves the project to "funded" status. This does a great deal to avoid "wish list" projects.

Where Else Do Projects Originate?

In addition to managing requests from departments and other agencies, a jurisdiction may have many other sources for potential projects.

Obviously, governing boards can raise the need for capital projects at any time, depending on current issues and concerns. For example, many counties have funded school security measures in the last decade, as the issue of school safety has come to the forefront. Governing boards also adopt annual goals and strategic plans, which may include capital projects. Public demand for facilities and amenities can also cause a jurisdiction to fund capital projects, and there are several ways to engage the public formally in the process, which are discussed below. Changes in the law can also create the need for capital projects. The Health Information and Privacy Protection Act (HIPPA) led to renovations of many local health departments' reception areas to ensure the privacy of clinic clients.

Some jurisdictions begin their capital planning process by conducting a needs assessment to systematically identify all potential capital projects. An example of this includes condition assessments that can help identify maintenance needs. About ten years ago, the Chatham County school system conducted a facility condition assessment that found most of its school roofs were in poor condition. Chatham County established a capital project and used a number of funding sources, including Qualified School Construction Bonds, motor vehicle taxes, and capital reserves, to fund the project. As a result, almost every school roof in the county has been replaced, which has been important in ensuring the ongoing viability of buildings constructed in the 1950s and 1960s. Another example is a comprehensive space needs assessment, which can help the jurisdiction identify short and long-term needs for additional space across the organization.

Master plans are another tool that jurisdictions use to identify the need for capital projects. Master plans are long-range planning processes that help communities determine how they would like to grow in the future. Processes often involve extensive community input and produce a set of goals and strategies to guide the desired growth. As such, master plans identify long-range capital needs and community desires for public facilities. Typically, the time horizon for these plans is much longer than that of a CIP. The most common example of a master plan is a parks and recreation master plan. If these plans are not integrated into a jurisdiction's CIP process, they have little chance of being realized. The City of Hickory has a number of such plans that inform its capital budgeting process, including (from the Fiscal Year 2016–2017 Budget Message)

- the Inspiring Spaces Connectivity Master Plan,
- the Landscape Master Plan,

- the Parks and Recreation Master Plan,
- the Hickory Horizons Strategic Plan,
- the Sidewalk and Bikeway Master Plan,
- the Business/Industrial Master Plan,
- the Water and Sewer Extension Plan,
- the Library Long-Range Plan,
- the Airport Master Plan,
- the Hickory by Choice Comprehensive Land Use and Transportation Plan, and
- Neighborhood Focus, which includes city grants for twelve self-identified neighborhoods to undertake neighborhood improvements.[7]

In addition to being a source of projects, long-range plans feature policy recommendations that guide what CIP projects a jurisdiction undertakes. The City of Raleigh is quite intentional about connecting its long-range planning processes to its capital projects, as seen in an excerpt from the city's 2017–2021 CIP:

> The city adheres to several policies and practices to ensure long-term financial sustainability, promote effective planning, and ensure appropriate use of capital funds. Below is a summary of major items:
>
> - Alignment with city-wide Strategic Plan: The Strategic Plan, adopted by City Council in April 2015, serves as the primary guide for capital investments.
> - Complementing the city's comprehensive plan: All capital projects should complement the comprehensive plan. The comprehensive plan includes specific policies that establish it as the city's lead growth and development guide and connect it to the CIP. Policies also require staff to consult the comprehensive plan when establishing capital priorities, share long-term plans with other city staff, and identify long-term planning opportunities.[8]

The City of Raleigh references these guiding documents in the description of specific projects, such as in the "Parks, Recreation and Cultural Resources" section of its 2017–2021 CIP:

> The City of Raleigh Comprehensive Plan, the City of Raleigh Strategic Plan, and the Parks, Recreation and Cultural Resources System Plan are the primary guiding documents for park maintenance and development, level of service and land acquisition. Existing feasibility studies, reports and strategic plans also guide staff on the timing, scope and location of

---

7. City of Hickory, North Carolina, *Fiscal Year 2016-2017 Recommended Budget* (May 2016), https://www.hickorync.gov/sites/default/files/hickoryncgov/Finance/Budget/Recommended%20Budget%202016-17.pdf.

8. City of Raleigh, North Carolina, *Adopted CIP FY2017-FY2021*. For more on Raleigh's plan, see the "2030 Comprehensive Plan" page on the city's website at https://raleighnc.gov/services/zoning-planning-and-development/2030-comprehensive-plan.

capital investments required to sustain a maturing Parks, Recreation and Cultural Resources system.[9]

In addition to plans that identify the need for projects, jurisdictions often adopt financial policies that establish important guidelines for the CIP process. These policies may cover when a jurisdiction will issue debt, how much debt it will issue, and the targeted level of fund balance, all of which affect preparation of the CIP. The Government Finance Officers Association (GFOA) recommends developing capital planning policies as a best practice.[10] Moore County's fiscal policy provides a comprehensive set of policies to guide preparation of the operating budget and CIP.[11] Some financial policies, such as those of Harnett County, include specific CIP preparation requirements, many of which are discussed above.

How Should You Decide Which Projects Are Funded and When?

Deciding which projects will be funded and when is a critical part of the CIP process. The first step in deciding whether a project should be funded is evaluating it on its own merits. Questions that should be considered include the following:

- What problem does the proposed capital project address, or what goal does it achieve?
- Is the need for the project well documented with facts and data?
- Have all other alternatives for solving the problem/achieving the goal been identified and discussed?
- Have all project costs been identified? Are those costs reasonable?
- Are impacts on the operating budget identified and quantified? Are those impacts reasonable and affordable? Have life cycle costs been identified for energy-efficiency measures?
- Is the project the least costly approach overall among the identified alternatives?
- How does the project affect other projects already included in the CIP?
- What potential partners exist for carrying out the project?
- What revenues are available for funding the project besides the general fund?
- Is the project feasible within the proposed time frame?

Submitting departments and outside agencies should address these questions in their requests. Using this information, the CIP staff should weigh the demonstrated benefits against the costs identified to determine if the project is justified.[12]

---

9. Ibid., 48.

10. See the Government Finance Officers Association's (GFOA) website for more information: https://www.gfoa.org/.

11. Moore County, North Carolina,, *Fiscal Policy Guidelines for Moore County, North Carolina* (amended July 15, 2014), https://www.moorecountync.gov/images/departments /financial-services/financial-policies/fiscal_policy_guidelines_adopted_7_15_14_signed.pdf.

12. William C. Rivenbark and Justin Marlowe, "Evaluation and Prioritization of Capital Assets," in *Capital Budgeting and Finance: A Guide for Local Governments*, 2nd edition, ed. Justin Marlowe, WIlliam C. Rivenbark, and John A. Vogt (Washington, D.C.:ICMA Press, 2009), 59–85.

Harnett County Fiscal Policy: Capital Improvement Plan (CIP) Policies.

1. It is the responsibility of the County Board of Commissioners to provide for the capital equipment and facilities necessary to deliver county services to the residents of the County, as well as provide necessary capital equipment and facilities for the Harnett County Public Schools and the Central Carolina Community College system.
2. North Carolina statutes charge the County Manager with preparation of the capital budget. It shall be his/her responsibility or that of his/her designee to coordinate the CIP process; receive requests from County departments, Harnett County Public Schools, and Central Carolina Community College; and propose a recommended CIP to the Board of Commissioners.
3. The Board of Commissioners is responsible for adopting a CIP annually and may amend it as needed.
4. All capital projects must be proposed through the County's CIP process.
5. The CIP includes all approved capital projects, including new construction, renovations, vehicles and heavy equipment, new software and other technology, and all other purchases and improvements that meet the threshold for definition as a capital project, currently $100,000 and above.
6. The County will develop a CIP of at least seven years and review and update the plan annually. The Harnett County Public Schools and the Community College System are strongly encouraged to submit their needs through this process, along with a prioritization of their requests.
7. After projects are approved in the CIP and before the project can begin, the project must be authorized through one of two means:

   A. Capital project ordinances: A separate capital budget ordinance shall be submitted to the Board of Commissioners for approval for all capital projects that are projected to span more than one fiscal year;

   B. All other capital projects will be budgeted in the operating budget.

8. All capital projects will be assigned a project code by the Finance Officer for tracking and reporting purposes.
9. The CIP will prioritize the maintenance of existing facilities and equipment, and otherwise protect the county's past capital investments. A maintenance and replacement schedule will be developed and followed as funding allows.
10. County departments will provide a written justification and identify the estimated project costs, potential funding sources, and impacts on the operating budget for each proposed capital project and include this information in their requests. The County Manager or his/her designee will review, modify as appropriate, and include this information in the recommended CIP.
11. The County will pursue the most cost-effective strategies for financing the CIP, consistent with prudent financial management.

Source: Harnett County, North Carolina *Fiscal Policy for Harnett County, North Carolina* (amended February 17, 2020), http://www.harnett.org/finance/downloads/fiscalpolicyproposedamendments2-17-20.pdf.

A robust review process that includes internal experts can help ensure projects are thoroughly vetted before they are included in the capital plan. In Chatham County, concept meetings are held with requesting departments before requests are formally submitted. Departments present their project "concepts" to an internal committee, which is made up of representatives of the manager's office and budget, finance, public works, IT, facilities, and central permitting and planning departments. The committee provides feedback on what information should be provided to justify the project, alternatives that should be explored, potential partners, the project's impact on internal departments and other projects, the regulatory framework surrounding the project, financial feasibility, and other considerations.

Once they have evaluated projects and justified them for inclusion in the CIP, jurisdictions often have to decide which of the worthy projects they can afford to move forward with and which project should be done first. Methods to prioritize and select these projects range from staff intuition to complex scoring systems.

The intuitive, or "gut-based," approach is a very common way to prioritize projects. It can be effective in small jurisdictions with few projects to decide among. Experienced managers and staff, who have the trust of the governing board and public and who thoroughly understand the jurisdiction and its goals, can easily recommend which projects among a few proposed projects best meet priorities. In such a setting, a more elaborate scoring process would require much more staff time and effort with questionable benefit.

In other circumstances, a formal prioritization system is called for. In 2014, Mecklenburg County N.C., (population 1,110,356) opened its CIP process to new projects for the first time since 2009. County departments and other partners submitted 149 projects for consideration, of which the board of commissioners ultimately included 116 in the capital plan at a cost of more than $1 billion. Obviously, the gut is not a reliable or publicly defensible approach for deciding what projects to include and when they should be scheduled. The county used a scoring matrix consisting of nine criteria, with point values assigned for the extent to which the project met the criteria. The matrix offers a sophisticated but easy-to-follow model for other jurisdictions that have a number of projects to prioritize.

Mecklenburg County Scoring Matrix
Source: Mecklenburg County, North Carolina, *Fiscal Year 2016 Adopted Budget*, 470,
https://www.mecknc.gov/CountyManagersOffice/OMB/PriorBudgets/Documents/FY2016.pdf.

If the gut is at one end of the prioritization strategy spectrum and the strategies of Mecklenburg are near the other end, then the prioritization strategies of Greely, Colorado, and the City of Clinton, North Carolina, lie closer to the middle of the continuum. In its 2007–2011 CIP, Greely used an uncomplicated, but effective, system. Projects were judged to fall into one of three categories:

- Priority 1: Imperative (must do): correct danger to public health and safety, meet legal obligation, alleviate immediate service/facility deficiency, prevent irreparable damage.
- Priority 2: Essential (should do): rehabilitate/replace obsolete facility, stimulate economic growth, reduce future operating costs, leverage grants.
- Priority 3: Important (could do): provide new or expanded service, promote intergovernmental cooperation, reduce energy use, enhance cultural or natural resources.[13]

In its 2017–2022 CIP, the City of Clinton, N.C. (population 8,454), used a slightly more complex 130-point system to prioritize its thirty-nine projects, which totaled just under $30 million:

1. Addresses Public Safety (20 points)
2. Legally Mandated (20 points)
3. Achieves Council Goal (15 points)
4. Achieves Community Goal (15 points)
5. Availability of Outside Funds (10 points)
6. Increases Service Efficiency (10 points)
7. Promotes Economic Development (10 points)
8. Protects/Maintains City Assets and Financial Stability (10 points)
9. Receives Economic Payback in Less Than 5 Years (10 points)
10. Links with Other Projects (10 points)[14]

As with many other parts of the CIP process, there is no "right" prioritization strategy. A formal system provides a greater level of transparency and better justification to governing boards and the public than an intuitive-based approach alone. A system that is overly complex for the jurisdiction might require more staff effort than is warranted. As demonstrated by the examples above, the strategy used should match the jurisdiction's particular needs and circumstances, and several precedents exist to help a jurisdiction establish a prioritization system. The International City/County Management Association's (ICMA) book on capital budgeting, *Capital Budgeting and Finance: A Guide for Local Governments*,[15] provides an extensive discussion and several more examples of prioritization strategies in the CIP process.

---

13. Ibid.

14. City of Clinton, North Carolina, *FY 2016-2017 Adopted Budget*, 7, https://www.cityofclintonnc.com/ArchiveCenter/ViewFile/Item/50.

15. Rivenbark and Marlowe, "Evaluation and Prioritization."

How Do You Build and Maintain Public Support?

Building public support for capital planning and particular projects is an important consideration in the CIP process. The most obvious reason is the need for voter approval of general obligation bonds. While jurisdictions may focus on the bond campaign at hand, success with voters requires maintaining public trust in the capital planning process. Jurisdictions in North Carolina have demonstrated a variety of methods for effectively engaging the public in this process.

The law is largely silent on the issue of public involvement in capital planning, except on the issue of general obligation bonds. Nationally, courts have ruled that public funds cannot be used to advocate for approval of bond referenda. While public funds can be used to educate voters about the need for bonds, public funds cannot be used to encourage an affirmative vote.

City of Fayetteville, N.C., 2016 Parks and Recreation Bond Referendum: A Case Study in Using Public Funds for Educating Voters

During its 2016 bond referendum on $35 million for parks and recreation projects, the City of Fayetteville used the tagline "Your Opinion Matters." The city spent about $50,000 to produce educational materials and utilized a variety of low-cost media, which included

- videos produced in house;
- use of all social media platforms that directed people back to the city's website;
- ads in diverse print publications in the city;
- table toppers at local fast-food restaurants, which were free except for the printing cost;
- information fliers included as inserts in the utility's monthly (mailed) newsletter;
- magnets for city parks and recreation vehicles, city buses, and city leaf collection trucks;
- city staff business cards that had QRV codes to link them back to the bond website;
- stickers printed for kids that were handed out before all recreation programs the week before the referendum;
- posters in all city recreation facilities;
- digital bulletin boards in major traffic areas;
- radio advertisements;
- presentations to many civic groups in the city; and
- a special web page that hosted all of the information about the bond and what it would accomplish.

Note: Parks & Recreation Bond Project Updates" page of the Fayetteville Cumberland Parks & Recreation website at https://www.fcpr.us/facilities/administrative/parks-recreation-bond -project-updates/.

According to Kevin Arata, City of Fayetteville Corporate Communications Director, the city attorney reviewed these materials before they were released to ensure the materials did not cross the line into advocacy. Ultimately, the referendum was successful, with approximately 59 percent of voters approving the bonds.[16]

---

16. Andrew Barksdale, "Fayetteville Voters Approve $35 Million in Parks & Recreation Projects," *Fayetteville Observer*, March 15, 2016, https://www.fayobserver.com/article /20160315/News/303159857.

Before a bond question is placed on the ballot, a jurisdiction should consider whether successful passage is likely. Some issues to consider include the following:

- Has polling been done that shows the bond would be successful? Contracting with a polling firm can be costly for small jurisdictions, but it provides more reliable information on whether a bond question will be approved by voters and can help jurisdictions avoid the expense of placing the question on the ballot if it is likely to fail, and polling may help jurisdictions know how best to educate voters.

- Have previous bond issues resulted in the projects promised? Are voters aware of the success of those bonds? Many jurisdictions take proactive approaches to keeping residents informed about their capital projects. The City of Charlotte has an interactive, searchable website that allows the public to view project progress.[17] The Town of Garner's website includes an interactive map that provides project updates.[18] The City of San Antonio, Texas, has a dashboard that shows a 2017 bond issue and its progress.[19]

- The City of Sanford posts signage during project construction and after completion to remind voters that bonds paid for improvements. All of these are examples of how jurisdictions keep the public informed after a bond issue has passed and projects are completed. While this is good public policy, it also helps maintain trust with voters for the next referendum.

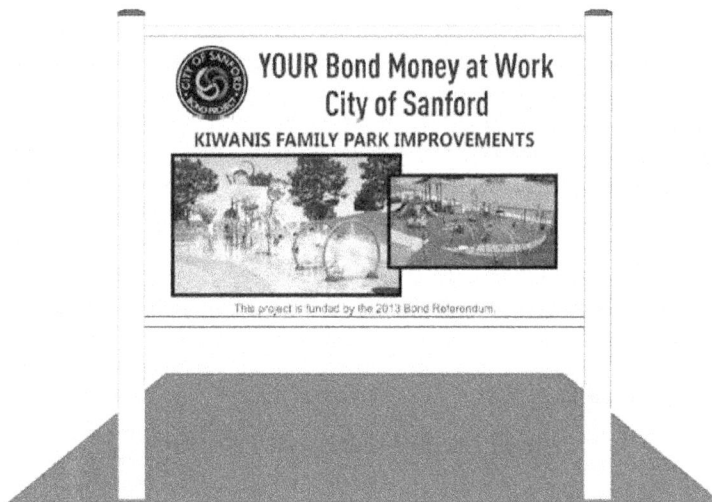

Drawing of sign placed at City of Sanford bond project to demonstrate to voters that the project was the result of an approved bond referendum

17. Capital Investment Plan," City of Charlotte, North Carolina, https://charlottenc.gov/charlottefuture/CIP/Pages/default.aspx.

18. "Garner Bond Program," Town of Garner, North Carolina, https://www.garnernc.gov/about-us/garner-bond-program.

19. "Bond Projects Status Dashboard," City of San Antonio, Texas, last updated April 22, 2021, https://www.sanantonio.gov/PublicWorks/Projects/Bond-Status-Projects-Dashboard.

- Has the jurisdiction had any financial scandals or issues that would cause concern about the integrity of the board or management? If so, the jurisdiction may need to do damage control and take measures to restore public trust before a bond question is placed before voters.
- Was the public involved in defining the projects included in the bond? Many jurisdictions propose bond projects that were identified in master plans that included public input. Making the connection back to the master plan can help the public see the value in such efforts and understand that their feedback was important in shaping the plan and the resulting projects.
- Can the jurisdiction demonstrate that the project cost is reasonable? Information comparing the cost to similar projects and steps taken to value-engineer the project can demonstrate to the public that costs are reasonable and justified.
- Is there any active opposition to the bond? Understanding what groups might be opposed to a bond can help a jurisdiction tailor its educational material to provide factual information.
- Are there potential community partners who could advocate for the bond? Non-public entities can advocate for passage of the bond as long as public funds are not involved. The Raleigh Chamber of Commerce advocated for passage of the city's 2017 transportation bonds in its Raleigh for Roads Campaign. The $206.7 million bond passed with overwhelming voter support.[20]

In addition to educating the public before, during, and after a bond referendum, strategies for engaging the public in a capital plan vary widely across the state. Unlike the operating budget, a capital plan does not require a public hearing. Some jurisdictions, like Harnett County, choose to hold a public input session as part of the CIP process. Other jurisdictions, like Hickory and Garner, engage neighborhoods in planning capital projects in their areas. Still others have citizen committees to provide input into the process. The City of Durham has a Citizen Capital Improvement Panel (CCIP) composed of business and community leaders. According to the Fiscal Year 2020–2025 CIP, the panel is charged with

1. helping city staff prioritize the right combination of new capital improvement projects,
2. advising the city council of the most critical CIP projects to meet the city's ongoing needs, and
3. evaluating and recommending projects for funding in the CIP.[21]

20. Richard Stradling, "Voters Easily Back Raleigh Transportation Bond," *News & Observer*, October 10, 2017, https://www.newsobserver.com/news/politics-government/article178176096.html.

21. City of Durham, North Carolina, *2020-2025 Adopted Capital Improvement Plan*, 5, https://durhamnc.gov/DocumentCenter/View/27413/FY20-Final-CIP.

Financing Capital Projects

Funding capital projects is often the most challenging part of implementing a capital plan. In general, jurisdictions have two options to pay for projects: borrowing money or paying for projects out of operating funds or cash reserves, often called "pay-as-you-go." Which should a jurisdiction use? It depends on a variety of factors, including the following:

- Does the jurisdiction have access to debt markets?
- Does the jurisdiction have debt capacity?
- Does the jurisdiction have other options for funding besides debt?
- What is the size of the project? A project may simply be too large for pay-as-you-go or too small for debt, as issuance costs would be too high to justify borrowing a small amount.
- Will the project mostly benefit current or future residents? Debt is typically and appropriately reserved for large projects with long useful lives. Constructing a project that will benefit future generations of residents justifies the use of debt that will be paid over a number of years.

Debt

Pay-as-you-go funding options are discussed later in the chapter. Debt is by far the most complex funding method and requires considerable planning for a jurisdiction to undertake. An in-depth discussion of the use of debt to fund capital projects is warranted, but as mentioned above, this chapter is not an exhaustive resource on the topic. The Local Government Bond Act,[22] the state constitution, Securities and Exchange Commission and IRS regulations, and court cases all contribute to the legal framework surrounding the issuance of debt. The most common types of debt and the major players in the debt issuance process are discussed to give the non-expert basic information and literacy. The most important step in deciding to issue debt is to seek guidance from financial and legal experts.

Those experts include first and foremost the jurisdiction's finance officer, especially one who has substantial experience in the borrowing process. If the jurisdiction's finance officer is new to the borrowing process, seeking guidance from other jurisdictions is a good first step. Second, with few exceptions, the State Treasurer's Office, through the Local Government Commission (LGC), oversees the issuance of debt by North Carolina local governments and can guide a jurisdiction through the borrowing process. The LGC website has helpful information for local governments issuing debt, including its guidelines.[23] Bond counsel and financial advisor are important resources, whose roles are discussed in the "Actors in the Debt Issuance Process" section.

---

22. G.S. 159-43 through -100.

23. The LGC's page on the State Treasurer's website can be accessed at https://www.nctreasurer.com/state-and-local-government-finance-division/local-government-commission; N.C. Department of State Treasurer, *Guidelines on Debt Issuance.*

Access to Debt Markets

Project size and the related amount to be borrowed, preferred amortization schedule (structure and length of time to pay off the debt), desire for tax-exempt interest, and project timing often dictate whether a jurisdiction should issue debt through public markets or borrow the funds directly from a bank.

One of the greatest benefits enjoyed by local governments is that interest paid on the debt they issue, with a few exceptions, is exempt from federal income taxes, which translates into lower interest rates for local governments. For the most part, as long as the debt is issued for a public purpose, the interest is tax exempt. However, the size of a debt issuance can remove this eligibility if the funds are borrowed directly from a bank. Under IRS Code Section 265, "bank-qualified" debt is available to "qualified small issuers," which refers to those who borrow no more than $10 million in a calendar year. Typically, this means that local governments issuing no more than $10 million in debt in a calendar year can borrow those funds from a bank (some exceptions apply) and the interest paid on that debt will be tax exempt. "Privately placed" debt issued directly from a bank usually has lower issuance costs, and the borrowing process can be completed more quickly than debt issued through public markets. However, privately placed debt may be limited to a shorter payment term and sometimes has higher interest rates.[24]

Issuing debt through the public markets is a more complicated process. Bonds are sold through an underwriter who places them with investors. More financing professionals are involved, often resulting in higher issuance costs. In addition, public issuances require the creation of a disclosure document (typically called an Official Statement) that takes time to create. As a result, public offerings tend to require a longer schedule than private placements to complete. Interest costs are generally lower than privately placed debt, and public offerings can accommodate a longer amortization schedule (term). In determining whether to issue publicly or privately, the jurisdiction should weigh all of these factors to determine which route best matches the local government's needs and provides the lowest overall cost of capital.

Debt Capacity

Four benchmarks are used in North Carolina to determine a jurisdiction's capacity for taking on new debt. The LGC guidelines state the following:

> The Unit should have a reasonable debt burden. A heavy debt burden may be evidenced by a ratio of General Fund Debt Service to General Fund Expenditures exceeding 15%, or Debt per Capita or Debt to Appraised Property Value exceeding that of similar units.[25]

The first indicator cited by the LGC, debt service as a percent of the operating budget, is reviewed to make sure jurisdictions are not issuing so much debt that they have little flexibility in their budgets for other expenses. The LGC guidelines state this indicator should be at 15 percent or less, though this is not a legal requirement and can be mitigated through repayment strategies, such as Chatham County's debt

---

24. Section 265 of the Internal Revenue Code, 26 U.S.C. § 265.

25. N.C. Department of State Treasurer, *Guidelines on Debt Issuance*.

model (which is discussed later in this section). Moore County's financial policies reference the LGC guideline and state the following: "Should the ratio of debt service expenditures as a percent of total governmental fund expenditures exceed 15.0% staff must request an exception from the Board of Commissioners stating the reason and length of time."[26]

The second indicator is debt per capita (debt divided by population or what each resident would owe to repay the debt today), though it is not a legal limit. Generally, this indicator is reviewed by rating agencies and potential bond holders to ensure that the jurisdiction is not issuing more debt than the population can repay. The N.C. Treasurer Analysis of Debt published by the LGC annually gives jurisdictions information on debt per capita of peer jurisdictions, which can be used to benchmark debt levels. Limits on per capita debt can be set by the governing board through adopted financial policies and should be reviewed as part of the decision to take on new debt.[27]

The third indicator flows from the state's legal limit on debt, which on its face has little practical utility for North Carolina governments deciding whether they can afford new debt. In North Carolina, total tax-supported debt (called "net debt") cannot exceed 8 percent of the jurisdiction's assessed property value. Debt that will be repaid through enterprise revenue is not included in this calculation. No jurisdiction is anywhere close to the legal limit. According to the 2019 LGC Debt Analysis, the highest percentage was 2.6 percent, meaning that the jurisdiction with the most debt as a percent of its property tax base could legally issue three times its current debt. Though the limit set by state law has little practical value, the LGC states in its guidelines that it will compare the jurisdiction's percentage to comparable units. Some local governments also have adopted a local debt limit. In its financial policies, Moore County restricts its tax-supported debt to no more than 2 percent of its estimated market value of county properties.[28]

Finally, though not cited specifically by the LGC, the ten-year payout ratio measures the percentage of total tax-supported debt that will be repaid in the next ten years. Rating agencies review this ratio to make sure a jurisdiction is retiring its debt in a responsible manner. Standard and Poor's (S&P) criteria state that a ratio above 65 percent will be a positive qualitative factor in its rating, while Moody's Investor Service wants to see that the ratio is not "too low." Generally, a jurisdiction should consider a minimum target for the ten-year payout ratio in its financial policies of between 50 and 60 percent repayment.[29]

As mentioned earlier, the LGC collects and reports information on debt issued by cities and counties in its annual debt analysis. According to the 2020 Debt Analysis,

26. Moore County, North Carolina, *Adopted Budget FY 2016-2017*, 55, https://test.moorecountync.gov/images/departments/administration/budget/2016-2017/FY_2016_2017_Adopted_Budget_Book.pdf.

27. N.C. Department of State Treasurer, State and Local Government Finance Division, *Analysis of Debt of North Carolina Counties at 6-30-2020* (February 4, 2021), https://files.nc.gov/nctreasurer/documents/files/SLGFD/LGC/LocalGovDebtMngmt/debtanalysisreport.pdf.

28. Moore County, North Carolina, *Adopted Budget*.

29. Mitch Brigulio (Senior Vice President, Davenport Public Finance), in discussion with the author, August 21, 2020.

North Carolina counties have issued a total of $12.6 billion in debt, while North Carolina cities have together issued $11.9 billion.[30] As Figures 9.1 and 9.2 show, counties more typically issue general obligation bonds, no doubt reflecting their obligation to fund schools. The majority of debt held by North Carolina cities is revenue bonds, reflecting water and sewer infrastructure needs. Both cities and counties also issue a substantial amount of installment debt. These three types of debt are the most common in the state. Each are governed by a different section of state statute, are secured by different sources of funds, and follow different approval processes.

Figure 9.1. North Carolina Counties

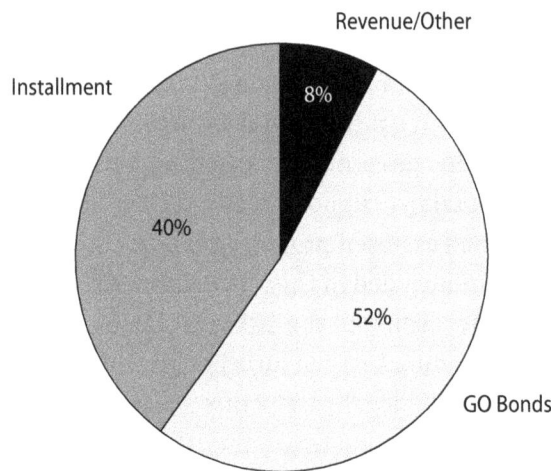

Figure 9.2. North Carolina Cities

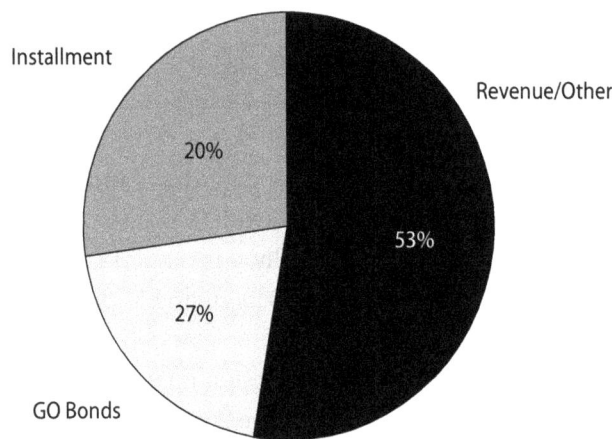

General obligation bonds, which are authorized by voters, are seen by lenders as the most secure because the public has voted in favor of the debt, and the jurisdiction pledges its "full faith and credit," or its taxing power. In case of default, the lender could compel the jurisdiction to raise its tax rate to cover the debt payments. In North Carolina, the state treasurer can step in and compel that taxes be increased.

---

30. N.C. Department of State Treasurer, *Analysis of Debt*.

North Carolina law also allows the tax rate to be increased above the statutory limit of $1.50 per $100 valuation to make debt payments. In deciding whether to use general obligation bonds as a financing mechanism, the jurisdiction should assess the likelihood of whether voters will approve the bonds.

Revenue bonds are appropriate only when the project is part of a revenue-generating enterprise. Revenue bonds are secured by a dedicated stream of revenues, typically those generated by the project itself or the larger enterprise system of which the project is a part. A jurisdiction must prove that its enterprise revenue or the project generates sufficient revenue to cover both its operations and the debt obligation. The ratio of excess revenue to the debt service is called debt-service coverage and, in general, the greater the coverage, the better the interest rate on the debt. To that end, the revenue bond process requires that detailed analysis be done prior to issuance of revenue bonds. A high-level summary of that analysis is typically provided in the jurisdiction's Official Statement, the document provided for investors and rating agencies. Some larger jurisdictions, such as the City of Greensboro, whose process is explained below, can perform the analysis in house, but it is more often contracted to consultants.

City of Greensboro Financial Analysis for Revenue Bonds

City of Greensboro internal staff performs financial analyses of the water/sewer utility throughout the year and, in particular, during the budget process and prior to each revenue bond sale.

Detailed debt models are created that follow required debt covenant calculations, (prescribed in trust documents) and include operating revenues, maintenance and operating expenses, debt service coverage, and cash projections. These debt models typically show performance over a five-year historical period and over a five-year projection. The foundation of the models include the following components:

1. the ten-year Utility Capital Improvements Plan (CIP), which forms the basis for debt planning and the timing of debt issuances;
2. ratings criteria for Moody's Investors Service, S&P Global Ratings, and Fitch's Ratings, along with comparative financial data for other similarly rated jurisdictions;
3. the regulatory climate and legislative changes that may impact the system; and
4. the economy's impacts on system development and the number of customers served.

In preparation for a bond issuance and corresponding credit ratings, staff prepares a one-page summary of key model details and presents information to credit rating analysts. The following topics are covered in this summary:

- the utility's CIP, showing pay-as-you-go and debt funding by year;
- planned debt issuances and the impact on total outstanding debt;
- historical and projected number of customers and water consumption;
- water and sewer rates and projected increases;
- gross revenues;
- total operating and maintenance expenses;
- debt service;
- debt service as percentage of total revenues;
- debt service coverage (The city's current goal is at least two times coverage.);
- unrestricted cash as a percentage of operating and maintenance expenses; and
- the number of days of expenditures cash on hand represents.

Source: Marlene Druga (Deputy Finance Director—Financial Services, Financial and Administrative Services, City of Greensboro, N.C.), email message to author.

For installment debt, the issuer's obligation to repay interest and principal is secured by a real property lien on at least some portion of the asset being financed. In reviewing the collateral, rating agencies will often judge the "essentiality" of the asset. The theory is that the jurisdiction is less likely to default on an essential asset, such as a water plant or jail, but more likely to default on a discretionary asset, such as a convention center. Jurisdictions should be prepared to discuss essentiality for projects that are perceived to be more discretionary. The most common instruments for installment debt issued through public markets are certificates of participation (COPs) and limited obligation bonds (LOBs), which sometimes require the use of a third-party financing corporation. Bank loans (private placement) are also common for installment debt and are issued as an installment financing contract directly between the bank and the issuer. North Carolina law requires that general obligation bonds be used for some facilities, such as athletic and cultural facilities, civic centers, convention centers, museums, historic properties, and urban redevelopment, public transportation, and cable television systems.[31] Installment debt cannot be used for these facilities.

The term of bonds, or the period of time over which the bond will be repaid, is another point for consideration. The bond's term should not exceed the useful life of the asset being financed, and the LGC will ensure this is the case when reviewing the proposed debt issuance. Generally, the LGC requires that general obligation and installment debt have a maximum term of twenty years. If the useful life of the asset being financed warrants it, revenue bonds can have terms of up to thirty years. Often jurisdictions will include in their financial policies a statement that the term will not exceed the useful life of the asset.

Debt repayment in North Carolina is typically structured with even principal payments throughout the term and interest calculated each period on the outstanding principal. This means debt payments for North Carolina jurisdictions are higher in the first years and decline over the term of the debt as principal remains the same and interest is calculated on a decreasing principal balance.

---

31. Kara Millonzi, "Two-Thirds Bonds," *Coates' Canons: NC Local Government Law* (blog), November 18, 2010, https://canons.sog.unc.edu/two-thirds-bonds/.

Figure 9.3. Example of Typical Debt-Service Structure in North Carolina with Even Principal Payments and Interest Calculated on the Outstanding Balance

County of Chatham, North Carolina October 31, 2016

2018 Board of Education Building

Par Amount $6,000,000   Issued July 2020

FY Ending	Principal ($)	Coupon (%)	Interest ($)	Fiscal Total ($)
6/30/2021	-	3.50	99,750	99,750
6/30/2022	600,000	3.50	199,500	799,500
6/30/2023	600,000	3.50	178,500	778,500
6/30/2024	600,000	3.50	157,500	757,500
6/30/2025	600,000	3.50	136,500	736,500
6/30/2026	600,000	3.50	115,500	715,500
6/30/2027	600,000	3.50	94,500	694,500
6/30/2028	600,000	3.50	73,500	673,500
6/30/2029	600,000	3.50	52,500	652,500
6/30/2030	600,000	3.50	31,500	631,500
6/30/2031	600,000	3.50	10,500	610,500
Total:	6,000,000		1,149,750	7,149,750

Source: Chatham County Debt Model Version 52B (October 31, 2016).

This contrasts with how personal debt is usually paid, which is in level payments (in the early years, the debt payment consists mostly of interest, and as payments continue, the proportion of principal increases, but the payment remains the same.) Sometimes the structure can be modified, for example to have interest-only payments for the first year or two, which is helpful if a jurisdiction is greatly increasing its debt-service requirements or a revenue-generating project needs time to come online.

Debt Issuance Process

There are several basic steps for issuing debt, which are listed below, but the process includes additional steps for issuing general obligation bonds approved by voters. That process is prolonged because deciding to hold a vote, scheduling the vote during a regular election as required by law, and receiving LGC approval must happen before the vote is held. Steps that apply only to voter-approved general obligation bonds are indicated in the list below. In addition, several steps are not required for private placements (debt issued through banks). Those steps are labeled as "public offerings only."

1. Plan the project. What is the scope, timing, and detailed cost estimate of the project?
2. Work with your financial and legal advisors to determine the best financing method and structure.
3. Meet with the LGC to hold preliminary discussions about the project. According to LGC guidelines, the jurisdiction should discuss both its overall capital plan and the specific project for which financing is being contemplated. If "innovative" financing is being contemplated, an early discussion is warranted. The LGC will be concerned primarily that the jurisdiction is

not taking on too much debt. Understanding the impact of the debt on the benchmarks discussed above is an important step in preparing for the meeting with the LGC.

4. Voter-approved general obligation only: Work with bond counsel to determine a calendar for the required approvals necessary to seek voter approval well in advance of the election. LGC approval typically occurs prior to voter consideration. With a few exceptions, the vote must be held during a regular primary or general election.

5. Voter-approved general obligation only: Hold the bond referendum vote.

6. Bid the project. Bids must be in hand before receiving LGC approval and ratings. For voter-approved general obligation debt, a significant amount of time may elapse between steps 5 and 6 if the referendum is on a general list of projects and the scope and budgets have not been specifically defined. (This will also impact the information shared with the LGC in step 3.)

7. When required, hold a public hearing and receive governing board approvals.

8. Seek approval from the LGC. A completed application, which a financial advisor typically prepares with assistance from the jurisdiction, must be submitted well in advance of the meeting during which LGC staff will present the application to the LGC for consideration. At this step, LGC guidelines state that the project must be ready, which is defined as follows: "Construction bids, required major permits and Phase I Environmental Studies should be received before the approval or, at the latest, before the sale of the debt. Other required sources of funding must be committed."[32] Make sure the project designer can meet the time frame for bids and knows how long bids need to be held. Knowing the LGC's calendar is important for ensuring project bids are in hand ahead of time, but the amount of time a contractor is willing to hold bids is not exceeded before the borrowing process can be concluded. Developing a calendar for steps 4 through 12 is a wise step to ensure all time frames can be met. A financial advisor, if used, can help the jurisdiction develop the calendar.

9. Public offerings only: Request and receive ratings from one or more ratings agencies. This step is discussed in more detail in the "Actors in the Debt Issuance Process" section.

10. Public offerings only: Finalize the Official Statement (OS). The OS provides potential investors detailed information on the jurisdiction, its finances and management, its local economy, indicators of population growth and community wealth, and the project being financed. Typically, in a public offering an underwriter will engage counsel who will spearhead the development of the OS with information provided by the jurisdiction. The jurisdiction works with its financial advisor and bond counsel to ensure all important issues are covered and the document is accurate. As a part of a public offering, the jurisdiction will be expected to certify that all information material to

---

32. N.C. Department of State Treasurer, *Guidelines on Debt Issuance.*

a potential investor has been included in the OS, and local governments should be diligent in their review of the OS before it is finalized.

11. Public offerings only: Sell the bond. General obligation bonds are typically sold competitively and coordinated by the LGC. Most installment debt and revenue bonds are sold on a negotiated basis and coordinated by an underwriter.

12. Close on the bonds/borrowing. This step is typically coordinated by bond counsel. Though historically handled in person, closings are now frequently done by email and regular mail.

13. Begin the project by giving the contractor notice to proceed.

Actors in the Debt Issuance Process

As mentioned, the public market debt issuance process is complex and requires that a jurisdiction work with multiple parties and advisors. A simplified list of parties and advisors is found in the sidebar below and is compared with parties and advisors in debt issued through private placements. The public market roles are discussed in more detail below.[33]

Actors in Public Market Offerings Compared with Actors in Private Placements

Public Market	Private Placement
• Jurisdiction's attorney and finance officer	• Jurisdiction's attorney and finance officer
• Local Government Commission (LGC)	• LGC
• Financial advisor (FA)	• FA (deals with bank, gets best interest rate, handles details)—not required
• Bond counsel	• Bond counsel
• Bond-rating agencies	• Bank
• Underwriter's counsel*	• Bank counsel
• Underwriter*	
• Trustee*	
• Feasibility consultant**	

*Applies to installment debt and revenue bonds; not always used for general obligation
**Applies to revenue bonds

Local Government Commission (LGC)

The importance of the Local Government Commission (LGC) cannot be overstated. The agency both oversees and approves the debt issuance and is a resource to guide a jurisdiction through the process. Early and ongoing discussions with the LGC are important, especially for those jurisdictions that are new to the debt issuance process. The LGC does charge a fee for the application and approval process. The fee is usually included in the financing cost and is part of the amount borrowed.

---

33. See Municipal Securities Rulemaking Board, *Roles and Responsibilities: The Financing Team in an Initial Municipal Bond Offering* (2018), http://msrb.org/msrb1/pdfs/Financing-Team.pdf for more information on these roles.

Bond Counsel

As highly specialized attorneys, bond counsel must have extensive knowledge of state and federal laws governing the issuance of debt, including state constitutional and statutory authority, federal tax regulations, and SEC regulations. Therefore, bond counsel must be carefully chosen to ensure they have the required expertise. Several North Carolina firms have attorneys who practice in this area. Bond counsel advise on how to structure a borrowing, draft and/or review documents required as a part of the issuance process, and render an opinion on whether the debt instrument (bond) is valid and enforceable under law and on the tax treatment (taxable or tax-exempt) of the debt instrument. Most local governments maintain ongoing relationships with their bond counsel who, in addition to providing service in connection with a bond issuance, provide advice and counsel on an ongoing basis on items, such as continuing disclosure, post-issuance tax compliance, and changes in applicable legislation or regulation. The bond counsel fee is usually included in the financing cost and is part of the amount borrowed.

Chatham County and Its Debt Model

Chatham County's population has nearly doubled in the past thirty years. For the first fifteen years or so of this growth, the county built two schools using general obligation bonds, but largely postponed other capital needs. As a result, in 2005 the county had a backlog of needed capital projects that, if funded, would increase the county's debt burden by $113 million, a six-fold increase in per capita debt. Commissioners, for obvious reasons, were reluctant to take on that level of debt without knowing how it would be repaid.

The county's finance officer engaged the county's first financial advisor. The advisor developed what the county now knows as the debt model. With assumptions validated by county staff, the advisor determined that the county could cover the debt by dedicating four cents on the property tax rate and setting aside those funds, along with interest earned and other revenues restricted for school capital in reserve. Courageously, in a revaluation year the Board of Commissioners raised taxes four cents above revenue neutral, and the county began its capital program.

When the Great Recession hit in 2008, the county completed three projects already underway but temporarily suspended its other projects because debt financing was largely unavailable. A year later, the finance officer was able to secure a bank loan and American Recovery and Reinvestment Act funding. When the county bid four projects either originally bid or costs estimated in 2008, it found that the cost of construction had declined substantially, with 13 to 19 percent resulting in a total savings of $10 million. That, along with historically low interest rates, allowed the county to leverage funds already being accumulated in the debt reserve and continue its capital program throughout the recession, while taking advantage of the low construction costs and historically low interest rates.

As projects have been added to the CIP, commissioners have exercised fiscal discipline and increased the contribution to the debt reserve. Today, the county contributes 9.2 cents annually to the debt model. Without the model, the county would have needed the equivalent of 12.8 cents on the property tax rate for debt service in FY 2020 and will need 21.7 cents in FY 2022. In addition to providing a sustainable funding source for debt-funded projects, the debt reserve is viewed by rating agencies as available fund balance. In 2014, Chatham County became the smallest county in North Carolina to achieve the highest bond rating given by S&P Global Ratings: AAA.

Source: N.C. Department of State Treasurer, State and Local Government Finance Division, *Analysis of Debt of North Carolina Counties at 6-30-2020* (February 4, 2021), https://files.nc.gov/nctreasurer/documents/files/SLGFD/LGC/LocalGovDebtMngmt/debtanalysisreport.pdf.

Financial Advisor

Though financial advisors (FA) are not required, FAs exclusively represent the jurisdiction's interest. In Chatham County, a financial advisor helped the county figure out how to repay debt for its entire CIP; the debt model is discussed as a best practice in the "Chatham County and Its Debt Model" sidebar. The FA can also advise the jurisdiction on the best time to sell its bonds, how to structure the debt, when to explore refinancing, whom to choose as an underwriter, the content of its OS, and presentation on the planned debt issuance to rating agencies. In summary, the FA guides the jurisdiction through the debt issuance process from start to finish. The FA may charge an annual fee for ongoing consulting services or may charge for services when debt is issued or both. Typically, the fee charged as part of the debt issuance process is included in financing costs and is part of the amount borrowed.

Bond-Rating Agencies

Rating agencies assess the quality of the jurisdiction's bonds and assign a rating, which is used by potential investors to determine the risk associated with purchasing bonds. North Carolina jurisdictions enjoy high ratings when compared to other states, in part because of the oversight of the LGC. North Carolina jurisdictions have typically sought ratings from Moody's Investor Service, S&P Global Ratings, and Fitch's, but many jurisdictions do not seek ratings from all three agencies. (The N.C. Debt Analysis shows ratings of every jurisdiction by rating agency).[34] Generally, bond-rating agencies review a jurisdiction's finances (liquidity, budget performance, budget flexibility), management, economy, and debt burden in determining a rating. Each agency has slightly different criteria and weighting. Once assigned, the ratings are monitored periodically by the agencies and may change to reflect an improvement or worsening of performance on rating criteria. In deciding to seek a rating from a particular agency, a jurisdiction should review the criteria and assess how well they perform. A financial advisor can help a jurisdiction assess the rating criteria, offer guidance for how to improve on those criteria under its control, and assist the jurisdiction in preparing its presentation to the rating agencies. Interestingly, S&P Global Ratings now include a jurisdiction's preparation for climate change in its ratings analysis.[35]

Underwriter

The underwriter markets and sells the jurisdiction's bonds. When voter-approved general obligation bonds are competitively sold in North Carolina, the LGC performs this role. For all other bonds, an underwriter is hired by the jurisdiction (often with assistance from the financial advisor) and the price (interest rate) of the bonds is negotiated between the underwriter and the jurisdiction. The underwriter is paid

---

34. N.C. Department of State Treasurer, *Analysis of Debt*.
35. "Through The ESG Lens: How Environmental, Social, and Governance Factors Are Incorporated into U.S. Public Finance Ratings," *S&P Global Ratings*, October 10, 2018, https://www.spglobal.com/ratings/en/research/pdf-articles/181010-through-the-esg -lens-how-environmental-social-and-governance-factors-are-incorporated-into-u-s -public-finance-ratings.

based on the difference between this negotiated rate and what the bonds ultimately sell for, which is called the spread. According to the Municipal Securities Rulemaking Board's (MSRB) publication on these roles, the underwriter:

- works with state or local government and municipal advisor to design the plan of finance,
- develops the bond structure,
- assists in determining timing to sell bonds based on market conditions,
- contributes to the development of the bond documents,
- helps in preparing any rating agency strategy and presentation,
- "runs numbers" to provide quantitative analysis of financing structure,
- manages the pricing process, and
- executes pre-sale marketing.[36]

The underwriter also has counsel who is part of the process and is typically responsible for the development of the OS with information provided by the jurisdiction.

Trustee

The trustee, which is usually a bank, receives the funds once bonds are sold and holds those funds until the jurisdiction needs them for the project. The trustee is the only party who must remain a part of the ongoing process of receiving funds and paying debt. The trustee's main obligation is its fiduciary duty to bondholders to ensure that the jurisdiction honors its debt obligation by enforcing the terms of the trust indenture. Throughout the debt term, the trustee makes sure the jurisdiction is complying with the terms of the bond documents, including insurance requirements and arbitrage compliance, which require ongoing disclosure by the jurisdiction. When funds are needed to pay project costs, and only after proper documentation is presented, the trustee transfers funds to the jurisdiction and invests any unspent funds. The trustee is also charged with receiving debt service paid by the jurisdiction and dispersing these funds to bondholders. The trustee is selected by the jurisdiction (with assistance from the financial advisor). The trustee's fee is charged as part of the debt issuance process and is included in financing costs.

Feasibility Consultant

For revenue bonds only, the feasibility consultant writes the feasibility report that is included in the OS. According to MSRB, the report "may evaluate the economic viability, or the adequacy of revenues generated by a capital project or program to repay debt. The report generally describes historic and projected demand for the services, economic trends, user base, user fees and rates that generate revenues pledged to cover debt service."[37] As mentioned above, some jurisdictions, such as the City of Greensboro, write the feasibility report in house.

In addition to the three debt instruments and the private placement options discussed above, jurisdictions that meet the demographic eligibility requirements, such

---

36. Municipal Securities Rulemaking Board, *Roles and Responsibilities.*
37. Ibid.

as rural population and/or low wealth levels, should consider United States Department of Agriculture (USDA) financing through the Rural Development Office. In some cases, jurisdictions may be eligible for partial grant funding. The USDA offers terms that are easier to afford than traditional financing, including level payments and terms longer than what is typically allowed by the LGC. The process is complex to navigate, though LGC approval is not required.[38]

Jurisdictions also refinance their debt when interest rates fall. This process, known as refunding, involves debt issuance steps 7 through 12, discussed above. As stated in its guidelines, the LGC wants to see at least a 3 percent overall savings as compared to the existing bonds. The guidelines also state that the term of the debt should not be extended.

Finally, two-thirds bond authority allows North Carolina local governments to issue general obligation bonds without voter approval in an amount equivalent to two-thirds of the principal retired within the preceding year.[39]

Pay-As-You-Go Funding

In an ideal world, jurisdictions would like to avoid issuing debt. Funding from current revenues or current revenues accumulated over time is the best way to do that. Avoiding debt means no interest costs, no issuance costs, and allowing accumulated funds to earn interest that the jurisdiction can keep. However, many projects are simply too large for pay-as-you-go funding, and accumulating funds for many years carries risk that political support may wane and costs may escalate at a rate greater than interest earnings. Additionally, projects that will benefit current and future residents are appropriate for debt finance, as both groups will pay a share of the project cost. The key is to balance between debt funding and pay-as-you-go funding so that a jurisdiction is not overly burdened with debt. Many jurisdictions include a statement to that effect in their financial policies. Grants, capital reserves, operating revenues, restricted revenues, and fund balance are common methods of paying for projects without issuing debt.

Grants are obviously the most attractive resource for financing capital projects. A number of sources exist in the state and nation. The following is a brief list of grants (and combination grant/loan programs) that are available and links to additional information:[40]

- Community Development Block Grant, a federally funded grant program through the United States Department of Housing and Urban Development (U.S. HUD) and administered by the state:

---

38. "Community Facilities Direct Loan & Grant Program," U.S. Department of Agriculture, Rural Development, https://www.rd.usda.gov/programs-services/community-facilities-direct-loan-grant-program.

39. Millonzi, "Two-Thirds Bonds."

40. See Rivenbark and Marlowe, "Evaluation and Prioritization," for a list of potential grant sources.

○ N.C. Department of Commerce, Rural Economic Development Division (building reuse, public infrastructure, demolition, disaster recovery, and community housing).[41]

○ N.C. Department of Environmental Quality, Division of Water Infrastructure (Drinking Water State Revolving Fund (DWSRF); Clean Water State Revolving Fund (CWSRF); Community Development Block Grant; Infrastructure, State Wastewater, and Drinking Water Reserve Programs; Merger/Regionalization Feasibility Grant Program; and Asset Inventory and Assessment Grant Program).[42]

- Parks and Recreation Trust Fund (parks development).[43]
- Golden Leaf infrastructure grants.[44]
- U.S. Department of Agriculture Rural Development (public facilities, economic development, housing, and utilities).[45]

With respect to federal grant funds, jurisdictions are required to follow the Davis-Bacon Act. According to the U.S. Department of Labor:

> The Davis-Bacon and Related Acts apply to contractors and subcontractors performing on federally funded or assisted contracts in excess of $2,000 for the construction, alteration, or repair (including painting and decorating) of public buildings or public works. Davis-Bacon Act and Related Act contractors and subcontractors must pay their laborers and mechanics employed under the contract no less than the locally prevailing wages and fringe benefits for corresponding work on similar projects in the area.[46]

These wage standards often result in higher project costs. The benefit of receiving federal grant funds must be weighed against this requirement. The act must be followed for the entire project, regardless of the amount of funding received.

Because grants funds are not readily available for every project, jurisdictions often have to fund small capital projects through other means, including capital reserves, operating revenues, fund balance, and restricted revenues.[47] Generally, North Carolina jurisdictions have fewer revenue options than jurisdictions in other states.

---

41. "Rural Economic Development Division," N.C. Department of Commerce, https://www.nccommerce.com/about-us/divisions-programs/rural-economic-development-division#public-infrastructure-support.

42. "Funding Programs and Application Information," N.C. Department of Environmental Quality, https://deq.nc.gov/about/divisions/water-infrastructure/division-water-infrastructure/funding-programs-and-application.

43. "Parks and Recreation Trust Fund," N.C. State Parks, https://www.ncparks.gov/more-about-us/parks-recreation-trust-fund/parks-and-recreation-trust-fund.

44. "Grant Seekers, How Can We Help You Move the Economic Needle in Your Community," Golden Leaf Foundation, https://www.goldenleaf.org/grant-seekers/.

45. "All Programs," U.S. Department of Agriculture, Rural Development, https://www.rd.usda.gov/programs-services/all-programs/.

46. "Davis-Bacon and Related Acts," U.S. Department of Labor, Wage and Hour Division, https://www.dol.gov/agencies/whd/government-contracts/construction.

47. To review the revenue options available for pay-as-you-go projects, see Kara A. Millonzi, *A Guide to County and Municipal Revenues in North Carolina* (Chapel Hill, NC: UNC School of Government, 2014).

The legal framework for capital reserves is discussed in the "Legal Framework" section above. The benefit of using capital reserves over annual appropriations for CIP projects is that the funds can be accumulated over time. The important step is ensuring the funds are set aside each year. In Chatham, when a new project enters the CIP, the county starts setting aside funds immediately for the project. For example, if a project enters the CIP in Year 7, the county will appropriate in its operating budget a contribution to capital reserve equal to one-seventh of the funding needed and does that each year until the project is ready to move forward. Each project is treated similarly, constituting the total contribution to the capital reserve. This conservative approach requires that the operating budget bear a heavier burden for funding in the early years of the CIP time frame, but the benefit is that the jurisdiction has capacity to add new projects without necessarily increasing the contribution to capital reserve. It also gives requesting agencies and departments some security that funding is already set aside for their projects.

Another approach is to model the pay-as-you-go requirements over the CIP time frame and determine an annual amount to be appropriated from the operating budget into the capital reserve. "Model" is a fancy way of saying "add up the total contribution needed and divide by the number of years in the CIP." This means that the contribution does not change from year to year unless new projects are added. In that case, the model is readjusted, and a new annual contribution is determined.

Deciding whether to have one capital reserve for all projects or a reserve for each project is a point for discussion. The approach of having one capital reserve (with broad authority for use) likely allows the jurisdiction much more flexibility and better cash flow for all projects. In addition, a jurisdiction does not have to establish a formal capital reserve for this purpose. It can keep these funds reserved as part of its fund balance. The obvious risk with this approach is that the funds can be more easily diverted for another purpose.

Jurisdictions can also fund the CIP through the operating budget as projects come up for funding. This more closely aligns CIP funding to the needs of the operating budget. However, funding can vary greatly from one year to the next, creating issues with being able to budget each year. In addition, the project's financial feasibility is not known until the funding year, which can create problems for project planning.

Jurisdictions can fund projects from fund balance. If this approach is used, jurisdictions should set an appropriate target for fund balance and ensure CIP spending does not cause the jurisdiction to fall under this target. Maintaining adequate fund balance is critical. The LGC requires that North Carolina jurisdictions maintain a minimum of at least one month of operating expenses, or 8 percent of the operating budget, in reserve. Most jurisdictions typically have much more than this amount (typically, the smaller the jurisdiction, the greater the ratio between fund balance and the operating budget). Rating agencies consider maintaining adequate fund balance a very important part of a jurisdiction's bond rating. Allowing fund balance to go much below the average of similar-sized jurisdictions jeopardizes a jurisdiction's ability to borrow at reasonable interest rates.

Some jurisdictions also require that the portion of fund balance over the targeted amount be transferred to the capital reserve. Moore County has this requirement in its policy: "Monies in excess of a 15.0% available fund balance will be transferred to a Capital Reserve Fund for future use for a specific purpose within a specified time frame."[48] This practice achieves several goals. First, it keeps fund balance from growing too much beyond the targeted level, which might create a negative public perception and political concerns. Second, it marries the contribution to the jurisdiction's ability to pay. However, if this is the only funding mechanism for the pay-as-you-go portion of the CIP, the variation in fund balance levels can cause difficulty in planning and funding projects, similar to that of funding projects from the operating budget.

A similar approach to using excess fund balance to fund the CIP is to earmark a portion of general fund revenues for this purpose. For example, a jurisdiction may set aside pennies on the property tax rate to fund capital. As long as the revenue source is relatively stable and has been projected for the CIP time frame, this poses less risk for CIP implementation.

Finally, North Carolina jurisdictions have a number of legally restricted revenue sources, such as water and sewer system development fees, 911 telephone surcharges, and recreation exaction payment-in-lieu funds, that must be accounted for separately and can only be used for projects allowed by the statutes governing their use.[49]

Summary

Capital planning is an important process for most North Carolina jurisdictions. Without it, large capital projects are difficult to achieve. Because most community services require capital facilities and equipment in order to deliver them, even the smallest jurisdiction is likely to be confronted with an expensive project it needs to figure out how to fund. Capital planning allows a jurisdiction to identify all such projects, weigh their relative merits, and decide on what projects should be done, when they should be conducted, and how to fund them.

Undertaking capital planning for the first time may seem like a daunting task, but many resources exist to help guide a jurisdiction through the process, including, hopefully, this chapter. While North Carolina law has little to say about capital planning, the variety of practices that exist within the state give jurisdictions, large and small, that are new to this process many different models to follow. Best practices would call for

- developing financial policies, including policies on fund balance, debt, and capital planning;
- setting a cost and useful life threshold for CIP projects;

---

48. Moore County, North Carolina, *Adopted Budget.*
49. Millonzi, *A Guide to County and Municipal Revenues.*

- ensuring the CIP is linked to master planning efforts and other guiding goals and plans, such as the jurisdiction's land use plan;
- designating a qualified staff person or department to develop the CIP;
- developing a calendar for preparation of the CIP and sharing that calendar with potential submitters;
- effectively evaluating projects by comparing the project's benefits to the capital and ongoing costs;
- deciding on a way to prioritize projects;
- effectively communicating the recommended CIP to the governing board and engaging the public in the CIP process;
- understanding the debt and pay-as-you go options and how to balance between the two so that the jurisdiction is not overly reliant on debt; and
- engaging appropriate experts to guide the jurisdiction through the debt issuance process.

Armed with these best practices, a jurisdiction can achieve a number of benefits by developing a capital improvements program.[50]

Other Resources

City of Greensboro: Marlene Druga, Deputy Finance Director, and Larry Davis, Assistant City Manager

City of Fayetteville: Kevin V. Arata, Corporate Communications Director

Jeremy Carter, Managing Director, DEC Associates Inc.

Mitch Brigulio, Senior Vice President, Davenport Public Finance

Vicki McConnell, Chatham Deputy County Manager

Bryan Thompson, Chatham Assistant County Manager

Paula Stewart, Harnett County Manager

Hal Hegwer, Sanford City Manager

Hardin Watkins, Burlington City Manager and former Garner City Manager

Please see the websites of the following municipalities/counties:

- Raleigh, N.C. (raleighnc.gov)
- Mecklenburg County, N.C. (mecknc.gov)
- Rocky Mount, N.C. (rockymountnc.gov)
- Moore County, NC (moorecountync.gov)
- Garner, N.C. (garnernc.gov)
- Charlotte, N.C. (charlottenc.gov)

---

50. For additional information, see Rivenbark and Marlowe, "Evaluation and Prioritization of Capital Assets"; N.C. Department of State Treasurer, *Guidelines on Debt Issuance*; and the other resources cited in this chapter.

- Wake County, N.C. (wakegov.com)
- Fayetteville, N.C. (fayettevillenc.gov)
- Hickory, N.C. (hickorync.gov)
- Harnett County, N.C. (harnett.org)
- Clinton, N.C. (cityofclintonnc.com)
- Durham, N.C. (durhamnc.gov)
- Greeley, Colo. (greeleygov.com)
- San Antonio, Tex. (sanantonio.gov)

Chapter 10

Performance Measurement and Performance Management*

David N. Ammons and William C. Rivenbark

Measuring a local government's performance is one thing. Using those measures to improve operations and services is another thing—a very different thing.

When governments decide what to measure, collect the data, and report their measures, they are engaged in *performance measurement and reporting.* When managers purposefully use their measures to improve operations and services, they are engaged in *performance management.* This chapter addresses both performance measurement and performance management. We turn first to performance measurement.

---

*Much of this chapter is drawn from David N. Ammons, "Performance Measurement: A Tool for Accountability and Performance Improvement," in *County and Municipal Government in North Carolina*, 2nd edition, ed. Frayda S. Bluestein (UNC School of Government, 2014). Used by permission.

Types of Performance Measures

Performance measures may be divided and categorized in different ways. For the most part, however, this short list covers the types of measures most relevant to tracking and improving performance in local government:

- output (workload) measures,
- efficiency measures,
- outcome (effectiveness) measures, and
- productivity measures.[1]

Output (Workload) Measures

When a department reports the number of applications processed, inspections made, or cases handled, it is reporting on its workload or output. These statistics are relatively simple to compile and report, but they are very limited in what they can say about a department or program. They say nothing about the quality or efficiency of the service. They only report how many units of a service were produced or how much of an activity was undertaken.

Although counting and tabulating workload numbers is the most common form of performance reporting in local government, the value of raw output measures for policy and management purposes is extremely limited. This is not to suggest that keeping track of output is unimportant. Comparing output from year to year provides an indication of growing or declining demand for a given service. More important, output numbers are often critical ingredients in the calculation of higher-order measures that hold greater value for managerial and policy decisions. Unfortunately, too many local governments depend almost entirely on raw output or workload measures to report their performance. With workload measures alone, the message conveyed by a department or program cannot be "We are efficient" or "We provide quality services." With raw workload measures alone, the only message is "We are busy!"

Efficiency Measures

Measures of efficiency report the relationship between resources used and services produced. Sometimes this relationship is expressed in terms of unit cost—for example, cost per application processed or cost per inspection—or units of service per $1,000. The relationship between resources and outputs also may be expressed as the ratio of outputs to staff hours—for example, staff hours per license application or curb miles swept per operator hour. When cost-accounting systems will not support precise unit-cost calculations and the calculation of employee output ratios is

---

1. Readers familiar with the literature on performance measurement will notice the omission of a category sometimes included on such lists: input measures. Raw input alone, typically in the form of dollars or personnel, does not measure performance. However, when input is measured in relation to output, the result is a measure of efficiency, which does measure performance. Hence, efficiency measures are included here, even as inputs alone are excluded.

impractical, many local governments opt for a less precise and comprehensive manner of gauging operational efficiency by tracking average turnaround time, average daily backlog, or similar operating characteristics.

Outcome (Effectiveness) Measures

Measures of outcome (also known as effectiveness measures) gauge the quality of services or the extent to which a program's objectives are being achieved. Suppose, for instance, that an objective of the solid waste department is to complete at least 95 percent of all refuse collection routes on the scheduled day of collection. If the department compiles statistics showing that 94 percent of the routes were completed as scheduled, this would be an outcome measure, for it measures the extent to which the objective was achieved. Among many other commonly reported types of outcome measures are various measures of responsiveness (for example, average response time to emergencies) and citizen satisfaction (for example, percentage of citizens who are "satisfied" or "very satisfied" with the local recreation program).

Productivity Measures

Productivity measures combine efficiency and effectiveness in a single index. These indices are rare in local government, but their absence is of little concern as long as good measures of efficiency and effectiveness are present to guide program efforts.

Examples of productivity indicators include measures produced by calculating unit costs more restrictively than a government calculates its efficiency measures. While an efficiency measure based on unit cost includes all costs in the numerator and all outputs in the denominator, the associated productivity measure would include only successes (that is, outputs of a specified quality or outputs yielding successful results) in the denominator. In essence, a program is penalized in this ratio for poor-quality outputs or unsuccessful results. The ratio reflects both cost and quality.

Developing a Good Set of Performance Measures

Good sets of performance measures include measures that are valid, reliable, understandable, timely, resistant to undesired behavior, sensitive to data-collection costs, and focused on important facets of performance.[2] A good set of performance measures reports not only how much service is provided but also how well and how efficiently. Even more important to local governments intent on truly managing their performance, a good set of such measures inspires managerial thinking by providing crucial performance data that cannot be ignored. To truly inspire managerial

---

2. C. K. Bens, "Strategies for Implementing Performance Measurement," *ICMA Management Information Service Report* 18 (November 1986): 1–14; C. Broom, M. Jackson, V. Vogelsang Coombs, and J. Harris, *Performance Measurement: Concepts and Techniques* (Washington, D.C.: American Society for Public Administration, 1998); H. P. Hatry, "Performance Measurement Principles and Techniques," *Public Productivity Review* 4 (December 1980): 312–39; H. P. Hatry, *Performance Measurement: Getting Results* (Washington, D.C.: Urban Institute Press, 1999); H. P. Hatry, D. M. Fisk, J. R. Hall Jr., P. S. Schaenman, and L. Snyder, *How Effective Are Your Community Services?* (Washington, D.C.: Urban Institute and International City/County Management Association, 2006), 3.

thinking, performance data must focus on important dimensions of service and must be compiled in a manner that either reassures operating officials and program personnel that services are being provided at suitable levels of quality and efficiency or, if not, causes them to investigate possible causes of shortcomings and consider options for improvement.[3] A fundamental test for a set of performance measures, then, is whether it provides data of sufficient importance and in a form that can inspire managerial thinking.

Examples of sets of performance measures for planning and inspection services are provided in Tables 10.1 and 10.2. Examples for fire and social services are shown in Table 10.3 and Figure 10.1.

Performance Measurement and Accountability

Recognizing their obligation to be accountable to governing boards and citizens, many city and county governments collect and report measures of performance. Some produce special reports devoted entirely to publicizing the performance measures of all the departments in the government. Others publish annual reports that include selected performance measures along with general program information and narrative about accomplishments. Many include performance measures in their annual budget documents—the most common vehicle for performance reporting.

A good set of performance measures is an important tool for building accountability not just to elected officials and citizens but also within the organization. By compiling key indicators of performance, supervisors can confirm that work crews are meeting expectations and delivering quality services—in short, they can ensure the accountability of front-line employees. Periodic reporting of selected measures allows supervisors to be accountable to department management for their work, department management to be accountable to central administration, and central administration to be accountable to the governing board. In turn, the periodic publication of key performance measures allows board members to be accountable to the citizenry for local government operations as a whole.

True accountability means more than just assuring the public that revenues are properly collected and reported and that expenditures are made in accordance with prescribed procedures. Accountability includes these important assurances but also entails assurances to the public that government resources are being spent wisely as well as legally and that services of good quality are being produced efficiently. Performance measurement offers a tool for providing such assurances.

The Value of Performance Measurement to Governing Boards

Even when the governing board hires a manager to handle matters of day-to-day administration, the board retains responsibility for providing general oversight of the local government as a whole and for establishing program priorities. It also retains responsibility for assessing the performance of the manager in directing local government operations. Good performance measures can be helpful in performing these

---

3. David N. Ammons, "Performance Measurement and Managerial Thinking," *Public Performance and Management Review* 25 (June 2002): 344–47.

Table 10.1. Example of Performance Measures for Planning

Service Goal	Two Years Ago Actual	Last Year Actual	Target
Encourage participation by a wide cross-section of area residents on advisory boards			
% of neighborhoods with at least one appointee to four standing advisory boards	78%	78%	75%
Integrate "green" buildings into development projects			
% of projects requiring town board review to incorporate green building standards	100%	0%	50%
Provide timely response to complaints and violations			
Average number of business days from receipt of complaint to site inspection	1	1.22	<5
% of violations brought into voluntary compliance	57%	83%	80%
Provide timely information to applicants			
% of development application submittals reviewed and sent comments within ten business days	79%	100%	90%
Improve departmental coordination through Technical Review Committee (TRC) review of new development			
% of applications for TRC review able to be approved or approved with conditions in the first meeting	75%	100%	75%
Promote professional development through certification			
% of zoning officials certified	25%	33%	33%
% of planners certified	66%	66%	100%
Represent the town on regional committees and efforts			
% of regional meetings attended where town had an appointed seat	67%	88%	80%

Source: Adapted from Town of Hillsborough, N.C., *FY13 Adopted Budget & Financial Plan*, 109. By permission.

duties. For instance, the governing board might ask the following questions in performing its oversight role:

- Are services being provided efficiently and equitably?
- Do they meet expectations for quality?
- Could better services be provided at a more reasonable cost by contracting out some functions?
- Have deficiencies been identified and are improvements being made where needed?
- Do service results indicate that programs are being properly managed?

Each of these questions can be answered adequately only if reliable data are available.

Table 10.2.   Example of Performance Measures for Inspections

Durham City-County Inspections

The City-County Inspections Department is a merged City and County department that administers and enforces the North Carolina State Building Codes and Durham City-County Zoning Ordinances.

	Last Year Actual	This Year Estimated	Target Adopted
Objective: To provide accurate and prompt plan review by reviewing 90% of all residential plans within five working days			
% of residential plans reviewed within five days	99%	95%	90%
% plan errors found in field	0.34%	1%	1%
Number of plans reviewed	2,625	2,324	2,324
Objective: To provide timely response to customer requests by responding to requested inspections within twenty-four hours 90% of the time			
% of inspections performed within twenty-four hours	98.2%	90%	90%
Number of inspections per inspector per day	17.3	17.3	16.0
Number of inspections performed	71,103	73,736	73,736
Objective: To provide for the safety and health of citizens by ensuring that all construction meets the North Carolina State Building Codes by performing two quality-control inspections of the work of each inspector per month			
Number of quality-control inspections per inspector per month	2.7	2.0	2.0
% inspections found to be accurate	99%	98%	98%
Number of quality-control checks	643	523	480

Source: Adapted from City of Durham, N.C., *FY 2012–2013 Adopted Budget*, VIII.4–VIII.6. By permission.

In recent years, many management experts have advocated more decentralized decision-making, allowing field unit supervisors and even front-line employees to make more of the service delivery decisions, as long as their decisions are consistent with the vision or culture established and nurtured by central authorities. Much can be said in favor of a strategy that places greater discretion in the hands of those who know the program best and are closest to the problems. However, without a dependable system for guaranteeing accountability, few governing boards will be willing to increase managerial discretion or encourage managers to permit greater discretion at lower levels of the organization. In the absence of a system for compiling and reporting evidence that programs are being run efficiently and effectively, top officials are more likely to believe that their oversight responsibilities require involvement in or approval of a large portion of the individual decisions made on behalf of the government. Upper management and governing boards are more likely to be receptive if greater supervisory discretion and reductions in administrative red tape are accompanied by clear evidence of favorable program results.

Table 10.3. Example of Performance Measures for Fire Services

	Last Year Actual	This Year Estimated	Next Year Projected
Effectiveness			
Average response time to fire/medical/rescue calls (target: < 4 minutes)	3.64 min.	3.60 min.	3.60 min.
Average turnout time (target: ≤ 1 minute)	0.85 min.	0.72 min.	0.75 min.
% of fire/medical/rescue calls responded to within 4 minutes	64.6%	65.0%	66.0%
Average response time to hazardous materials (HazMat) incidents (target: ≤ 10 minutes)	10.05 min.	10.5 min.	10.5 min.
% of HazMat incidents responded to within 10 minutes	62%	60%	60%
% of structure fires contained within the room of origin (target: ≥ 70%)	78%	70%	70%
% of fires where cause was determined (target: ≥ 85%)	96%	97%	95%
Fires per 1,000 population (target: ≤ 5)	3.86	5.0	5.0
% of commercial properties inspected annually (target: 100%)	99%	98%	98%
Workload			
Building fires	321	300	310
Medical calls	17,638	18,000	18,000
HazMat calls	139	150	200
Participants in fire prevention education events	36,902	60,000	60,000
Annual inspections performed by suppression companies	6,211	6,000	6,000
Annual inspections performed by inspectors	3,039	3,200	3,500

Source: Adapted from City of Winston-Salem, N.C., *FY 2012–2013 Adopted Budget*, 118. By permission.

The expense of administering a good performance measurement system is not trivial, but neither are the benefits of a good system. Because of its value to board members, appointed administrators, supervisors, and the general citizenry, performance measurement has been endorsed by a host of professional associations, including the International City/County Management Association, the Government Finance Officers Association, the Governmental Accounting Standards Board, and the National Academy of Public Administration.

Performance Management

Performance management is the purposeful use of performance information to improve operations and services, and more generally, to make better decisions. Some local governments engage in performance management only to a modest extent, using performance information for a few decisions affecting a few programs. Others claim to be more heavily engaged in performance management and often have nice charts showing how performance information *should influence decisions*, but they

Figure 10.1.   Example of Performance Measures for Social Services (Annual Trend Data)

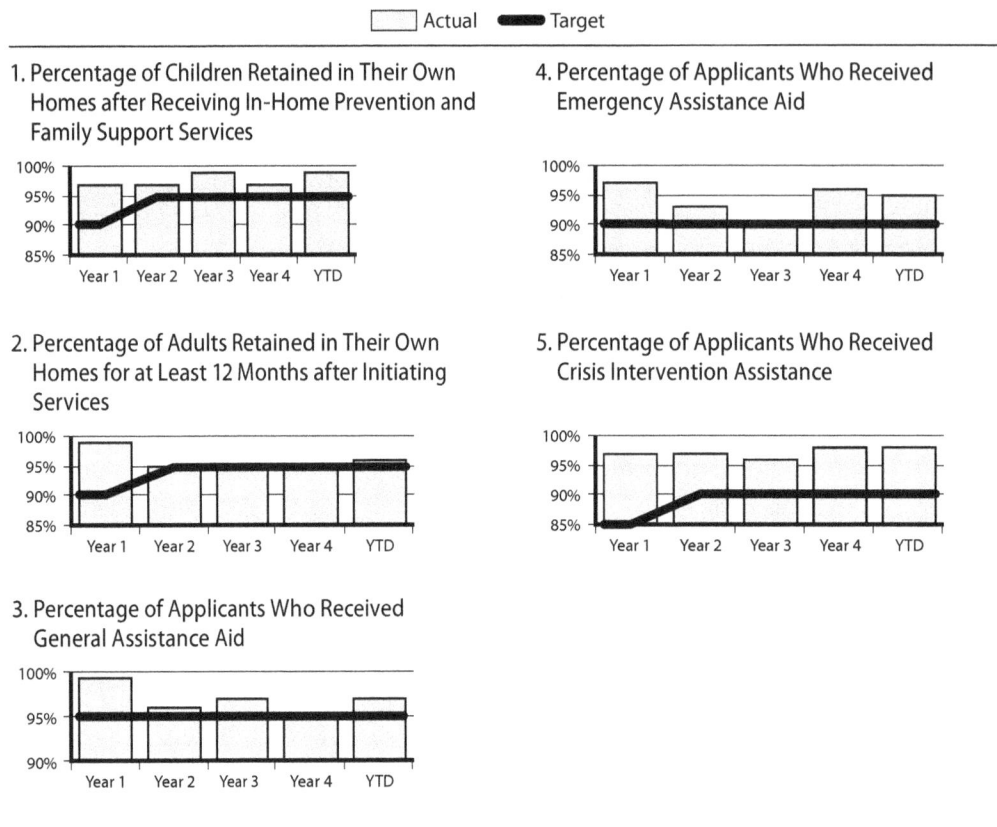

Actual ⬜   Target ▬

1. Percentage of Children Retained in Their Own
   Homes after Receiving In-Home Prevention and
   Family Support Services

4. Percentage of Applicants Who Received
   Emergency Assistance Aid

2. Percentage of Adults Retained in Their Own
   Homes for at Least 12 Months after Initiating
   Services

5. Percentage of Applicants Who Received
   Crisis Intervention Assistance

3. Percentage of Applicants Who Received
   General Assistance Aid

Source: Adapted from Rockingham County, N.C., *Rockingham County Performance Management Program: Comprehensive 2011–2012 Mid-Year Report*, 22, http://www.co.rockingham.nc.us/docview.aspx?docid= 28205. By permission.

sometimes are able to muster little evidence to show that it *actually does have* that influence. City and county governments that actually do engage meaningfully in performance management typically take some of the following approaches:

- *Use of performance information in the budget process.* Performance measures in such engaged governments are more than simply "decorations" in the budget document.
- *Benchmarking as a catalyst for performance improvement, not as a defense of the status quo.* Benchmarkers who are serious about performance management willingly expose gaps between their organization's performance and that of top performers and seek ways to close those performance gaps.[4]

---

4. David N. Ammons, "A Proper Mentality for Benchmarking," *Public Administration Review* 59 (March/April 1999): 105–9.

- *Regularly scheduled performance strategy sessions.* Performance information is reviewed regularly in these sessions, problems are identified, and strategies for improvement are developed.
- *Meaningful integration of performance information into influential management processes.* Key processes, such as budgeting, human resource development, and strategic planning, draw routinely on performance information.
- *Individual acts of performance management throughout the organization.* Most of the documented successes of performance management have occurred at the program level, where departmental managers have identified opportunities for improvement and have had the authority to make operational changes.

Use of Performance Information in Budgeting

The budget process provides an opportunity to influence program design and priorities within and across various services. The budget itself is a financial document, but in fact it is much more than that. It is a financial document that reflects program planning and service priorities in financial terms and also, ideally, in terms of performance expectations.

Some public sector budgets retain a strictly line-item format, listing appropriations for each detailed expenditure category. Many governments, however, have adopted formats more conducive to management or policy deliberations. Program budgets, for example, omit most of the object-of-expenditure details that characterize line-item budgets. Instead, they are organized around programs or types of service and report only broader categories of anticipated expenditures like personal services, operations, and capital outlay. Program budgets often include several measures of performance that reveal past performance and reflect performance expectations for the future.

Another prominent budget format is the performance budget. Once again, many line-item details are omitted from the document itself, and broader categories of expenditure are organized around departments, activities, or programs. In the case of performance budgeting, measures of performance become the central focus of budget deliberations as governing boards and managers discuss performance successes and disappointments, hammer out plans for performance improvement and resource reallocation, and focus on budgetary decisions that will enable operating units to achieve desired performance levels.

A local government's decision to choose a performance budget format over a line-item format does not guarantee a change in the focus or nature of budgetary debate. However, it does set the stage for budget deliberations that focus a little less on office supplies, fuel, insurance premiums, and other categories of expenditure, and a lot more on services and program results. Budget formats that incorporate good performance measures—especially efficiency and outcome measures—recognize and advance the planning and managerial opportunities of the budgetary process. They are designed to equip elected and appointed decision makers with the performance facts and figures for a given program, as well as the resource facts and figures, that will help them plan wisely and manage prudently.

Although the Government Finance Officers Association (GFOA) refrains from endorsing one particular budget format over another, it nevertheless advocates the use of performance measurement. Included in the guidance accompanying the GFOA's Distinguished Budget Presentation Award criteria are recommendations regarding unit goals, objectives, and performance measures.[5]

The unit goals and objectives criterion encourages each local government to document a given program's stated goals and quantifiable objectives, including a timeframe for accomplishment. The performance measures criterion encourages each local government to track and report on performance data that are directly related to the stated goals and quantifiable objectives, and more importantly, performance data that focus on results and accomplishments rather than inputs. Despite all the advantages that performance measurement offers and the numerous endorsements it boasts, the act of incorporating performance measures into the budget process will not make the often arduous task of budget decisions suddenly simple. Performance measures will help identify operational strengths and weaknesses and will gauge changes in efficiency and progress toward meeting objectives, but they can neither formulate the perfect budget nor prescribe remedies for operational deficiencies. Governing boards will still struggle to set priorities—and struggle to stretch resources to fund those priorities—and operating officials must still design program-improvement strategies. But performance measures can provide a baseline and a manner of gauging the success or failure of those strategies.

Rarely will budget decisions be made solely on the strength of performance measures. Well-intentioned strategies of rewarding good performance with budgetary increases and penalizing poor performance with budget reductions inevitably deteriorate when crucial programs, struggling and seemingly losing ground to intractable problems, might be helped by a budgetary boost. When crime statistics are climbing, should the governing board penalize the police department or sheriff's office with a blanket reduction, or should it reinforce law enforcement efforts with a budgetary increase?

Even if performance measures rarely yield clear budgetary direction, they almost always contribute positively to the process. Difficult decisions are best made with clear evidence of program performance and realistic expectations of future impact. Perhaps more important, awareness of downward performance trends often prompts managers to design remedies prior to budget deliberations. These suggested remedies may then be presented in the budget process. Furthermore, meaningful performance measures can enhance communication between governing boards and managers regarding performance expectations and service priorities.

---

5. Government Finance Officers Association, *GFOA Detailed Criteria Location Guide: Distinguished Budget Presentation Awards Program*, http://www.gfoa.org/sites/default /files/BudgetDetailedCriteriaLocationGuideFY2015.pdf.

Benchmarking as a Catalyst for Performance Improvement

Most of the benchmarking done in the public sector takes one of two forms:

- best-practice benchmarking or
- comparison of performance statistics as benchmarks.

The first of these forms, best-practice benchmarking, is used much less commonly by governments than is the second. Best-practice benchmarking follows the private sector's formal benchmarking model, popularized when corporate giants such as Xerox and Motorola analyzed the procedures of benchmarking partners from other industries to improve their own practices. A local government applying this best-practice benchmarking model focuses on a single process in its operation (e.g., the procurement process, the issuance of permits, or the development review process), identifies other organizations that achieve superior results from that process, carefully analyzes the process in its own organization and the process in its benchmarking partners' organizations, identifies factors that contribute to the superior results achieved by its partners, and figures out how to modify its own process to improve results. Because this approach focuses on processes and identifies performance leaders, it is linked to the search for best practices and carries that label.

The second form is the most common type of benchmarking in the public sector. In this form of benchmarking, government units compare their own performance statistics with performance standards or with the performance targets and actual results of other units. For example, a property appraisal unit in one county government might compare its appraisal accuracy, based on the degree to which appraised values match market prices from actual sales, with the appraisal accuracy of other counties, or it might compare the daily workload of its appraisers with the typical production rates reported by the International Association of Assessing Officers.[6] Occasionally, major cooperative projects of considerable scope are developed around this form of benchmarking. Longstanding examples include a multi-jurisdictional performance measurement project involving more than a dozen cities and towns in North Carolina, coordinated by the University of North Carolina's School of Government, and similar projects in Florida and Tennessee.[7]

---

6. Richard R. Almy, Robert J. Gloudemans, and Garth E. Thimgan, *Assessment Practices: Self Evaluation Guide* (Chicago: International Association of Assessing Officers, 1991).

7. Carla Pizzarella, "Achieving Useful Performance and Cost Information in a Comparative Performance Measurement Consortium," *International Journal of Public Administration* 27, nos. 8 & 9 (2004): 631–50; William C. Rivenbark ed., *A Guide to the North Carolina Local Government Performance Measurement Project* (Chapel Hill, N.C.: Institute of Government, University of North Carolina at Chapel Hill, 2001). For current information on the three projects listed here, see (1) the School of Government's searchable "Resources" index at http://www.sog.unc.edu/resources/microsites/north-carolina -benchmarking-project; (2) the Florida Benchmarking Consortium's website at http:// www.flbenchmark.org/; and (3) the University of Tennessee Knoxville's "Tennessee Research and Creative Exchange (TRACE)" web page at http://trace.tennessee.edu /utk_mtas_tmbp/.

Comparison of performance statistics differs from best-practice benchmarking in three major ways. First, it typically focuses broadly on multiple services or operations, rather than narrowly on a single key process. Second, it focuses primarily on results and only secondarily, if at all, on the details of the processes that produce these results. Third, it is diagnostic rather than prescriptive. Comparing performance statistics reveals performance strengths and weaknesses vis-à-vis performance standards or the performance results achieved by others. This is a diagnostic function; it does not tell officials how to improve results. In contrast, best-practice benchmarking is designed to reveal the practices of top performers that account for their superior performance results. The intent is to identify best practices for adaptation and use by the benchmarking organization. This is a prescriptive function.

Local government officials who choose to compare performance statistics rather than to use best-practice benchmarking accept a trade-off. They trade the depth of analysis associated with best-practice benchmarking for the breadth of coverage that comes with the comparison of performance statistics across several government operations. Those who make this trade-off do not necessarily rule out more detailed analysis at a later point. In fact, the broad comparison of performance statistics across several departments may help identify functions that would benefit most from best-practice benchmarking, operations analysis, or the application of other managing-for-results strategies.

Performance Strategy Sessions

The odds that performance data will actually be used go up when managers establish performance management routines that, on a regular basis, prompt the use of performance information. One such routine is the practice of holding regularly scheduled performance strategy sessions to discuss performance information and brainstorm ideas for improving results.[8]

The most well-known examples of performance strategy sessions in local government are the New York City Police Department's CompStat system and the city of Baltimore's CitiStat system, but many other varieties of performance strategy sessions operate elsewhere. The characteristics that performance strategy sessions hold in common as performance management routines are the regularity of their occurrence (i.e., more often than just annual events); their reliance on solid performance information; their focus on goals, objectives, and performance results; and their usual practice of engaging operating personnel in the discussion rather than relying solely on the insights of managers and analysts. Although many systems have been modeled on

---

8. Performance strategy sessions have also been called "how-are-we-doing sessions" and "learning forums." *See* Blaine Liner, Harry P. Hatry, Elisa Vinson, Ryan Allen, Pat Dusenbury, Scott Bryant, and Ron Snell, *Making Results-Based State Government Work* (Washington, D.C.: Urban Institute, 2001); Donald P. Moynihan, *The Dynamics of Performance Management: Constructing Information and Reform* (Washington, D.C.: Georgetown University Press, 2008); and Donald P. Moynihan, "Goal-Based Learning and the Future of Performance Management," *Public Administration Review* 65, no. 2 (March/April 2005): 203–16.

CompStat or CitiStat—for instance, Louisville (Kentucky) has LouieStat, Somerville (Massachusetts) has SomerStat, and King County (Washington) has KingStat—most of these *stat systems* deviate in various ways from the originals.

The original CompStat and CitiStat systems (both systems have changed and evolved over time) were acclaimed for the performance improvements they achieved. Both required heavy time commitments from executives—i.e., the police commissioner in New York City and the mayor in Baltimore. Several of the variations modeled on these systems sought ways to lighten the executive load and also to reduce the confrontational aspects of CompStat and CitiStat meetings that had been highlighted—some say exaggerated—by the media. The performance gains reported by these alternative stat models have not always matched those secured by the originals.

Whether the chief executive—the city manager in council-manager cities—must be in attendance for performance strategy sessions to succeed is a difficult question to answer without first knowing the performance culture of a given local government. The presence of the executive signals the session's importance to everyone involved and increases the likelihood that the discussion and follow-up assignments will be taken seriously. Without the executive's presence, would these sessions slide into "show and tell" presentations? Some do, even with the executive in attendance.

The keys to the success of performance strategy sessions are preparation and the seriousness of participants about performance improvement. Must the chief executive be present for these to occur? Careful analysis of Baltimore's CitiStat revealed that much of the real performance management action occurred not at the grand CitiStat meetings with the mayor and top executives but at the AgencyStat meetings of the departments, which began as dress rehearsals for the CitiStat meetings but soon became the standard method of managing individual departments.[9] The mayor was not present at AgencyStat meetings. If the culture is right, the department head can be the executive presence needed for a good performance strategy session at the department or program level.

Integrating Performance Information into Management Processes

Only when performance information truly adds value to fundamental management processes and *for that reason* is regularly integrated into those processes will data-driven decisions become the norm. For this to happen, performance measures must be relevant to the process at hand and they must address important dimensions of performance—service quality, efficiency, and effectiveness. The performance information must bring something important to the decision-making table.

Local governments that have effectively integrated performance information into key management processes—budget administration, human resource management, strategic planning, etc.—are more likely to use their performance information and

---

9. Robert D. Behn, *The PerformanceStat Potential: A Leadership Strategy for Producing Results* (Washington, D.C.: Brookings Institution Press, 2014).

demonstrate benefits from its use.[10] For instance, solid performance information has been integral to gainsharing and other incentive programs used effectively in the human resource management strategies of several local governments. Differing in important ways from the profit-sharing programs common in the private sector, gainsharing programs incentivize public employees to save taxpayer dollars while maintaining service quality. Although there are different approaches to implementing gainsharing plans in local government, the basic idea involves paying employee bonuses when budget surpluses are realized and performance targets are met. Any payment comes from the surplus, not from a special appropriation. Performance information must confirm that performance targets have been met. While there can be controversy over this type of management tool, it does integrate performance information into a key management process—human resource management—and increases employee buy-in to monitoring, managing, and improving the performance of service delivery.[11]

Strategic planning, in which elected officials and administrators work together to develop and adopt long-term goals for their communities, is widely accepted as a best practice in local government. Although each strategic plan is expected to be community-specific, common goals often include community safety, infrastructure, economic and community development, environmental sustainability, and quality of life. The greatest challenge for strategic planning often lies at the follow-through stage, where the task of monitoring progress and managing results opens the door for the use of performance information. Crime rates and response times collected and reported for police services, for example, can be used to track progress toward the goal of community safety. The high-profile use of key measures in strategic planning increases the likelihood that they will be used for other policy and management decisions as well.

An approach to performance management called the *balanced scorecard* is often tied closely to the goals established in a community's strategic plan. Originally designed for the private sector, the balanced scorecard replaces corporations' traditional emphasis on financial metrics with a broader focus on four performance perspectives: financial, customer, internal process, and learning and growth. The balanced scorecard provides balance between "short- and long-term objectives, between financial and non-financial measures, between lagging and leading indicators, and between external and internal perspectives."[12] In public sector applications, the four perspectives often have been modified slightly to better reflect public sector priorities. The strength of the balanced scorecard for local governments adopting this approach has been the focused effort it has elicited from managers and elected officials to

---

10. David N. Ammons and William C. Rivenbark, "Factors Influencing the Use of Performance Data to Improve Municipal Services: Evidence from the North Carolina Benchmarking Project," *Public Administration Review* 68, no. 2 (2008): 304–18.

11. David N. Ammons and William C. Rivenbark, "Gainsharing in Local Government," *Popular Government* 71, no. 3 (2006): 31–37.

12. Robert S. Kaplan and David P. Norton, *The Balanced Scorecard* (Boston: Harvard Business School Press, 1996), viii.

connect performance measures with long-term community goals through the four perspectives of this management tool.[13]

Local government officials often make the decision to pause and evaluate the success of a selected program based on the established goals and objectives for which the program was created. Evaluation requires a good set of performance measures to assess whether the program is meeting expectations, whether its scope or design needs to be changed, and even whether it should be continued or discontinued.[14] Consider, for example, a local government that decides to implement a new approach to street cleaning, hoping to increase the percentage of citizens assessing this function favorably. After a selected period, the next step would be to evaluate the success of this change. Evaluation of this basic type benefits from the baseline data available if performance measurement already was integrated into management processes.

Individual Acts of Performance Management

As city and county governments have become more and more interested in the potential benefits of performance management, some have adopted elaborate performance management systems designed to channel performance information to elected officials and senior management teams to be used for decisions made at that level. The real action in performance management, however, often is found elsewhere. Many of the performance management successes of governments occur not at the top of the organization but down in the ranks, where decision makers at the program level use performance information to improve operations and services. Cumulatively, these individual acts of performance management can have a big effect.

The manager of the parks and recreation program in a medium-sized North Carolina community was committed not only to collecting and reporting performance measures for the purpose of accountability but also to the use of performance information to manage her program. One of the effectiveness measures she reported each year was the "rate of repeat registrations," which demonstrated—perhaps even more than end-of-program satisfaction surveys—just how much participants liked the programs being offered. Another effectiveness measure she relied upon was the "external participation rate," providing feedback on service demand from individuals outside the city limits. While the rate of repeat registrations had remained steady over the past several years, the external participation rate had continued to increase. Based on this external demand, the program manager then decided to offer a policy recommendation to the city manager and ultimately to the governing board to implement different rates for program fees—one for municipal residents and a higher one for non-municipal residents. The governing board balked at the different rates proposed but appreciated the staff's action in calling attention to the need for additional resources to cover the costs of non-citizen users. The decision was made to

---

13. William C. Rivenbark and Eric J. Peterson, "A Balanced Approach to Implementing the Balanced Scorecard," *Popular Government* 74, no. 1 (2008): 31–37.

14. Robert D. Behn, "Why Measure Performance? Different Purposes Require Different Measures," *Public Administration Review* 63, no. 5 (2003): 586–606.

request an annual payment from the county to help offset the cost of program delivery. This request was approved by the county, which resulted in program expansion and slightly higher repeat registration and external participation rates.

The manager of recycling services in another North Carolina community was also committed to using performance information to manage his operation. Recycling had long been highlighted as a priority in the community's strategic plan, but despite supportive pronouncements few advances had occurred in recent years. Key performance measures, such as recycling set-out rate and solid waste diversion rate, remained fairly stagnant. The recycling manager used this performance information to press for additional resources to mount a comprehensive education campaign on the importance of recycling for becoming a "green" community. The effectiveness of the education campaign would be gauged by progress on key performance measures. Funds were authorized and the strategy worked—so well, in fact, that additional resources were needed. Not only did the community see major gains in the recycling set-out rate and solid waste diversion rate, it also experienced major demand for new recycling bins to meet the needs of a citizenry energized about household recycling services.

There are three elements in these two individual acts of performance management that are common in successful performance data use. First, line managers took responsibility for using performance information to drive change. They did not assume that performance management was the work of senior management alone. Second, each manager was inspired to make changes in the current operating strategy by a good set of performance measures—a set that included more than rudimentary measures of inputs and outputs. Third, the performance measures inspired changes and then were used not only to support the recommended changes but also to document the success of those changes, once adopted.

Conclusion

Many local governments have undertaken performance measurement with the best of intentions. Most managers have been pleased with the contributions their performance reports have made to their government unit's accountability, but many have been disappointed that the measures have had less influence on the quality and efficiency of services than they anticipated. Therefore, we conclude this chapter with some parting thoughts on how local government officials can increase the utility of their performance measurement systems and increase the likelihood of embracing performance management at all levels of the organization.

The likelihood that performance measures will be used as a management tool is greater when the following steps are taken:

- *Align performance measures with goals and objectives.* Performance measures should focus on important dimensions of service and should gauge progress on key objectives.
- *Measure efficiency and effectiveness—not just workload.* Output (workload) measures are the most rudimentary form of performance measurement. In contrast, systems that also report a department's efficiency, the quality of its

services, and the effectiveness of its programs receive a lot more attention from managers—and these systems deserve to receive more attention because they are much more valuable.

- *Present performance measures in context.* A performance measure reported out of context is "just a number" to all but the best-informed consumers of that information. Last year's numbers provide the easiest context for this year's numbers, but a more informative context would be any widely accepted and applicable standards of service quality and efficiency or the performance marks of respected counterparts. Presented in context, performance statistics become more valuable—and to a much broader audience, even interesting!
- *Link the performance measurement system to important policy processes and to other management systems.* High-impact performance measurement systems are linked to important processes and contribute meaningfully to major and minor policy and managerial decisions.

Additional Resources

A Performance Management Framework for State and Local Government. Chicago: National Performance Management Advisory Commission, 2010.

Ammons, David N. (ed.), *Leading Performance Management in Local Government.* Washington, D.C.: International City/County Management Association, 2008.

——.*Municipal Benchmarks: Assessing Local Performance and Establishing Community Standards*, 3rd ed. Armonk, N.Y.: M. E. Sharpe, 2012.

——.*"Getting Real* about Performance Management." *Public Management* 97, no. 11 (December 2015): 8–11.

Fountain, James, Wilson Campbell, Terry Patton, Paul Epstein, and Mandi Cohn. *Reporting Performance Information: Suggested Criteria for Effective Communication.* Norwalk, Conn: Governmental Accounting Standards Board, 2003.

Hatry, Harry P. *Performance Measurement: Getting Results*, 2nd ed. Washington, D.C.: Urban Institute Press, 2006.

Hatry, Harry P., D. M. Fisk, J. R. Hall Jr., P. S. Schaenman, and L. Snyder. *How Effective Are Your Community Services? Procedures for Performance Measurement*, 3rd ed. Washington, D.C.: Urban Institute and International City/County Management Association, 2006.

Poister, Theodore H., Maria P. Aristigueta, and Jeremy L. Hall, *Managing and Measuring Performance in Public and Nonprofit Organizations: An Integrated Approach*, 2nd ed.. San Francisco: Jossey-Bass, 2015.

Chapter 11

Economic Development

Jonathan Q. Morgan

1. Introduction: What Is Economic Development?

Local governments promote Economic-Development to ensure that their residents have access to jobs and to build vibrant and prosperous communities. With most elected officials reluctant to increase tax rates, municipalities and counties often turn to economic development as a way to generate new tax revenue. New private investment within a jurisdiction is the essential mechanism through which job creation and tax base expansion occur. An expanded tax base creates new revenues that local governments need to fund public investments in amenities, education, and infrastructure that make their communities attractive to businesses, workers, and residents.

Economic development is both a process and a set of desired outcomes that communities seek to achieve. At its core, economic development is what communities do to stimulate private investment, job creation, and wealth creation. The extent to which communities engage in this process can vary considerably based on local preferences, resources, and capacity. There is empirical evidence to suggest that local governments with greater capacity tend to do more in support of economic development.[1] Some localities intervene directly in trying to encourage economic development by offering financial incentives and various types of assistance to businesses. Others take a more passive, indirect approach and focus on creating a local environment that is conducive to business investment through lower taxes and streamlined regulations.

---

1. Jonathan Q. Morgan, Michele Hoyman, and Jamie McCall, "Everything but the Kitchen Sink: Factors Associated with Local Economic Development Strategy Use," *Economic Development Quarterly* 33, no. 4 (November 2019): 267–78.

In defining economic development, it is useful to draw a distinction between *growth* and *development*. Growth refers to quantitative increase in terms of more people, rooftops, businesses, and the like. In the short run, this sort of expansion in a local economy can produce jobs and higher business and tax revenues. However, rapid unbridled growth can also strain existing infrastructure and cause negative externalities or unintended consequences, such as traffic congestion, overcrowded schools, and environmental pollution. In other words, growth may not always be unquestionably good for a community. For example, attracting industries that create a lot of low-wage jobs will not do much to reduce poverty and raise incomes. Adding more businesses that pollute the air and water can jeopardize the natural environment and negatively affect public health. By contrast, the concept of development is about making qualitative improvements in a local economy and using growth as a means to achieve that end. Development seeks to ensure that having more/getting bigger (i.e., growth) is sustainable and actually makes a community better off in the long run. The bottom line is that growth can be good, but development is better. Development indicators will gauge the extent to which the needle moves on income, wealth, and the standard of living for residents.

In many small, rural communities and high-poverty urban areas, the prospects for economic development are inextricably linked to efforts to build the local assets and capacity needed to succeed. It may be important for these communities to address challenges with respect to the fundamental building blocks of prosperity, such as education, workforce, and infrastructure. Economic development in low-resource communities may be sorely constrained until the foundational prerequisites of development are in place. In this sense, economic development relies on community development efforts that build local capacity and help communities become "development-ready."[2] A capacity-building approach to economic development can also emphasize social equity and aim to enable everyone to fully participate in the economy and realize their potential.[3]

The Context for Economic Development

The process of economic development does not happen in a vacuum. It occurs within a larger context comprised of dynamics that are, for the most part, beyond the control of local officials. These include

- fluctuating economic cycles,
- uncertain fiscal conditions,
- rapid technological innovation and automation,
- pressures of electoral politics,

---

2. Rhonda Phillips and Robert H. Pittman, "A Framework for Community and Economic Development," in *An Introduction to Community Development*, 2nd ed., ed. Rhonda Phillips and Robert H. Pittman (New York: Routledge, 2015), 3–21.

3. M.P. Feldman, T. Hadjimichael, T. Kemeny, and L. Lanahan, "The Logic of Economic Development: A Definition and Model for Investment," *Environment and Planning C: Government and Policy* 34 (2016): 5–21.

- globalization and trade policies,
- ongoing threats to national security,
- periodic natural disasters, and
- increasing economic disparities.

When there is a downturn in the national or global economy, the effects at the local level are readily apparent. Like a contagion, a major slowdown in one sector or geographic area can quickly spread elsewhere, causing economic mayhem. Companies shed jobs, lay off workers, shut down plants, and scrap plans for making new capital investments. The Great Recession of 2007–2008 is a case in point that illustrates how a slowing economy creates fiscal pressures for government. A drop-off in economic activity almost always puts downward pressures on tax revenues, which can leave public officials with budget gaps to fill. In tough fiscal times, economic development takes on an even greater sense of urgency, even though many communities will have fewer resources available in the near term to jump-start the local economy.

New technologies are changing many aspects of everyday life and are rapidly disrupting multiple sectors of the economy. Innovative products and services come along that make existing ones obsolete through a process of "creative destruction."[4] For example, the once-dominant Blockbuster Video, with its brick-and-mortar rental model, got put out of business by Netflix movies-by-mail, Red Box kiosks, and online streaming. Similarly, the rise of digital photography totally transformed the way people take and share pictures, causing industry leaders like Kodak to fundamentally reinvent themselves. Consider how modernized ATMs and online banking have drastically altered how customers interact with financial institutions. Many aspects of manufacturing are now highly automated and technology-based, which has significant ramifications for the nature of jobs in that sector and its prospects for boosting employment. As manufacturing companies invest more heavily in technology and automate production processes, they typically will need fewer workers. Technology-driven gains in productivity enable manufacturers to make more widgets with fewer people. The employment displacement effect of technology/automation hits workers in lower-wage, labor-intensive parts of manufacturing the hardest.

The timing of political election cycles can create uncertainty and make it difficult to take a longer-term view of economic development. When political control shifts significantly or when there is a sizable influx of newly elected officials, there is often a push to do things differently. At the state level in North Carolina, changing political leadership resulted in a new regional development framework and the formation of a new public-private partnership tasked with doing many vital economic development functions.[5] At the local level, wholesale changes in county and municipal elected boards can spur interest in reshaping the way jurisdictions

---

4. Joseph Schumpeter, *Capitalism, Society, and Democracy* (Harper & Brothers, 1942).

5. Jonathan Q. Morgan, *Economic Development Handbook*, 4th ed. (North Carolina Economic Development Association and UNC School of Government, 2016).

structure and implement economic development. Partly as a response to changes in the makeup of governing boards in recent years, many North Carolina localities have instituted new structural arrangements for doing economic development. While causing some short-term uncertainty, these sorts of changes can possibly result in innovative approaches that work better than the status quo.

The intersection of national and global forces also shapes the context in which communities try to promote economic development. The election of a new U.S. president in 2016 ushered in a somewhat different approach to international trade than recent administrations have taken. The Trump administration's harder line on trade imbalances with major countries like China and the proposed imposition of tariffs can have significant ramifications for U.S. businesses, workers, and consumers. The decisions of nations who are major trading partners with the United States can create unexpected disruptions to well-established practices and systems. For example, in 2018, China instituted a major policy change with respect to the recyclable waste materials it imports. By placing more stringent limits on the amount of contamination allowed in the mixed paper and plastics recyclables it takes in from other countries, China's new policy is drastically altering the global markets for recyclable commodities. In response, many U.S. municipalities are re-examining their recycling programs, and some have substantially curtailed, if not abandoned, curbside recycling.[6]

The occurrence of extreme weather events such as hurricanes, tornados, flooding, drought, and other natural disasters (e.g., earthquakes, wildfires, etc.) is another part of the context for local economic development in many regions of the United States. These weather-related events can wreak havoc on local economies, and the process of rebuilding is time-consuming and costly. The frequency and severity of extreme weather events in recent years have caused many communities and regions to more explicitly incorporate disaster resilience into their strategies for economic development.

Entrenched economic disparities, especially along the lines of race and geography, are becoming prominent features of the modern knowledge-based economy. As the economy morphs into one that is increasingly driven by higher-order knowledge, technology, and creative talent, certain people and places are at risk of falling even further behind. Workers with limited educational attainment and technical skills who are concentrated in low-wage sectors are finding it particularly difficult to get ahead. The economic challenges persist for low-income minority communities that have suffered from institutionalized discrimination and disinvestment. Many small, rural communities continue to lose industries and population and face an uncertain future in this dynamic new economy.

Against this daunting backdrop, local efforts to promote economic development will require strategic direction and a sustained level of commitment if a jurisdiction hopes to achieve desired outcomes. The multifaceted context for economic

---

6. Corinne Rico and Cooper Martin *Rethinking Recycling: How Cities Can Adapt to Evolving Markets*, (National League of Cities, 2018).

development poses significant challenges for public officials. But it also presents many potential opportunities that communities can exploit if they have a proactive vision and overarching strategy in place to navigate this arduous terrain.

2. How Does the Process of Economic Development Work?

Understanding the process of economic development requires an examination of the specific mechanisms through which new private investment occurs. Various theoretical perspectives attempt to identify these mechanisms and explain how they contribute to the formation of private investment and the prosperity it brings.[7] Two classical theoretical perspectives have had a lasting impact on how we think about the economic-development process: location theory and economic base theory.

Traditional location theory sought to pinpoint which factors drive the location decisions of firms and tended to emphasize transportation costs.[8] The early consensus was that, all else being equal, firms will choose to locate where they can minimize transport costs. Contemporary research suggests that the list of priority location factors varies by industry and includes items such as market access, the availability of skilled labor, labor costs, available land and buildings, corporate tax rates, state and local incentives, and quality of life. The practical application of location theory is evident in state and local efforts to influence business location decisions by enhancing their competitive position with respect to one or more of the location factors thought to be highly important.

The other classical approach that has deeply shaped policy and practice is economic base theory (also known as export base theory).[9] A fundamental tenet of economic base theory is that exports—goods and services sold outside the local economy—are the primary drivers of growth. Firms that export comprise the basic sector, while those serving local markets are considered non-basic. Basic/export industries bring new money into the local economy, some of which ripples throughout many other sectors by way of what is called the "multiplier." The multiplier captures linkage between the basic and non-basic sectors and indicates how much a direct investment/expenditure in the basic sector will impact the local/regional economy.[10] In practice, economic/export base theory is part of the reason manufacturing has been a primary target for industrial recruitment. Manufacturing is the

---

7. Emil E. Malizia and Edward J. Feser, *Understanding Local Economic Development* (New Brunswick, N.J.:Center for Urban Policy Research, Rutgers University, 1999).

8. John P. Blair and Michael C. Carroll, *Local Economic Development: Analysis, Practices, and Globalization*, 2nd ed. (Los Angeles: Sage, 2009).

9. Homer Hoyt, "Homer Hoyt on the Concept of the Economic Base," *Land Economics* 30 (1954): 182–86. *See also* Hans Blumenfeld, "The Economic Base of the Metropolis," *Journal of the American Institute of Planners* 21 (1955): 114–32; Charles Tiebout, *The Community Economic Base Study* (Committee for Economic Development, 1962).

10. Malizia and Feser, *Understanding Local Economic Development*.

quintessential export industry and typically creates a higher multiplier effect than non-basic industries such as retail, construction, and many services. The thinking is that expanding the manufacturing sector will spur economic activity in the non-basic sector among firms that primarily serve local markets. A shortcoming of economic base theory is that industries do not always fit neatly into the basic or non-basic sector, plus there are exceptions to the norm. For example, there may be instances in which large-scale or highly specialized retail and health care facilities function as basic/export industries, although in most cases those activities would be classified as non-basic/local-serving. Another concern is that the primacy of exports as the driver of growth neglects important indigenous or "homegrown" sources of private investment and job creation.[11]

As the U.S. economy has transformed structurally and become more knowledge-based and innovation-oriented, economic-development professionals have embraced alternative theories of growth and development. One is based on the idea that innovative entrepreneurs and small firms are substantial job creators. In fact, some research shows that small firms create more jobs than large businesses. One of the most influential studies examined U.S. business establishments and found that firms with twenty or fewer employees created two-thirds of all net new jobs and firms with 100 or fewer employees created about 80 percent of net new jobs.[12] Another study points to a subset of small firms—startups—as the dominant source of job creation. This study found that firms younger than one year old create an average of 3 million jobs annually, while more mature existing firms are "net job destroyers" and lose 1 million jobs net each year.[13]

Other research casts doubt on the job-creation potential of small businesses. While one study demonstrated that small firms (those with fewer than twenty employees) created nearly 80 percent of all net new jobs over a thirteen-year period, it attributed this mostly to substantial gross job losses among larger firms rather than huge amounts of job creation by small firms.[14] Among small businesses, the study found that job creation is fueled by expansions of existing firms to a much greater extent than the formation of startups. One of the more recent studies concluded that small businesses account for higher levels of job creation than larger firms, but only slightly so.[15] Yet another recent study was unable to establish a definitive connection between the presence of small businesses and job growth, leading the author to suggest that

---

11. Blair and Carroll, *Local Economic Development.*

12. David Birch, "Who Creates Jobs?," *The Public Interest* 65 (1981): 7, http://www .nationalaffairs.com/public_interest/detail/who-creates-jobs.

13. Tim Kane, "The Importance of Startups in Job Creation and Job Destruction" (Ewing Marion Kauffman Foundation, 2010), http://www.kauffman.org/uploadedFiles /firm_formation_importance_of_startups.pdf.

14. Kelly Edmiston, "The Role of Small and Large Businesses in Economic Development," *Economic Review* (Federal Reserve Bank of Kansas City, 2007), http://www.kansascityfed .org/publicat/econrev/pdf/2q07edmi.pdf.

15. D. Neumark, B. Wall, and J. Zhang, "Do Small Businesses Create More Jobs? New Evidence for the United States from the National Establishment Time Series," *Review of Economics and Statistics* 93 (2011): 16–29.

small businesses may have the most potent effect on economic development when they grow and become larger establishments.[16]

The mixed and inconclusive research results on the relationship between small businesses and jobs have not deterred communities from instituting programs to support entrepreneurship. A key takeaway from the latest studies on this topic is that such efforts should focus on helping small, growth-oriented firms, often referred to as "gazelles," expand and grow to the next level with their operations. In many cases, these high-growth gazelle firms are innovators in their respective sectors working to launch new products, services, and technologies.

The concept of industry clusters has greatly influenced our thinking about economic development. It is the idea that having a concentration of related industries in a location can benefit firms and regions in ways that enhance their competitive advantage.[17] When firms in related industries are located in close proximity and reach a critical mass, they will likely attract supplier firms and enjoy lower transaction costs as a result. The cluster will also draw workers with specialized skills and produce knowledge spillovers that benefit firms. The host region can support the cluster by enlisting local organizations to ensure that a skilled labor force exists and by providing the specialized talent, services, technologies, and infrastructure that firms may need. The linkages and interdependencies among firms, industries, and supporting organizations we observe in many high-performing regional clusters are thought to be essential. Clusters tend to form and grow in regions where the specialized assets and resources exist (or could exist) to boost the competitiveness of firms and industries. Some prominent clusters in the United States are auto production in Detroit; financial services in New York City and Charlotte; carpet manufacturing in Dalton, Georgia; biotech and pharmaceuticals in Research Triangle, North Carolina; and information technology in Silicon Valley. In practice, the cluster framework helps regions to identify industrial specializations and better understand the linkages among firms, sectors, and the organizations that support them. Many states and regions use clusters to target their business attraction efforts. The extent to which regions can intentionally create clusters from scratch is the subject of ongoing debate.

A final conceptual lens through which to consider how growth and development occur is human capital. The supposition that human capital matters for economic development centers on how educational attainment, skill levels, and specialized knowledge influence the prosperity of both regions and workers. Much of the research literature has found formal educational attainment (e.g., years of schooling, having a college degree, etc.) to be an important predictor of wages, productivity, economic

---

16. Todd M. Gabe, *The Pursuit of Economic Development: Growing Good Jobs in U.S. Cities and States* (Palgrave Macmillan, 2017).

17. Michael Porter, "Location, Competition, and Economic Development: Local Clusters in a Global Economy," *Economic Development Quarterly* 14 (2000): 15–34; Jonathan Q. Morgan, "Clusters and Competitive Advantage: Finding a Niche in the New Economy," *Popular Government* 69, no. 3 (2004): 43–54.

activity, and growth.[18] A contemporary stream of work on human capital examines the role of creative talent and specific occupational/skills clusters in economic development. Studies in this vein have established that creative talent and certain higher-order skills are positively associated with various indicators of growth and development.[19] The practical application of human capital and creative talent theories is apparent in local, regional, and state efforts to enhance the education and skill levels of workers and better meet the workforce needs of employers. These perspectives are also prompting communities to devise strategies for becoming more attractive places for highly-skilled knowledge workers and people with creative talent. In this sense, human capital relates to the placemaking strategy discussed later.

While the various theoretical perspectives provide alternative explanations for how economic development works (or should work), they do not always demonstrate how the private investment that gets created, often at taxpayer expense, materially benefits a community and its residents in meaningful ways. This is partly why the North Carolina Supreme Court, in a landmark decision, ruled that local government support for economic development must fulfill a public purpose and not merely serve to benefit private businesses.[20]

3. The Relationship between Economic Development and Local Government Fiscal Concerns

Economic development is a concrete way for local governments to expand the local tax base. When businesses locate, expand, or start up in a jurisdiction; purchase real property, machinery, and equipment; and hire workers, they boost the revenues from local property and sales taxes. The base of taxable property and purchasing expands, which increases government revenue without having to raise tax rates. Increased tax revenue enables local governments to provide high-quality services and amenities in a cost-effective way, which helps reinforce the community's status as an attractive location for businesses, workers, and residents.

On the expenditure side of the ledger, there are cost dynamics that public officials will encounter in implementing economic development. One has to do with the "opportunity cost" of offering business incentives—the idea that public dollars spent

---

18. Gabe, *The Pursuit of Economic Development*. *See also* Jaison Abel and Todd M. Gabe, "Human Capital and Economic Activity in Urban America," *Regional Studies* 45, no. 8 (2011): 1079–90; J. Rauch, "Productivity Gains from Geographic Concentration of Human Capital: Evidence from the Cities," *Journal of Urban Economics* 34, no. 3 (1993): 380–400.

19. Gabe, *The Pursuit of Economic Development*; Richard Florida, Charlotta Mellander, and Kevin Stolarick, "Inside the Black Box of Regional Development—Human Capital, the Creative Class, and Tolerance," *Journal of Economic Geography* 8 (2008): 615–49.

20. Maready v. City of Winston-Salem, 342 N.C. 708 (1996). *See also* Tyler Mulligan, "When May NC Local Governments Pay an Economic Development Incentive?," *Coates' Canons: NC Local Government Law* (blog), December 17, 2013, https://canons.sog.unc.edu /when-may-nc-local-governments-pay-an-economic-development-incentive/.

on incentives are not available for other critical uses such as education, infrastructure, amenities, and the like. Another issue is that the costs of providing public services varies based on the type of land use and development being contemplated.[21] In most cases, commercial and industrial development projects will generate more than enough tax revenue to cover the costs of needed public services. By contrast, residential development projects typically do not produce sufficient tax revenue to offset the costs local governments incur to provide them with public services. This may depend on the density of the development, but residential projects usually exert higher demand for school facilities, water and sewer, road improvements, police and fire services, and transportation access, etc. This relates to another fiscal consideration with respect to economic development: how to pay for and finance the long-term infrastructure and capital improvements that will eventually be needed to support growth.

An important fiscal question concerns how taxes affect a jurisdiction's competitiveness for economic development. Practically speaking, taxes are but one component of the state and local business climate that shapes private investment and must be examined in this context. Considering taxes along with other key business climate variables, industry trade publications consistently rank North Carolina among the top five states with respect to its attractiveness for business locations. For example, North Carolina earned top honors as the number 1 state for business in a 2018 ranking by Forbes and garnered the overall number 2 spot in Site Selection's *2018 Top State Business Climate Rankings*.[22] The various business climate rankings are based on multiple criteria, including executive surveys, cost factors, labor supply, regulatory environment, tax policies, quality of life, and infrastructure. The Forbes state ranking includes taxes as part of business costs, along with labor and energy costs. The Site Selection ranking measures taxes as the state tax burden on mature and new firms.

In recent years, the North Carolina General Assembly has gradually reduced the corporate income tax rate in North Carolina to one of the lowest in the nation. One rationale for doing so is the sense that a lower corporate rate makes the state more competitive for business investment and job creation. While lowering the rate of a single tax can make a difference, most analysts recognize that businesses may also care about the total tax burden in a jurisdiction. The tax burden consists of multiple levels and types of taxes, including state, local, corporate, individual, sales, property, and unemployment insurance. Using these various taxes, the Tax Foundation's 2019 *State Business Tax Climate Index* ranks North Carolina as the third-best state on corporate taxes alone and number 12 overall with all taxes combined.[23]

---

21. Jonathan Q. Morgan, *Analyzing the Benefits and Costs of Economic Development Projects*, Community and Economic Development Bulletin 7 (UNC School of Government, April 2010), https://www.sog.unc.edu/sites/www.sog.unc.edu/files/reports/cedb7.pdf.

22. Mark Arend, "An Oasis of Opportunity," *Site Selection*, November 2018, https://siteselection.com/issues/2018/nov/business-climate-ranking-an-oasis-of-opportunity-cover.cfm.

23. Jared Walczak, Scott Drenkard, and Joseph Bishop-Henchman, "2019 State Business Tax Climate Index," *Tax Foundation*, September 26, 2018, https://taxfoundation.org/publications/state-business-tax-climate-index/.

North Carolina appears to be in a competitive position when it comes to taxes and business climate. But what evidence exists to support the notion that low taxes stimulate economic activity and private investment? As it turns out, numerous studies spanning decades have examined the relationship between taxes and economic growth. Although early research downplayed the role of taxes, the consensus among more recent studies is that taxes are generally detrimental to growth.[24] There is solid empirical evidence to show that states and regions with higher taxes experience lower levels of job growth and business activity, and vice versa.

Despite this verdict, there are reasons to consider taking a more nuanced view on the impact of taxes. First, in reality, it is difficult to isolate how taxes affect growth without also looking at government spending. When taxes go up or down, it is not safe to assume that spending will be unchanged. Some observers note the likelihood that tax decreases will lead to spending reductions in certain instances.[25] Moreover, if tax increases result in greater spending, it is certainly possible that the additional spending could diminish some of the negative effects of taxes on growth. Also, higher taxes may be the price to pay for more and better public services and amenities.[26] And, as Charles Tiebout suggests, some firms and individuals will prefer that mix of high taxes and greater public services, while others will not.[27]

Returning to the distinction made previously between growth and development, it is worth pondering how taxes, government spending, and public services come into play. On the one hand, the preponderance of empirical evidence indicates that high taxes stifle job growth and business activity and low taxes do the opposite. On the other hand, it is conceivable that higher taxes may be needed to support the provision of high-quality services and amenities. Economist Todd Gabe attempts to reconcile the taxes/services conundrum by examining the effects of being a low-tax/low-cost region on income levels and broader indicators of economic development, in addition to employment growth.[28] He found that low business costs (composite index of tax, labor, and energy costs) positively influence job growth but have no effects on income or broader development indicators. These findings led to the conclusion that being a low-tax/low-cost region is beneficial as a short-term growth strategy but is not at all useful as a long-term approach to economic development. A long-term strategy for economic development may rely on the better services and amenities that higher taxes, combined with higher government spending, make possible.

---

24. Gabe, *The Pursuit of Economic Development*; Walczak, Drenkard, and Bishop-Henchman, 2019 "State Business Tax Climate Index."

25. Michael Bell et al., "State and Local Fiscal Policy and Economic Growth and Development" (working paper no. 26, George Washington Institute of Public Policy, 2005).

26. Gabe, *The Pursuit of Economic Development*, above at note 16.

27. Charles Tiebout, "A Pure Theory of Local Public Expenditure," *Journal of Political Economy* 64 (1956): 416–24.

28. Gabe, *The Pursuit of Economic Development*.

4. Economic-Development Tools and Strategies

Much of economic-development practice focuses on helping prospective and existing businesses find feasible solutions for their real estate and workforce needs. As the economy continues to expand, tightening regional labor markets are increasing the demand for housing in many communities. Cities and counties employ several tools and strategies in their efforts to assist businesses with these issues and make their communities competitive for private investment. The rationale for using many of them can be traced to some of the previously discussed theoretical perspectives that help us understand how economic development is thought to take place.

Tools of the Trade

Numerous financial, tax, policy, and program tools are available for local governments to employ as part of their various strategies for economic development. These tools are the levers cities and counties can use to induce private investment. Financial incentives include cash grant payments to businesses and direct expenditures to defray or offset certain real estate development costs, such as the land/building purchase, infrastructure upgrades, and site preparation. Cash grants are paid annually and should be contingent on the business meeting its targets for capital investment and job creation. The amount of the grant may be determined based on the projected tax revenues the company generates.

When combined with state-level inducements and tax relief, the financial incentives local governments offer can help close the deal on a major business location or expansion project. The use of business incentives in this way has always been somewhat controversial for a variety of reasons. Over the years, critics have raised legitimate concerns about the legality, fairness, accountability, efficiency, and effectiveness of incentives.[29] On the question of effectiveness, a recent review of thirty studies found that incentives directly influence less than 25 percent of business investment decisions.[30]

The practice of enticing businesses with hefty incentives has received heightened scrutiny in the wake of Amazon's high-profile location search for a second corporate headquarters in 2018. Although Raleigh was one of twenty finalist communities, Amazon ultimately announced that it would split the $5 billion investment and 50,000 jobs between Long Island, New York, and Arlington/Northern Virginia. The "win" for Long Island was short-lived, as intense local outcry and pushback against the estimated $2.6 billion incentive package that was offered caused Amazon to scrap its plans in the Empire State.[31] Uncertainty about Wisconsin's $3 billion incentive deal

29. Jonathan Q. Morgan, "Using Economic Development Incentives: For Better or for Worse," *Popular Government* 74, no. 2 (2009): 16–29.

30. Timothy J. Bartik, " 'But For' Percentages for Economic Development Incentives: What Percentage Estimates Are Plausible Based on the Research Literature?" (working paper 18-289, W.E. Upjohn Institute for Employment Research, 2018), https://doi.org/10.17848/wp18-289.

31. See Nathan M. Jensen, "Report: Five Economic Development Takeaways from the Amazon HQ2 Bids," *Brookings.edu,* March 4, 2019, https://www.brookings.edu/research/five-economic-development-takeaways-from-the-amazon-hq2-bids/.

with Foxconn has also raised some red flags. In 2017, the company initially pledged to create as many as 13,000 jobs in Mt. Pleasant/Racine County and construct a $10 billion plant, but the company has more recently signaled that it may scale back its investment and job creation in the state.[32] Despite the controversy around financial and tax incentives, they are practically useful in the final stage of the site-selection process when a prospective business has narrowed the list of potential locations to the "final few" that meet all of its essential requirements. At that point, it can come down to which of the finalist communities offers the best incentive package.

Beyond providing direct financial inducements, local governments can also employ certain tax-related development finance tools to stimulate private investment. Tax increment financing (TIF) is a mechanism that enables cities and counties to issue bond debt to raise money to pay for public improvements that are necessary for attracting private investment to designated areas.[33] TIF bonds are considered to be "self-financing" because the new (incremental) tax revenues generated by higher property valuations resulting from the new private investment in the TIF district are used to repay the bond debt. North Carolina's version of TIF is called project development financing (PDF). TIF/PDF is a way for local governments to finance the capital costs of critical public investments in infrastructure and amenities that are needed to support private investment in specified areas. Although widely used in other states, the uptake of conventional TIF in North Carolina has been slow, as cities and counties turn to "synthetic TIF" instead.[34]

Some cities create a special taxing district and require all property owners within the district to pay extra taxes in order to fund downtown revitalization.[35] In North Carolina, these special taxing districts are called municipal service districts but they are more commonly known as business improvement districts (BIDs). The tax revenue a BID generates can be used to pay for a range of enhancements and activities that help revitalize a downtown area.

Historic preservation tax credits (federal and state) encourage the rehabilitation of certified historic structures. They can be an important tool in efforts to revitalize and redevelop historic portions of downtown and main street areas. The federal New Markets Tax Credit is designed to attract investment capital to low-income communities.

---

32. Robert Channick, "As Foxconn Changes Wisconsin Plans, Job Promises Fall Short," *Chicago Tribune*, February 8, 2019, https://www.chicagotribune.com /business/ct-biz-foxconn-plant-hiring-target-20190205-story.html; Molly Beck, "Foxconn Must Meet Job Creation Goals to Get Subsidies," *Milwaukee Journal Sentinel*, April 21, 2019, https://www.jsonline.com/story/news/politics/2019/04/21/tony-evers -floats-lowering-job-creation-goals-foxconn-wisconsin/3533746002/.

33. *See* Tax Increment Financing in North Carolina (microsite, UNC School of Government), https://www.sog.unc.edu/resources/microsites/tax-increment -financing-north-carolina.

34. Kara Millonzi, "What is a Synthetic Project Development Financing (aka Synthetic TIF)?," *Coates' Canons: NC Local Government Law* (blog), April 5, 2013, https://canons.sog .unc.edu/what-is-a-synthetic-project-development-financing-aka-synthetic-tif/.

35. Kara Millonzi, "A Guide to Business Improvement Districts in North Carolina," *Coates' Canons: NC Local Government Law* (blog), April 1, 2010, https://canons.sog.unc .edu/a-guide-to-business-improvement-districts-in-north-carolina/.

Designated community development entities apply to the U.S. Treasury Department to receive an allocation of tax credits. These tax credits are sold to investors to raise capital that is invested or loaned to qualified businesses and nonprofits operating in low-income areas. The newest federal tax incentive intended to steer investment to distressed communities is the "opportunity zone" program.[36] Opportunity zones are part of the Tax Cuts and Jobs Act legislation passed by the U.S. Congress in late 2017. The program offers a capital gains tax deferral to investors who reinvest the capital gains earned from the sale of an asset in one of 8,700 opportunity zones nationally that have been certified by the Treasury Department, including 252 in North Carolina.[37] While many observers are hopeful that opportunity zones will spur much-needed private investment in the designated areas, some fear that the program may fail to benefit low-income-zone residents and possibly displace them due to eventual gentrification.[38]

A final set of tools available for communities to use in promoting economic development helps meet the specific needs of small and mid-sized businesses at different stages. These include revolving loan funds, facilitation of networking, and business incubation. A revolving loan fund is typically able to offer lower-cost and more flexible financing with better terms than a conventional bank. In many cases, the fund is initially capitalized with dollars from multiple public, private, and philanthropic sources, which spreads the default risk among lenders.[39] The fund replenishes itself when loans are repaid. Some local governments partner with chambers of commerce and other organizations to sponsor formal networking events for entrepreneurs and facilitate informal interactions. These networking opportunities enable entrepreneurs to socialize with peers, exchange ideas, discuss business trends, share resources, and explore the possibility of joint ventures. Business incubation programs provide physical space to house fledgling firms, along with a range of support services needed to grow, such as managerial and technical assistance, bookkeeping and accounting, access to financing options, networking, and linkages to external resources and strategic partners.

Local governments employ these tools as part of their broader strategies intended to stimulate private investment and job creation through recruiting/attracting new businesses, retaining and growing existing employers, supporting the startup of new firms, developing workforce skills and talent, and making place-based enhancements to their communities. Localities may emphasize some strategies more than others.

36. Anne Kim, "How 'Opportunity Zones' Could Transform Communities," *Governing*, November 2018, https://www.governing.com/columns/public-money/gov-opportunity-zone.html.

37. Tyler Mulligan, "Federal Opportunity Zones: What Local Governments Need to Know," *Coates' Canons: NC Local Government Law* (blog), September 21, 2018, https://canons.sog.unc.edu/federal-opportunity-zones-what-local-governments-need-to-know/.

38. Timothy Weaver, "The Problem with Opportunity Zones," *CityLab* (May 16, 2018), https://www.citylab.com/equity/2018/05/the-problem-with-opportunity-zones/560510/.

39. Janet R. Hammer and Jessica Farr, "Community and Economic Development Finance," in *An Introduction to Community Development*, 2nd edition, ed. Rhonda Phillips and Robert H. Pittman (New York: Routledge, 2014), 383–97.

Table 11.1. Priorities for Local Economic Development in North Carolina

	Percent Reporting		
	All	**Municipalities**	**Counties**
Retain existing business	68.1	59.8	89.2
Job creation	67.7	60.8	85.1
Expand tax base	64.3	62.4	68.9
Recruit new business	63.5	59.3	74.3
Quality of life	44.1	50.3	28.4
Diversity of economic base	30.4	31.2	28.4
Small-business development	27.0	26.5	28.4
Increase workforce skills	26.6	20.6	41.9
Wealth creation	8.0	7.4	9.5
Environmental sustainability	6.8	7.9	4.1
Social/economic equity	5.7	6.9	2.7
N	263.0	189.0	74.0

Source: J.Q. Morgan, *2015 Survey of Local Government Economic Development Activities* (UNC School of Government, 2015).

The results in Table 11.1, drawn from a 2015 survey conducted by the UNC School of Government,[40] show that North Carolina local governments, overall, tend to prioritize both business retention and business recruitment, with counties being more fervent than municipalities. Cities and towns recognize the value of being desirable places to live, work, and play. Half of the municipal survey respondents view enhancing the quality of life in their communities as a priority for economic development, compared to just 28 percent of counties. This finding is relevant to the "placemaking" strategy discussion detailed later. The survey responses suggest that small-business development is a lower priority for local governments in the state and that counties see workforce development as a higher priority than do municipalities. Relatively few responding jurisdictions indicated that the broader development goals of wealth creation, sustainability, or equity are priorities.

Industrial Recruitment/Business Attraction

Industrial recruitment/attraction is a logical outgrowth of location theory, which emphasizes the various place-based factors a business considers in its search for an area in which to operate a new facility. Public officials and economic developers want to know what is required for their communities to be competitive in this search process. A good starting point is to understand which factors businesses prioritize as being most important in making their location decisions. One source for this information is *Area Development* magazine, which conducts a corporate survey every year in order to gauge the relative importance of the many variables firms take into

40. Jonathan Q. Morgan, *2015 Survey of Local Government Economic Development Activities* (UNC School of Government, 2015).

Table 11.2. Local Business Attraction/Recruitment Tools and Activities in North Carolina

	Percent Reporting		
	All	Municipalities	Counties
Respond to business inquiries	67.7	60.8	85.1
Zoning/permit assistance	60.5	60.8	59.5
Community website	55.5	50.3	68.9
Host site visits	51.3	41.8	75.7
Call on prospective businesses	48.3	39.7	70.3
Promotion/advertising	42.6	33.9	64.9
Retail incentives	35.7	31.2	47.3
Cash grants for new businesses	33.5	26.5	51.4
Trade shows	30.8	20.6	56.8
Regulatory flexibility	28.5	29.1	27.0
One-stop permitting	27.4	21.2	43.2
Target industry clusters	22.4	16.9	36.5
Subsidized land/buildingss	15.6	13.2	21.6
Subsidized worker training	13.3	7.9	27.0
N	263.0	189.0	74.0

Source: J.Q. Morgan, *2015 Survey of Local Government Economic Development Activities* (UNC School of Government, 2015).

account when choosing a location for a new facility. The 2018 ranking of location/site-selection factors indicated that the following factors matter the most (top ten out of twenty-eight) to respondents: availability of skilled labor (90.5 percent), labor costs (89.1 percent), highway accessibility (87.2 percent), corporate tax rate (86.7 percent), tax exemptions (83.0 percent), quality of life (82.8 percent), state and local incentives (82.5 percent), energy availability and costs (77.8 percent), available buildings (76.7 percent), and occupancy or construction costs (76.1 percent).[41]

Marketing and place branding are important aspects of business recruitment, as they enable communities to get on the radar of prospective companies and pitch the advantages they offer. As shown in Table 11.2, many of the tools and activities associated with business attraction that North Carolina local governments utilize are marketing related. The marketing activities most frequently reported by participants in the 2015 School of Government survey are responding to inquiries from prospective businesses, maintaining a community website, hosting visits from prospective businesses, calling on prospective businesses to sell their communities, promotion/advertising, and attending trade shows. The keen interest in cluster-based development

41. Geraldine Gambale, "33rd Annual Corporate Survey & the 15th Annual Consultants Survey," *Area Development*, Q (Quarter) 1, 2019, https://www.areadevelopment.com/Corporate-Consultants-Survey-Results/Q1-2019/33nd-annual-corporate-survey-15th-annual-consultants-survey.shtml.

Table 11.3. Local Product-Development Tools and Activities in North Carolina

		Percent Reporting		
		All	Municipalities	Counties
Improve infrastructure		67.7	64.6	75.7
Building/sites inventory		51.3	42.9	73.0
Industrial/business park		40.7	32.8	60.8
Land/building acquisition		35.4	30.2	48.6
Site preparation		31.9	23.8	52.7
Shell buildings		16.0	12.7	24.3
	N	263.0	189.0	74.0

Source: J.Q. Morgan, *2015 Survey of Local Government Economic Development Activities* (UNC School of Government, 2015).

discussed earlier does not appear to be translating into widespread application locally in North Carolina, as only 22 percent of survey respondents indicated that they target industry clusters.

In addition to marketing, North Carolina local governments support business attraction by taking steps to create a more business-friendly climate. The survey results show that assisting businesses with zoning and permitting is the tool of choice in this regard. Fewer local governments reported using regulatory flexibility and "one-stop" permitting. As for financial incentives, retail incentives and cash grants for newly locating firms are most prominent, especially for counties. To a lesser extent, local governments also subsidize the costs of real estate purchases (land and buildings) and worker training for businesses.

What economic developers refer to as product development is a prerequisite for success in business attraction. Product development refers to the real estate aspects of a business recruitment project. Companies seeking to locate a new facility pay attention to community attributes such as educational attainment, quality-of-life amenities, taxes, etc., but they absolutely must have an industrial site and, ideally, a building that meets their operational requirements. Communities that make "shovel-ready" sites and existing buildings available to prospective businesses are a step ahead in the intensely competitive processes of business recruitment and site selection. Upgrades and expansions of the existing physical infrastructure are usually necessary in order to turn raw land into viable industrial and commercial sites. According to the results in Table 5.3, drawn from the 2015 School of Government survey, investing in infrastructure improvements is the most frequently cited product-development activity in which North Carolina local governments engage. Half of all survey respondents and nearly three-quarters of counties maintain an inventory or database of local buildings and sites in order to facilitate a company's search for a suitable property.

Forty percent of all local governments and 60 percent of counties that responded to the survey reported using an industrial/business park to promote economic development. Proactively assembling and preparing multiple contiguous land parcels to be used as interconnected industrial sites is one indicator that a community is development ready. However, it is a speculative real estate undertaking with no guarantee of success. The landscape has no shortage of industrial parks that have sat idle without a tenant for years. Some local governments in North Carolina have partnered with neighboring localities to form multi-jurisdictional industrial parks. The General Assembly enacted Chapter 158, Section 7.4 of the North Carolina General Statutes to authorize and encourage this sort of regional collaboration on product development. The statute allows local governments to enter into interlocal agreements to share the costs of developing a joint business park and to divvy up any tax revenues that arise when companies locate in the park. For example, three municipalities in North Mecklenburg County—Cornelius, Davidson, and Huntersville—joined forces to build an industrial park called Commerce Station. Four counties—Franklin, Granville, Vance, and Warren—engaged in a formal partnership to develop a specialized industrial park in each respective county that they have collectively branded "Triangle North."

Business Retention and Expansion (BRE)

A strategy of working to retain and grow the businesses that already exist in a community is worthwhile for a variety of reasons. A business retention and expansion (BRE) program is a formalized way to reach out to existing employers, identify what they need locally to stay competitive, and connect them to valuable resources and expertise. BRE is a smart move, both symbolically and substantively. It creates symbolic value by making existing firms, which employ residents and pay taxes, feel appreciated and connected to the community. The strategy is important substantively because research shows that existing, small, growth-oriented companies are an important source of new private investment and job creation. The odds of generating new private investment and job creation are better with an existing business than they are with a prospective one because, as the adage says, "a bird in the hand is worth two in the bush." It is worth noting that product development and incentives can be equally important to BRE as they are to business recruitment. Existing companies seeking to expand their operations need workable real estate options, and incentives can sway their decision about staying versus finding a location elsewhere. The point of incentives is to induce private investment and job creation, irrespective of whether the business is new or existing. Economic-development organizations determine their success with BRE based on the number of businesses expanded, assisted, and retained; jobs retained; amount of financing provided; ratings of the local business climate; and the retention and growth of at-risk businesses.[42]

Local governments in North Carolina are not as active in business-retention and expansion activities as they are with recruitment/attraction. As shown in Table 11.4, the highest percentage (53.6 percent) of all jurisdictions, and more than two-thirds (68.9 percent) of counties responding to the 2015 School of Government survey indicated that they visit local businesses. Lesser-used BRE-related tools and activities

---

42. Jonathan Q. Morgan and Crystal Morphis, "Defining Success in Business Retention and Expansion: What Do Economic Development Organizations Measure and Why?," *Community Development* 48, no. 2 (2017): 299–316.

Table 11.4. Local Business Retention and Expansion Tools and Activities in North Carolina

	Percent Reporting		
	All	**Municipalities**	**Counties**
Visit local businesses	53.6	47.6	68.9
Existing business surveys	30.8	24.9	45.9
Regulatory flexibility	28.5	29.1	27.0
One-stop permitting	27.4	21.2	43.2
Business-recognition awards	25.1	20.6	36.5
Target industry clusters	22.4	16.9	36.5
Cash grants for retention	22.1	18.0	32.4
Subsidized land/buildings	15.6	13.2	21.6
Subsidized worker training	13.3	7.9	27.0
Promote technology	13.3	9.0	24.3
Vendor/supplier training	11.0	6.9	21.6
Low-cost financing	9.1	5.3	18.9
Business ombudsmen	7.6	6.3	10.8
Export assistance	5.3	3.7	9.5
N	263.0	189.0	74.0

Source: J.Q. Morgan, *2015 Survey of Local Government Economic Development Activities* (UNC School of Government, 2015).

include surveys of existing businesses, regulatory flexibility, one-stop permitting, business-recognition awards, target-industry clusters, and cash grants for business retention. The discrepancy between the percentage of survey respondents who use cash grants specifically for BRE (22.1 percent) versus the share using cash grants for recruitment (33.5 percent) is telling.

Business Creation and Entrepreneurship

As previously noted, there is evidence to suggest that small firms in growth-oriented sectors can create a lot of jobs. However, the benefits and contributions of small businesses to the economy extend beyond job creation. For example, self-employment ventures typically do not produce large numbers of jobs, but they enable individuals to provide a valued good or service, earn a living, pay taxes, and meaningfully participate in the economy.

A business-creation strategy involves building an entrepreneurial ecosystem that cultivates the startup of new firms and helps them grow. The role of local governments in supporting entrepreneurs and small businesses is not always clear. Small firms, particularly those on a high-growth trajectory, have a variety of needs with respect to financial capital, managerial and technical expertise, market development and access, workforce development, and innovation and technology. Local governments may be better suited to assist entrepreneurs and small firms with some needs more than others. In order to find a niche in supporting business creation, it helps to

Table 11.5. Local Business Creation and Entrepreneurship Tools and Activities in North Carolina

	Percent Reporting		
	All	Municipalities	Counties
"Buy local" campaigns	40.3	35.4	52.7
Business networking	36.5	30.2	52.7
Business-recognition awards	25.1	20.6	36.5
Small-business technical assistance	23.2	16.4	40.5
Small-business centers	19.4	13.2	35.1
Revolving loan funds	18.6	12.2	35.1
Business incubators	14.1	9.0	27.0
Promote creative sectors	14.1	9.5	25.7
Promote technology	13.3	9.0	24.3
Vendor/supplier matching	11.0	6.9	21.6
Low-cost financing	9.1	5.3	18.9
Business ombudsmen	7.6	6.3	10.8
Export assistance	5.3	3.7	9.5
Micro-enterprise program	4.9	3.2	9.5
Executive mentoring	3.8	2.6	6.8
N	263.0	189.0	74.0

Source: J.Q. Morgan, *2015 Survey of Local Government Economic Development Activities* (UNC School of Government, 2015).

understand which other local organizations are working to assist the different types of small businesses and entrepreneurs.

North Carolina local governments are engaged in activities and programming to support entrepreneurship and small-business development, but to a lesser extent than their involvement in business attraction. Counties are more likely than municipalities to employ business-creation tactics. As shown in Table 11.5, the most frequently used activities among respondents to the 2015 School of Government survey are "buy local" campaigns and business networking. Local governments also report using business-recognition awards, which could be a way to promote small businesses in the community. Nearly a quarter of all survey respondents and 40 percent of counties provide technical assistance to small businesses. Counties are much more inclined than cities to use small-business centers at community colleges, revolving loan funds, and business incubators. Roughly a quarter of counties indicated that they promote creative sectors of the local economy and technology as part of their economic-development efforts, while less than 10 percent of municipalities are leveraging these two potentially important aspects of a local entrepreneurial ecosystem.

An example of a small town's strategy for promoting business creation is Star, North Carolina, in Montgomery County.[43] The Town of Star worked with a regional nonprofit to open a small-business incubator called STARworks. Located downtown in a former textile mill building, STARworks rents studio space to local artisans, potters, and glass blowers.

Workforce and Talent Development

Informed by the aforementioned theories of human capital, local strategies to enhance workforce skills and cultivate talent are an indispensable part of the formula for economic-development success. As the economy becomes more knowledge-based and technology-driven, companies increasingly need to hire people with specialized expertise and technical skills. Communities and regions pursue workforce- and talent-development strategies to meet this demand. Institutions of higher education, such as community colleges and universities, are central players in building the workforce pipeline, along with the K–12 education system. There is also growing appreciation for the value of pre-K and early childhood programs in workforce development, especially for at-risk youth.

Workforce and talent development are important components of both business recruitment and retention/expansion strategies, as prospective new and already exist-ing firms in a community cannot operate, much less grow, without a properly edu-cated and skilled pool of labor from which to hire. It behooves a locality to implement a successful workforce-preparedness strategy in order to attract and retain businesses. Many companies, particularly those in technology-related sectors, need specialized talent that can be hard to find. In response, some communities and regions are start-ing to focus on attracting talent almost as much they do on recruiting companies. Placemaking, discussed below, is a big part of the way communities intend to become magnets for talent.

North Carolina local governments, for the most part, tend to rely on core workforce-development programs in their efforts to build human capital (see Table 11.6). Other reported activities that fit within a human capital/workforce/talent strategy are much less frequently used and include attracting retirees and creative people as well as supporting affordable housing.

Placemaking

When a community engages in a concerted effort to become a high-quality place that provides the amenities, infrastructure, cultural experiences, and opportunities that people and businesses desire, the strategy is called placemaking. This approach often includes plans for physically redeveloping and revitalizing a particular area, such as a downtown/main street, a waterfront property, a vacant industrial facility, or a dis-tressed neighborhood. The idea is to create well-designed and aesthetically appealing physical spaces that connect to a community's distinctive sense of place. Placemaking

---

43. "Star, NC," Homegrown Tools for Economic Development, UNC School of Gov-ernment, accessed June 19, 2019, http://homegrowntools.unc.edu/index.php/studies/star/.

Table 11.6. Local Human Capital Development Tools and Activities in North Carolina

		Percent Reporting	
	All	**Municipalities**	**Counties**
Workforce development	41.8	27.5	78.4
Attract retirees	20.2	15.9	31.1
Attract creative people	19.8	16.9	27.0
Affordable housing	17.5	18.5	14.9
N	263.0	189.0	74.0

Source: J.Q. Morgan, *2015 Survey of Local Government Economic Development Activities* (UNC School of Government, 2015).

can involve coming up with a brand for the community to use in communicating its place narrative to residents, visitors, tourists, and prospective companies.

A placemaking strategy may target different local assets or economic sectors around which to create a distinctive sense of identity. Many small towns and rural areas emphasize arts and crafts trades. Agriculture and local food are popular placemaking focuses for some localities. Other communities play up what makes them special in terms of tourist attractions, recreation and sports, cultural amenities, creative sectors, and craft breweries.

There are obvious connections between placemaking and the quality-of-life investments that local governments are responsible for supporting. In addition, placemaking can draw inspiration from human capital and creative talent theories to the extent that businesses are thought to increasingly go where they can find talent—and talented people increasingly choose to live in high-quality places they consider to be desirable.

As shown in Table 11.7, the 2015 School of Government survey revealed that the top placemaking-related tool for North Carolina local governments is investing in public parks and recreation. Other frequently reported economic-development tools and activities that align with a placemaking strategy include promoting tourism, downtown development, arts/cultural amenities, and "buy local" campaigns. Nearly 40 percent of all local governments reported using historic preservation in support of economic development, and 40 percent of municipalities indicated that they employ façade grants. Based on the survey results, North Carolina local governments make very little use of two previously discussed tax-related financing tools often associated with place-based redevelopment and downtown revitalization: tax increment financing and business improvement districts.

The Town of Ayden, North Carolina, is pursuing placemaking through downtown revitalization.[44] Momentum for reviving downtown Ayden gained steam in 2006, when the town applied to become a participant in the NC Main Street Program and formed a community-based vision for the effort. Local officials decided early on to

---

44. "Ayden, NC," Homegrown Tools for Economic Development, UNC School of Government, accessed June 19, 2019, https://homegrowntools.unc.edu/index.php/studies /ayden/.

Table 11.7. Local Placemaking Tools and Activities in North Carolina

	Percent Reporting		
	All	Municipalities	Counties
Public parks and recreation	63.1	62.4	64.9
Promote tourism	51.3	41.8	75.7
Develop downtown	46.0	49.2	37.8
Arts/cultural amenities	44.9	40.7	55.4
"Buy local" campaigns	40.3	35.4	52.7
Historic preservation	38.4	39.2	36.5
Façade grants	34.6	40.7	18.9
Main Street Program	31.2	31.7	29.7
Sporting events	23.6	23.8	23.0
Affordable housing	17.5	18.5	14.9
Promote creative sectors	14.1	9.5	25.7
Mass transit development	12.2	14.8	5.4
Tax increment financing	11.4	10.1	14.9
Business improvement district	8.4	10.6	2.7
N	263.0	189.0	74.0

Source: J.Q. Morgan, *2015 Survey of Local Government Economic Development Activities*, UNC School of Government.

expand an existing façade-improvement grant program that encourages businesses located downtown to renovate their properties and storefronts. The town came up with a new brand and logo to use in marketing downtown Ayden's authentic and distinctive attributes. Since 2006, Ayden has won grants to help renovate vacant buildings in the downtown area in order to repurpose them for retail and commercial uses. Local officials are planning to develop a food-processing facility and host more festivals and special events in downtown Ayden, such as the annual BBQ and Collard Festival.

5. Conclusion: Economic Development as a Strategic Public Investment

Local governments engage in a wide range of activities and use numerous tools in their efforts to promote economic development. The involvement of cities and counties in this process rests on the assumption that it yields a net positive return and serves a public purpose. How can local governments ensure that their expenditures on economic development are a strategic investment of tax dollars and not corporate welfare or the unnecessary subsidization of private enterprise that critics claim?

The first step in making sure economic-development expenditures are strategic is to have an overarching vision and road map to guide the process. This can be achieved with a regularly updated strategic plan for economic development devised with substantive community input about goals and priorities. A strategic-planning process provides a platform for assessing development strategies in order to determine whether the investment portfolio needs to be rebalanced.

Smart public investments in economic development are structured to be cost-effective and maximize public benefits—they try to avoid overpaying and underperforming. Local governments can make better-informed decisions in this regard by conducting appropriate analyses in order to determine the economic and fiscal impacts of development projects.[45]

Strategic public investments in economic development consider how today's decisions will affect a community in the long run. They seek to promote growth in the short term that leads to long-term development in the form of qualitative improvements that make a community substantively better off. A useful framework for connecting growth decisions to the development outcomes communities want to achieve is "triple bottom line" investing, which explicitly integrates economic, environmental, and equity/social well-being considerations.[46]

Finally, a strategic approach to making public investments in economic development represents accountability to the public. This is particularly important for the somewhat controversial practice of using business incentives to stimulate private investment and job creation. Financial and tax incentives are most defensible when public officials can demonstrate that they pass the "but for" test—that is to say, they induce private investment and job creation that would not occur in the absence of such incentives. Local governments should always execute performance-based contractual agreements with companies that clearly specify the terms of an incentive deal. The contract should include clawback provisions that force the company to return incentive payments if investment and employment numbers fall below what was promised.

Economic-development programs that are accountable to taxpayers get evaluated so that public officials can determine what works (and what does not) and make any necessary adjustments. They also strive to get the metrics right by moving beyond simple workload measures to capture the tangible outcomes that program activities can be expected to produce.[47] As previously stated, the ultimate end goal for economic development is to see communities and their residents make substantive gains in income and wealth, become more prosperous, and be in a qualitatively better place in terms of well-being.

---

45. Morgan, *Analyzing the Benefits and Costs.*

46. Janet Hammer and Gary Pivo, "The Triple Bottom Line and Sustainable Economic Development Theory and Practice," *Economic Development Quarterly* 31, no. 1 (2017): 25–36, https://doi.org/10.1177/0891242416674808.

47. David Ammons and Jonathan Q. Morgan, "State-of-the-Art Measures in Economic Development," *PM Magazine* 93 no. 5 (2011): 6–10.

Chapter 12

Public School Financing

Kara A. Millonzi

Introduction

The North Carolina Constitution guarantees each child in the state the opportunity to receive a sound basic education. The constitution and state statutes establish a complex policy-making, funding, and administrative framework to meet this constitutional duty. The state legislature sets broad educational policies and allocates funding responsibilities between the state and local sources. The North Carolina State Board of Education (SBE) is responsible for supervising and administering the free public-school system. It sets education policy, within constitutional and statutory guidelines, and enacts regulations to carry out state law. The board sets the salary schedules for school employees, adopts a standard course of study, and develops accountability measures for school systems. The Department of Public Instruction, overseen by the independently elected Superintendent of Public Instruction, administers the day-to-day operations of the state public-school system. Local education agencies (LEAs) administer school systems.[1] A local school board supervises school personnel, sets educational policy within the guidelines set by state statute and the SBE, and manages the LEAs' budgets. Although LEAs are the primary public-school unit, there are other public-school structures, including charter schools, innovation schools, regional schools, lab schools, and the N.C. Virtual School. Finally, local taxing entities provide funding directly to LEAs and indirectly to other public schools.[2]

Funding public schools is a responsibility of both state and county governments. (The federal government also provides limited funding for certain targeted programs.)[3] The basic structure of school finance has not changed since the 1930s. In aggregate, the state continues to be responsible for the majority of operating expenses necessary to maintain the minimum nine-month term, while counties are responsible for financing construction and the maintenance of school facilities. In this respect, North Carolina's approach to financing its public schools differs from that of most other states, where the basic financial backing for public schools comes from local rather than state revenues. In North Carolina, state income and sales taxes, rather than local property taxes, constitute the primary revenue sources for financing schools. Although, like other states, North Carolina also relies on lottery proceeds to fund education. There has been a blending of funding responsibilities over time. The state appropriates funds for school construction, and counties must provide funds for operating expenses. In fact, the aggregate county share of school funding has increased significantly in recent years. (And, as of 2018, municipalities are allowed, but not required, to contribute to schools, too).[4]

But what are counties legally required to fund? And how much control do counties have over school expenditures? These are complicated questions, and their answers will vary by county/LEA and by fiscal year. Funding factors include state and federal funding levels and matching requirements, student population and makeup, state and

---

1. The state's public schools are divided into 115 local school administrative units and one regional school. Each county has at least one local school administrative unit; some counties have up to three. Note that throughout this chapter, the terms *school unit*, *school system*, and *LEA* are used interchangeably.

2. Chapter 160A, Article 30 of the North Carolina General Statutes (hereinafter G.S.).

3. Although public education is a state and local responsibility, since the 1950s the federal government has assumed a significant role in public education, primarily by providing funds to states. The United States Congress generally conditions a state's receipt of federal funds on the state's compliance with federally defined conditions. Most federal moneys are categorical funds, which means they are appropriated by Congress to the states for specific educational purposes. These funds are channeled through the North Carolina State Board of Education for distribution to local units, but the board has little control over the programs themselves. In general, poorer school units receive more federal dollars relative to their enrollment than wealthier units do.

4. G.S. 160A-700.

local educational policies, and county fiscal policy. This chapter provides a detailed look at the local budgeting process for schools and explains the legal framework for navigating the local funding process for public schools.

Local Budgeting Process

Each year, a county engages in a detailed budgetary process to estimate revenues and make appropriations for the forthcoming fiscal year. A county includes its appropriations to its local school unit(s) for capital outlay and current expenses in its annual budget ordinance. The Local Government Budget and Fiscal Control Act,[5] as supplemented by the School Budget and Fiscal Control Act,[6] prescribes the procedural and substantive requirements for adopting the county's budget ordinance and appropriating money to its local school unit(s). The budgeting process can be broken down into the following ten steps:

Step 1: County board and local school board(s) communicate on an ongoing basis

Step 2: Superintendent submits proposed budget

Step 3: Local school board considers superintendent's budget

Step 4: Local school board submits budget request to county board

Step 5: County board makes appropriations to local school unit(s)

Step 6: Local school board initiates dispute resolution process (optional)

Step 7: Local school board adopts school budget resolution

Step 8: County distributes appropriated funds to LEA

Step 9: Local school board amends school budget resolution

Step 10: County board reduces appropriations to local school unit(s) during fiscal year (optional and limited authority)

Each step is analyzed more thoroughly in the subsequent sections.

Step 1: County Board and Local School Board(s) Communicate on an Ongoing Basis

A county board and school board must work together to ensure a successful school budgeting process. Although this may seem obvious, it is not always easy to accomplish in practice. In some counties, the only time the two boards communicate is when the school board presents its budget request each year. Without proper context, county commissioners and school board members may not fully understand the legal

---

5. G.S. Ch. 159, Art. 3.
6. G.S. Ch, 115C, Art. 31, Pt. 1.

and practical requirements and fiscal constraints under which each board is operating. Recognizing the complexity of the school budgeting process, the law actually envisions and encourages both boards to engage in ongoing communication during the fiscal year.[7] The boards (or staff from each organization) should communicate about the fiscal needs of the LEA and the fiscal resources of the county. Doing so will prevent surprises to either board at budget time and will help staff identify potential issues early on, providing more time to work through them. Counties and LEAs have also found it helpful to educate each other on their respective budgeting, financial administration, and accounting processes. Counties and schools have separate charts of accounts, different cash flows, and different operational processes. School units, in particular, have a complex array of funding sources and timing issues. It is helpful for county commissioners to understand the nuances of school budgets and school financial reports, particularly as they pertain to the expenditure of county funds. (At a minimum, county commissioners should be familiar with an LEA's chart of accounts and reporting structure (purpose and function codes, object codes, and program report codes)).[8] County commissioners also should understand state funding mechanisms, requirements, and limitations.[9] School boards, likewise, benefit from understanding a county's fiscal policies and constraints, as well as a county's strategic plans. These discussions will not only help each side recognize the legal and financial constraints but also provide opportunities for better coordination, planning, and innovation. In practice, counties and LEAs that communicate regularly and build trust are able to find creative ways to get needed funding to schools without overburdening counties.

Some county boards and local school boards agree to adopt multiyear funding agreements for operational expenses, indexed to such things as enrollment growth, percentages of low-wealth or special needs students, or state funding averages. These funding agreements are not legally enforceable, but they can serve as a useful tool for financial planning. Other counties and schools have adopted detailed joint capital planning processes, folding school needs into a county's capital improvement program (CIP). Regardless of the method, counties and schools should strive to communicate more and identify opportunities to work together, while respecting each other's respective roles and responsibilities, with the aim of building trust and avoiding unnecessary conflict.

---

7. *See* G.S. 115C-426.2.

8. The current chart of accounts for LEAs in N.C. is available at https://www.dpi.nc.gov /districts-schools/district-operations/financial-and-business-services/school-district -finance-operations/chart-accounts.

9. For information on the state funding framework for schools, see Kara A. Millonzi, "Financing Public Schools," in *Introduction to Local Government Finance*, 3rd ed. (UNC School of Government, 2018). *See also* N.C. Department of Public Instruction (NC DPI) Division of School Business, *Highlights of the North Carolina Public School Budget* (Raleigh, N.C.: NC DPI, May 2020), https://files.nc.gov/dpi/documents/fbs /resources/data/highlights/2020highlights.pdf.

Step 2: Superintendent Submits Proposed Budget

Although the budgeting process starts well before this date, May 1 is the first statutory deadline. By May 1, the superintendent of public schools must submit a budget and budget message to the local board of education (superintendent's budget).[10] A local school board may direct the superintendent to follow certain specified guidelines and processes in preparing the proposed budget. A copy of the superintendent's budget must be filed in the superintendent's office and made available for public inspection.[11] The superintendent may, but is not required to, publish notice that the superintendent's budget has been submitted to the local board of education.

Step 3: Local School Board Considers Superintendent's Budget

The local board of education may hold a public hearing on the superintendent's budget, but it is not required to do so.[12] With or without public input or support, the board is free to make any changes to the proposed budget before submitting it to the county for consideration. Most years there is a great deal of uncertainty at this point about state funding for schools. There also will be some uncertainty about student head-count numbers (formally referred to as *average daily membership* or ADM)[13] and thus staffing needs for the forthcoming school year. A school board must make its best estimates but also prepare for financial contingencies. (Note, however, that state law does not allow either a school board or the county to adopt contingency budgets.)

Step 4: Local School Board Submits Budget Request to County Board

By May 15, the local board of education must submit its entire proposed budget (not just its request for county funding) to the board of county commissioners.[14] The county's budget officer must present the local board of education's requests to the county board, even if the budget officer's proposed county budget recommends different funding levels for the school unit.

The board of county commissioners may request further information from the local school administrative unit about its proposed budget request. In fact, the county board has broad authority to obtain from the local board of education "all books,

---

10. G.S. 115C-427.

11. G.S. 115C-428.

12. Ibid.

13. For more information on ADM, see NC DPI, *School Attendance and Student Accounting Manual 2020–2021*, accessed April 26, 2021, https://www.dpi.nc.gov /media/10117/download.

14. G.S. 115C-429.

records, audit reports, and other information bearing on the financial operation of the local school administrative unit."[15] It also may specify the format in which the financial information must be presented. This is where advanced planning and communication are key. If a county board fully understands school financials, it will know exactly what to ask for and how to interpret it. School units should provide context, where necessary, to help county commissioners understand budget requests, particularly those for new money.

A county board can (and often does) invite the school unit's superintendent or the local school board to present the school's budget proposal at a county board meeting or during the public hearing on the county's budget. This affords the county board an opportunity to ask questions about certain expenditure items and to obtain further clarification on a local school board's policy goals and needs.

Step 5: County Board Makes Appropriations to Local School Unit(s)

The board of county commissioners makes its appropriations for capital and operating expenditures to the local school administrative unit(s) in the county's annual budget ordinance.

What Guides the County Board in Making Its Funding Decision?

The question of what guides a county board in making its funding decision is a great one with a complicated answer. G.S. 115C-408 specifies that "it is the policy of the State of North Carolina to provide from State revenue sources the instructional expenses for current operations of the public school system as defined in the standard course of study. It is the policy of the State of North Carolina that the facilities requirements for a public education system will be met by county governments."[16] On its face, this statute articulates a clear demarcation of funding responsibility between the state and county governments. The statute, by its terms, is merely aspirational, however. It does not actually assign any specific funding responsibilities. Neither does it reflect funding realities. As detailed below, counties are required to fund both school operational and capital expenditures.

Unfortunately, the constitutional and statutory frameworks for public-school funding do not provide much guidance for county and public-school officials wrestling with tough budgetary decisions. Except as delineated below, what a county funds (and how much it spends) for both capital and operating expenses will depend on the unique facts and circumstances facing the county and its local school unit(s) in any given fiscal year. There are, however, several identifiable factors that influence

---

15. G.S. 115C-429(c). A board of county commissioners automatically receives a copy of the annual audit report for the local school administrative unit. G.S. 115C-447(a).
16. G.S. 115C-408.

the amount a county is legally required to appropriate to its public schools for capital and operational expenses. These include

- the budget request for capital and operational expenses from the county's local school administrative unit(s),
- the amount of funding a county's local school administrative unit(s) receives from other sources—including the state and the federal government,
- the educational policies of the state and the county's local school administrative unit(s),
- the size and composition of the student populations in the county's local school administrative unit(s),
- the financial resources of the county, and
- the fiscal policies of the county's board of commissioners.[17]

Note that the listed factors are in no particular order; presumably, they are all equally important. The factors simply provide some rudimentary guidelines for county officials as they work with their local school board officials to make difficult appropriation decisions relating to public schools.

County Funding for Operating Expenses

State law explicitly assigns to counties responsibility for funding some operational expenditures—specifically, school maintenance and repairs,[18] instructional supplies and reference books,[19] school property insurance,[20] and fire inspections.[21] Counties commonly fund a variety of other school costs, such as teacher supplements, teacher and teacher assistant positions, and special school programs. The legislature has mandated a funding floor of sorts for operational expenses, albeit in a complicated way. As discussed below, if a school board believes it has not received sufficient funds to meet its constitutional responsibility, it may initiate a dispute process with the county. If the process results in an impasse between the two boards, the legislature has imposed a "per pupil maintenance of effort plus inflation" county funding requirement for school operational expenses.[22] Although this mandate is only triggered with a formal dispute process, it provides a guide to both counties and school boards when making budgeting decisions. It also may negatively influence a county's willingness to fund new operational expenses in any given year, because doing so sets a new funding floor.

---

17. *See* G.S. 115C-431.
18. G.S. 115C-524.
19. G.S. 115C-522(c).
20. G.S. 115C-534.
21. G.S. 115C-525(b).
22. *See* G.S. 115C-431.

County Funding for Capital Outlay

State law assigns to counties responsibility for funding capital outlay expenditures, including school facilities, furniture, and apparatus;[23] buildings for bus and vehicle storage;[24] library, science, and classroom equipment;[25] water supply and sanitary facilities;[26] and maintenance and repair of school buildings.[27] Although some of these expenses (such as maintenance and equipment/furniture purchases) are regular, most capital expenditures are costly and more sporadic.

Long-term planning is essential to an effective capital strategy. School boards must report annually on capital needs over a five-year horizon.[28] Schools, however, are only mandated to communicate their capital needs to counties on an annual basis. And a county is only obligated to fund the capital items that are necessary to meet the school unit's needs in a particular fiscal year. The law leaves it to county and school personnel to determine how best to coordinate longer-term planning efforts. To the extent possible, a school unit should avoid requesting a major capital project at budget time without any forewarning to the county. Likewise, the county should keep school officials abreast of any financial issues or constraints that will impact the scope and/or timing of school capital funding. In terms of the yearly budget request, as with operational expenses, if a school board believes that it has not received sufficient appropriations from the county in any given year to meet its minimum capital needs, the school board may institute a dispute process, which could result in litigation.[29] This is discussed in more detail in the following sections of this chapter.

School Fund Balance

Questions often arise at budget time about the propriety of a local school unit maintaining a fund balance. Most state funds allocated to school units revert at the end of a fiscal year if not spent. Thus, a school unit's fund balance is comprised primarily of county appropriations from previous years. Unlike for counties and municipalities, the state's Local Government Commission (LGC) does not prescribe a minimum fund balance level for local school units. That does not mean that an LEA does not need fund balance. Schools experience emergency expenditures and also have cash flow issues related to the state (and federal) funding processes. Some of the cash flow issues may be more acute than those faced by counties because of the nature and timing of these other revenues. The amount of fund balance needed by a particular LEA depends on a number of factors. A county board may not force a school board to expend its fund balance for capital or operating expenditures. And a school unit is not authorized to return all or a portion of its fund balance to the county. A county board, however, may consider the amount of fund balance available to the school

23. G.S. 115C-521.
24. G.S. 115C-249.
25. G.S. 115C-522(c).
26. Ibid.
27. G.S. 115C-524(b).
28. G.S. 115C-521(a).
29. *See* G.S. 115C-431.

unit when making its yearly county appropriations for operating expenses.[30] This is an issue that is ripe for conflict between the two boards. It may be helpful for an LEA to detail its specific need for fund balance (factoring in cash flow needs as well as providing a sufficient cushion for unexpected expenses based on past data). And both boards should strive for mutual agreement on the purposes for which fund balance may or may not be expended.

How Are Appropriations Made?

A county board of commissioners makes its appropriations for both school capital and operating expenses in the county's annual budget ordinance. Appropriations for capital are allocated to the LEA's Fund 4: Capital Outlay Fund. Appropriations for most operating expenses are allocated to the LEA's Fund 2: Current Expense Fund (otherwise known as the LEA's general fund). Occasionally, a school unit will request county funding for a special program, such as a pre-K program. Funding for that and a few other special programs is allocated to the LEA's Fund 8.[31]

May a County Direct How a School Unit Spends County Appropriations?

Allocating Local Current Expense Appropriations

A board of county commissioners may appropriate a lump sum to the local current expense fund to support operating expenses. If a county appropriates moneys to the local current expense fund with no further direction, the local board of education has full discretion over the expenditure of those moneys.[32]

A county is authorized, however, to allocate part or all of its appropriation for operating expenses within the local current expense fund by purpose or function, as defined in the uniform budget format.[33] The uniform budget format (now the uniform chart of accounts) defines "purpose code" to include the activities or actions that are

---

30. G.S. 115C-426(e) allows a county board to consider "other moneys available or accruing to the local school administrative unit," which provides some justification for a county board to consider a school unit's uncommitted fund balance when making its yearly appropriation decisions. Note, however, that practically a county is still bound by the statutory minimum appropriation requirement for operating expenses in G.S. 115C-431.

31. For more information on Fund 8, see Kara A. Millonzi, "Allocating Operating Monies among Local School Unit Funds: Local Current Expense Fund vs. Fund 8," *Coates' Canons: NC Local Government Law* (blog), June 10, 2014, https://canons.sog.unc.edu /allocating-operating-monies-among-local-school-unit-funds-local-current -expense-fund-vs-fund-8/.

32. A local school unit must distribute the per-pupil proportional share of certain local current expense appropriations (along with certain state appropriations) to each charter school (G.S. 115C-218.105(c); G.S. 115C-426(b)), University of North Carolina (UNC) Lab School (G.S. 116-239.11), and/or Innovative School District (G.S. 115C-75.10) that is attended by a child who otherwise would attend school in the local school unit.

33. G.S. 115C-429. The county board may specify that the local school board submit its budget request according to these purpose and function codes.

performed to accomplish the objectives of the school unit.[34] Function codes are first-level subdivisions of purpose codes and represent the greatest level of specificity to which a county may allocate funds for operating expenses. County appropriations may be allocated to the following purpose (first level) and function (second level) codes:

- 5000—*Instructional Services.* Includes the costs of activities dealing directly with the interaction between teachers and students.
  - 5100—Regular Instructional Services
  - 5200—Special Populations Services
  - 5300—Alternative Programs and Services
  - 5400—School Leadership Services
  - 5500—Co-curricular Services
  - 5600—School-Based Support Services
- 6000—*Supporting Services Programs.* Includes the costs of activities providing system-wide support for school-based programs, regardless of where these supporting services are based or housed.
  - 6100—Support and Development Services
  - 6200—Special Populations Support and Development Services
  - 6300—Alternative Programs and Services Support and Development Services
  - 6400—Technology Support Services
  - 6500—Operational Support Services
  - 6600—Financial and Human Resource Services
  - 6700—Accountability Services
  - 6800—System-Wide Pupil Support Services
  - 6900—Policy, Leadership, and Public Relations Services
- 7000—*Ancillary Services.* Includes activities that are not directly related to the provision of education for pupils in a local school administrative unit.
  - 7100—Community Services
  - 7200—Nutrition Services
  - 7300—Adult Services
- 8000—*Non-programmed Charges.* Includes conduit-type payments to other local school administrative units in the state or in another state, transfers from one fund to another fund in the local school administrative unit, appropriated but unbudgeted funds, debt-service payments, scholarship payments, payments on behalf of educational foundations, and contingency funds.
  - 8100—Payments to Other Government Units
  - 8200—Unbudgeted Funds
  - 8300—Debt Services
  - 8400—Interfund Transfers

---

34. NC DPI, *DPI Purpose Codes*, accessed April 26, 2021, https://www.dpi.nc.gov/media/10539/download?attachment.

- ○ 8500—Contingency
- ○ 8600—Educational Foundations
- ○ 8700—Scholarships
- 9000—*Capital Outlay.* Includes expenditures for acquiring fixed assets, including land or existing buildings, improvements of grounds, initial equipment, additional equipment, and replacement of equipment.[35]

A board of county commissioners may request that a local board of education refrain from using county appropriations for certain items of expenditure within a purpose or function code. However, it may not legally restrict these expenditures at the line-item level. Furthermore, if a county board allocates its appropriations according to a purpose or function code, the local school board may modify up to 25 percent of an allocation for operating expenses. The board of county commissioners may reduce the local school board's discretion to modify allocations if it so specifies in the county budget ordinance, but not to less than 10 percent.[36]

Allocating Capital Outlay Appropriations

According to the uniform budget format (now the uniform chart of accounts), there are three categories of expenditures to which a county may appropriate capital funds to its public school(s).[37] A county may appropriate moneys for Category I expenditures for a specific capital project or projects. Moneys appropriated for Categories II and III expenditures, however, are allocated to the entire category, not to individual expenditure items.

The following details the authorized capital outlay expenditures in each category:

- Category I: Acquisition of real property and acquisition, construction, reconstruction, enlargement, renovation, or replacement of buildings and other structures for school purposes
- Category II: Acquisition or replacement of furnishings and equipment
- Category III: Acquisition of school buses, activity buses, and other motor vehicles

If the board of county commissioners allocates part or all of its capital appropriations by project, the local school board must obtain approval from the county for any changes in the allocation for specific Category I expenditures—acquisitions of real property for school purposes and acquisitions, construction, reconstruction, enlargement, renovations, or replacement of buildings and other structures.[38] However, a local board of education has full discretion to reallocate funds within Categories II and III.

---

35. Ibid.
36. G.S. 115C-433.
37. G.S. 115C-426.
38. G.S. 115C-433.

Apportionment of County Funds among Multiple School Units

If a county supports more than one local school unit, county appropriations to the local current expense funds of the local school administrative units (to support operating expenses) must be apportioned according to the average daily membership of each unit.[39] There is an exception for appropriations funded by voted supplemental taxes levied less than countywide. This occurs when a county has more than one local school administrative unit. These funds do not need to be apportioned equally among local school administrative units.

This uniform apportionment requirement does not apply to capital funds. A county may allocate unequal amounts of capital funding to different school units within a fiscal year. Furthermore, under certain circumstances a county may appropriate moneys to special funds for particular programs at one local school administrative unit without appropriating an equivalent amount to other units. The local school administrative unit must budget and account for these moneys in a fund other than the local current expense fund.

What Moneys Are Available for Appropriation?

Moneys for School Operating Appropriations

Counties fund most school operating appropriations with general fund moneys School expenditures typically comprise the largest percentage of a county's general fund expenditures. Because of that, occasionally county commissioners seek to earmark or dedicate a certain portion of the property tax rate to school expenditures. This may provide political cover to justify the county's general property tax rate or even an increase in the rate. There are two methods by which a county may legally dedicate property tax proceeds for public-school purposes: dedicated county general tax and voted supplemental tax.

Dedicated County General Tax

The first method is by obtaining voter approval to dedicate a portion of the general property tax for public-school purposes. If the referendum is successful, the board of county commissioners decides each year whether or not to levy the dedicated property tax rate, along with the county's general rate. If it levies the portion of the property tax dedicated to schools, it can then use the proceeds from that tax to either supplement or supplant its appropriations to the school unit(s) from other sources for capital and/or operating expenses.[40]

Voted Supplemental Tax

The second method requires a joint effort between the local board of education and the board of county commissioners. It is the closest thing to a local school board having its own taxing authority. The local board of education may petition the county commissioners to hold a voter referendum to authorize a voted supplemental school tax.[41] If the county commissioners receive a valid petition, the county must hold

---

39. G.S. 115C-430.
40. G.S. 153A-149(d).
41. *See* G.S. Ch. 115C, Art. 36.

the referendum. The petition must state the maximum authorized supplemental tax rate, up to $0.50 per $100 valuation for school units having a population of less than 100,000 and $0.60 per $100 valuation for all other school units.[42] If a supplemental tax is approved by the voters, a local board of education may request that the county levy a tax each year up to the maximum rate approved by the voters.[43] The county decides whether or not to levy the tax and at what rate (the rate is capped at the level requested by the local board of education).[44]

The county does not have any control over how the supplemental tax proceeds are spent by the school unit. That decision rests with the local school board, subject only to the terms of the ballot measure under which the tax was approved. The board of county commissioners, however, may consider the availability of the supplemental tax revenue when determining the county's annual appropriations.

Moneys for School Capital Appropriations

Counties will also fund some school capital with general fund moneys Due to the nature of capital outlay, in particular the large sums typically involved, counties also have to rely on additional funding mechanisms.

County Borrowing

For some large capital outlay a county will need to borrow money to front the costs. Counties typically issue general obligation bonds (which required voter approval) or do installment financings to fund school projects. Borrowing money is not a revenue source. Borrowed moneys are repaid with either unrestricted general fund revenues, sales- and use-tax proceeds, or other special revenues (such as state or federal grants). Borrowing is merely a mechanism to leverage future revenues.

State Aid

Over the years, the state has provided direct and indirect support through additional revenue generation methods primarily for school capital, although occasionally for school operating expenses. Currently, these include local sales and use tax authority and school construction funds.

Local Sales- and Use-Tax Authority

In 1983, the legislature authorized counties to levy a one-half-cent sales and use tax[45] (Article 40 tax) with a specified percentage of the resulting revenue earmarked for school capital outlay, including retirement of existing school indebtedness (30 percent of the proceeds are currently so earmarked). In 1986, the legislature authorized counties to levy another one-half-cent tax (Article 42 tax), this time with 60 percent of the revenue earmarked for school capital outlay expenses.[46] Because traditionally sales and use taxes have been a state revenue source, these local sales taxes may reasonably

---

42. G.S. 115C-502.
43. G.S. 115C-511.
44. Ibid.
45. G.S. Ch. 105, Art. 40.
46. G.S. Ch. 105, Art. 42.

be viewed as a form of state revenue sharing for school construction. All counties levy both taxes.[47] Counties may hold the moneys generated from the earmarked portion of the taxes in a capital reserve fund for future projects; any interest earned must be earmarked for school capital outlays.[48] A county has discretion to determine how much of these earmarked funds to appropriate each year and for what capital projects. A county board may appropriate all of the available funds each fiscal year, or it may place the money into a capital reserve fund for future expenditure. This allows a county to save moneys over several years to finance large capital outlays for its school unit(s). As with county appropriations of other general fund revenues, a county board may exercise some control over how its local school unit(s) expends these funds. A county may seek permission from the Local Government Commission (LGC) to use part or all of the earmarked local sales- and use-tax proceeds for any lawful purpose if the county demonstrates that it can satisfy all of the capital outlay needs of its school unit(s) from other sources. In order to apply to the LGC for an exemption from the statutory earmarks on the Article 40 and Article 42 tax proceeds, a board of county commissioners must adopt a resolution and then submit it to the LGC. The resolution must indicate that the county can provide for its public-school capital needs without restricting the use of part or the entire designated amount. The LGC must consider both the school unit's capital needs and those of the county generally in making its decision. The LGC must issue a written decision detailing its findings and specifying what percentage, if any, of the earmarked proceeds may be used by the county for any lawful purpose. Counties also are free to allocate the unrestricted portion of their local sales- and use-tax proceeds to fund public-school capital and operating expenses.

In 2007, counties received authority to levy an additional quarter-cent tax, subject to voter approval.[49] The proceeds of the tax can be used for any county expenditure item, including public schools. Beginning in July 2016, certain counties began receiving additional sales- and use-tax revenues, pursuant to G.S. 105-524. This revenue results from a redistribution of a portion of the proceeds generated from county sales and use taxes. A county may use this additional revenue to fund public-school capital and operating expenses, community colleges, or economic development.

---

47. Counties have additional sales and use tax authority. All counties levy a one-cent tax pursuant to G.S. Ch. 105, Art. 39. Several counties also levy a quarter-cent tax pursuant to G.S. Ch. 105, Art. 46. Neither of these taxes is earmarked for school funding, though.

48. A county may petition the North Carolina Local Government Commission (LGC) for authorization to use part or all of the earmarked revenues for other purposes. The LGC will approve a petition only if the county demonstrates that it can provide for school capital needs without the earmarked revenue. A local board of education also may petition the LGC if it believes that the county has not complied with the intent of sales- and use-tax laws. G.S. 105-502 and -487.

49. G.S. Ch. 105, Art. 46.

State School Construction Funds

In 1987, the legislature enacted the School Facilities Act, which created the Public School Building Capital Fund (PSBCF).[50] The PSBCF was established to provide aid to all counties for school construction projects. It too was originally funded by a portion of the state's corporate income tax proceeds,[51] which were allocated among the 100 counties on the basis of ADM. A county and its local school administrative unit(s) could jointly apply to the Department of Public Instruction to use the county's allocation for capital outlay and technology projects. A county was required to match moneys allocated for capital outlay projects on the basis of one dollar of local funds for every three dollars of state funds.

Beginning in 2005, the legislature also allocated a portion (roughly 40 percent) of the state's lottery proceeds to the PSBCF.[52] These funds could be used to fund capital outlay projects for school buildings and were allocated among the counties according to a detailed statutory formula.[53] No local match was required.

In 2013, the General Assembly repealed the statutory distributions of both corporate income tax proceeds and lottery proceeds to the PSBCF.[54] New appropriations to the PSBCF will be subject to yearly state budget appropriations. According to G.S. 115C-546.2(d), if funds are appropriated to the PSBCF from the state lottery, those moneys must be allocated for school construction projects based on ADM.[55] A county and its local school administrative unit(s) will jointly apply to the Department of Public Instruction for a distribution of the moneys "to fund school construction projects and to retire indebtedness incurred for school construction projects."[56] No county matching funds are required. For the past several years, the legislature has appropriated $100 million to the fund.[57]

In 2017, the General Assembly established a second public-school capital fund, known as the Needs-Based Public School Capital Fund (NBPSCF). This fund is managed by the Superintendent of Public Instruction and is used to award grants to counties designated as a development tier one or tier two area to assist with public school building capital needs. The grant funds are subject to a county match based

50. S.L. 1987-622. The legislature also enacted the Critical School Facility Needs Fund (CSFNF). The CSFNF, funded by corporate income tax proceeds, aided counties and school units with the most pressing needs in relation to their resources, as determined by the CSFNF Commission. Moneys were distributed to high-need counties from 1988 through 1994, at which time the fund was abolished. S.L. 1995-631, § 14.

51. G.S. 115C-546.1(b) (repealed 2013).

52. G.S. 18C-164(d) (repealed 2013).

53. G.S. 115C-546.2(d)(1) and (2) (repealed 2013).

54. S.L. 2013-360, § 6.11.

55. G.S. 115C-546.2(e) allows the North Carolina State Board of Education to use up to $1.5 million of the funds appropriated each year to support positions in the North Carolina Department of Instruction.

56. G.S. 115C-546.2(d)(4).

57. The General Assembly has indicated an intent to increase the amount of lottery revenue dedicated to assist local governments in meeting capital needs to 40 percent of the net lottery revenue collected no later than fiscal year 2028–2029. See S.L. 2017-57, § 5.3(d).

on the development tier. For tier one counties, the match is three dollars in lottery funds for every one dollar in county appropriations, and grants may not exceed fifteen million. For tier two counties, the match is one dollar in lottery funds for every one dollar in county appropriations, and grants may not exceed ten million. There are some significant restrictions in the NBPSCF grant program.[58]

Other Local Funding Sources

In addition to appropriations from a county's general fund, a local school unit also may receive revenue derived from locally collected penalties and fines. Under Article IX, Section 7 of North Carolina's constitution, "the clear proceeds of all penalties and forfeitures and of all fines collected in the several counties for any breach of the penal laws of the state, shall belong to and remain in the several counties, and shall be faithfully appropriated and used exclusively for maintaining free public schools."[59] Several locally collected fines and penalties are subject to this constitutional mandate.[60] If a county collects penalties or fines that are subject to this constitutional requirement, it must remit the clear proceeds (gross proceeds minus up to 10 percent in collection costs) to the local school unit(s) within the county within ten days after the end of the month in which the money was collected.

A county does not include these funds in its appropriations to the school unit(s), and the county board has no control over their expenditure. The board of county commissioners, however, may consider the amount of fine, penalty, and forfeiture revenue received by a local school unit when determining the county's annual appropriations.

Step 6: Local School Board Initiates Dispute Resolution Process (Optional)

If the local school board "determines that the amount of money appropriated to the local current expense fund [for operating expenses], or the capital outlay fund, or both, . . . is not sufficient to support a system of free public schools," it may initiate a

---

58. For more detail on grant criteria, see N.C. State Superintendent, *Needs-Based Public School Capital Fund 2020 Grant Application*, https://go.boarddocs.com/nc/wcpsnc/Board.nsf/files/BTAJMU4AF412/$file/Needs-Based%20Public%20School%20Capital%20Fund%20-%202020%20Grant%20Application%20-%20Wayne%20County%20Public%20Schools.pdf.

59. N.C. Const. art. IX, § 7.

60. *See* G.S. 115C-437. For a detailed discussion of the categories of locally collected penalties and fines that are subject to this constitutional provision, see Kara A. Millonzi, "Locally-Collected Penalties & Fines: What Monies Belong to the Public Schools?," *Coates' Canons: NC Local Government Law* (blog), November 17, 2011, https://canons.sog.unc.edu/locally-collected-penalties-fines-what-monies-belong-to-the-public-schools/.

dispute resolution process with the board of county commissioners to challenge the appropriation (dispute resolution process).[61]

There are a number of steps in the dispute resolution process. First, to trigger the process, a local school board must so notify the county board, and the chairs of the respective boards must arrange a joint meeting of the boards within seven days of the adoption of the county budget ordinance. The boards then are required to meet and make a good-faith effort to try to resolve their differences. A mediator presides over the meeting and acts as a neutral facilitator.[62]

If the meeting is not successful, the boards proceed to official mediation. Unless the two boards agree otherwise, the participants in the mediation are the chairs, attorneys, and finance officers of each board; the public-school superintendent; and the county manager. The compensation and expenses of the mediator are shared equally by the local school administrative unit and the county. The mediation is conducted in private, and statements and conduct are not discoverable. The mediation must end by August 1, unless both boards agree otherwise. If the mediation continues beyond August 1, the county must appropriate to the local current expense fund a sum equal to its appropriation for the previous fiscal year.

If mediation ultimately fails, what happens next depends on the nature of the funding dispute.

Dispute over Operational Funding

If the dispute at least partially involves operational funding amounts, to be appropriated to the school unit's local current expense fund, then a failed mediation triggers a default funding formula (for operational funding). The funding formula is the final determination of the local current expense appropriation amount for that fiscal year. Neither the local board of education nor board of county commissioners may file any legal action challenging the determination. There is a detailed (and confusing) formula to calculate the minimum funding requirement. As stated above, the result is essentially a *per-pupil maintenance of effort plus inflation*. In other words, the minimum appropriation must be the equivalent of the per-pupil current expense appropriation from the prior year that was actually spent multiplied by an inflationary factor and the budget year student head count (or projected head count). The specific formula is detailed on the next page.

---

61. G.S. 115C-431(a).

62. Ibid. The mediator is either selected by agreement of both boards or appointed by the Senior Resident Superior Court Judge.

Local Current Expense Funding Formula if Statutory Funding Formula Not Triggered for the Prior Two Years

The funding formula differs depending on whether or not the funding formula had been triggered in the prior fiscal year. If the statutory funding formula was not triggered in the prior two fiscal years, the county's appropriation to a local school unit's local current expense fund derives from the following formula:

1. Start with the amount of county appropriations allocated to the local current expense fund in the prior fiscal year that was actually expended by the local school unit or transferred to a charter school, innovative school, regional school, or laboratory school. In other words, begin the calculation with the amount of county appropriations that were actually spent for the year immediately preceding the budget year. Note that because county appropriations are commingled with other local revenue sources in the local current expense fund, it is incumbent on the local school board to separately track the expenditure of county appropriations and report on this information to the county.

2. Divide the amount from step (1.) by the sum of the average daily membership of the local school administrative unit from the prior year plus the share of the average daily membership of any innovative, charter, regional, or laboratory school whose students reside in the local school administrative unit from the prior year. This number represents the per-student allocation of moneys actually spent.

3. Multiply the amount from step (2.), rounded to the nearest penny, by the sum of one plus the twelve-month percent change in the second quarter Employment Cost Index for elementary and secondary school workers as reported by the Federal Bureau of Labor Statistics. Unfortunately, the law does not precisely designate the data required to make this calculation. It is unclear if the reference is to the Employment Cost Index for total compensation for elementary and secondary school workers or the Employment Cost Index for wages and salaries for elementary and secondary school workers. (Note that second quarter data is released on July 31.) The new law also does not indicate whether seasonally adjusted or non-seasonally adjusted data should be used. It will be up to the county to determine which set of data to use in the calculation.

4. Multiply the adjusted per-student allocation in step (3.), rounded to the nearest penny, by the sum of the allotted average daily membership of the local school administrative unit from the budget year in dispute plus the share of the average daily membership of any innovative, charter, regional, or laboratory school whose students reside in the local school administrative unit from the budget year in dispute. Again, it is not clear what number should be used to determine the total number of students for the budget year in dispute. At the point in time that the statutory formula is likely to be triggered, a local school unit likely will only have its estimated average daily membership for the year.

The resulting figure from step (4.), rounded to the nearest penny, is the statutorily mandated local current expense appropriation for the budget year.

Local Current Expense Funding Formula if Statutory Funding Formula Triggered in Prior Two Fiscal Years or More

If the statutory funding formula is triggered a second year in a row, the formula is altered to increase the inflationary factor. The formula then becomes the following:

1. Start with the amount of county appropriations allocated to the local current expense fund in the prior fiscal year that was actually expended by the local school unit or transferred to a charter school, innovative school, regional school, or laboratory school. In other words, begin the calculation with the amount of county appropriations that were actually spent for the year immediately preceding the budget year.

2. Divide the amount from step (1.) by the sum of the average daily membership of the local school administrative unit from the prior year plus the share of the average daily membership of any innovative, charter, regional, or laboratory school whose students reside in the local school administrative unit from the prior year. This number represents the per-student allocation of moneys actually spent.

3. Increase by 3 percent the twelve-month percent change in the second quarter Employment Cost Index for elementary and secondary school workers as reported by the Federal Bureau of Labor Statistics. This provision, again, leaves a great deal of ambiguity. As stated above, it is unclear if the reference is to the Employment Cost Index for total compensation for elementary and secondary school workers or the Employment Cost Index for wages and salaries for elementary and secondary school workers. (Note that second quarter data is released on July 31.) The new law also does not indicate whether seasonally adjusted or non-seasonally adjusted data should be used. It will be up to the local school board and board of county commissioners to determine which set of data to use in the calculation. Finally, it is not clear how to interpret the mandate to increase the percentage change by 3 percent. It could mean that you add 3 percent to the percent change. It could also mean that you multiply the percent change by 3 percent. The former interpretation seems the most consistent with legislative intent. (To illustrate how that calculation would work, if the twelve-month percent change is 2.38 percent, you add 3 percent to that for a total of 5.38 percent or 0.0538.)

4. Multiply the amount from step (2.), rounded to the nearest penny, by the amount in step (3.), rounded to the nearest penny. Note that statutory language appears to indicate that the percent change calculated in step (3.) be rounded to the nearest penny before it is multiplied by the amount from step (2.) (To illustrate how the calculation would work, if the amount from step (2.) is 211.3823 and the amount from step (3.) is .0538, you round both numbers and then multiply 211.38 by .05.)

5. Multiply the modified per-student allocation in step (4.) by the sum of the average daily membership of the local school administrative unit from the budget year plus the share of the average daily membership of any innovative, charter, regional, or laboratory school whose students reside in the local

school administrative unit from the budget year. Note that at the point in time that the statutory formula is likely to be triggered, a local school unit likely will only have its estimated average daily membership for the year.

The resulting figure from step (5.), rounded to the nearest penny, is the statutorily mandated local current expense appropriation for the budget year.

Dispute over Capital Funding

If the dispute is over the amount of capital funding, the local board of education may file an action in superior court. The action must be filed within five days of the failed mediation. Either side may demand a jury trial. The judge or jury must determine (1) "the amount of money legally necessary from all sources" to maintain a system of free public schools "as defined by State law and the State Board of Education policy" and (2) "the amount of money legally necessary from the board of county commissioners."[63] In making this determination, a judge or jury must consider

> the educational goals and policies of the State and the local board of education, the budgetary request of the local board of education, the financial resources of the county and the local board of education, and the fiscal policies of the board of county commissioners and the local board of education.[64]

In *Union County Board of Education v. Union County Board of Commissioners*, the court of appeals held that the amount "legally necessary" is the amount needed to enable the local school board to fulfill its constitutional duty to provide every child with the opportunity for a sound basic education. The court also clarified that the judge or jury is limited to considering the needs of the school unit, and resources available to the school unit and the county, in the fiscal year in which the dispute arose.[65]

If the school board succeeds in the litigation, the court will order the board of county commissioners to appropriate a specific amount to the local school administrative unit and, if necessary, to levy property taxes to cover the amount of the appropriation. Any payment by the county may not be considered or used to deny or reduce appropriations to a local school administrative unit in subsequent fiscal years.

Either board may appeal the superior court's judgment in writing within ten days after the entry of the judgment. Final judgments at the conclusion of the appellate process are legally binding on both boards.

Although the statute directs the trial court to take up the matter as soon as possible, it is silent as to the timing of appellate review. In practice, the appellate review process often takes over a year or more to complete. Thus, even if a judge or jury determines that a local school board needs additional capital funds from the county

---

63. G.S. 115C-431(c).

64. Ibid.

65. Union County Board of Education v. Union County Board of Commissioners, 771 N.C. App. 590 (2015).

to meet its constitutional and statutory educational responsibilities for a particular school year, the school unit may not receive those additional funds that school year. In fact, the school unit may not receive the funds until well into the following school year. And, from a county's perspective, it may end up paying more money in a future fiscal year to its local school unit than is needed to support the school unit that year. In addition, both boards incur the (often substantial) costs of litigating the issue. For these reasons, most dispute resolution processes do not proceed beyond mediation.

Step 7: Local School Board Adopts School Budget Resolution

If the local board of education does not formally dispute the county's budget appropriations, or upon successful resolution of any dispute, then the local board of education adopts a budget resolution.[66] The budget resolution reflects the county's appropriations for capital and operating expenses as well as those from the state and federal governments. It also incorporates revenues from other local sources. G.S. 115C-432 imposes several requirements and limitations on a school unit's budget. Among other things, the school unit's budget must conform to the county's budget allocations. The budget resolution must be entered into the minutes of the local board of education. Within five days of adoption of the budget, copies are to be filed with the public-school superintendent, school finance officer, and county finance officer.[67]

The Local Government Budget and Fiscal Control Act requires that adoption of the budget ordinance take place by July 1.[68] However, sometimes county boards are unable or unwilling to adopt a budget ordinance by this date. In such cases, a county board must adopt an interim budget that appropriates money to cover necessary expenses for county departments and the local school unit(s) until the budget ordinance is adopted.[69] In an extreme situation, the state's LGC is authorized to assume the financial duties of the county board and to adopt the budget ordinance.[70] If the county's budget is delayed beyond July 1, a local school board also must adopt an interim budget resolution to pay salaries and the "usual ordinary expenses" of the school unit.[71]

---

66. G.S. 115C-432.
67. Ibid.
68. G.S. 159-13; G.S. 115C-429.
69. G.S. 159-16.
70. G.S. 159-181.
71. G.S. 115C-434.

Step 8: County Distributes Appropriated Funds to Local Education Agencies (LEAs)

By statute, a county must distribute one-twelfth of its local current expense appropriation each month. A county has more flexibility to distribute capital appropriations. There is likely to be variation in how these funds are distributed based on the nature of the capital project. Most counties will distribute at least some capital funding as a lump sum to the LEA after the budget is adopted. These funds likely will be used for maintenance and repair projects and equipment and furniture purchases. For major construction or land acquisition projects, the flow of funds will depend on a variety of factors. If a county must borrow money to fund the project, the county may pay the school unit or pay the contractor/vendor directly based on submitted invoices. The county and school board may work out alternative disbursement arrangements even if the county is not borrowing money, though. Regardless of the flow of funds, as discussed below, once the funds are appropriated to the LEA they are legally earmarked for LEA purposes (even if the full amount of the appropriation is not expended within the fiscal year). There are limited circumstances under which a county may reduce its school appropriation once the budget ordinance is adopted.[72]

Step 9: Local School Board Amends School Budget Resolution (Optional)

A local school board is free to amend its budget resolution any time after its adoption. The budget resolution must continue to meet the requirements specified in G.S. 115C-432, and if the county board has allocated funds by purpose or function code, the school board must continue to honor those designations except as allowed by statute.

Prohibition against Capital Outlay Fund Transfers

Occasionally during a fiscal year, a local school board will want to move moneys from its capital outlay fund to its current expense fund, or vice versa, in order to cover unexpected expenditures. A local school board is prohibited, however, from transferring money between these two funds, except under limited circumstances. A transfer may occur if all of the following conditions are met: (1) the funds are needed to cover emergency expenditures that were both "unforeseen and unforeseeable" when the school budget resolution was adopted, (2) the local board of education receives approval from the county board of commissioners, and (3) the local board of education follows certain procedural requirements.[73]

A local board of education may initiate a transfer between its capital outlay and current expense funds by adopting a resolution that states (1) the amount of the pro-

---

72. G.S. 159-13(b)(9).
73. G.S. 115C-433(d).

posed transfer, (2) the nature of the emergency, (3) why the emergency was unforeseen and could not have been foreseen, (4) what objects of expenditure will be added or increased, and (5) what objects of expenditure will be reduced or eliminated.

The local board of education must send copies of the resolution to the board of county commissioners and any other local school administrative units in the county. The board of county commissioners must allow any other local boards of education to comment on the proposed transfer. The board of county commissioners must then approve or deny the request within thirty days. The board of county commissioners must notify the requesting local board of education and any other local boards of education in the county of its decision. If the board of county commissioners does not act within the thirty-day period, its approval is presumed, unless the local board of education that submitted the request explicitly agrees to an extension of the deadline.[74]

Capital Outlay and Current Expense Fund Balance

If county moneys appropriated to the LEA for either capital or operating expenses are not expended within the fiscal year, they do not revert back to the county. They remain legally earmarked for either school current expense or school capital outlay, depending on the original appropriation. If the county's original appropriation allocated funds by purpose, function, project, or category (as discussed above), those designations remain even if the moneys become part of the LEA's fund balance at the end of the fiscal year.

Step 10: County Board Reduces Appropriations to Local School Unit(s) during Fiscal Year (Optional)

A county may reduce its appropriations to a local school unit only under limited circumstances. The board of county commissioners may not reduce its appropriations for capital outlay or operating expenses after it adopts the county budget ordinance unless (1) the local board of education consents to the reduction or (2) it is pursuant to a general reduction in county expenditures due to prevailing economic conditions.[75] If the board of county commissioners reduces its appropriations to its school unit(s) pursuant to a general reduction in county expenditures, it must hold a public meeting and afford the local school board an opportunity to present information on the impact of the reduction and then take a public vote (that is, a vote in an open session of a public meeting) on the decision to reduce the appropriations.

---

74. Note that if a board of county commissioners and a local board of education seek to use the local sales- and use-tax proceeds that are specifically earmarked by state statute for capital outlay expenses to fund operating expenses, the county also must seek approval from the Local Government Commission according to the procedures set forth in G.S. 105-487 and -502.

75. G.S. 159-13(b)(9).

PART IV

COMMUNICATING WITH STAKEHOLDERS

Chapter 13

Citizen Engagement through the Budget Process

Whitney B. Afonso

I. Introduction

Citizen engagement, defined in more detail in the subsection immediately below, involves employing a method or methods to involve citizens in community decision-making. Such engagement can be an effective tool for educating and informing citizens about numerous aspects of their local governments. For example, it can provide resources to help citizens better understand (1) the laws and policies that govern their counties or municipalities, (2) the missions and priorities of their local governments, and (3) the cost and scope of services provided by those governments. A local government's budget is an especially powerful tool for creating community engagement.

Depending on the needs and preferences of your governmental unit, you may have specific goals regarding citizen engagement. To attain these goals, certain questions must be raised and addressed. For example: "What type of information are we trying to convey?" Are you hoping to better inform citizens about the types and degrees of spending in your unit that are mandatory versus discretionary? Are you interested in giving them more information about the breadth of services provided? Another critical question: "What type of feedback do we want from citizens?" Perhaps the answer is "none" and your goal is simply to supply information. Or maybe you do want feedback, e.g., about competing budget proposals. Your answers to these types of questions will shape the approach you take toward citizen engagement.

A. What Is Citizen Engagement?

First things first: What, exactly, is citizen engagement? There is no one correct answer to this question, nor does the term contemplate a single type of engagement. In fact, there is a great deal of disagreement about what citizen engagement is.

The three major stakeholders in the creation of a local budget are citizens, practitioners or government employees, and elected officials. Each of these groups has different perceptions of what citizen engagement means and what outcomes can and should be achieved when it comes to the budget. This subsection focuses on identifying stakeholder perceptions of citizen engagement, exploring the efficacy of citizen engagement, and highlighting examples of citizen engagement.

Elected officials probably have the broadest notion of what citizen engagement means. Many officials see town hall meetings and budget workshops as providing sufficient citizen engagement in the budget process. They believe that these forums produce genuine citizen engagement and that such engagement can assist the budget process. Additionally, many elected officials see their elections and subsequent re-elections as the strongest forms of citizen engagement. They are mindful, however, that active (or vocal) citizens do not necessarily represent the community as a whole and that, as elected officials, they have a responsibility to consider the views of the entire community instead of just the opinions of the most engaged citizens.[1]

Practitioners and government employees, for their part, also see citizen engagement as an important part of the budgeting process. They view their role as providing information to citizens and encouraging them to act as macro-level community advocates. They understand that local government budgets are highly complex and technical, making them difficult to explain to citizens who may not have the time to get into the necessary details or to consider the needs of the entire community when assessing the budget (they also may not understand those larger needs). Fortunately, practitioners/employees believe that engaged citizens can be effective agents for explaining tough and controversial budget decisions to their fellow citizens. Government employees and local practitioners also appear to ascribe to the view that supporting citizen engagement can translate into the development of key citizen support for difficult budget decisions. Citizen leaders who are engaged in and supportive of local government decisions can be crucial in the passage of local referendum items like bond and tax measures, as well as in creating popular support (as opposed to popular opposition) for difficult budget decisions.[2]

In contrast with the other relevant stakeholders, citizens define engagement as an open dialogue between all stakeholders wherein they are given information but also provided the opportunity to inform practitioners/employees and/or elected officials of their priorities and concerns. Citizens value such opportunities for involvement in the decision-making process. Further, citizens understand that the later their participation in the budget process, the less influence they will have. Knowing this makes the fact that it can often be difficult to become engaged early in the process especially frustrating. Thus, ensuring adequate citizen engagement requires

---

1. For further discussion of stakeholder attitudes toward citizen engagement, see Maureen M. Berner, Justin M. Amos, and Ricardo S. Morse, "What Constitutes Effective Citizen Participation in Local Government? Views from City Stakeholders," *Public Administration Quarterly* 35, no. 1 (2011): 128–63.
2. Ibid.

> "Community engagement refers to the connections between governments, citizens and communities on a range of policy, program and service issues. It encompasses a wide variety of government-community interactions ranging from information sharing to community consultation, and, in some instances, active participation in government decision making processes."
>
> ---
>
> *Source:* Queensland Government, Department of Communities, *Engaging Queenslanders: An Introduction to Community Engagement* (2005), 5, https://naaee.org/sites/default/files/intro_ce.pdf.

increased outreach efforts, and more effort overall, on the part of administrators and elected officials.[3]

B. Does Engagement Matter?

Now that we have discussed what engagement means to different stakeholders, it is important to consider the tangible benefits that pursuing additional citizen engagement may bring to your local government and community.

Many local governments spend considerable time and resources trying to identify ways to make their citizen engagement efforts more effective. Some see positive results, while others discover that, despite their best efforts, the level of citizen engagement in the community remains unchanged. The academic evidence on the efficacy of dedicating resources to achieve higher citizen engagement is inconclusive. Some of the traditional literature indicates that such endeavors may not be effective, while some suggests that resource allocation to this end may be worthwhile. Therefore, it is advisable to be mindful of your community and its needs, to consider multiple options for how best to reach citizens, and to have realistic expectations when it comes to engagement.

The studies finding merit in government efforts to increase citizen engagement highlight the fact that the type and frequency of government conduct affect the level and quality of engagement. For example, in North Carolina, local governments that publish only that budget information that is required by law and host only the legally mandated number of public hearings should expect to see lower levels of citizen engagement when compared with communities that actively solicit engagement, e.g., by providing citizens with multiple sources of budget information and holding multiple hearings.[4] Local government leaders must home in on the type of engagement their communities need and then create policies that promote that

---

3. Ibid.

4. The North Carolina Local Government Commission (LGC) mandates that (1) a local government hold one public hearing before its proposed budget can be adopted and (2) the proposed budget that has been presented to elected officials be made immediately available to the public for review. *See* LGC, *Audit Manual for Governmental Auditors in North Carolina, Checklist Notes* (rev. March 2016), https://www.nctreasurer.com/slg/Audit%20Manual/Excel159checklist.pdf.

Local Government Must-Haves

Q: What are some of the things you need to develop citizen engagement?

1. Time

2. Resources and support from elected officials and/or practitioners

3. Interested and willing citizens

4. A representative group of citizens

Q: What else do you think your community might need?

_____

_____

_____

_____

---

engagement. (The next section provides an overview of several types of engagement strategies.)

A new research study suggests that engaging citizens, using a broad notion of engagement, helps local governments make the hard decisions they often face. Examining specifically the effect of engagement on budget outcomes during economic downturns, this study finds that in terms of expenditure cutting, citizen involvement (and approval) is associated more with the adoption of "high loss and high conflict" choices than with "slight loss[es] that lead to low conflict" strategies. This contradicts previous research findings that citizens generally do not favor high-loss budget-cutting strategies. This same study also finds that citizens are more willing to pay for local government services when revenue-raising mechanisms link such payments to service consumption and when the citizens understand (1) why the additional revenues are needed and (2) the relationship between how the revenue will be used and the presented needs.[5]

As previously mentioned, the creation of a local government budget is a complex process for deciding how to spend limited funds. Completing this process requires technical education and training, a desire to understand the budget as a whole and not merely specific parts of it, and a neutral mindset focused on serving the entire community. Expecting all citizens to meet these requirements is likely not reasonable, as evidenced by the relatively small number of citizens seen by local leaders at budget hearings. Consequently, if local practitioners and elected officials want to truly engage citizens in the budget process, they must reach out to as many of them as possible, across all demographics, and consider mechanisms for providing them the education and encouragement they need to become involved in the process.

---

5. Benedict S. Jimenez, "Raise Taxes, Cut Services, or Lay Off Staff: Citizens in the Fiscal Retrenchment Process," *Journal of Public Administration Research and Theory* 24, no. 4 (October 2014): 923–53.

Numbers Do Matter

It may sound obvious to say that you need to reach out to a broad base of citizens to attain high levels of citizen engagement, but this point cannot be stressed enough. Some statistics from a recent national survey to keep in mind:

- 89 percent of citizens between the ages of 18 and 24 did not attend a single public meeting over the course of the year covered by the survey, while just 65 percent of 65–74 year olds failed to do so.
- 10 percent of Asian Americans reached out to elected officials in the twelve months studied; the same numbers for African Americans and white Americans were 22 and 19 percent, respectively.
- Such differentials were also observed between low- versus high-income earners. Only 16 percent of those making less than $25,000 had reached out to elected officials in the past year, while 22 percent of those making $150,000 or more made the effort.

Source: Mike Maciag, "The Citizens Most Vocal in Local Government," *Governing*, July 2014, https://www.governing.com/archive/gov-national-survey-shows-citizens-most-vocal-active-in -local-government.html.

Training and education are not the only potential roadblocks that citizens may encounter when engaging in the budget process. For many citizens, the time commitment required to become actively engaged and acquire necessary knowledge may not be possible, or even considered worthwhile, given their busy schedules. Thus, if local government leaders want to increase citizen engagement, they must find methods for educating and inspiring the public that don't require intensive time commitments on the part of citizens.[6] Failing to do so may restrict local governments' engagement successes to only small groups of citizens.

Even in cases where the level of citizen engagement is high, however, elected officials and local practitioners should acknowledge that certain populations will be more difficult to engage in the budget process and that they, the officials and practitioners, should avoid overlooking the valid concerns, needs, and preferences of those groups.

C. Citizen Engagement Goals, Effectiveness

The literature identifies many reasons why local governments might want to engage their citizens. For example, they may need or want to

- meet legal requirements,
- advance democratic ideals of citizen participation,
- advance notions of social justice,
- educate and inform the public,
- encourage innovation and the creation of new ideas,

---

6. School of Government faculty member John B. Stephens has written extensively on such methods. See, for example, *Creating Effective Citizen Participation in Local Government Budgeting: Practical Tips and Examples for Elected Officials and Budget Administrators*, Public Management Bulletin 6 (UNC School of Government, June 2011).

- improve processes,
- create a sense of community, or
- generate greater public support.[7]

Given that there are various goals for, and many reasons behind, citizen engagement efforts, it is not surprising that the literature on whether such efforts are effective is mixed. This may be attributable, at least in part, to the fact that there is disagreement on just what effectiveness means in this context. Researchers Carol Ebdon and Aimee Franklin have gauged the effectiveness of citizen engagement in the budget process by referencing the following criteria:

- participants reflect the community as a whole,
- the process is open to a large number of participants,
- citizen input is collected in the early stage of the budget process,
- there is two-way communication between citizens and government officials,
- citizen input is not merely symbolic but is actually taken into consideration, and
- citizens reveal their true preferences.[8]

When one takes that definition of "effective" and expands it to include additional goals, advocates of citizen engagement see the potential for many positive outcomes. For example, supporters view citizen engagement as an educational tool and see effective engagement in this sense as leading to strengthened notions of civic responsibility and citizenship. Supporters also believe that effective citizen engagement can introduce people to other perspectives and help them understand the common good. Engagement can also decrease feelings of alienation and legitimize the role of government from the citizen's perspective.

Many of these additional goals for citizen engagement relate to building up trust in government, which has been steadily declining over the last sixty years (see Figure 13.1). The engagement goals also include, broadly speaking, achieving a more equitable and just society. To these ends, supporters view citizen engagement as giving voice to the have-nots and the politically weak.[9]

---

7. *See* Carol Ebdon and Aimee L. Franklin, "Citizen Participation in Budgeting Theory," *Public Administration Review* 66, no. 3 (May/June 2006): 437–47; Tina Nabatchi, "Addressing the Citizenship and Democratic Deficits: The Potential of Deliberative Democracy for Public Administration," *American Review of Public Administration* 40, no. 4 (2010): 376–99; Brian W. Head, "Australian Experience: Civic Engagement as Symbol and Substance," *Public Administration and Development* 31, no. 2 (May 2011): 102–12; John M. Bryson et al., "Designing Public Participation Processes," *Public Administration Review* 73, no. 1 (January/February 2013): 23–34; Alfred T. Ho, "Citizen Engagement in the New Normal Fiscal Environment: Time for Participatory Performance Budgeting (PPB 2.0)" (paper, International Conference of the Institute of Public Administration Australia (IPAA), Melbourne, Australia, September 18–20, 2012).

8. Carol Ebdon and Aimee Franklin, "Searching for a Role for Citizens in the Budget Process," *Public Budgeting & Finance* 24, no. 1 (March 2004): 32–49.

9. Nancy Roberts, "Public Deliberation in an Age of Direct Citizen Participation," *American Review of Public Administration* 34, no. 4 (December 2004): 315–53.

Figure 13.1. Citizen Trust in U.S. Federal Government (April 2019)

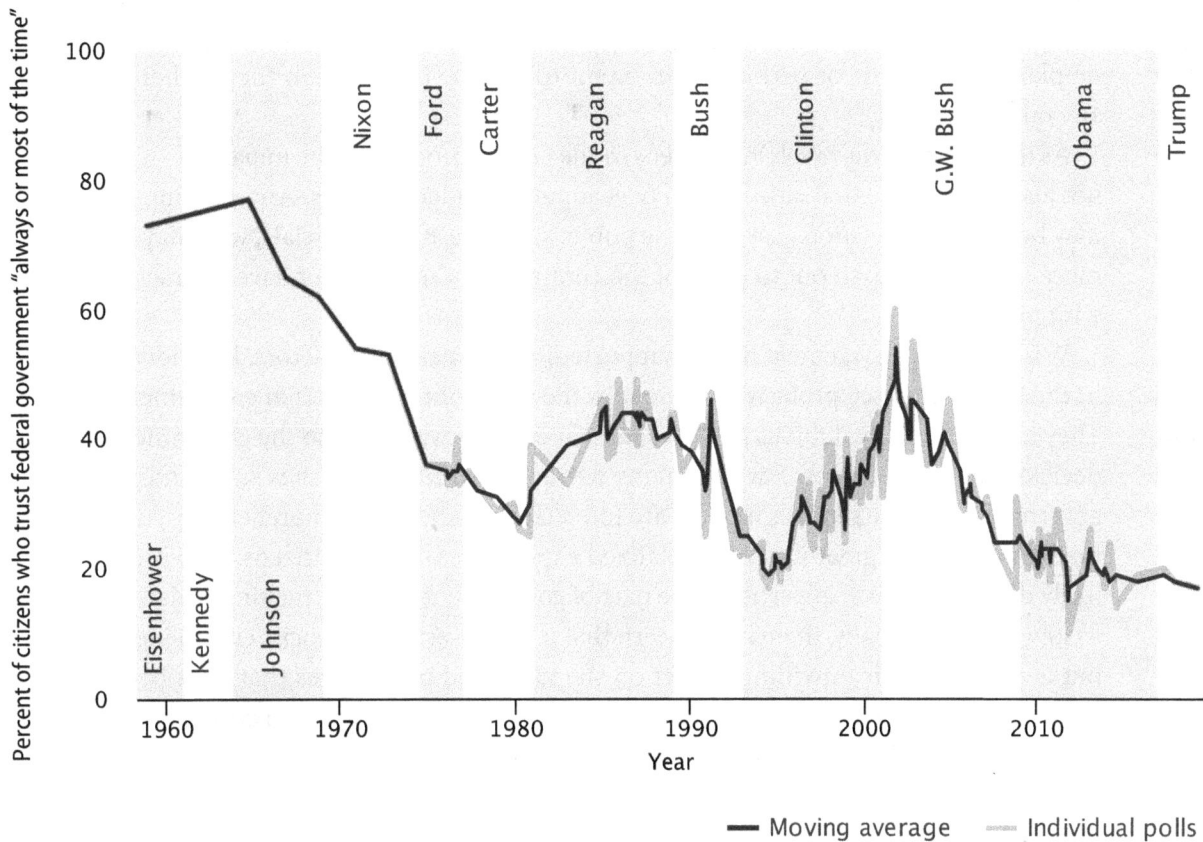

Source: "Public Trust in Government 1958–2019," Pew Research Center, accessed April 11, 2019, http://www.people -press.org/2019/04/11/public-trust-in-government-1958-2019/.

Another reason for soliciting citizen participation is to improve the performance of the agency or department involved in the decision-making at issue. As a general proposition, agency performance can be improved through better allocation of resources. For example, citizens providing input on new bus routes and placement of bus stops may improve the effectiveness of a public transit agency in reaching its desired constituents. More specifically, research has shown that the timing of citizen participation makes a great deal of difference in the results of the budget process— and in agency effectiveness. Public engagement at the beginning and the end of the process appears to carry the greatest weight. In particular, public input has the greatest potential to change outcomes in the information-sharing and program assessment stages of the budget process. Citizen involvement at the budget discussion or budget decision phases of the process has not been shown to improve agency performance.[10]

___

10. Hai (David) Guo and Milena I. Neshkova, "Citizen Input in the Budget Process: When Does It Matter Most?," *American Review of Public Administration* 43, no. 3 (2012): 331–46.

When it is taken seriously, citizen engagement has been found to benefit both citizens and public officials alike.[11] Unfortunately, it is not always taken seriously. Often, officials view reaching out to citizens as a symbolic gesture. They do so with no plan, mechanism, or perhaps even intent to use the information they gather in any meaningful way.

As discussed above, involving citizens in the budget process can be impactful—and not just in the sense that citizens will have input on budget choices. Another impact may be improved relations between the public and government officials, who may be more inclined to reach out to parts of the community they may not have interacted with previously.

While citizen engagement has its supporters, it also has its detractors. Individuals in the latter camp see problems inherent in the very concept of citizen engagement. They are particularly dubious of the value that citizens will bring to the government decision-making process. Further, many detractors argue that issues surrounding government and the services it offers are too technical and that comprehending such matters requires a great deal of specialized expertise. Allowing citizens, who most likely do not have such expertise, to be part of government decision-making is viewed as unwise. Additionally, there is a concern that if the government solicits citizen input but is not able (or is unwilling) to act on the ideas and preferences that have been expressed, then citizen engagement will lead to even greater distrust in government.

On top of the concerns about engagement discussed immediately above, critics argue that citizen engagement practices can be inefficient, slow, and burdensome. For example, many critics worry that citizen engagement will lead to a larger divide between the haves and have-nots because the ability to participate will require resources that the wealthy are more likely to possess, such as time, money, and other resources. There are also concerns regarding direct participation by citizens in the decision-making process.[12] (See sidebar.)

All of these concerns must be carefully considered and weighed against the potential value created by citizen engagement.

---

11. *See* Brian Adams, "Public Meetings and the Democratic Process," *Public Administration Review* 64, no. 1 (January-February. 2004): 43–54; Wendy L. Hassett and Douglas J. Watson, "Citizen Surveys: A Component of the Budgetary Process," *Journal of Public Budgeting, Accounting and Financial Management* 15, no. 4 (2003): 525–41; Nai-Ling Kuo, "Citizen Dissatisfaction Leads to Budget Cuts, or Not: A Case Study of a Local Taiwanese Government," *Australian Journal of Public Administration* 71, no. 2 (June 2012): 159–66.

12. Roberts, "Public Deliberation in an Age of Direct Citizen Participation."

Direct citizen participation is viewed with skepticism and even wariness. Representative democracy, or indirect citizen participation, has its advantages. It protects citizens from the dangers of direct involvement. It buffers them from uninformed public opinion, it prevents the tyranny of the majority, and it serves as a check on corruption. It also meets the needs of a complex, postindustrial society that requires technical, political, and administrative expertise to function. Unlike public officials, citizens do not have the time or the interest to deliberate for the purpose of developing informed public judgment. Given the size and complexity of the modern nation state, direct citizen participation is not a realistic or feasible expectation.

Source: Nancy Roberts, "Public Deliberation in an Age of Direct Citizen Participation," *American Review of Public Administration* 34, no. 4 (December 2004): 316.

D. The Role of Government Leaders

The value of citizen engagement is, as stated in the sections above, determined through factors such as engagement goals and the effectiveness of efforts to achieve them. How government leaders approach and advocate for citizen engagement can bear on the effectiveness of engagement efforts. What leads to successful citizen participation outcomes? Research has cited several factors, including

- reaching out to citizens through repeated advertisements of engagement events,
- treating citizens with courtesy and respect when engaging with them, and
- following up with citizens after an event has concluded.[13]

Additionally, there is evidence that the nature of the champion matters, i.e., whether the individual pushing for citizen engagement is a passionate or a passive advocate. The political environment and the attitude of the manager of the jurisdiction involved in the governmental decision-making are especially critical. If the manager has a strained relationship with elected officials, those officials are less likely to seek ways to innovate and to engage with citizens. This strained relationship will also lead to a general sense of distrust and to the allocation of fewer resources that could be devoted to citizen engagement. Research has shown that to successfully foster citizen engagement, particularly engagement that goes beyond mere information-sharing, the manager has to be passionate and intentional.[14]

But, while government can improve the engagement process, it can also undermine it. Researcher Matt Leighninger argues that the laws currently governing citizen participation are outdated and obsolete and that this leads to higher levels of distrust

---

13. William H. Baker, H. Lonn Addams, and Brian Davis, "Critical Factors for Enhancing Municipal Public Hearings," *Public Administration Review* 65, no. 4 (July 2005): 490–99.

14. Yuguo Liao and Yahong Zhang, "Citizen Participation in Local Budgeting: Mechanisms, Political Support, and City Manager's Moderating Role," *International Review of Public Administration* 17, no. 2 (2012): 19–38.

in government.[15] Jyldyz Kasymova's examination of multiple engagement efforts in New York suggests similar outcomes. When citizen engagement is used ineffectively, Kasymova observes, it may "result in [a] more suspicious and skeptical citizenry."[16] Citizens get frustrated when they feel like engagement efforts are simply symbolic. A common example of this would be a local government that hosts a budget hearing right before the budget is adopted.[17]

II. Phases of Citizen Engagement

The citizen engagement process can be broken down into three distinct phases that fall across a broader spectrum of engagement and involvement. Phase 1 is the information-sharing phase. This phase contemplates a one-way relationship in which government leaders share information with citizens. Phase 2 is the consultation phase. In this phase, government leaders prompt a two-way conversation with citizens wherein the leaders solicit feedback on an agenda that the government has set. Phase 3 is the active participation phase. In this final phase, government leaders and citizens collaborate on a set of policy issues, and citizens are able to shape policy and outcomes. While citizens have a large role in Phase 3, the government maintains final decision-making authority and is not obligated to heed and incorporate citizen perspectives.[18] These three phases will be discussed in more detail in the following sections.

A. Phase 1: Information-Sharing

In the information-sharing phase, local government leaders create a one-way relationship focused not on receiving input but, rather, on providing citizens with information. Examples include making budget documents available to the public and creating websites that citizens can access to find information on the budget and other matters of interest. The activity in this phase aligns closely with how most elected officials, and to a lesser extent practitioners, tend to view citizen engagement.[19] There are

---

15. Matt Leighninger, "Want to Increase Trust in Government? Update Our Public Participation Laws," *Public Administration Review* 74, no. 3 (May/June 2014): 305–6.

16. Jyldyz Kasymova, "Analyzing Recent Citizen Participation Trends in Western New York: Comparing Citizen Engagement Promoted by Local Governments and Nonprofit Organizations," *Canadian Journal of Nonprofit and Social Economy Research* 5, no. 2 (2014): 59.

17. Maureen Berner, "Current Practices for Involving Citizens in Local Government Budgeting: Moving Beyond Method," *Public Administration Quarterly* 27, no. 3/4 (Fall 2003/Winter 2004): 410–32; Ebdon and Franklin, "Searching for a Role for Citizens in the Budget Process"; Kasymova, "Analyzing Recent Citizen Participation Trends in Western New York."

18. State of Queensland, Department of Public Works, "Queensland Government Enterprise Architecture (QGEA) Online Community Engagement Guideline" (December 2010), https://www.qgcio.qld.gov.au/documents/online-community-engagement-policy.

19. Berner et al., "What Constitutes Effective Citizen Participation in Local Government?"

Figure 13.2. Citizen Engagement Process

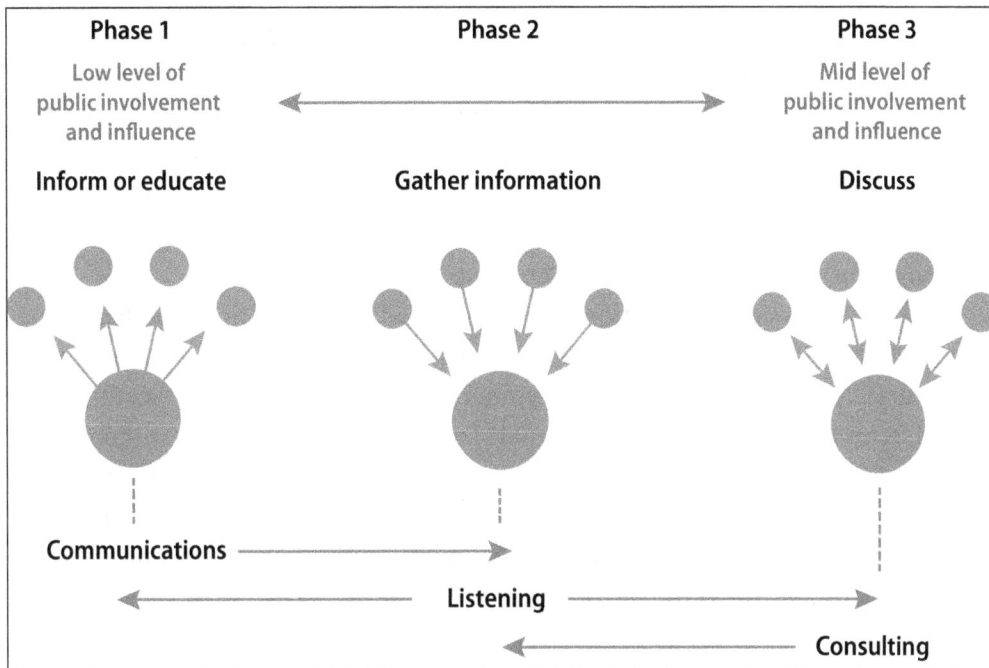

Source: Health Canada Policy Toolkit for Public Involvement in Decision Making.

several benefits to the information-sharing relationship found in Phase 1 of the citizen engagement process. First, both the costs and the efforts demanded from government leaders and practitioners are low. Second, the relationship can be an effective vehicle for communicating important budget information. In a time of budget shortfalls and limited resources, creating this information-sharing relationship is a relatively easy way to fulfill citizen engagement needs and ensure that practitioners are able to focus on the daily operation of local government.

However, this phase of citizen engagement does have its drawbacks. The most important one, arguably, is that it creates a solely one-way avenue of communication from local government leaders to citizens. Citizens may be directly given, or may be provided with the means to access, the information, but they have limited (if any) ability to give local leaders feedback that could be helpful in guiding local budget decisions. Another shortcoming of the information-sharing phase is that, typically, only a small portion of citizens will seek out the information provided by the government, meaning that the average citizen will remain uninformed about where his or her taxes go and what his or her local government does.

1. Examples of Budget Information-Sharing

There are three common methods of information-sharing employed by many local governments. The first is simply making budget information available to the public online, at the local government unit's offices and/or at places in the community such as public libraries. This is a basic and, in North Carolina, a mandated method for sharing information and ensuring transparency. It also requires very limited time and resource commitments from local government leaders, which makes it a very attractive information-sharing option. The main shortcoming of this method is that the information shared will likely be too complicated and overwhelming for the average citizen, and thus the public is probably not going to gain a great deal from it. For example, citizens may not understand their local government's revenue streams, debt constraints, levels of mandatory spending, specific program functions, or budget terminology. The fact that this approach only reaches citizens who are proactive in attaining information is another shortcoming.

Another often-used information-sharing method is the creation and dissemination of budget fact sheets. A major advantage of using fact sheets to convey budget data is that it allows local government leaders to communicate complicated information in an easy-to-understand manner. For instance, a local government's fact sheet might contain "Budget at-a-Glance," "Key Items to Know," and "Community Priorities" sections. The primary disadvantage of this method is that creating even a brief fact sheet from a lengthy budget document requires significant practitioner time. Also, the work involved in doing so—e.g., synthesizing all of the necessary information, providing context—is quite complex. Practitioners tend to find it difficult, if not impossible, to provide a full picture of the budget in a single fact sheet, raising concerns that this method of information-sharing may actually misinform or mislead citizens. Additionally, creating a fact sheet that is purely neutral and does not advance certain arguments/budget choices over others by highlighting—or choosing not to highlight—specific areas of spending can be a huge challenge. Practitioners should be aware of any fact sheet element that may incite an argument when information within it is presented in a particular way, however subtle. The use of terms such as "myth", "truth", and "reality" are examples of elements that could imply a position or amount to advocacy. Local governments that use budget fact sheets should exercise due diligence and ensure that they are producing neutral, information-centric fact sheets.

Videos are becoming an increasingly common means for sharing information. In today's digital age, conveying budget information in a video is an easy and appealing approach. Creating informational videos can be a time- and cost-effective process that results in highly informational products. Many municipal governments in North Carolina have public access television channels dedicated to government programming. These channels would be a great avenue for educating the public about budget information. On the down side, only one-third or so of the public gets its news from local television channels, so it would not be much of a leap to presume that even fewer citizens would be proactive and interested enough to watch budget briefings on public access television.[20] To reach more citizens, local practitioners are going to have to be creative and develop multiple mediums through which to disseminate

20. Katerina Eva Matsa, "Fewer Americans Rely on TV News: What Type They Watch Varies by Who They Are," *FactTank: News in the Numbers* (Pew Research Center), January 5, 2018, http://www.pewresearch.org/fact-tank/2018/01/05/fewer-americans -rely-on-tv-news-what-type-they-watch-varies-by-who-they-are/.

informational budget videos. Tech-savvy local leaders and practitioners (or college interns in their offices) should consider leveraging YouTube, Facebook, and Twitter (among other platforms) to reach a broader audience. When creating video content, local leaders should keep the public's potential responses in mind. The leaders should be striving to make a positive impression on citizens and working hard not to leave them with the feeling that the government has wasted precious resources on an overly complicated video.

Open data[21] and transparency efforts by local governments could arguably be considered forms of information-sharing. While such efforts by the government are laudable, when local leaders only share documents and data, citizens may not fully understand what they are seeing. Even worse, they may be outraged by what they are seeing because the information has been presented in a vacuum—i.e., there is no context for it. Therefore, when putting budget information out to the public, your organization should take steps to provide context for the facts, figures, and numbers presented by, for example, benchmarking a jurisdiction's expenditures against peers and explaining how they are similar and how they are different. Doing this can help residents better understand the typical scope and cost of government services. Additionally, discussing associated legal constraints might also be useful. For example, there may be pertinent laws that govern how revenues may be used (e.g., as in the case of some local sales taxes). Offering context for budget information is becoming a best practice (and will likely be required by law in the near future).

Providing taxpayers with receipts is another way for local governments to share budget information with citizens. With a tax receipt, the government can break down a citizen's tax burden and connect it to what he or she is receiving in return. A receipt template for an Orange County taxpayer created for a recent School of Government bulletin serves as a good example, showing that just over a dollar of the taxpayer's average monthly property tax burden goes to public transportation.[22] While I would, in many cases, caution against treating citizens like customers, this approach has been an effective tool in other contexts at the federal and state levels and, more and more commonly, at the local level.[23]

An extremely innovative budget information-sharing mechanism was created right here in the state of North Carolina. The city of Asheville developed what it calls its "Adopted Budget Dashboard,"[24] a user-friendly method for presenting city expenditure and revenue data by category. The dashboard conveys this data visually, allowing the user to first see and compare the size of various types of expenditures and then dive more deeply into the different categories of expenditures and revenues,

---

21. *Open data* is data that is readily accessible to the public and is provided to citizens at no cost. *See* "What Is Open Data?," Open Data Handbook, http://opendatahandbook .org/guide/en/what-is-open-data/.

22. Whitney Afonso, *Would You Like a Receipt with That? An Information-Sharing Tool for Enhancing Citizen Engagement*, Public Management Bulletin 8 (UNC School of Government, February 2014), http://sogpubs.unc.edu/electronicversions/pdfs/pmb08.pdf.

23. For more information, see the bulletin cited in note 22.

24. "Adopted Budget 2017-2018," City of Asheville, N.C., Dashboards, http://dashboards.ashevillenc.gov/budget/details?mode=expenditures&nodePath=root.

progressing to more specific areas of spending. The dashboard also allows users to download data and provides links to the city's full budget document and to a helpful "Understand this data" option. It is an excellent and straightforward way to present budget information and make it accessible to residents.

A final information-sharing method involves reaching out to our youngest citizens. I encourage local government leaders to go into the public schools in their communities and talk to students about government. The subject of civics is being taught less and less frequently in our classrooms, and many students may lack even a basic understanding of how government works, especially local government. These conversations will often be challenging, given this gap in knowledge and the age of many students, but by going into the schools you will have a captive audience and, generally speaking, a fairly representative portion of the population. Students are not merely citizens; they are the future of our communities, and building relationships with them early on and encouraging them to be engaged from a young age has the potential to pay large dividends.[25]

B. Phase 2: Consultation

The second phase of citizen engagement is consultation. Whereas information-sharing involves a one-way relationship, consultation creates a two-way dialogue based on citizen feedback. It relies on a fundamental assumption by local leaders that citizen feedback is beneficial to the budget process. This engagement phase provides for and encourages citizen input while still allowing local leaders to define the agenda. The key at this stage is for practitioners and elected officials to solicit input on a set of issues and questions that they have created and over which they exert control.

Like information-sharing, consultation, in some form, regarding the budget is required by state law. For example, each local government must hold a budget hearing where the proposed budget is presented and citizens have the opportunity to

---

25. For a discussion of the lessons I learned by going into the classroom to talk with upper elementary school– and middle school–aged children about budgeting, see Whitney Afonso, "Engaging Our Future: A Guide to Going into the Classroom," *Death & Taxes* (UNC School of Government public finance blog), September 25, 2017, https://deathandtaxes.sog.unc.edu/engaging-with-our-future-citizens-a-guide-to-going-into-the-classroom/. *See also* "Project Citizen," Center for Civic Education, http://www.civiced.org/programs/project-citizen, a program whose mission is as follows:

> Project Citizen is a curricular program for middle, secondary, and post-secondary students, youth organizations, and adult groups that promotes competent and responsible participation in local and state government. The program helps participants learn how to monitor and influence public policy. In the process, they develop support for democratic values and principles, tolerance, and feelings of political efficacy.

Project Citizen is a program to consider, and one that could be implemented with the help of your local budget office, although it has a broader scope than just financial concerns.

comment on it.[26] While these budget hearings are often wide in scope, covering the entire budget, there are specific issues that (1) will frequently be of particular interest to citizens and (2) officials will be more interested in explaining, discussing, and receiving feedback on.

Providing the public with venues (such as public hearings and town hall meetings) where information is shared and citizens are offered opportunities to give local leaders their opinions and suggestions is a common form of consultation. Beyond information-sharing, an additional benefit of the consultation phase is that, to be successful, it requires a limited investment of time and money on the part of the local government. Consultation as a form of citizen engagement aligns with both practitioners' and elected officials' view of what constitutes engagement (more so with the practitioner view, which seeks to inform citizens and create community liaisons).

One of my favorite examples of consultation comes from our neighbors to the north. A few years ago, Fairfax County, Virginia, asked its citizens to create a better budget. The county asked citizens to suggest increases and decreases to key areas of government expenditure. Citizens could share their views either on hard copy documents that could be mailed back to the county or via dynamic PDFs[27] that automatically calculated changes in both tax burdens and expenditures. Both forms not only allowed citizens to change expenditures (in select areas) but also allowed the government to provide explanations for why certain decreases or increases might be warranted. Citizens could change key spending areas (by indicating an increase or a decrease, for example, in spending for education or public safety) and then would be asked to balance the budget, either through cuts or tax increases (let's be honest here—most people believe that some aspects of government deserve more funding than others).

Fairfax County's efforts are a great example of a method that satisfies not only the information-sharing phase of citizen engagement, but the consultation phase as well, owing to the two-way dialogue that was facilitated and achieved. Citizens chose to share their budget choices with the county, providing county officials with a good deal of information about citizen priorities and preferences as to expenditures and the preferred mechanisms for financing them.

While this type of consultation process can be very informative for local governments, leaders should bear in mind that there is a high likelihood that the citizens who choose to participate in such activities reflect a segment of the population that may not be representative of the citizenry as a whole. Therefore, local leaders must balance what they hear from participants with what they believe are the needs of the greater population. Establishing this balance is no easy task; it requires much work and dedication from elected officials and practitioners.

---

26. Chapter 159, Section 12 of the North Carolina General Statutes.
27. The author has a copy of the PDF in her files.

C. Phase 3: Active Participation

In the third phase of citizen engagement, active participation, local government leaders maintain final decision-making authority over the budget but citizens are permitted and encouraged to actively shape budget options. When active participation efforts are successful, elected officials, local practitioners, and citizens become engaged collaborators, working together interactively to shape and create a budget. When properly executed, active participation activities allow local governments to make budget decisions that are truly aligned with the priorities of their citizens. This is what citizens think of when they think of citizen engagement.

Unfortunately, there are some significant difficulties and drawbacks associated with the active participation phase of citizen engagement. First, this phase demands a time commitment on the part of local practitioners and elected officials that is significant and that may interfere with their daily duties. Additionally, it requires that citizens commit no small amount of their own time in order to gain the necessary information, understand the information, and then engage local leaders throughout the budget process. This time requirement will in all likelihood result in a group of participating citizens that is far less representative of the population as a whole and far less representative than the citizens groups that participated in the consulting phase. Accordingly, local leaders will need to be especially conscious of the needs of non-represented population segments. Further, if citizens (and practitioners) are being asked to make such a large time commitment, the information that is generated from their efforts must, in some form, be integrated into the budget document. If input from citizens/practitioners is not used in this way, you risk alienating them and losing their willingness to participate in any future engagement.

Active participation is not a commonly used form of engagement in the United States, and thus there are few examples of it to draw upon and highlight in this textbook. This section will briefly discuss two examples of active participation employed by local governments. The first comes from East Lansing, Michigan, which was faced with the decision of how to repurpose a public building to best serve resident needs. Rather than go through the typical process and do things such as conducting a study, having local government departments submit proposals on how they could use the space, or limiting such proposals to those identified by the city manager, East Lansing chose to actively involve residents in the decision-making process about the future of the building. The city solicited proposals from citizens and held roundtable discussions on the feasibility of the proposed options, managing in the process to engage many people who had never before interacted with their government leaders. The city partnered with a nonprofit that was able to integrate many of the proposed uses for the space that had been put forward by the citizens. The project garnered high levels of support from the community as a whole and was deemed very successful.[28]

---

28. For more information, see "Case Study: How East Lansing Increased Public Trust by Using Online Input to Give an Old Building New Life," *Alliance for Innovation*, August 22, 2015, http://www.transformgov.org/articles/case-study-how-east-lansing -increased-public-trust-using-online-input-give-old-building-new.

The second example of a local government engaging citizens using active participation comes from a place closer to home. It is an example many of you may have heard something about: participatory budgeting efforts undertaken by the city of Greensboro.[29] The city has chosen to allocate $500,000 to its participatory budgeting process. Each of Greensboro's five city council districts will be given $100,000 for capital projects. Spending decisions will be made by district residents using an active participation method wherein (1) participating citizens "brainstorm ideas for improvement [project]s," (2) "budget delegates" convert those ideas into proposals, (3) district residents cast votes for their preferred projects, and (4) the projects tallying the most votes receive funding.

Greensboro put a lot of time into determining participation criteria, ultimately establishing an inclusive set of people who qualify to submit ideas for how to best use the allocated money. The city also developed a careful process for vetting submitted ideas, ensuring compliance with stated criteria (e.g., legal and feasibility mandates).[30]

Winning projects from the first cycle (fiscal year 2016) of Greensboro's participatory budgeting endeavor included bus shelters, pool shades, bike lanes, and crosswalks.[31] Though the process is still in its infancy, qualifying projects thus far have only included capital projects without large amounts of recurring expenses. The financed projects ideally will involve one-time costs, since the initiative's money is only allocated through this one process.

III. Conclusion

The budget process is a natural place to engage citizens. It provides an overview of government; it is, essentially, a set of policy choices and directions toward/at which the government is working to arrive; and it is a venue wherein citizens can both learn about the scope and services of government and possibly change them.

There are many ways for local government leaders to engage citizens in the budget process. In North Carolina specifically, all local governments engage with their citizens regarding the budget to some degree. For example, each local government is required by state law to hold a budget hearing before the proposed budget is adopted. However, there is no one-size-fits-all strategy for achieving successful citizen engagement in the budget process. How you, as local leaders, will best engage your citizens

---

29. For more information, see "Greensboro Participatory Budgeting," Greensboro, N.C., http://www.greensboro-nc.gov/index.aspx?page=4796.

30. For more context on the Greensboro example, as well as on the advantages and disadvantages of participatory budgeting generally, see Whitney B. Afonso, "Citizens Engaging Government: Participatory Budgeting in Greensboro, North Carolina," *Public Administration Quarterly* 41, no. 1 (2017): 7.

31. For more information, see "Greensboro PB: Cycle 1 Project Implementation Update, 4th Quarter," Greensboro, N.C., August 2017, http://www.greensboro-nc.gov/modules/showdocument.aspx?documentid=35324.

will depend on many factors, such as your goals for engagement and the demographics of your community. Below is a quick guide for thinking about what citizen engagement might look like in your jurisdiction.

First, start the engagement process by being mindful of your community's needs and of the diversity that exists within it. Local governments that are truly interested in citizen engagement will implement multiple strategies for attaining it because not all citizens are the same and, thus, not all approaches will work. So, for example, if you decide to hold town hall meetings, you need to be sure to think about transportation issues. Does the majority of your residents have a way to get to meetings? How about the timing of the meeting? Are you excluding a large population group because the citizens within it have family responsibilities or perhaps second jobs that make attendance at certain times impossible? How can you advertise town hall meetings to reach different segments of the population?

One solution to some of the above-raised concerns is to hold a combination traditional-virtual town hall.[32] The virtual version of the meeting can include much of the same information as the live event, be "open" for a longer period of time, and be more accessible to multiple segments of the population. Of course, holding only a virtual town hall would likely exclude some populations, such as the elderly (who are typically less comfortable with technology) and those without access to the Internet. How would you get the word out to as many citizens as possible? The most common ways are to advertise the meeting in newspapers, hang notices in public libraries, and post about it on social media platforms. Some local governments go a step further by reaching out to community groups within their jurisdictions, hoping that, if the leadership of such groups is made aware of the meeting, they will, in turn, reach out to their members and encourage them to attend.

If a town hall meeting does not seem like the best way for your community to engage citizens in the budget, an Internet or phone survey might be a worthwhile endeavor. When compared with holding a town hall meeting, each of these approaches would be lower in cost, less burdensome, and perhaps more effective.[33]

Do you live in a community with a large non-English-speaking population? If so, and if you are thinking about using a survey to engage your citizens about the budget, you will need to have survey materials available in other languages. If you plan to conduct a telephone survey, a method which tends, for several reasons, to rely upon non-cellular phone numbers, this could introduce other concerns. What percentage of the population has landlines these days? Certainly not younger citizens,

---

32. For a brief description of virtual town halls, see Matt Crozier, "What Is a 'Virtual Town Hall'?," *Engaging Local Government Leaders* (blog), October 14, 2016, https://elgl.org/what-is-a-virtual-town-hall/.

33. For additional resources on surveying citizens, see Ritu Nayyar-Stone and Harry P. Hatry, "Using Survey Information to Provide Evaluative Citizen Feedback for Public Service Decisions" (IDG Working Paper No. 2010-03, Urban Institute Center on International Development and Governance, June 2010), https://www.urban.org /sites/default/files/publication/29161/412215-Using-Survey-Information-To -Provide-Evaluative-Citizen-Feedback-For-Public-Service-Decisions.PDF; Tom Miller, "Best Practices for Local Government Citizen Surveys" (webinar, April 27, 2017).

so using this engagement method could skew your results. On a related note, what about (once again) citizens who don't have computers/access to computers or who are uncomfortable with technology? You could use a mixed method to get the surveys out, expanding your approach to include hard copy/paper surveys. One drawback with this survey tactic is that it might end up reaching the same people more than once and, because most surveys are designed to be anonymous, you will not be able to control for whether a portion of your responses are from passionate citizens who are willing to engage across multiple platforms (and survey instruments).

It should have become clear, even with just these few examples, that reaching your entire community effectively with just one form of engagement outreach is close to impossible. This is why it is advisable to have multiple outlets for engagement and feedback. You must also regularly evaluate whether you are hearing from certain parts of your community, even if you have employed your best efforts to engage all citizens. Again, reaching out to community leaders and asking them how you might better reach their members, or inquiring as to whether there is a meeting or function their members might favor, are effective strategies for better soliciting and integrating feedback on the budget from those populations. Sounds like a lot of work, doesn't it? I won't lie: it can be.

Bottom line: as local leaders and practitioners, make sure you are being thoughtful about where and how you engage citizens about the budget process. You NEVER want to get feedback from citizens that you do not plan on using. It is a waste of your time and theirs. Instead of building bridges and strengthening your communities, this behavior will leave people more frustrated and distrustful.

This is especially important advice for the second and third phases of citizen engagement, consultation and active participation. Providing information and helping citizens better understand government, the budget, and taxes can be challenging, but it does not have to be daunting. (Doing so carries the additional benefit of helping to prevent "fiscal illusion,"[34] which involves the public not understanding the true cost of government. This may manifest itself in citizens not understanding their actual tax burdens and/or not understanding the full cost of government provisions and expenditures.) You should never avoid the consultation and active participation phases of engagement simply because they might present some difficulties. You will be successful so long as you choose the correct types and levels of engagement that suit your community's needs (as opposed to taking an approach that seems like something you should be doing). Citizen engagement may appear to be an uphill battle, but there are many great resources out there about how to do it successfully, so do not lose heart! Ultimately, it is all about strengthening your community, and for public servants, there is no greater ambition!

---

34. For more on fiscal illusion, see Whitney Afonso, "It Was an (Im)Perfect Illusion: Fiscal Illusion and You," *Death & Taxes* (UNC School of Government public finance blog), May 22, 2017, https://deathandtaxes.sog.unc.edu/it-was-an-imperfect-illusion-fiscal-illusion-and-you/.

Chapter 14

The Role of Local Elected Officials in the Budget Process

Patrice C. Roesler

Introduction

Adopting a budget is one of the most important responsibilities of local elected officials. They must consider the ongoing operational needs of the unit of government they serve as well as the future investments needed in their local government's human capital and infrastructure assets. To the elected officials, the budget process is a carefully choreographed and sometimes fragile balancing act.

On one hand, citizens need and deserve public services; on the other hand, the burden of taxation must be carefully weighed in the context of local economic drivers, such as business and industry, prevailing wage rates, property values, population growth or migration, and overall financial capacity.

The roles of local elected officials in this balancing act fall principally into two categories: legal responsibilities and leadership responsibilities. This chapter covers five primary responsibilities in each of these categories.

Legal Role of Local Elected Officials in the Budget Process

The legal responsibilities of local elected officials in the budget process are outlined in various statutes, including those related to general county government, general municipal government, and the Local Government Budget and Fiscal Control Act (hereinafter Fiscal Control Act).[1] These legal responsibilities can be summarized in five primary actions:

1. appoint a budget officer,
2. follow the statutory processes,
3. levy taxes,
4. revalue property, and
5. receive and discuss the annual audit.

1. Appoint a Budget Officer

A primary role of local elected officials is to appoint a budget officer and direct the fiscal policy of the unit of government.[2] Additional parts of laws that apply here include G.S. 153A-82(5) for counties,[3] G.S. 160A-148(5) for municipalities,[4] and the Fiscal Control Act. Specifically, G.S. 159-9 states that "each local government and public authority shall appoint a budget officer to serve at the will of the governing board."[5]

The county and municipal laws give governing bodies authority to establish the manager form of government and define the duties of the manager. The duties are required to include the preparation and submission of the annual budget and capital program to the governing board and delivery of a completed annual report of the unit of government to the governing body and the public.

G.S. 159-9 requires the governing boards to appoint a budget officer and further specifies that the county or city manager SHALL BE that officer for local governments that have the manager form of government.[6] In North Carolina, all one hundred counties have the manager form of government, and almost half of the municipalities operate under the manager form of government.

There is an alternative organizational structure for municipalities that do not have managers, and in North Carolina this form is typically referred to as the mayor/council form of government. Most of the municipalities operating under this structure are relatively small, with populations below one thousand.[7] For municipalities that do not have the manager form of government, the Fiscal Control Act spells out the process for appointing persons, including the mayor, who can serve as the budget officer. Cities that do not have the manager form of government may impose the duties of the budget officer on any city officer or employee, including the mayor, if they agree to undertake them.[8]

---

1. Chapter 159, Article 3 of the North Carolina General Statutes (hereinafter G.S.).
2. G.S. 153A-101.
3. G.S. 153A-82 is Powers and Duties of Manager, and (5) specifies, "He shall prepare and submit the annual budget and capital program to the board of commissioners."
4. G.S. 160A-101.
5. G.S. 159-9.
6. Ibid.
7. Forms of North Carolina City Government," UNC School of Government, https://www.sog.unc.edu/resources/microsites/forms-north-carolina-city-government/current-forms-government.
8. G.S. Ch. 159, Art. 3.

It is the role of elected officials to ensure that the appointed budget officer or manager is qualified and capable of fulfilling their budget duties as described in the law; elected officials also must hold that person accountable for managing the day-to-day finances of the local government in accordance with the law and the policies established by the governing board.

2. Follow the Statutory Processes

While it may seem redundant to point out that local elected officials have a responsibility to follow the law, the reason to state it specifically here is that governing boards have statutory duties related to the budget that go beyond simply appointing a budget officer. Understanding and respecting budget timelines is a key responsibility of the governing body. To some extent, these timelines are spelled out in the Fiscal Control Act. G.S. 159-8(b) defines the fiscal year to begin on July 1 and end on June 30,[9] and G.S. 159-11(b) states that the budget, together with the budget message, must be submitted to the governing board each year no later than June 1.[10]

While these dates could lead to an assumption that the elected officials' role in the budget process starts on June 1, that is far from the case in real life. Elected officials are ultimately accountable for making sure budget development is proceeding in a timely manner and that all the relevant deadlines are likely to be met. In the interest of accountability, most governing boards begin working on their budgets around the middle of the fiscal year in December or January.

During this period of time, elected officials are regularly receiving reports from staff about anticipated revenues and expenditures, talking about potential operating needs that could impact operations or capital expenditures, and generally establishing an ongoing dialogue with the manager and finance officer about the needs of individual local government departments. These discussions may take place during the governing body's regularly scheduled meetings or in special meetings held for this purpose.

Often the local government managers ask their governing boards to schedule additional meetings throughout the spring, specifically to hear from individual department heads and other related agencies about their anticipated budget needs and desires. These additional meetings add a layer of complexity to the role of the elected officials and place significant additional demands on their calendars. For elected officials, it is their duty to make sure the statutory timelines are being met and to take the lead in providing whatever policy guidance is needed as the proposed budget comes together.

3. Levy Taxes

One of the more politically charged roles of elected officials is to levy taxes in a sufficient amount to provide full funding for a balanced budget. In many ways, elected officials bear the brunt of public schizophrenia about the role of government in our

---

9. G.S. 159-8(b).
10. G.S. 159-11(b).

daily lives. Nobody likes to pay taxes, and property is the primary means of generating tax revenues at the local government level.

Most citizens appreciate having safe water to drink, fire and law enforcement protection, emergency medical services, libraries, and parks. Most citizens want to go to local polling places to vote in elections and want a quality education for their children. They are conflicted about how much they want to pay for these and other services. The role of the governing board is to balance the current and future needs with the citizens' ability or willingness to pay taxes, and this is not an easy role.

Local elected officials must also consider the balance of the tax burden, or how much of the necessary tax revenues are paid by property owners, as compared to the amount contributed by non-property owners through sales taxes, fees, or other revenues. Local governments have limited authority to create sources of revenue, and the primary source over which they have some control is the property tax. It stands to reason that discussions about the property tax levy can be highly charged.

The Fiscal Control Act is explicit in stating that the governing board must adopt a budget ordinance making appropriations and levying taxes in amounts that the board considers "sufficient and proper."[11] It further stipulates that the budget ordinance has to levy taxes on property at rates that will produce the necessary revenue to balance the budget.[12]

Governing boards must levy taxes in a sufficient amount to meet the ongoing needs of the local unit and must also plan for future needs. Protecting the capital assets of citizens and planning for future necessary improvements should always be a part of their budget discussions. Local elected officials serve an important role in balancing the present and future needs of their citizens with the willingness or ability of the taxpayers to pay.

4. Revalue Property

The county board of commissioners is charged with revaluing property every eight years under the taxation laws of North Carolina. These statutes are sometimes known as the Machinery Act, as they set out the "machinery" of taxation in North Carolina, including both state and local taxation.[13]

The part of this statute that governs reappraisal of property establishes the norm of an eight-year cycle of revaluation, specified by county, with specified counties revaluing properties every year (roughly twelve counties each year, but in some years the number is slightly higher). Following this prescription, all one hundred counties

---

11. G.S. 159-13(a). "Not earlier than 10 days after the day the budget is presented to the board and not later than July 1, the governing board shall adopt a budget ordinance making appropriations and levying taxes for the budget year in such sums as the board may consider sufficient and proper, whether greater or less than the sums recommended in the budget."

12. G.S. 159-13(c). "The budget ordinance of a local government shall levy taxes on property at rates that will produce the revenue necessary to balance appropriations and revenues, after taking into account the estimated percentage of the levy that will not be collected during the fiscal year."

13. G.S. 105-286(a)(1).

will have revalued property over an eight-year cycle. At their option, boards of commissioners can choose to revalue more frequently, and many counties have opted to revalue property every four years.

The role of elected officials in revaluation is to ensure that financial resources are available to cover the cost of the revaluation process itself, to appoint a county assessor, to approve the schedule of values proposed by the assessor, and to provide an opportunity for citizens to appeal their property values. It is not the role of elected officials to assess or value property—their role is to ensure that property is revalued at a minimum of every eight years by a qualified assessor and to levy a tax rate based on those values that is sufficient to generate a balanced annual budget.

5. Receive and Discuss the Annual Audit

Local elected officials are responsible for hiring a certified public accountant to conduct an independent audit of the local government's financial records every year. The auditor is hired by and reports directly to the governing body. While the budget officer, manager, finance officer, and other staff will work closely with the auditor to gather the necessary information and reports during the audit process, the reporting relationship with the auditor is directly to the governing body.

The elected body should receive the audit in open session, require the auditor to explain their findings, and ask for a full discussion of any details in the management letter. Setting these expectations of the auditor in advance is a part of the role of the elected officials. After the audit is completed and the findings have been reported, it is then the responsibility of the elected officials to resolve any issues raised.

Periodically, the governing body should also consider whether to issue Requests for Proposals (RFPs) and discuss establishing new auditor relationships. Ultimately it is the responsibility of the governing body to ensure that the applicable laws are being adhered to and that the unit is financially stable.

While these five legal responsibilities provide an umbrella for the principle statutory roles of local elected officials, there are also important leadership roles in the budget process.

Leadership Responsibilities of Elected Officials in the Budget Process

Leadership is about behaviors—how you act and interact with others, treat colleagues and staff, voice concerns, raise questions, and generally exercise the responsibilities of serving in elected office. Leadership means showing respect and being diligent in the act of governing.

There are five primary leadership responsibilities that elected officials should embrace in the area of the budget, not because any law requires them to but because these actions create a culture of trust in local government. And the value of citizens' trust in local governments and their local elected leaders extends far beyond the single realm of the budget.

The following are five leadership responsibilities of local elected officials, which are described in more detail in this chapter:

1. do their homework,
2. be at all times aware of their local government's financial condition,
3. build trust with each other and with staff,
4. think strategically, and
5. openly share a vision for the future.

1. Do Their Homework

Elected officials are not expected to come into office knowing and understanding the complexities of local government finance. They are, however, expected and even required to become well informed about their financial responsibilities and liabilities and to give regular consideration to the financial reports of the unit of government. As local government leaders, it is important for them to take the time to do their homework. They need to read the financial reports, ask questions, and seek out others who can help them understand anything that is not clearly apparent. Elected officials have a responsibility to act from a place of understanding, and reviewing financial reports for understanding requires discipline. They must exercise curiosity, approach the financial statements with an inquiring mind, and come to meetings prepared to actively engage in the discussions.

2. Be at All Times Aware of the Financial Condition of Their Local Government

Elected officials have a responsibility to know their local government's financial position and condition. They cannot rely on the annual audit to disclose their financial condition. Having a "clean" audit simply means the budget is balanced, that the local government followed generally accepted accounting principles (GAAP), and that funds were generally spent in accordance with the budget ordinance. This leadership responsibility is about doing more than the law requires; it is about asking for and receiving regular financial reports from the manager or designated budget officer, knowing that the bank statements are being reconciled every month, making sure the bills are being paid on time, and setting the expectation that the elected body is holding the budget officer accountable for the financial condition.

If there is an enterprise function, the elected officials are responsible for making sure the enterprise is financially stable, that the accounts payable are up to date, and that the condition of the enterprise assets is being maintained. The elected officials need to know and understand where the revenues come from, know their cash flow position, and understand the purpose of fund balance. They should also have a fairly good understanding of their local economy, so they can be confident their local government services and workforce as well as revenues and expenditures can withstand any unforeseen challenges, such as hurricanes or pandemics.

Being a responsible leader means learning and understanding financial conditions and being prepared to take the right steps to ensure financial solvency, even when hard decisions must be made.

3. Build Trust with Each Other and Staff

Responsible leaders create an atmosphere of trust between members of the board or council and staff. In developing, adopting, and implementing the budget, the role of local elected officials is to assume a mindset that their managers and staff are approaching their responsibilities from a good place. The elected officials are responsible for oversight and accountability; they are not responsible for the day-to-day management of the budget. The budget is a planning tool; expenditures and revenues vacillate up and down over the course of the fiscal year. It is the manager's job, or the designated budget officer's job, to make sure the finances are managed appropriately.

Depending on the size of the local government, the lines of authority can become blurred, especially if the mayor is designated as the budget officer. In these circumstances, the mayor may be more actively engaged in the budget management than would otherwise be expected. As leaders, the role of the elected officials is to establish financial policies, be clear about their goals and priorities, and let the manager do the job of carrying out the budget and making sure priorities are being met.

4. Think Strategically

An important leadership role for elected officials is to think strategically about the future of their local government, their community, and their citizens. Leaders engage in strategic discussions about goals and priorities to meet future needs. Besides the actual preparation and adoption of the budget, having a strategic focus is one of the most important roles of elected officials.

Thinking forward is no longer a luxury for local governments—it is a necessity. Citizens want to know that their future needs are going to be met, whether that means new water pipes or new schools, paving potholes, or opening another library. Preparing for the future is what effective leaders do; they think ahead and have a plan for continuity and growth in both human and capital infrastructure. Many local governing boards develop strategic plans to establish these future priorities and policy directions. Thinking beyond one budget year at a time is a critical role for elected officials in the budget process.

5. Openly Share a Vision for the Future

Sharing a vision for the future of their communities is an important role for local elected officials in the budget process. Financial resources are precious commodities, and citizens want to know that their taxes are being spent wisely. Citizens also appreciate knowing their elected officials have a future for them in mind.

Being willing to set long-term goals and show progress toward meeting those goals as each budget gets adopted builds trust with citizens. Effective local leaders have a vision for the future, and they openly talk about it and promote it. They advocate for the future they see, and they build support for the goals that will actuate it.

Conclusion

Helping local elected officials learn and grow into their roles and responsibilities with the budget is a significant gift professional staff can offer. Most local elected officials are not budget or finance professionals, but the majority of them can easily relate to the value of knowing where the money comes from and understanding where it goes. Whether staff works with them routinely or occasionally, directly or indirectly, helping elected boards and councils translate the budget into realized accomplishments leads to more effective governing.

Chapter 15

Communicating Financial Condition to Elected Officials in Local Government*

William C. Rivenbark, Gregory S. Allison, and Dale J. Roenigk

Introduction

The public expects much of its elected officials in local government, who in many cases assume their positions facing a steep learning curve on a wide range of complex issues. A critical part of this learning curve involves *financial management*, where elected officials possess the ultimate responsibility for the fiscal matters of their organizations.[1] To carry out this responsibility, the law requires an annual independent audit of each local government unit's financial statements and requires that an auditor be selected by and report directly to the unit's governing board.[2] One goal of this process is for the locality to receive an "unmodified audit opinion," meaning that its financial statements were prepared in conformity with generally accepted accounting principles (GAAP) and present, in all material respects, the *financial position* of the organization. Another goal, which may be overlooked by elected officials, is to analyze and interpret the financial statements to determine the *financial condition* of the local government.

---

*Much of this chapter is drawn from William C. Rivenbark, Dale J. Roenigk, and Gregory S. Allison, "Communicating Financial Condition to Elected Officials in Local Government," *Popular Government* 75, no. 1 (Fall 2009): 4–13. Used by permission.

1. For a complete definition of "financial management," see Jerome B. McKinney, *Effective Financial Management in Public and Nonprofit Agencies*, 4th ed. (Santa Barbara, Calif.: Praeger, 2015). Chapter 160A, Section 67 of the North Carolina General Statutes (hereinafter G.S.) states that "the government and general management of the city shall be vested in the council." G.S. 153A-101 is even more specific, stating that the "board of commissioners . . . shall exercise the responsibility of developing and directing the fiscal policy of the county government."

2. *See* G.S. 159-34(a).

Administrators play an extremely important role in helping elected officials manage the fiscal matters of local governments. They ensure that professional management practices are used to budget and account for the *financial resources* of the organization, to prepare monthly financial reports for elected officials to review budget-to-actual variances, and to ensure that annual financial statements are prepared in conformity with GAAP. In 1999, as part of their role, administrators were responsible for implementing Governmental Accounting Standards Board (GASB) Statement No. 34, *Basic Financial Statements—and Management's Discussion and Analysis—for State and Local Governments*. This pronouncement expanded the financial-reporting model for local governments to include government-wide and fund-level statements. One reason for expanding the model was to provide a more complete picture of financial position.[3] Another reason was to increase a local government's ability to compare itself financially with other local governments and thus to help readers of financial statements evaluate the financial condition of local governments through benchmarking.[4]

The purpose of this chapter is to present administrators with an approach for analyzing, interpreting, and communicating financial condition to elected officials. We begin by defining *financial condition*—responding to the lack of agreement on this concept in our profession—before presenting the criteria that we identified for creating our approach to evaluating financial condition.[5] We then describe how the approach relates to the financial-reporting model, the dimensions and the indicators that we selected to measure financial condition, and the ability to communicate financial condition to elected officials with the state's web-based dashboard. We conclude with a summary of our approach for communicating financial condition in local government.

Defining Financial Condition

The definitions of "financial condition" in the professional literature are either specific in nature or broad in scope.[6] Therefore, in search of middle ground, we turned to the work of Robert Berne and Richard Schramm to guide our approach for evaluating financial condition.[7] These scholars maintain that there are two basic reasons for the

---

3. Dean Michael Mead, *An Analyst's Guide to Government Financial Statements*, 2nd ed. (Norwalk, Conn.: GASB, 2012).

4. GASB Statement No. 34, *Basic Financial Statements—and Management's Discussion and Analysis—for State and Local Governments* (Norwalk, Conn.: GASB, 1999). Although GASB Statement No. 34 applies to both state and local governments, this article focuses solely on local governments.

5. Xiaohu Wang, Lynda Dennis, and Yuan Sen (Jeff) Tu, "Measuring Financial Condition: A Study of U.S. States," *Public Budgeting & Finance* 27, no. 2 (2007): 1–21.

6. Ibid.

7. Robert Berne and Richard Schramm, *The Financial Analysis of Governments* (Englewood Cliffs, N.J.: Prentice Hall, 1986).

way resources are presented in financial statements: to report on the flow of resources during a given period and to report on the stock of resources at a given point. Operating statements report on the inflow and outflow of financial resources during the fiscal year. Balance sheets report on the stock of assets, liabilities, and net position or fund balances at the end of the fiscal year. We concluded that a logical definition of *financial condition* would align with resource flow and stock as reported in the annual financial statements.

Berne offers a definition that is closely related to the concept of resource flow and stock: the probability that a government will meet, currently and in the future, (1) its financial obligations to creditors, consumers, employees, taxpayers, suppliers, constituents, and others as they become due and (2) its service obligations to constituents.[8] The probability that a local government can meet these obligations, as interpreted from financial statements, increases with adequate resource flow to meet current obligations and with adequate resource stock to meet obligations over time.

An implied but missing element of Berne's definition is provision of capital assets. In response to this and other considerations, we offer the following definition of *financial condition*: a local government's ability to meet its ongoing financial, service, and capital obligations based on the status of resource flow and stock as interpreted from its annual financial statements. Although a local government's ability to meet its ongoing financial, service, and capital obligations is broad in scope, the specific focus of our definition is how a local government's ability to meet them aligns with resource flow and stock as interpreted from the annual financial statements.

Another important aspect of our definition is that it focuses solely on financial condition. One of the most frequently cited definitions of *financial condition* comes from the International City/County Management Association (ICMA): a government's ability to finance its services on a continuing basis.[9] This definition aligns with financial factors that show financial condition and with economic factors that affect financial condition, presenting a different form of analysis and requiring data from sources outside annual financial statements.[10]

---

8. Robert Berne, "Measuring and Reporting Financial Condition," in James L. Perry, ed., *Handbook of Public Administration*, 2nd ed. (San Francisco: Jossey-Bass, 1996), 66–96.

9. International City/County Management Association (ICMA), *Evaluating Financial Condition*, 4th ed. (Washington, D.C.: ICMA, 2003).

10. A financial factor that shows financial condition is fund balance as a percentage of expenditures. An economic factor that affects financial condition is the annual growth rate of the assessed value of the community's property.

Criteria for Creating an Approach to Evaluating Financial Condition

Similar to the situation with defining financial condition, our profession does not have an agreed-on approach for analyzing, interpreting, and communicating financial condition in local government. Again, the approaches that exist are either specific in nature or broad in scope. As an integral part of the development of our model, we reviewed and analyzed approaches contained in the literature. Ken Brown created a ten-point test (which was updated in response to GASB Statement No. 34) as an easy-to-use approach to evaluate the financial condition of a local government.[11] An advantage of the ten-point test is the use of benchmark data for interpreting each financial indicator. A disadvantage is the limited analysis across all major funds.

A model by the ICMA, on the other hand, provides a comprehensive approach to evaluating the financial condition of a local government, similar to bond-rating agencies' approach to evaluating a local government's ability to manage systematic and unsystematic risk in the repayment of debt over time.[12] The disadvantage of this approach is the sheer number of indicators used to analyze both financial and economic factors of financial condition, making it a feasible tool for larger local governments only.

Because of the broad continuum of current methods for evaluating financial condition in local government, we started with the following criteria to guide our approach: systematicness, comprehensiveness, flexibility, comparability, and manageability. We based the criteria on a literature review and on our own professional backgrounds.

Designing a systematic approach to evaluating a local government unit's financial condition was paramount, given the expanded financial-reporting model created by GASB Statement No. 34. More specifically, the approach had to (1) systematically evaluate the financial condition of the organization as a whole as reported in government-wide statements and (2) systematically evaluate the financial condition of each major fund. The approach also had to be comprehensive, providing a thorough analysis of resource flow and stock at the government-wide and fund levels of the organization. The focus on resource flow and stock supported our definition of *financial condition*.

The criterion of flexibility acknowledged that administrators might want to augment our approach with additional financial indicators or even replace a financial indicator selected by us with another. We have used the *quick ratio* to analyze the liquidity of a local government, whereas others support the use of the *current ratio*.[13]

---

11. For information on the original test, see Ken W. Brown, "The 10-Point Test of Financial Condition: Toward an Easy-to-Use Assessment Tool for Smaller Cities," *Government Finance Review* 9, no. 6 (1993): 21–26. For information on the updated test, see Dean Michael Mead, "A Manageable System of Economic Condition Analysis for Governments," in Howard Frank, ed., *Public Financial Management* (Boca Raton, Fla.: Taylor & Francis, 2006), 383–419.

12. ICMA, *Evaluating Financial Condition*.

13. The quick ratio represents a more conversational approach to evaluating an organization's ability to meet its short-term obligations, preventing current assets like inventory

Although we relied on the most prevalent indicators in the literature, individual circumstances might warrant change.

Comparability was one of the primary reasons for the passage of GASB Statement No. 34. Calculating a financial indicator like the quick ratio at one point would provide only limited information. Calculating it over time for trend analysis and benchmarking it against other local governments would provide the necessary context for interpreting the results. The reality is that evaluating financial condition is relative, requiring comparative information for analyzing, interpreting, and communicating it to elected officials.

Evaluating financial condition also had to be manageable, a criterion the ICMA's model does not satisfy. Local governments of all sizes had to be able to implement our evaluatory approach accurately from financial data taken from their annual financial statements—consistent with our definition of *financial condition*—and had to have the organizational resources to manage it over time. Another important aspect of this criterion was the ability to use our approach successfully to communicate financial condition to elected officials. Doing so would require a careful balance of financial indicators selected for the evaluation. If the approach relied on a limited number of financial indicators, then communicating a comprehensive analysis to elected officials would not be possible. If the approach relied on too many financial indicators, then communicating the analysis would be unwieldy.

Understanding the Financial-Reporting Model

Because our approach is designed to be systematic across both government-wide and fund statements, to use it elected officials must possess some understanding of the model of financial reporting used in local government. (For the model in which our approach is applied, see Figure 15.1.)

Elected officials must have a basic understanding of three important aspects of this model before they can be expected to use financial-condition information effectively. First, financial statements in local government have two levels of reporting: the government-wide level and the fund level. Second, financial statements for government-wide activities and enterprise funds measure *economic resources* using the *accrual basis* of accounting, whereas financial statements for governmental funds measure *financial resources* using the *modified accrual basis* of accounting.[14]

---

from increasing a local government's liquidity. For more information on quick and current ratios, see Earl R. Wilson, Susan C. Kattelus, and Jacqueline L. Reck, *Accounting for Governmental and Nonprofit Entities*, 14th ed. (Boston: McGraw-Hill Irwin, 2007).

14. *See* Robert J. Freeman, Craig D. Shoulders, and Gregory S. Allison, *Governmental and Nonprofit Accounting*, 10th ed. (Upper Saddle River, N.J.: Prentice Hall, 2012). *Economic resources* reflect the measurement of all assets and liabilities on a balance sheet, regardless of form or maturity. The associated *accrual basis* primarily reflects a timing issue, most notably of revenue recognition. In this case, revenue is recognized when it is

Third, all North Carolina counties and municipalities are required to have a general fund, which is the main operating fund and one of several potential governmental funds. However, not all local governments have enterprise funds, which are used to account for the resource flow and stock of utilities (for example, water, wastewater, electricity, and natural gas).

Figure 15.1. Revised Financial-Reporting Model for Analysis of Financial Condition

Financial Statement Reporting Level	Activity Type (Resources Measured)	
Government-Wide Level	**Governmental Activities** (Economic Resources)	**Business-Type Activities** (Economic Resources)
Fund Level	**Governmental Funds** (Financial Resources)	**Enterprise Funds** (Economic Resources)

Figure 15.1 does not contain fiduciary funds because the resources accounted for in pension trust, investment trust, private-purpose trust, and custodial funds are owned by parties other than the local government. Figure 15.1 also does not contain internal service funds, one of the two types of proprietary funds (the other type being enterprise funds), because they inherently create redundancy in financial reporting.[15] To overcome this problem, the accumulated resources of these funds are disbursed back to either governmental activities or business-type activities at the end of the fiscal year on the basis of which group of activities used them the most. The profits or losses of these funds then are divided between governmental activities and business-type activities on the basis of actual use.

We acknowledge that local governments may want to use our approach to evaluate the financial condition of selected internal service funds on a case-by-case basis. Internal service funds that account for activities like fleet services may be appropriate for this form of analysis. An actuarial analysis may be more appropriate for internal service funds that account for activities like health benefits, given the known and unknown risks involved with them.

---

earned, regardless of when it is actually collected. *Financial resources* reflect the measurement of only financial assets—those that are in the form of cash or readily convertible to cash. Likewise, only current liabilities are recognized—those that are immediate draws on financial resources. The associated *modified accrual basis* reflects revenue recognition only when it becomes available.

15. Stephen J. Gauthier, *Governmental Accounting, Auditing, and Financial Reporting* (Chicago: Government Finance Officers Association, 2012).

Selecting Financial Dimensions and Indicators

Fortunately, the literature contains a large number of financial dimensions and indicators from which to choose in evaluating financial condition.[16] Our task was to pare them down so that our approach would result in a comprehensive financial evaluation but be manageable for local governments of all sizes in North Carolina. We began the selection process by using our definition of *financial condition*, which focuses on the status of resource flow and stock as interpreted from annual financial statements. We then identified fundamental financial dimensions that support the analysis of resource flow and stock.

Our intent was to identify one set of flow indicators and one set of stock indicators for evaluating the financial dimensions we selected. Doing so was not possible, however, given that certain financial statements measure economic resources, whereas other statements measure financial resources. We responded by selecting one set of flow and stock indicators for evaluating the financial condition of government-wide activities and enterprise funds, given that their financial statements measure economic resources. We then selected another set of flow and stock indicators for evaluating the financial condition of governmental funds, given that their financial statements measure financial resources. Although some overlap exists between the two sets of flow and stock indicators, there are some fundamental differences between them because of the accounting differences.[17]

We selected four financial dimensions and four financial indicators for evaluating resource flow for government-wide activities and enterprise funds (see Table 15.1). The first dimension, *inter-period equity*, addresses whether a government lived within its means during the fiscal year.[18] The *total margin ratio* indicator is used to evaluate this dimension. It represents the total inflow of resources divided by the total outflow of resources for government-wide activities and for enterprise funds. A ratio of 1.0 or higher indicates that the government lived within its means for the respective activity or fund. For government-wide activities, resource inflow includes the net of transfers in and out between governmental activities and business-type activities. For the enterprise funds, transfers in from other funds are included as resource inflow, and transfers out to other funds are included as resource outflow. These assumptions are consistent with the GAAP reporting format.

Whereas the total margin ratio analyzes the relationship between total resources available and total resources consumed, the financial indicator of *percentage change in net position*, used to evaluate our second financial dimension, *financial performance*, provides feedback on the extent to which a government's net position improved or

---

16. See, for example, Wilson, Kattelus, and Reck, *Accounting for Governmental and Nonprofit Entities.*

17. If a local government chooses to include an internal service fund in its analysis, it would use the set of financial dimensions and indicators selected to evaluate the financial condition of government-wide activities and enterprise funds, given that financial statements for internal service funds measure economic resources using the accrual basis of accounting.

18. Wilson, Kattelus, and Reck, *Accounting for Governmental and Nonprofit Entities.*

Table 15.1. Resource Flow for Governmental Activities and Enterprise Funds—Operating Statement (Economic Resources and Accrual Basis of Accounting)

Financial Dimension	Description	Financial Indicator	Governmental Activities		Enterprise Funds	
			Calculation	Data Source	Calculation	Data Source
Inter-period equity	Addresses whether or not a government lived within its financial means during the fiscal year.	Total margin ratio	Total resource inflow (program revenues plus total general revenues and net transfers) divided by total resource outflow (total expenses)	Statement of activities	Total resource inflow (operating and nonoperating revenues plus transfers in) divided by total resource outflow (operating and nonoperating expenses plus transfers out)	Statement of revenues, expenses, and changes in fund net position
Financial performance	Provides the magnitude of how a government's financial position improved or deteriorated as a result of resource flow.	Percentage change in net position	Change in net position divided by net position, beginning	Statement of activities	Change in net position divided by net position, beginning	Statement of revenues, expenses, and changes in fund net position
Self-sufficiency	Addresses the extent to which service charge revenues covered total expenses.	Charge to expense ratio	Charges for services (fees, fines, and charges for services) divided by total expenses	Statement of activities	Charges for services divided by operating and nonoperating expenses	Statement of revenues, expenses, and changes in fund net position
Financing obligation	Provides feedback on service flexibility with the amount of expenses committed to annual debt service.	Debt-service ratio	Debt service (principal and interest payments on long-term debt) divided by total expenses plus principal[a]	Statement of activities[b]	Debt service (principal and interest payments on long-term debt) divided by operating and nonoperating expenses plus principal[c]	Statement of revenues, expenses, and changes in fund net position[d]

a. Principal is added to the denominator because it is not included in expenses.

b. Interest payments on long-term debt for governmental activities are located on the statement of activities. Principal payments on long-term debt for governmental activities are located in the notes of financial statements.

c. Principal is added to the denominator because it is not included in expenses.

d. Interest payments on long-term debt for enterprise funds are located on the statement of revenues, expenses, and changes in fund net position. Principal payments on long-term debt for enterprise funds are located on the statement of cash flows or in the notes of financial statements.

deteriorated as a result of resource flow.[19] A positive percentage change indicates that a government's financial position improved from the resource flow that occurred during the fiscal year. Periodic modest fluctuations are generally to be expected. Fluctuations that are significant in nature (in either direction) should be obvious and evaluated accordingly.

The financial dimension of *self-sufficiency* addresses the extent to which the government used service charges to cover total expenses. This dimension is especially important to business-type activities and to enterprise funds, for which the goal often is to cover total expenses on a charge-for-service basis. The *charge-to-expense ratio* indicator is used to analyze this dimension. A ratio of 1.0 or higher indicates that the activity or fund was self-sufficient. An argument could be made that this financial dimension is not applicable for governmental activities because governmental services with public-good characteristics are not designed to be self-supporting. However, elected officials and administrators often are interested in the mix between general taxation and user-fee revenue when preparing and adopting budgets for the forthcoming fiscal year. To this end, the financial indicator calculation does not include grants and contributions, which are an inherent part of program revenues in the government-wide financial statements.

Our final dimension for resource flow for government-wide activities and enterprise funds is *financing obligation*. This dimension is analyzed with the *debt-service ratio* indicator, which is calculated by dividing annual debt service of principal and interest payments by total expenses plus principal. Because of their measurement focus, both government-wide activities and enterprise funds do not report principal repayments on debt as an expense. To achieve a proper calculation of this debt-service ratio, the principal amounts must be included in both the numerator and the denominator. The purpose of this ratio is to provide feedback on service flexibility, which decreases as more resources are committed to annual debt service.

We selected four financial dimensions and four financial indicators for evaluating resource stock for government-wide activities and enterprise funds (see Table 15.2). An advantage of the stock indicators over the flow indicators is that they tend to be more recognizable in the profession because they are associated with the balance sheet, which more often is used to evaluate financial condition in the public and private sectors. In other words, balance sheets report on equity, or net position, at a given point.

Liquidity is the financial dimension used to analyze an organization's ability to meet short-term obligations. It is calculated with the *quick ratio* indicator: cash and investments divided by current liabilities. A high ratio suggests that the government is more likely to meet its short-term obligations. *Solvency*, on the other hand, is the financial dimension used to analyze an organization's ability to meet long-term

---

19. Financial performance represents a relatively new financial dimension in local government. For more information, see Stephen J. Gauthier, "Interpreting Local Government Financial Statements," *Government Finance Review* 23, no. 3 (2007): 8–14.

Table 15.2. Resource Stock for Governmental Activities and Enterprise Funds—Balance Sheet (Economic Resources and Accrual Basis of Accounting)

Financial Dimension	Description	Financial Indicator	Governmental Activities		Enterprise Funds	
			Calculation	Data Source	Calculation	Data Source
Liquidity	Government's ability to address short-term obligations	Quick ratio	Cash and investments divided by current liabilities[a]	Statement of net position	Cash and investments divided by current liabilities[b]	Statement of net position—proprietary funds
Solvency	Government's ability to address long-term obligations	Net position ratio	Unrestricted net position divided by total liabilities[c]	Statement of net position	Unrestricted net position divided by total liabilities	Statement of net position—proprietary funds
Leverage	Extent to which total assets are financed with long-term debt	Debt-to-assets ratio	Long-term debt divided by total assets	Statement of net position	Long-term debt divided by total assets	Statement of net position—proprietary funds
Capital	Condition of capital assets as defined by remaining useful life	Capital-assets-condition ratio	1–.0 (accumulated depreciation divided by capital assets being depreciated)	Statement of net position or notes to financial statements	1–.0 (accumulated depreciation divided by capital assets being depreciated)	Statement of net position or notes to financial statements

a. Restricted cash is not part of cash and investments for this calculation. This ratio also excludes the current portion of compensated balances from current liabilities. Another potential exclusion is bond anticipation notes. The current portion of long-term debt is included.

b. Restricted cash is not part of cash and investments for this calculation. This ratio also excludes the current portion of compensated balances from current liabilities. Another potential exclusion is bond anticipation notes. The current portion of long-term debt is included. It should be noted that the Local Government Commission uses a different ratio for calculating the current ratio for enterprise funds—current assets (less inventory and prepaid expenses) are divided by current liabilities.

c. The value of unrestricted net position for governmental activities is often negative for North Carolina counties because the value of school assets financed with county debt is not included on the statement of net position. While the interpretation of the financial indicator remains the same, it should be footnoted for explanation.

obligations. It is calculated with the *net position ratio* indicator: unrestricted net position divided by total liabilities. As with the quick ratio, a high ratio suggests that the government is more likely to meet long-term obligations.

Some advocate using total assets as the denominator for this calculation rather than total liabilities.[20] We believe that standardizing unrestricted net position with total liabilities provides a stronger indication of an organization's ability to meet

---

20. Wang, Dennis, and Tu, "Measuring Financial Condition."

long-term obligations. Furthermore, we believe that restricted net assets should not be a part of this equation because such assets are typically not directly related to an entity's ability to meet current or long-term obligations.

Leverage is the financial dimension that addresses the extent to which total assets are financed with long-term debt. The financial indicator used to analyze this dimension is the *debt-to-assets ratio*: long-term debt divided by total assets. If a government becomes too reliant on debt financing to secure capital assets, it may compromise service flexibility as it commits more resource flow to annual debt-service obligations. An overreliance on debt also may have unfavorable implications for bond ratings.

This financial indicator may present challenges for North Carolina counties because school debt is included on their financial statements and the value of school infrastructure financed with that debt is not. One approach to getting around this problem is to use the flexibility criterion (see the "Criteria for Creating an Approach to Evaluating Financial Condition" section in this chapter), eliminating or replacing the debt-to-assets ratio. The preferred approach is to calculate the indicator on the basis of the data contained in the financial statements, footnoting the discrepancy for the reader.[21] The reality is that counties are responsible for school debt but do not own the related infrastructure.

Capital, the final financial dimension of resource stock for government-wide activities and enterprise funds, is used to analyze the condition of capital assets as defined by their remaining useful life. The financial indicator to measure this dimension is the *capital-assets-condition ratio*. The data used for this calculation are located in the capital assets section of the notes to financial statements. To calculate the indicator, accumulated depreciation is first divided by capital assets subject to depreciation. The resulting percentage is then subtracted from 1.0, which results in the remaining useful life of the total capital assets being depreciated. A high ratio suggests that a government is investing in its capital assets.

We selected three financial dimensions and three financial indicators for evaluating resource flow for governmental funds (see Table 15.3). This evaluation applies primarily to the general fund. At times, a local government may want to analyze the financial condition of special revenue funds, debt-service funds, capital project funds, or permanent funds. Our indicators may be used to evaluate the financial condition of these funds. However, we propose that they be captured as part of governmental activities unless a local government has a specific reason for disaggregating them. For example, a local government may have a major special revenue fund that it wants to disaggregate, given the amount of resources involved or the importance of services and activities being accounted for in the fund.

Service obligation is the first financial dimension for evaluating the resource flow for governmental funds. The *operations ratio*, representing total revenues divided by total expenditures, is used to analyze this dimension. The data for this calculation come directly from the statement of revenues, expenditures, and changes in fund balances, and a ratio of 1.0 or higher indicates that a government lived within its means.

---

21. The authors, in consultation with the Local Government Commission, recommend this approach.

Table 15.3. Resource Flow for General Fund—Operating Statement (Financial Resources and Modified Accrual Basis of Accounting)

Financial Dimension	Description	Financial Indicator	Calculation	Data Source
Service obligation	Addresses whether a government's annual revenues were sufficient to pay for annual operations.	Operations ratio	Total revenues divided by total expenditures (plus transfers to debt-service fund and less proceeds from capital leases and installment purchases)	Statement of revenues, expenditures, and changes in fund balances
Dependency	Provides the extent to which a government relies on other governments for resources.	Intergovernmental ratio	Total intergovernmental revenue divided by total revenue[a]	Statement of revenues, expenditures, and changes in fund balances
Financing obligation	Provides feedback on service flexibility with the amount of expenditures committed to annual debt service.	Debt-service ratio	Debt service (principal and interest payments on long-term debt, including transfers to the debt-service fund) divided by total expenditures (plus transfers to debt service fund and less proceeds from capital leases and installment purchases)[b]	Statement of revenues, expenditures, and changes in fund balances

a. Intergovernmental revenue includes restricted and unrestricted.

b. Debt service may be part of expenditures, may be a transfer to the debt service fund, or may be both.

Transfers out are not part of this calculation unless the given transfer is to a debt-service fund. GAAP also require governmental funds to report the present value of the minimum payments on capital leases or installment purchases as an expenditure in the year of an agreement's inception. If the total expenditures do include this amount (as would be evidenced by another financing source of an equal amount), they should not be included for purposes of this calculation and should be subtracted from total expenditures.

The remaining two dimensions capture important aspects of revenues and expenditures. *Dependency* is used to determine the extent to which governments rely on other governments for resources, as measured by the *intergovernmental ratio* indicator: intergovernmental revenue divided by total revenue. *Financing obligation* is used to provide feedback on service flexibility by measuring, with the *debt service ratio* indicator, the amount of resources committed to annual debt obligations. If transfers to a debt-service fund have been made by the governmental fund, the transfer should be included in both the numerator and the denominator.

We selected three financial dimensions and three financial indicators for evaluating resource stock for governmental funds (see Table 15.4). The financial dimension of

**Table 15.4. Resource Stock for General Fund—Balance Sheet
(Financial Resources and Modified Accrual Basis of Accounting)**

Financial Dimension	Description	Financial Indicator	Calculation	Data Source
Liquidity	Government's ability to address short-term obligation	Quick ratio	Cash and investments divided by current liabilities[a]	Balance sheet
Solvency	Government's ability to address long-term obligation	Fund balance as a percentage of expenditures	Available fund balance divided by total expenditures (less proceeds from capital leases) plus transfers out[b]	Balance sheet
Leverage	Extent to which a government relies on tax-supported debt	Debt as a percentage of assessed value	Tax-supported, long-term debt divided by assessed value[c]	Notes to financial statements[d]

a. Restricted cash is not part of cash and investments for this calculation.

b. G.S. 159-8 defines available fund balance for appropriation as the sum of cash and investments minus the sum of liabilities, encumbrances, and deferred revenues arising from cash receipts.

c. This calculation is the same calculation used by the Local Government Commission when issuing its annual report. *Analysis of Debt of North Carolina Counties and Municipalitie*s, where the sum of outstanding general obligation (GO) debt, authorized and unissued GO debt, and installment purchase debt is divided by the assessed property valuation as reported to the N.C. Department of Revenue (NCDOR) (this calculation excludes debt associated with enterprise funds). This percentage is used as an approximation for the 8 percent of assessed valuation.

d. Tax-supported, long-term debt comes from notes to financial statements. Assessed value comes from NCDOR.

liquidity uses the *quick ratio* indicator, which follows the same philosophy and calculation as the liquidity dimension for government-wide activities and enterprise funds.

The financial dimension of *solvency* is evaluated with one of the most recognized financial indicators in local government: *fund balance as a percentage of expenditures,* as calculated with available fund balance divided by total expenditures plus transfers out.[22] Transfers out is included in the denominator because the Local Government Commission standardizes available fund balance for comparison purposes by dividing it by expenditures and transfers out less the present value of any capital leases or installment purchases entered into during the fiscal year.[23]

The final financial dimension for evaluating resource stock for governmental funds is *leverage*, which is supported with the financial indicator of *debt as a percentage of assessed value.* The definition of "debt" is tax-supported, long-term debt, which is

22. G.S. 159-8(a) defines "available fund balance" as the sum of cash and investments minus the sum of liabilities, encumbrances, and deferred revenues arising from cash receipts.

23. The Government Finance Officers Association (GFOA) standardizes available fund balance by dividing it by general fund operating revenues. For more information, see *Fund Balance Guidelines for the General Fund,* which was adopted by the executive board of the GFOA in September 2015. It can be found at https://www.gfoa.org/materials/fund-balance-guidelines-for-the-general-fund.

the amount prepared for a local government's sworn statement of debt.[24] The debt is standardized by dividing it by assessed value. State law prevents local governments from issuing debt that would result in net debt exceeding 8 percent of assessed value.[25] This financial indicator also plays a major role with bond-rating agencies when they are conducting a general-obligation-rating assignment.[26]

Using the State's Web-Based Dashboard

As part of providing extensive oversight of the financial management practices in North Carolina local government, counties and municipalities are required by law to submit their annual audited financial statements to the Department of State Treasurer.[27] Because of this requirement, the Department of State Treasurer collects audited financial data from all local governments annually and makes them available via its website. Therefore, local governments have two options regarding the financial condition model presented in this chapter. One approach is for local officials to calculate, analyze, and present their respective financial indicators to elective officials, relying primarily on internal data.

Another approach is to use the Benchmarking Tool for Municipalities and Counties, the Department of State Treasurer's web-based dashboard, to make the calculations, relying on internal data and external data from other local governments.[28] This web-based tool allows a user to create dashboards for analyzing the financial condition of local governments in North Carolina. Each dashboard contains the respective flow and stock financial indicators tracked over a five-year period for trend analysis, and, if desired, a comparison to peer local governments for benchmarking. To begin, the user selects the desired county or municipality from the drop-down menu, which is organized in alphabetical order.

The user then selects the type of report for analysis. All local governments have data to populate the first two types—governmental activities and general fund—but not all local governments have water and sewer funds or electric funds. If these latter two choices are not applicable to the desired local government, the user will not be able to select them. The four report types are listed below.

- **Governmental Activities.** The financial statements for governmental activities are reported at the government-wide level of the financial-reporting model and measure economic resources on the accrual basis of accounting. They combine all governmental funds at the fund level, which measure

---

24. *See* G.S. 159-55.

25. G.S. 159-55(c).

26. Linda Hird Lipnick and Yaffa Rattner, *The Determinants of Credit Quality* (New York: Moody's Investors Service, 2002).

27. *See* G.S. 159-34.

28. The Benchmarking Tool can be accessed, via hyperlink, on the Department of State Treasurer's website: https://www.nctreasurer.com/slg/Pages/default.aspx.

financial resources on the modified basis of accounting, and recast them on the accrual basis.

- **General Fund.** The financial statements for the general fund are reported at the fund level of the financial-reporting model and measure financial resources on the modified accrual basis of accounting. It accounts for all transactions of a local government not accounted for in other funds, representing the primary fund for most local governments.
- **Water and Sewer Fund.** The financial statements for the water and sewer fund, which is an enterprise fund, are reported at the fund level of the financial-reporting model and measure economic resources on the accrual basis of accounting.
- **Electric Fund.** The financial statements for the electric fund, which is an enterprise fund, are reported at the fund level of the financial-reporting model and measure economic resources on the accrual basis of accounting.

After designating a report type, the user then has two options: moving directly to the final step of calculating the respective financial indicators or including peer local governments for benchmarking. Because financial-condition analysis is relative, peer comparisons are encouraged to allow the user to build external context for analysis in addition to the five-year-trend data. Users may select up to five (5) benchmarking peers. We offer the following four criteria for guidance when selecting benchmarking peers.

- **Similar Services.** The user should select local governments with similar services, particularly water and sewer funds or electric funds. Even if the user is looking at the general fund or governmental activities, which all local governments have, utility funds can play an important role in shaping overall finances. The peer selection tool shows whether a given government has a water and sewer fund or an electric fund.
- **Similar Population.** Local governments of similar size often make good benchmarking comparisons because size can affect certain indicators. The management tool provides the population for each local government.
- **Geographic Area.** Smaller local governments may want to compare themselves against local governments of the same region, as this may reflect similar economic and social conditions. Larger local governments may be unable to use the region criterion given the limited number of larger counties and municipalities in North Carolina.
- **Other Preference.** Elected officials and administrators may have other criteria for selecting benchmarking partners. For example, some local governments are destination communities, while others have high bond ratings. These possible preference criteria will require additional research by the user of this management tool.

After selecting benchmarking peers, the user must choose either a PDF file or a Text/CSV (comma-separated values) file for the report format. If the PDF file is selected, the dashboard is created along with tables showing the data used to calculate the indicators. If the Text/CSV file is selected, the financial data become available in a spreadsheet program, which allows the user to create customized reports.

The dashboard identifies the local government chosen for the analysis and the benchmark peers selected for comparison. The dashboard then groups the financial dimensions by resource flow (operating statement) and resource stock (balance sheet), including the financial indicators used to analyze the financial dimensions. A bar graph is used to display the data of each financial indicator over a five-year period. Underneath each graph, the actual result of each indicator is provided for the most recent fiscal year. Each bar graph also contains a comparative line when benchmark peers have been selected for the analysis. The line represents the annual average for the benchmark peers selected; therefore, the line adjusts as the annual average changes for each fiscal year. Also underneath each graph, the actual result of the annual average benchmark is provided for the most recent fiscal year.

We explain how the dashboard is designed because it is not simply a collection of financial indicators. It is specifically designed to increase the ability to communicate financial condition effectively to elected officials in local government. It also is designed to support our definition of *financial condition* and the financial dimensions that we have selected to analyze resource flow and stock in annual financial statements.

Summary

Local officials, both elected and non-elected, may never reach a consensus on a professionally accepted set of financial indicators for evaluating the financial condition of local governments. Although there are pros and cons associated with any individual financial indicator (or any set of indicators), our focus is on providing administrators with an effective approach for analyzing, interpreting, and communicating financial condition to elected officials. We have offered the following definition of *financial condition* to guide our approach: a local government's ability to meet its ongoing financial, service, and capital obligations based on the status of resource flow and stock as interpreted from annual financial statements.

We selected financial dimensions and indicators that supported the analysis of resource flow and stock as shown on the numerous operating statements and balance sheets contained in annual financial statements. Unlike previous models for evaluating the financial condition of local governments, our approach recognizes that financial reporting contains government-wide and fund statements and that some financial statements measure economic resources while others measure financial resources. This recognition provides a more systematic and comprehensive approach to evaluating financial condition, responding to the complexities of local government financial statements. We also capitalize on the strengths of a dashboard for communicating financial condition to elected officials, using trend and benchmark data for a more robust interpretation of each financial indicator.

Historically, more attention has been placed on financial position in local government than on financial condition. With the implementation of GASB Statement No. 34, an opportunity has been created to allow for a dual focus, one that looks at both financial position and condition in local government. This represents the ultimate goal of our approach: to give administrators a management tool that facilitates their including financial condition when they are helping elected officials embrace the responsibility of managing the fiscal matters of local governments.

Chapter 16

Budget Presentation: How Format Can Improve Decision-Making

Eric J. Peterson, Emily H. Bradford, and Jen Della Valle

Introduction

An often-overlooked part of the budget process is the way the budget document is formatted. A well-formatted budget document can improve decision-making by increasing focus on key issues, decreasing the time spent in the weeds debating lower priorities, and improving an organization's ability to manage a disaster, recession, or crisis. A clear presentation also allows traditional and social media outlets to report on the budget more accurately, thus reducing confusion and time spent correcting mistakes reported to the public. There are many other benefits that make it worth the investment to design budget documents with end users in mind.

There is no one right way to format a budget. What is successful in one local government may not work in another. If you are looking to improve an organization's budget document, there are many examples of excellent budget documents in North Carolina, which are discussed in this chapter. Modifying a format from another local government can be an effective and easy way to improve your budget presentation. The key is finding a design that fits your organization's needs, priorities, culture, and staff's ability to prepare the budget document annually.

When searching for examples to improve your format, do not limit your search to documents from local governments that are in similar size to yours. There are many sophisticated and effective documents from small and medium-sized organizations that can be adjusted to work in larger governments. On the flip side of the coin, small governments should not shy away from looking at models from larger governments, as such models can work and be adapted for smaller governments' situations, too.

A budget presentation should succeed in the eight areas listed below. The rest of this chapter will dive deeper into each area.

1. Help the governing body with decision-making
2. Serve as a work plan and information resource
3. Anticipate questions
4. Include multiyear forecasting
5. Provide continuity
6. Change and adapt with the times
7. Be easy to understand and navigate
8. Build credibility and trust

1. Help the Governing Body with Decision-Making

Regardless of a municipality's or county's size, all local governments have one thing in common: The governing body needs clear, relevant information in its budget document in order to make well-informed decisions. Another key function of the budget document is ensuring all members of the governing board are on an even playing field. This is accomplished by providing the same information to all elected officials, so everyone is aware of key issues, challenges, opportunities, and alternatives. This fosters a productive environment for deliberating issues and providing direction.

The budget is the Super Bowl of decision-making for local governments. Most critical decisions that occur during the year take place during the budget process. Thus, budget adoption is the biggest and most important vote on policy the governing board makes annually. It is also important for the manager and staff to remember, while they prepare the document and make recommendations, that the budget is the overarching policy document of the governing board. Elected officials are ultimately held accountable by the public and not just during elections. Ask any elected official, and they will tell you how they regularly hear from citizens during trips to the grocery store, when out at a restaurant with their families, at community events, at church, and pretty much anywhere they go, as well as via email and social media. The document is also essential to help the manager, budget team, departments, and public understand needs and new requests, develop options and priorities, consider unintended consequences of proposals, and craft solutions, all in a fiscally responsible plan for the government body to consider.

2. Serve as a Work Plan and Information Resource

A budget document primarily full of revenue and expenditure line items is a missed opportunity. When crafted well, the document is a primary reference source that is used throughout the fiscal year for a variety of topics. For a document to qualify for a Distinguished Budget Presentation Award from the Government Finance Officers Association,[1] it must be proficient in four categories: policy document, financial plan, communications device, and operations guide. These categories appropriately recognize the various functions of the budget. In short, the budget is the "go-to" resource for many of the organization's and public's information needs, such as operations, financial condition, debt, personnel allocations, and performance data.

Any local government that goes through a bond-rating or large debt financing process quickly discovers the strengths of and gaps in its budget document. During a bond rating or major debt issuance, the budget, especially if it has an integrated multiyear planning component, can act as the source for much of the critical information staff needs to respond to requests from the Local Government Commission, bond-rating agencies, financial advisors, bond counsel, bond brokers, and others. The quality of the document impacts how successful the local government will be in terms of the bond rating and corresponding interest rate the local government receives. In addition to being a critical depository of information, the budget is a gauge of a local government's professionalism, strategic thinking, and financial management skills.

Hillsborough, North Carolina, has used a strategy map for many years to identify the initiatives, priorities, and performance measures necessary to carry out its mission and vision. Together these elements serve as the town's strategic plan. Local governments use various means of linking goals, objectives, and specific actions to performance measures and associated targets. This work plan guides departmental actions throughout the year. To achieve key goals, there must be a system serving as the GPS, or navigational guide, for the local government, in which the route and destination are identified.

People are often more motivated when they know what is expected of them, such as in the form of clear goals, objectives, and action items.[2] A successful document improves accountability by listing goals and action items expected to be completed by the end of the fiscal year. This paints a picture of what departments should be focusing on given their available resources, so there is no question at the end of the year as to what should have been accomplished. This also makes it easier to make midyear course corrections that are necessary to adjust to ever-changing conditions and priorities.

---

1. For more information about the Government Finance Officers Association's (GFOA) Distinguished Budget Presentation Awards Program, see https://www.gfoa.org/budget-award.

2. Greg McKeown, *Essentialism: The Disciplined Pursuit of Less* (New York: Crown Business, 2014). "If a team does not have clarity of goals and roles problems will fester and multiply. … When there is a serious lack of clarity about what the team stands for and what their goals and roles are, people experience confusion, stress, and frustration. When there is a high level of clarity on the other hand, people thrive. When there is a lack of clarity people waste time on the trivial many. Clarity gives people opportunities for greater innovations and breakthroughs."

3. Anticipate Questions

Potential questions are the most important consideration to build into a budget presentation. Due to the volume of information in a budget, a well-designed document still requires substantive thought and digging to understand what is being requested and why. Even smaller jurisdictions can have documents with many pages of line items, explanations, justifications, and other supporting documentation. Reviewing all this information naturally raises questions from elected officials, the media, and the public, especially when there is a proposal to increase tax or utility rates. Management and department heads regularly have questions during the review process as well.

Figuring out ways to answer questions before they arise helps everyone. The biggest benefits are managing time more effectively and allowing even more valuable questions to be asked. People have limited attention spans and energy, especially in meetings. A disproportionate amount of time in budget workshops is often spent on small items, thus unnecessarily depleting the energy and attention span of the group. The cost of these distractions is that insufficient time is spent discussing and learning about critical items that will have the biggest impacts on the organization and community. The big question is how best to format the budget document to minimize distractions and their consequences. Listed below are several approaches and examples that have been successful in helping elected officials and staff focus on the most critical information and decision points in the budget:

- **Budget message.** Some organizations opt to have a short message and rely on an executive summary to provide greater detail. The best approach is the one that works for your situation. For the purpose of this chapter, the term *budget message* will be used interchangeably with *executive summary*. In addition to providing an overview of key expenses, issues, changes, goals, strategies, and challenges, the budget message is a place to anticipate and respond to questions that may arise. The budget message is often the only part of the budget that gets read because people do not want or have the time to wade through hundreds of pages of detail—they want to get to the bottom line quickly.

  It is important to be transparent and make readers aware of significant issues, rather than bury those issues in the document. This is especially the case for bad news. For example, in the first year that a new budget format was being used in Hillsborough, the manager recommended exceptionally high increases for taxes and utility rates. The budget message included a heading that drew attention to the issue, which was something to the effect of "Why are rates rising so high?" Using such headings brings attention to the topics in which readers are most interested and then walks readers through the rationale for the recommended steps. While it is not fun dealing with negative or emotional reactions from unpopular recommendations, it is the first step in informing everyone and starting deliberations.

Raising major issues also sets the context for other key decisions in the budget, such as tax or rate increases, sluggish revenues, rebuilding after a hurricane or floods, paying for an upgrade to a water or wastewater plant, building a new fire or police station, or increasing employee pay and benefits to remain competitive with the market. Seemingly unrelated items in a budgetary fund can have major impacts on each other and what gets funded. The budget message must point out connections that are not obvious, so stakeholders understand the situation, interconnection of issues, and impact on their individual issues of interest. For an example of a budget message, see Appendix A, "Budget Message for Fiscal Year 2019, Town of Hillsborough, N.C.," at the end of this chapter.

The following are examples of Hillsborough anticipating questions in the budget message:

○ During the Great Recession, the Hillsborough town manager recommended eliminating 10 percent of the positions in the general fund. This included a significant reduction in the Hillsborough Police Department (HPD) personnel. While position cuts are never popular, position cuts in public safety have traditionally been more likely to raise objections from the public than other types of position cuts. Anticipating that this was going to be greeted with serious concern and opposition, the budget message included an explanation as well as a basic table comparing the HPD's resources to those of other agencies in North Carolina. The chart showed that despite the cuts, the HPD was still well ahead of the state average in officers per 1,000 population and per capita spending. The day after the budget was released to the public, the town manager received a call from a citizen who was a planning board member and active in the community. He started off by stating that he was not happy about the cuts to the HPD for several reasons. He then went on to say after reading the comparison chart and explanation in the budget message he understood and supported the decision but wanted those positions added back as soon as possible once the town was financially able. That conversation could have gone a much different way had the question not been anticipated and the rationale shared in the budget message.

Table 16.1. Police Department Resource Comparison

Measures	N.C. Police Department (FY10 Average)	FY12 Proposed HPD Budget	Difference
Full-time equivalent police per 1,000 population	2.8	4.14	47.8%
Police services costs per capita	$243	$348	43.2%

Note: Data retrieved from the School of Government at the University of North Carolina, Chapel Hill Benchmarking Group. FY = fiscal year

○ During the Great Recession, one of the headlines in the budget message was "How can we still have deficits with all these cuts?" The question was followed with a bullet list of reasons why that was happening.

○ The main heading for the "Water and Sewer Fund" section was "Significant rate increases likely for several years." This section began by explaining the process of raising sewer rates 8.8 percent over five years to pay for an exceptionally expensive upgrade to the town's wastewater treatment plant. Hillsborough and several of its neighbors in the Upper Neuse River Basin are under some of the strictest nitrogen discharge limits in the country. Communicating this and other key information was essential in gaining support from the town board and water and sewer advisory committee, as well as helping the public understand why such rate increases were necessary over a five-year period. The rate increases were unpopular, and many residents were upset, but clearly communicating the cuts up front in the budget message set the stage for deliberating, responding to inquiries, and exploring alternatives to help the town board make a well-informed decision.

○ The budget message can also use the "restaurant menu approach." It is easy to anticipate you will be asked why the park, public works building, sidewalk, additional planner, or take-home police vehicles are not included in the budget. Providing a list (or "restaurant menu") of significant unfunded requests makes it easy to identify these requests and their potential impact on the budget. The list should include costs, annual cost if debt payments are used, and, most importantly, the corresponding property tax or rate increase necessary to pay for it. Because "wants" always exceed available funding for new requests, the list makes it easy for readers to identify the cost of funding these requests in terms of both the impact on the government's bottom line as well as potential rate impact on citizens.

If there is a recommendation to raise taxes, questions naturally focus on how to avoid an increase. Providing a list of items that are included in the proposed budget, as well as those that are unfunded, can focus deliberations on what the governing board, public, and staff ultimately want to see funded. To add context to these discussions, it is helpful to see not just the dollar amount of each budget item under consideration, but how much the tax or utility rates would need to be raised to fund that request. Conversely, identifying the tax rate equivalent cost helps determine the impact of removing items from the budget to reduce or avoid a tax rate increase. For instance, if there is a desire to build a park, then either taxes will have to be raised X cents, or corresponding cuts and savings need to be made elsewhere. To avoid a tax rate increase, decision makers can go to the list in the budget message, or "menu," to determine what they are willing to cut or defer. The menu approach helps focus attention and discussion on specific options so the merits and potential downsides of those options can be considered. Debates often boil down to something tangible, like whether to fund a police officer or build a sidewalk. A menu that features cost equivalents can help direct debates in a productive direction.

- **Include a "comments" column for line items or cost centers.** In Hillsborough's document, all the revenue and departmental budget pages have a column on the far right titled "Comments." If a line item increases or decreases by a significant amount from one year to the next, it is a safe bet someone is going to question it. This comments column provides space for a succinct explanation or elaboration of the change. For example, if the "Water Treatment Plant, Contract Services—Alum Sludge Removal" line item is expected to increase significantly, a quick explanation for the increase can be added in the "Comments" column such as, "Dredging ponds annually to maintain permit compliance." It is amazing how much information can be included in a small area, especially when using a small font, abbreviations, and some creativity. The comments answer many questions that would otherwise have come up in a budget meeting. This leads to greater understanding of budget items by the governing board, far fewer questions during the meeting, superior questions to be asked due to enhanced context, and thus more time to discuss priorities. For an example of a comments column on a budget document, see Appendix B, "Police Patrol Budget Page (Hillsborough, Fiscal Year 2020)."

    When questions are asked by elected officials during budget workshops, it is common for them to be answered not by staff but by fellow elected officials. One elected official may respond by pointing out the column or justification form that addresses the inquiry. When this occurs, it helps keep the discussion centered among the board and is less disruptive to the rhythm of the meeting, often creating a more effective response than if it had come from a staff member. Keep in mind that no matter how diligent one is in reviewing a document, there is a lot of information to digest, so everyone misses or forgets something.

    The comments are also highly beneficial during internal review meetings between the manager, budget staff, and departments. They provide reminders and clarification throughout the year about what funds are allocated for. It is easy to forget where, what, or why something was done months after budget adoption. Hillsborough's mayors and commissioners have been big supporters of the comments columns since the 1990s. As the town's budget has grown larger over the years due to growth, the comments have become increasingly important for the board, manager, and staff, as there are more items and issues to monitor.

Time Savings in Budget Workshops

The comments column is highly effective in freeing up significant blocks of time. During the town manager's first year in Hillsborough, he changed the budget format to what had been used in his prior manager's job in Topsail Beach, N.C. The prior year, Hillsborough's budget ordinance had been done on a typewriter, and a memo from the manager was attached to a list of line items with no historical data—only what was budgeted in the current year along with the requests from the budget year. When the budget calendar came out, the finance director stated she noticed there were only two budget workshops scheduled. She stated that the prior year they had had five or six workshops and did not think there was a way the board would get through everything in just two meetings.

Even though the budget recommended significant tax, water, and sewer rate increases, the board completed the review process with one long meeting and another shorter one, so actually about one-and-a-half meetings. How did this happen? Changing the budget message to an easy-to-understand format and anticipating questions by incorporating a comments column into all the summary and departmental budget spreadsheets played big roles. Questions were anticipated in other ways, including through key information about operations, departmental goals and objectives, finances, performance measures, and a budget message that explained the overall situation. Together, these changes led to focused discussions with far less time spent in the weeds, despite dealing with an exceptionally challenging budget year.

After going through the process, the board had a far better understanding of the town's operations, issues, and paths to achieving their goals than in prior years. This helped build trust and credibility both ways between the town board and staff. The board appreciated and understood that staff was trying to be detailed and help the board make tough decisions. Staff appreciated the board's willingness to ask difficult questions and make unpopular decisions, but ones that were best for the organization and community.

- **Departmental narrative/summary pages.** These provide a quick overview for the fiscal year and include the following: key operations/functions, prior year's major accomplishments, noteworthy changes for the budget year, key issues in the future or in the multiyear financial forecast, action plan items, summary of expenses by major cost area, and informational graphics. For an example of departmental narrative/summary pages, see Appendix C, "Wastewater Treatment Plant—Budget Highlights (Hillsborough, Fiscal Year 2019)."

- **Departmental expenditure pages.** These pages display line items or programmatic cost centers broken down by categories, such as personnel, operations, capital outlay, and debt. Hillsborough adds sub-line items to provide more detail on some of the expenses. This is helpful for the governing board, public, and departments, as it clarifies what is included in a line item. For instance, line items like "Travel and Training" or "Supplies and Materials" can include a wide variety of activities that are often costly. Departments and divisions in Hillsborough rely on the sub-lines throughout the year to quickly ascertain where and how their funds are allocated. This not only aids in transparency but also improves internal management and monitoring of funds.

- **Budget justification forms.** This is another area to anticipate questions and increase awareness of needs, challenges, risks, and opportunities. Justifications for new or additional personnel, equipment, projects, programs, systems, operational changes, and others should address the traditional who, what, when, where, why, and how questions. Unfortunately, this level of thought and detail is often not achieved. It is not uncommon to see a request for additional staff only make generalized comments and lack detail, something to the effect of, "Staff is busy and can't keep up with the workload."

  Why are inadequate justifications submitted? Staff turning in the requests often see the primary reviewer of the justification as the department head, budget staff, or town manager. Therefore, they may believe detail is not needed because the reviewers may be familiar with the request and need. It is important to remember that this is the governing body's budget. The staff's job is to help the governing body make well-informed decisions. Thorough and clear explanations are essential. In addition, residents, businesses, and the media are going to be looking at requests, so clarity is essential to ensure that the budget is reported on accurately.

  Anticipating questions likely to arise during a budget workshop, from the public, media, and social media, and then figuring out ways to answer those questions before they are even asked is the goal. It does take additional time to prepare a thorough explanation for why a request is needed, but the "slower is faster" motto applies here as well. The justification should also discuss what other options were considered or could be implemented if the request is not funded.

  Local governments deal with a wide range of unique services and operations, so many requests are going to be unfamiliar to management, elected officials, the media, and the public. Painting a clear picture is a must, as there is a limited amount of money available to fund new requests. If your department is putting together a budget request, have someone outside of the department review the request and give you feedback. Having someone unfamiliar with your operations read through your request can help ensure that the request is easy to understand. While it may not be fair or best for the organization, lower-priority needs can get funded because staff making those requests prepared a more convincing case than staff from another department, even though that other department had a more pressing need. Budget staff and management will coach departments on ways to bolster their cases, but there is only so much they can do to help.

  Pictures, maps, charts, diagrams, other graphics, and links to videos are often the best ways to explain a request or at least key parts of it. Again, towns, cities, and counties deal with so many different functions that graphics are a quick way to familiarize decision makers with items they do not deal with frequently. It helps to see items like a knuckle boom truck, spectrometer, and sewer line cleaning vacuum truck.

Showing diagrams, pictures, or even videos of how pipe bursting techniques work in water line replacements and slip-lining of sewer lines goes a long way in explaining why a request is important. Maps are another great way to orient reviewers, as well as show how complex or simple a project might be.

Often a budget justification form may not provide the space needed to adequately explain a request. In those cases, get creative and figure out a way to make your case. Something as simple as a supplementary memo, an attachment with examples from other locations, or a link to a video can be a big help.

4. Include Multiyear Forecasting

Incorporating a multiyear component into the budget presentation has many benefits. North Carolina local governments can only adopt a one-year legally binding budget, but nothing prevents an entity from making it part of a multiyear financial plan. Combining the budget, capital improvement program (CIP) items, and financial forecast in one layout makes it easier to see a more complete financial and operational picture. This improves decision-making capacity by making the impact of today's decisions on future years clear, which is far more difficult using a traditional annual budget. The multiyear format is yet another way to anticipate questions and respond more swiftly to potential problems.

A well-respected government budget and finance expert, Allen J. Proctor, stated, "All financial forecasts have one thing in common, they are all wrong."[3] The purpose of the multiyear budget and financial plan is not to precisely predict future revenues and expenses but to anticipate and rationally plan for situations that may be looming on the horizon. This "fiscal radar" gives a local government more time to get ready for an approaching storm, recession, or financial challenges; seize good opportunities; and avoid or mitigate rate increases. It is easier to develop effective solutions and options and solicit and receive feedback when one's back is not against the wall. The goal is to identify and mitigate problems while they are still manageable.

Preparing a multiyear budget and financial plan the first time takes a little extra effort but is not complicated. Simply adding two additional columns beyond the budget year for Year 2 and Year 3 and then completing projections using available prior years', the current year's, and budget estimate data is all that needs to be done. It is even easier the next year because much of the work has already been completed. This means departments are not starting from scratch in preparing their budget, and they immediately have complete drafts for the first two years for the upcoming budget and financial plan. The focus becomes editing, updating, and refining the first two years

---

3. This quote is taken from a presentation Proctor gave at the N.C. Budget Officers Association's summer conference in Atlantic Beach, North Carolina, sometime between 1992 and 1994. Proctor was the executive director of the Financial Control Board that was created to help get New York City out of bankruptcy.

of the forecast, as well as the justification forms for new personnel, programs, and capital, which save significant time. Year 3 is the only one that needs to be completed from scratch, but this is simplified due to the availability of several years of historical and projected data to help with those estimates. Once staff members go through the annual cycle once, they quickly see the benefits of preparing a multiyear budget and financial plan.

Over the years, Hillsborough has used three, five, and seven-year formats for its financial plan. The board liked the three-year format so much they wanted it increased to seven years. In addition to putting too much information on one page, going that far out created too much information to view at once, and accuracy of projections suffers in longer forecast windows. It was quickly cut back to five years and then back to three, which seems to be a sweet spot of forward thinking, reasonable accuracy, and manageable workload.

Local governments can still include a longer forecast window for their CIP that can also be included in the budget document. For example, Hillsborough has a seven-year CIP. If your organization is considering moving to a multiyear format, but there is concern about two years being too much, try just adding one year as a pilot and then adjust accordingly. Even by adding just one year to the budget document, an organization will still experience many of the benefits discussed in this section.

How the multiyear format improves the budgeting process:

- **Focus.** Prior to implementing the multiyear format in Topsail Beach, North Carolina, the board already functioned effectively during its budget workshops. Still, with the adoption of the multiyear format, the level of focus improved, less time was spent on minor issues, and the board allocated more time and energy to discussing key issues. As mentioned earlier, the first year Hillsborough implemented the multiyear plan, budget discussions went much faster even though there were two additional years to review. Seeing several years of critical information in sequence widens one's field of view by revealing the bigger picture and improves one's ability to lead and think strategically. Just as important, it limits instances of getting sidetracked by relatively minor issues.

- **Awareness of fiscal condition.** A traditional one-year format can create "tunnel vision" on doing what is necessary to get through the budget adoption, as long as things do not look too bad (e.g., taxes, rates, fees plus fund balance, deficit, and other metrics that may be used by a local government). It is easier to kick the can down the road in terms of equipment and infrastructure when the future years are invisible. When using a multiyear format, the goal is not just to produce a plan that is acceptable at the end of the budget period (Year 1) but also produce a plan that is fiscally responsible through the last year of the plan, such as Year 3. Because the multiyear format shows what the financial picture looks like in the out-years directly to the reader, that picture is harder to ignore. When elected officials, management, and departments are aware of and understand a situation, they will usually do the right thing, even if it means making unpopular decisions, like raising taxes or rates and saying no to or delaying expenditure requests.

There have been many instances of elected officials using this longer-range view in their questioning and decision-making calculus. In Topsail Beach, during the budget process that followed Hurricane Fran, one of the commissioners, Robert V. Richards, stated he knew the town could afford to buy a new fire truck today, but his concern was how that would affect the fund balance in three years. This long-range thinking is a common perspective and approach seen in local governments (i.e., elected officials, management, department heads, and other key staff) that use a multiyear format.

- **Communication.** Realistically, there are going to be times when the outer years of the plan are not acceptable, such as deficits being too large three years from now. Even in these cases, this "fiscal radar" lets everyone know they need to be working on solutions now, but they have time before the situation becomes a crisis. When more difficult decisions must be made in subsequent years, it is no longer a surprise. Constraints or limited resources are a critical part of creative problem-solving. Consistently viewing the financial condition from a multiyear perspective increases awareness of resource limitations over time.

  It is easier for everyone to understand the organization's situation and see how they can contribute by sharing innovative ideas, developing alternatives, finding and eliminating waste, improving efficiency, and communicating this information with co-workers, the public, media outlets, and social media outlets. Talking in trends and using charts, especially showing increasing deficits and decreasing savings levels, is an easy and effective way to communicate key information to stakeholders to gain support and understanding and encourage engagement.

Quick Case Study: Communication Leads to Problem-Solving

Early in the Great Recession, sharing the financial challenges the town was facing and asking the employees and elected officials for assistance by generating ideas to reduce the budget deficits was the approach used when Hillsborough's town manager and budget director visited all departments to explain the crisis the town was facing. The multiyear plan indicated significant shortfalls if corrective action was not taken. The employees generated over 160 ideas to help address the projected deficits over the next three years. This assisted the mayor and town board in explaining and defending these challenges to the community, especially when some of the ideas resulted in decreasing service (e.g., reducing weekly bulk item and brush pickup to once per month and biweekly due to eliminating several positions in public works and the code enforcement officer position). Had the multiyear plan not been in place, which allowed the organization to act early, the situation would have been significantly harder to manage, as the Great Recession started shortly thereafter. Hillsborough was able to address sizeable projected deficits without raising property taxes by finding many smaller cuts, deferments, and creative solutions that served as bridges and "band-aids" until things got better.

- **Multiyear savings increase options.** Every year presents similar challenges in developing a balanced and fiscally responsible budget: (1) eliminate the inevitable deficit the organization begins with or reduce it to a manageable amount, (2) fund as many requests as possible, and (3) avoid tax, rate, or fee increases if possible. When searching for savings in terms of items to cut or defer, and identifying less expensive alternatives, it is natural to initially pass over relatively small dollar amounts as not making a substantive dent in the deficit. Instead of viewing the total savings or cost as a one-year amount, it should be viewed as multiplied over a multiyear period to see a more accurate impact of the decision.

  Reviews take place during the current budget year, starting with internal reviews as early as January or February. Decisions can sometimes be made then (midyear) to make cuts and deferments for the current year, the proposed budget (Year 1), and the forecasted years (e.g., Years 2 and 3). For example, identifying a $12,500 savings in the current year that can also be carried out through Years 1–3 is a $50,000 impact. A $100,000 savings or cost avoidance decision over five years finds an organization $500,000. This deficit reduction approach clarifies the impact of a dollar as well as the local government's decisions over time. When applied to the hundreds or thousands of line items in a local government's budget, this can have a major impact, regardless of the size of the organization.

  The same principle of identifying cost over time applies when considering funding new expenses or increasing revenues. This makes it easier to identify the opportunity cost (i.e., what you are giving up, missing out on, or could do) by funding another item. For example, adding a new position for a department may mean not being able to pay for a new building because the annual debt service on the installment-purchase agreement may be similar. Anytime a decision can be boiled down to something tangible, it is less abstract and more easily understood by participants, who can then more easily compare merits and deliberate.

  The combination of a significant population increase in Hillsborough; high rates; pressure to address many capital facilities' needs; taking care of existing assets; tackling needs, such as climate change; and pursuing many other priorities has created complex challenges in trying to balance the budget, remaining fiscally sound, and addressing the community's needs. This situation is like what many local governments in North Carolina are facing today. Having a multiyear plan to increase awareness, identify options, and buy time to solve these complex problems greatly increases the likelihood of developing a successful and fiscally responsible plan. Multiplying the impact of a change over the multiyear forecasting window provides additional opportunities for identifying ways to pay for priorities or simply eliminating a deficit to balance the budget.

- **Morale.** Each year, well-justified needs do not get funded due to resource limitations. When requests are cut, departments naturally ask management, "When are we going to get the additional position we requested?" In a typical one-year budget format, the answer will be something to the effect of, "We don't know, put in the request next year, and we'll see what happens." This leaves the department in limbo, and no one likes uncertainty. Departmental staff can understandably feel like management, along with the governing board, do not understand or appreciate the challenges and adversity they are dealing with throughout the year.

  When the same question is asked in local governments that use a multiyear format, the answer is often much different. A typical response is, "It did not get funded in Year 1, but it will be in Year 2 or 3." Department heads can go back to their employees and communicate that while it is not in the upcoming budget, it is on the radar. That conveys quite a different and more understanding message to the department. Employees are far more likely to feel they have been heard, their situation acknowledged, and there is a light at the end of the tunnel. Hence, the multiyear format elevates the level of communication and understanding from stakeholders in the budget process. Departments understand that just because a request is in Year 2 or 3, it is not a guarantee that it will automatically move up and get funded next year, as it is a plan, and conditions change.

- **Enhanced response to disasters, crises, and recessions.** Unlike the typical budget cycle that provides months to make decisions, events like hurricanes, tornadoes, floods, ice storms, unexpected damage to critical infrastructure, recessions, and sudden close of a large business or industry come with little to no warning. This often requires quick action. In these cases, having a combined budget and multiyear financial plan is an invaluable tool in managing significant challenges. The story in the "Topsail Beach's Response to Hurricane Fran" sidebar is just one example of how the format is beneficial.

5. Provide Continuity

The biggest changes that happen to a local government usually occur with turnover or transitions of positions. This is usually due to elections or departures of managers, department or division heads, and other key staff. It takes time for new elected officials and key staff to get oriented. Having a budget document that is easy to understand, contains key information, and is in a multiyear format accelerates their familiarity with issues, the organization, challenges, future projects, capital purchases, and the rationale behind previously made plans. This saves everyone a lot of time moving forward. Newly elected officials and staff naturally ask many questions

Chapter 16 | Budget Presentation: How Format Can Improve Decision-Making | 363

Topsail Beach's Response to Hurricane Fran

Seven weeks after Topsail Beach, N.C., was struck by Hurricane Bertha in 1996 and the eye of the Category 2 storm passed directly over the town, Hurricane Fran hit with even greater power as a Category 3. About one-third of the homes in the town were either severely damaged or destroyed. The southern half of the five-mile-long town was buried in two to five feet of sand. Because the road to Topsail Beach, through Surf City, was either washed out or blocked by damaged homes crumpled onto the roadway, the only way to get in and out of town was by using a four-wheeled drive vehicle during low tide on the beach for over four miles.

One of the first challenges was removing the immense amount of sand deposited from the storm surge across the southern half of town. This was essential to opening roadways, allowing property owners to access their homes, repairing lines and valves to get the water system operational again, and making it more manageable for mutual aid crews from outside the area to assist with recovery. Shortly after the storm, a contractor bid on a project to remove the sand, which involved filtering to clean out the large volume of debris and then placing it back on the beach in the form of a rebuilt dune line. The cost was equivalent to 25 percent of the annual general fund budget and would take ten days.

This was a massive expense, and the manager knew the board would ask the next day whether they could afford to proceed. The multiyear plan made crafting a plan and options to pay for this and other storm-related expenses much easier. This was done by identifying expenses that could be delayed and eliminated as well as transfers from other funds and fund balances to cover the cost. This gave the board and manager a high level of confidence they could proceed with this project and other efforts to expedite the recovery efforts. This was important, as tourism was the main economic driver for the community and the town needed to be ready for business by the following spring. Other communities in the area did not respond nearly as fast, primarily because they did not have clarity on their budgetary and financial situations.

The first year the multiyear plan was implemented in Hillsborough, the plan clearly showed the town was about eighteen months away from being bankrupt in the general and water and sewer funds. The focus of prior boards had been to keep taxes and utility rates as low as possible. Just using a traditional annual budget gave them little to no warning of the financial mistakes they were making by spending fund balance to avoid rate increases. The multiyear format made it easier for the new town manager to show and explain the situation. Most importantly, elected officials, departments, employees, and the public were able to see the trends, understand the crisis, and take appropriate action in the form of cutting expenses and adopting significant rate increases.

---

to get acclimated during their first year. Not only does a good budget presentation address many questions in advance, but it also allows officials to ask deeper and more nuanced questions and offer insight on alternative ways to approach matters.

The budget document should be part of a package of information provided to all candidates running for office. Candidates for office, whether they were elected or not, have commented to the Hillsborough town manager during his thirty years as a manager in three towns about how helpful it has been to read explanations for what is being done, why, and when. It is evident during election campaigns when candidates for office have read the budget document. They often have a better grasp of the issues and mechanics of the organization. An ineffective budget document is a missed opportunity to help candidates when they take office and sends a message that the organization may not be organized or thorough in its decision-making process.

A well-presented budget is an important part of the recruitment and selection process for key members of the local government staff. The quality of the document says a lot about the professionalism of the local government. It helps candidates decide whether the organization may be the right fit for them, makes a statement about the quality of work expected, and paints a clear picture of the issues, challenges, and opportunities they will be tackling in the job. In addition, a good selection process or assessment center will use relevant parts of the budget in various exercises to evaluate candidates.

Another way the budget aids in continuity is in succession planning, especially if there is a multiyear operational and capital planning component. An effective budget document identifies upcoming issues, challenges, resource gaps, and opportunities. This helps identify skill sets and resources needed as part of the succession planning process. Key recommendations from the succession plan can then be included in the multiyear budget, as preparations often take more than a year or years to effectively implement, such as allocating resources for training to develop employees, restructuring departments or the entire organization, adding new positions, and implementing technology and other efficiency improvements.

6. Change and Adapt with the Times

In his book, Thriving on Chaos (1988), noted management expert Tom Peters said: "Excellent firms don't believe in excellence—only in constant change and constant improvement." Local government is a dynamic environment, like navigating white water rapids in a kayak that are often swirling, changing directions, and tossing you around. Listen and look down the road to anticipate potential changes that may be needed. Spotting changes and charting an alternative course correction early allows the organization to make adjustments manageable and less disruptive. Just like driving a car on the highway, if you are looking far down the road and see trouble ahead, a small correction such as lightly pushing on the brake pedal to slow down or turning early can easily avoid the situation without much issue. Failing to look ahead or waiting too late to act then requires a drastic maneuver that is more likely to fail.

Waiting until the problem has nearly arrived creates more pressure due to time constraints and erases options. While many people have a natural reluctance to change, it is better to do it early and on your organization's terms. Waiting until something becomes a hot-button issue risks having rashly thought out or emotional responses being imposed on the organization.

While changes to the budget format or process may not occur every year, there should be continual evolution over time. Adjusting to conditions, personalities, skill and experience sets, and opportunities; applying lessons learned; and modifying ideas taken from other local governments are all good reasons to make these improvements.

An opportunity to regularly improve your documents exists through the GFOA's Distinguished Budget Presentation Award program. The most valuable part of the review process is the comments and suggestions made by the reviewers on ways to make your local government's budget document better. Also, consider being a reviewer for the program. Seeing other budgets, how things are done in other areas of the country, and the issues they are dealing with is a great way to get ideas to improve your document and process.

7. Be Easy to Understand and Navigate

Due to negative perceptions about government, we sometimes start off with two strikes against us in the areas of trust and credibility. Having a confusing, cluttered, or numbers-heavy document just reinforces that perception. Therefore, it is essential a local government's documents are user-friendly. Listening to complaints to identify barriers readers are working through when reading your local government's budget creates opportunities to improve everyone's ability to contribute to the process.

One example of a small formatting change to make the document easier to review involves the three-year budget and financial forecast format used previously in Topsail Beach and for the past twenty-three years in Hillsborough. Adding the additional two years of information created what appeared to be a sea of numbers. The simple addition of highlighting the budget year column in gray made those numbers jump out and become easy to find. The reviewer's eyes naturally lock on that column. It provides an easy reference point when reviewing any revenue, expense, fund balance, or other summary data. Plus, the gray column breaks up the page, making it more visually appealing.

Each year in Hillsborough's citizen's academy there is a presentation and exercise that uses the town budget. Participating residents frequently get excited when they understand how to find information and use the budget document, as well as participate in the process. This enthusiasm continues, as many participants move on to serve on many of the advisory boards as well as the governing board.

8. Build Trust and Credibility

If the budget is relatively easy to understand, information of interest can be found, and many key questions are anticipated and answered in advance. Moreover, if the finances and operations are planned in a multiyear format, the process of developing the local government's most important policy document becomes more transparent. This can increase stakeholders' overall confidence, which carries over to interactions with the local government on other issues, services, and needs. At the very least, this gives skeptics less to worry about and attack, thus setting the table for improved future interactions.

Addressing even some of the topics covered in this chapter can go a long way toward breaking down barriers and perceptions that government is untrustworthy or inefficient. The number of challenges local governments deal with today is overwhelming. To be successful, increased engagement with stakeholders in the budget process and other issues is essential. This makes it easier to share stories of how local government works and the challenges it is facing; identify gaps and problems; and bring more people together in a constructive manner to improve the community's problem-solving power.

Even when information in the budget is being used by groups to argue against your local government's goals, operations, or policies, you have still been successful in presenting the information in way that is accessible, is understandable, and allows open deliberation on the topic. One of the major villains of decision-making is not getting wide-ranging feedback, and thus relying on a narrow inside view. Getting differing views is essential to sound decision-making.

Appendix A. Budget Message for Fiscal Year 2019, Town of Hillsborough, N.C.

Budget Message

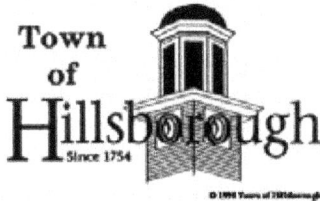

Town
of
Hillsborough
Since 1754

© 1998 Town of Hillsborough

May 11, 2018 (revised June 11)

Honorable Mayor Stevens and Board of Commissioners:

I am pleased to submit Hillsborough's FY19 Annual Budget Workbook and FY19-21 Financial Plan. The budget is prepared in accordance with the North Carolina Local Government and Budget Fiscal Control Act. As this proposed document is transmitted from the town manager to the Board of Commissioners, it now becomes the governing body's budget to review, debate, adapt and ultimately adopt. It is expected that changes will be made to the proposed budget as new information becomes available and alternatives are considered. Town staff is ready to provide whatever information the board deems necessary to help it make well-informed decisions on the budget and financial plan.

It is important to note that this first draft is not the final word on Hillsborough's budget and financial plan. Rather, it's intended to serve as a "starting point" in the process. Therefore, the mayor, Board of Commissioners, Water & Sewer Advisory Committee, other advisory boards and community are strongly encouraged to share their views regarding what should be funded, eliminated, reduced, added, or altered because this is ultimately **your** budget!

The Budget as a Decision-Making Tool

This is the 21st year a multi-year financial planning format has been used in reviewing the town's budget and operations. It is the 12th year the balanced scorecard has been used to implement and communicate the board's mission, vision, strategic priorities and core values. The scorecards are a response to the town board's strategy map through initiatives, performance measures and targets pursued by departments in their daily operations. This system was designed to help the organization become more analytical, adaptive and responsive to the lessons it learns while trying to achieve its goals. Strategies are tested through trial and error via the performance measures in the scorecards.

These businesslike techniques (used by more than half of the Fortune 1,000 companies) determine how to prioritize needs and allocate town resources. While the scorecard is a typical tool in the business world, Hillsborough is one of only about a

few local governments in North Carolina using this system that links goals, actions, measures, and targets.

This is also the third year "top priority" maps have been included to identify departmental priorities and the steps needed to achieve those goals. In addition, seeing the priorities makes it easier to ensure the budget provides departments the resources necessary to be successful.

The multi-year forecasting component of this document encourages the town to look forward to identify, address, and mitigate potential problems while they are still manageable. The plan allows readers to better see how today's decisions affect the town's financial condition in the future. The financial plan functions as a "fiscal radar," giving Hillsborough more time to proactively plan responses to problems and needs. This is crucial in avoiding unwanted surprises!

Using only an annual budget process, as most local governments do, to manage financial and departmental operations provides little advanced warning of problems looming on the horizon. If the town board, staff, and community is aware of a potential problem in advance, it has greater flexibility and time to develop reasonable solutions. Hillsborough is one of the only local governments in North Carolina that uses a multi-year budget format. While only the first year of the budget is legally binding, Years 2 and 3 of the financial plan provide critical information that provide a more accurate picture of the fiscal and operational challenges facing the town.

FY19-21 Budget & Financial Plan Strategy

The pressure of new development bringing more residents, businesses, and visitors to Hillsborough tests the strategy of assembling a budget that meets current and future demands. In recent years, a simple approach has been used to categorize and help balance the various wants and needs facing our town. In addition to the Town Strategy Map, the following three principles are used as a guide in developing this budget and financial plan:

1. Take care of what we already have
2. Invest in Hillsborough's future
3. Minimize rate impacts on the community

1. Take care of what we already have (infrastructure, equipment, employees, and organizational structure)! The town's mission, vision, strategic priorities and objectives can't be implemented if these basic tools of service implementation are not in working order. The longer a municipality waits to address, repair or replace these assets (tangible and intangible), the more expensive it becomes in the long term. Federal, state and local governments are notorious for building capital assets and not adequately maintaining them. For example, ensuring the organizational structure and resources are in place to maintain parks is equally as important as

Budget Message, Town of Hillsborough (*continued*)

Budget Message

building the parks themselves. Hence, construction of new assets must be balanced with the personnel, equipment, and organization to operate and maintain them, which is critical in avoiding the overextension of resources.

2. Invest in Hillsborough's future! Identify specific projects, programs, services and/or infrastructure improvements likely to make Hillsborough a better place to live, work, visit and start a new business. Sound growth is necessary to support the improvements and services desired by the citizenry, and to make Hillsborough an affordable place to live.

3. Minimize rate impacts on the community! If rate increases are deemed necessary, work to keep those costs on tax and rate payers as low as can reasonably be managed. A few efforts that demonstrate these principles are highlighted below.

✓ No property tax or stormwater rate increases are proposed for FY19!

✓ Decreasing water costs for low-volume users was accomplished in 2016 via the four-year plan, which started in 2013 to lower the minimum charge from 3,000 to 2,500 gallons per month. This was done without raising rates on customers using above the minimum. Please see the chart below for the cost savings impacts experienced by lower volume users during this period.

Cost Reduction Benefits
Change From 3,000 to 2,500 GPM Minimum Charge
(Savings for Customers Using 2,500 Gallons/Month or Less)

In-Town	Month	Year
Water	$ 4.04	$ 48.42
Sewer	$ 6.07	$ 72.78
Combined	**$ 10.10**	**$121.20**
Out-of-Town		
Water	$ 7.87	$ 94.44
Sewer	$ 11.83	$141.90
Combined	**$ 19.70**	**$236.34**

FY19 BUDGET EXPENDITURES	
General Fund	$ 10,803,480
Stormwater Fund	$ 647,000
Water/Sewer Fund	$ 11,186,257
Total	**$ 22,636,737**

TAX & RATE HIGHLIGHTS

Property Tax Rate: *No change*, tax rate remains at 62 cents for FY19. This will be the sixth consecutive year without a property tax rate increase. In FY18, the property tax rate was slightly reduced, even below the "revenue neutral" rate as part of the countywide revaluation process.

Stormwater Fee: *No change*.

Water Rates: 9.25% *increase*. Water rates were last raised six years ago, in July 2012. The in-town rate increases from $8.07 to $8.82 per 1,000 gallons. For the average residential customer using 3,864 gallons per month this equates to a $2.90 increase per month. Out-of-town rates increase from $15.74 to $17.20 per 1,000 gallons, or $5.64 per month for the average customer.

Sewer Rates: 7.5% *increase*. Sewer rates were last raised two years ago, in July 2016. The in-town rate increases from $12.13 to $13.04 per 1,000 gallons. For the average residence, this equates to a $3.52 increase per month. Out-of-town rates increase from $23.65 to $25.42 per 1,000 gallons, or $6.84 per month for the average customer.

Water & Sewer System Development Fees Update (capital facility fees). These are one-time charges assessed to new water and/or wastewater customers, developers, or builders to recover a proportional share of capital costs incurred to provide service availability and capacity for new customers. **These fees are not charged to current customers with existing services – this is for new development.** Fees for water are increasing, primarily due to the reservoir expansion. Fees for sewer are decreasing. The table below shows a cost comparison for a new residential customer.

	Current	New	% Change
Water	$2,993	$3,864	29.1%
Sewer	$3,488	$3,243	-7.0%

For detailed explanations on how these fees are proposed to change depending on meter size, please see the report from Raftelis Financial Consulting under Supplemental Information. The North Carolina General Assembly passed legislation in 2017 requiring that all water and sewer systems update their system development fee charges through an engineering or similar analysis to ensure fees are being fairly assessed. The report and proposed fee increases are posted on the town's website and comments are being accepted for 45 days through June 4. The town board will conduct a public hearing on June 11 at 7 p.m. at the Town Barn to consider additional comments before adoption.

Budget Message

SNAPSHOT: GENERAL & STORMWATER FUNDS

The mayor and town board directed the town manager at the April 7 budgetary planning retreat to take all reasonable steps to avoid raising property taxes and stormwater fees in FY19. That directive has been fulfilled. While three overdue positions are added in this year's budget, FY19 is more of a continuation that focuses on core operational needs. With that said, several key needs and opportunities are not funded. Those are discussed later in this message.

SNAPSHOT: WATER & SEWER FUND
Why are Rates Increasing?

The FY19 budget and three-year financial forecast project raising water rates by 9.25% and sewer rates by 7.5% over each of the next three years. Hillsborough already has high water and sewer rates, so why are they increasing? Below are several key reasons:

✓ Reservoir expansion. The approximate $16 million expansion project will ramp up to about $1 million dollars of annual debt payments over the next three years. Completing the expansion now, under the original Army Corps of Engineers permit issued 20 years ago, which will soon expire, will save the town millions of dollars. If the town were to have to secure a new permit, the cost of complying with today's standards would drive the cost much higher. More than doubling the current capacity of the reservoir provides protection against future droughts, which is important during a time of unpredictable weather fluctuations. Most communities are located close to an affordable water supply (e.g., lake, river, or wells that yield plenty of water). The Eno River yields a relatively small amount of water for a community of Hillsborough's size. Or, as happens for many small towns, their water and sewer systems are absorbed by a larger or big city system. Hillsborough does not appear to have those options available, hence this long-term investment to secure a stable water supply is essential.

✓ Wastewater Treatment Plant debt. While not new, the 2014 upgrade to the plant was done to comply with some of the strictest nitrogen discharge limits in the country, if not the strictest. These were imposed on Hillsborough per the Falls Lake Rules. This project alone more than doubled the annual expenses for the plant. Over $1.2 million dollars in annual debt is a big burden to pay for a small-town wastewater plant.

✓ Loss of Efland-Cheeks Sewer Customers in October will cost the fund $372,000 annually, or the equivalent of 8.5% of sewer revenues. The Efland-Cheeks customers are connecting to the City of Mebane's system. Over the long-run, the loss of these customers will be beneficial as this area of the system appears to be a large source of costly "inflow & infiltration" into the wastewater collection system and wastewater plant. In the short term, the loss of this revenue source alone necessitates a rate increase to replace those funds.

✓ Water and sewer system repairs and upgrades. In addition to what was already on the capital improvement program (CIP) radar, additional system needs were recently identified as being a high priority over the next three years. Some of these projects include:

  o Sewer line replacements ($1.1 million projected) for South Churton Street, Orange Grove Road, and Exchange Club Park Lane.
  o Wastewater collection system model ($100,000). This is the first step in attempting to find ways to eliminate, defer or reduce the cost of a $5 million replacement of the River Pump Station over the next few years.
  o I-40 water main relocation ($500,000) to place an underground casing to prevent interstate collapse in the event of a line break.
  o Water main replacement downtown ($230,000)

✓ Six years without a water rate increase, in combination with decreasing the monthly minimum charge from 3,000 to 2,500 gallons. Customers using 2,500 or less per month experienced a 20% decrease in their water bills since 2013. This dramatically slowed revenue growth generated from water and sewer sales during this period. Many low volume customers benefited from this change. Six years is a long time for a utility system or a business to go without raising prices.

✓ Minimize use of non-recurring revenues to balance the budget. During the recent building boom, Hillsborough has been fortunate to generate substantial capital facility fee revenues. These revenues also stop or slow when the economy loses steam. Hence, while things are good, the system needs to wean itself off these revenues, as well as the use of savings (i.e., fund balance or retained earnings) to balance the budget. If we do not do this now, while the economy is good, it will be even harder to do in the future. In addition, some economists contend we are overdue for a recession. The water and sewer fund is in good financial shape, as evidenced by the strong AA bond rating issued by Standard & Poor's in April. To keep that strong financial position, the use of non-recurring revenues should ideally be limited to paying cash for capital projects to limit future debt and balancing a conservative budget (i.e., appropriate retrained earnings at the beginning of the year, even though it may not be used and thus returned to savings). This means raising operating revenues to match the cost of operating expenses.

Budget Message, Town of Hillsborough (*continued*)

Budget Message

In summary, any small-town utility system would consider themselves highly unlucky to either 1) pay the significant cost of building/expanding a reservoir to ensure adequate future water supply, or 2) have the cost of treating their wastewater to meet some of the strictest discharge limits in the United States. Hillsborough doesn't just have one of those challenges - we have both! Those costs, coupled with a desire to take care of our water and sewer infrastructure, to provide clean and safe drinking water to the community, then safely discharge it back into the Eno River is an expensive endeavor that clearly puts a financial strain on its customer base.

The town's sale of revenue bonds on May 9 for the reservoir means the town's finances will be reviewed annually by both bond rating agencies and the bond trustees. This "higher bar" or standard is set to ensure the financial health of the water and sewer fund, guarantee that key debt coverage ratios and other key fiscal metrics are being met, and protect against short-sighted decisions that could jeopardize the fund's ability to make annual debt payments to the bond buyers.

The recommended 9.25% increase to water rates and 7.5% increase to sewer rates in FY19, FY20 and FY21 are designed to meet the standards discussed above. The utility consultant from Willdan Financial Services who conducted the required five-year financial analysis for the revenue bond sale, arrived at a similar recommendation regarding the rate increases needed over the next three years to meet the key financial standards in which the AA bond rating was based, as well as the indentures in the Master Trust Agreement in which the Town of Hillsborough must abide by.

Town staff is eager to continue working with the mayor, town board, Water & Sewer Advisory Committee, and others to explore fiscally responsible ways to reduce projected rate increases in the future.

GENERAL FUND – PROJECTS & INITIATIVES

Expenses increase by 6.7% in FY19

✓ Street Repaving – $350,000 keeps the town on pace to repave about 5% of streets or on a 20-year cycle. ($185,000 is funded from the Streets Division and $165,000 from Powell Bill revenues).

✓ Police Radio Replacements – $70,000 in FY19 replaces about half of the 10-year old radios in the department and includes some additional units for back up and reserve officers. The current models are discontinued, starting to experience failures, and requiring repair on a regular basis. The handheld radios are one of the officers' most critical pieces of equipment and are an important aspect of the job and officer safety.

✓ Police Additional Overtime – $12,000 provides resources to form problem-solving teams amongst police staff to address specific community concerns and problems as they arise during the year.

✓ Stamped Crosswalks at Downtown Intersections – $95,000. The Churton Street Access Plan included a recommendation for stamped crosswalks at Tryon, King, Margaret, and Nash & Kollock Streets for increased visibility, traffic calming, and safety. This will be done after NCDOT repaves Churton Street in FY19 and completes the multi-year project.

✓ Public Space Enhancements – $36,000 funds the following projects: expand parking and improve visibility at King's Highway Park, add newspaper containment area on West King Street, make improvements at Murry Street and Turnip Patch Parks, fund public art, and add interpretive signs at the Old Town Cemetery and the Gold Park Pollinator Garden/Bee Hotel.

✓ Sidewalks & Riverwalk Connections - Constructs the final portions of Riverwalk in the town's jurisdictions and makes related sidewalk and safety connections to the surrounding neighborhoods. The project includes the greenway portion from Gold Park to Allison Street, a sidewalk along Allison Street to connect to the Occoneechee State Natural area trails, intersection improvements at Eno and Nash Street, removal of on-street parking and sidewalk widening on South Nash Street, and the extension of a sidewalk along Calvin Street. The town's $221,062 match leverages an additional $362,200 in Congestion Air Mitigation Quality program funding through NCDOT to complete this project.

✓ Sustainability Efforts – $10,000 continues planning efforts to achieve the town's goal of going carbon-free by 2050.

Personnel – New Positions, Merit, Pay Plan, Etc.

✓ Administrative Support Specialist – assistance to human resources, town clerk and safety and risk management operations. The human resources team is particularly stretched to provide support and training to employees. The position would also greet the public once the human resources/town clerk offices move to the Town Barn.

✓ IT Manager – The budget director has taken on many functions related to IT over the past several years (e.g., liaison with IT contractor, point of contact for employees when many issues arise, phone system upgrades, fiber project, representative on TJCOG IT group, etc.). This has become exceptionally time consuming and the responsibilities keep growing, thus taking time away from

Budget Message

budget. Adding a position that would supplement the IT contractor, providing on-site support to town departments, providing a higher level of in-house expertise and sharing the workload with the budget director are all critical needs as IT has a direct impact on the productivity of all town operations.

✓ Planning Technician – The Planning Department currently has more work than they can complete and there are tasks that are not receiving the attention needed. This position will initially focus on general permitting and initial public contact and will evolve with time.

✓ Merit System – 3.25% average raise, which appears to be in-line with surrounding local governments at this point. General Fund: $109,000. Water/Sewer Fund estimate: $35,000.

✓ Market Rate Salary Adjustments – During the past fiscal year, human resources completed a market update for all town positions to ensure the town's classification and pay plan remains competitive with area employers. Salary grade adjustments to position classifications as well as salary increases for some employees will be implemented in FY19 based on the results of the study. Projected costs for the adjustments are $38,500 and $12,300.

Unfunded Requests – General Fund

While current service levels along with some new items are funded for FY19, there are still requests and needs that are not included in the proposed budget and three-year financial plan. The list below includes some items the town board may want to discuss and re-evaluate. Additional information on these and other unfunded items are listed at the end of most departmental budget sections.

- *Public Works Facility and Fleet Maintenance Expansion* – $2.88 million with $217,256 annual debt payments.

- *Fiber Connection Project* – $2.05 million with annual debt payments of $253,363.

- *Public Safety Station* – approximately $7 million to relocate the downtown fire and police stations to their future homes at the North Campus property on North Churton Street.

- *Parks & Facilities Repair Coordinator* – $70,529 total cost, plus vehicle in first year of hire.

- *Exchange Club Park acquisition and improvements* – ($380,000).

- *Exchange Club* – requesting an additional $1,000, over the $7,500 already included in the continuation budget, for maintenance at the park.

- *Equipment Operator* – Streets/Public Works ($51,539).

- *311 Software System for Public Works & Public Spaces* – $24,000, then $12,000 recurring expense. Allows staff in vehicles to quickly record service and repairs via GPS, etc.

- *Latimer Boardwalk* – connects south end of Latimer and Hayes Streets ($131,900).

- *Hillsborough Arts Council* – requesting an additional $4,500 to fund a full-time coordinator position.

- *North Campus Right-of-Way/Pedestrian Projects*:

    o Crosswalks along North Churton Street at Queen, Union, and Orange Streets ($205,000).

    o Sidewalk along North Churton Street from Corbin Street to Highway 70 ($120,000).

WATER/SEWER FUND – EXPENSE HIGHLIGHTS

Expenses decrease by 10.9% in FY19.

Projects/Facilities/Initiatives

✓ Reservoir Phase II ($16 million) – Construction started in April on the reservoir expansion. The first series of two revenue bonds were sold on May 9 providing over $11.1 million in funding for the project. The remaining funds will be raised through another revenue bond sale in early 2019 to pay for the remaining two road projects required to finish the project. Debt payments for the project are estimated at $563,038 for FY19, $849,550 in FY20 and $1,011,640 in FY21.

✓ Master Plan/Preliminary Design for Old Water Plant: Line Crew & Operations Building ($40,000) – There is currently one bathroom for 17 personnel, only three offices, limited to no central heat/air in parts of the building, and other current and future space needs. Welding operations are limited due to space and safety regulations. Construction is planned for FY20 at approximately $600,000. This project cannot move forward until public works is relocated to the NC Highway 86 North location.

✓ Sewer Line Repairs ($60,000) – Continues annual inflow & infiltration ("I&I") reduction program. Funds for this need increase by $10,000 annually. Starting in FY20, an additional $100,000 is provided for contracted I&I repairs.

Budget Message, Town of Hillsborough (*continued*)

Budget Message

✓ Churton Street Water Main Replacements – $230,000, in combination with $200,000 from FY18, to replace old cast iron lines in the downtown area.

✓ I-40 Water Main – Place in Casing – ($100,000 in FY19 for design and $400,000 in FY20 for construction). Once the 16-inch main acquired from OWASA goes into service south of I-40, it should be relocated to the pre-installed casing to prevent damage to the interstate should a break occur.

✓ Sewer Camera Video Inspection System ($140,000) – Replace nine-year old system that has been experiencing regular break downs and hindering staff efficiency.

✓ Wastewater Collection System Modeling/Evaluation & Capacity Study ($100,000) – The model will identify areas that are currently hydraulically overloaded, predict the impact of additional flows created by development, and plan for future needs. This is also a critical step in minimizing inflow & infiltration into the wastewater plant, as well as identifying options to delay or reduce the estimated $5 million River Pump Station replacement.

✓ Sewer Main Replacement Project ($440,000) – Installs new main that crosses South Churton at Orange Grove Road. The current line has several problems, such as sagging and reverse grading and it is too small to service this area. The next step will be replacing much of the Exchange Club Park Lane sewer main in FYs20-21 that's expected to cost $600,000.

✓ Rate study ($30,000) – Evaluate and explore various rate structures that could provide a more equitable way to charge customers for water and sewer.

✓ Merchant Processing Fees – Beginning Fall 2018, when utility billing moves back inhouse with implementation of new utility billing software, merchant processing fees will be passed on to customers wishing to pay via credit card. These fees continue to grow each year and are expected to cost the town approximately $77,000 in FY18. If these fees are not passed on, rates may need to be adjusted to cover this expense. Customers will still have the option to pay via cash, check or bank draft at no charge.

STORMWATER FUND – EXPENSE HIGHLIGHTS

A separate Stormwater Fund and fee was created in FY17 to fund approximately $1.1 million in improvements necessary to comply with Stage I of the Falls Lake Rules. These rules are required by the State of North Carolina over the next five to seven years to protect and restore the lake's water quality. The fund will also pay for in-town stormwater and drainage system maintenance.

Expenses decrease by 6.9% in FY19.

✓ *Stormwater infrastructure ($32,500)* – System maintenance, repairs, projects, inspections, cost share projects with property owners, and street sweeping. Prioritize high priority needs and develop plans to address water quality and drainage issues throughout town.

✓ *Capital Projects ($64,622)* – Falls Lake nutrient reduction as well as reserves for future projects.

✓ *Valley Forge Stormwater Project ($120,000)* – Replace 3 90" pipes crossing under Valley Forge Road. The pipes have deteriorated due to age, current flow, and damage from debris. Failure to replace the pipes could lead to road failure.

NOTABLE CHANGES FROM WORKBOOK TO ADOPTED BUDGET

General Fund
Revenue
- Current Tax Levy increased by $15,000 – increase due to updated projections.
- Food & Beverage Tax increased by $31,000 – decrease due to updated projections.
- Cable Access Fee (PEG) increased by $27,000 – town is expected to receive fee because the government access channel will be in operation for a portion of the fiscal year.
- Fund Balance Appropriation increased by $72,000 – increase due to updated expenditure and revenue projections.

Expenditures
- Departmental Salaries and Benefits due to updated salary projections.
- Governing Body
  - Auditor Fees decreased by $20,000.
  - Attorney Fees increased by $10,000.
- Administration
  - Insurance increased by $18,000 due to updated projections in Workers Compensation and Property and Liability insurance.
- Government Access Channel (PEG)
  - Training, Postage, Data Processing Services, and Miscellaneous increased by almost $6,000 – increase due to maintaining government access channel for a portion of the fiscal year.
- Accounting
  - Utilities decreased by $9,000 – decrease due to utilities being moved to Ruffin-Roulhac with new Town Hall Annex.
- Ruffin-Roulhac

Budget Message

- o Utilities increased by $8,000 – increase due to Accounting utilities being moved to Ruffin-Roulhac with new Town Hall Annex.
- Information Services
  - o Data Processing Services increased by $24,000 – increase due to additional funds toward routine maintenance, anti-ransomware agent, dark web monitoring, and moving investigations to Old Annex.
- Fleet Maintenance
  - o Cost Allocation updated to reflect update in number of vehicle and major equipment breakdown between funds.
- Economic Development
  - o Payments – Tourism Board decreased by $29,000 – decrease due to updated revenue projections.
- Special Appropriations
  - o Community Reinvestment increased by $2,000 – additional funding was awarded to the Hillsborough Arts Council.
  - o Transfer to Capital Project Fund increased by $3,000 – increase due to revised downtown access improvements projection.

Water & Sewer Fund
Revenue
- Water Charges increased by $70,000 – increased rate increase from 7.5% to 9.25%.
- Retained Earnings Appropriation decreased by $424,000 – reduction due to increased Water Charges revenue and a reduction in expenditures.

Expenditures
- Administration of Enterprise
  - o Cost Allocations decreased by $450,000 – reduction due to updated General Fund budget amounts and to correct a typo.
- Billing & Collections
  - o C.S./Billing & Collection Service increased by $88,000 – increase due to delay in implementation of new utility billing software and need to extend Fathom contract for several more months.
- Wastewater Collection
  - o Capital – Vehicles reduced by $7,000 – reduction due to purchase of utility bed for truck #213 in FY18.

Stormwater Fund
Revenue
- No notable change.
Expenditures
- *Not notable change.*

Closing
Quality of Life, Superior Services, Community Safety, and Strategic Growth are listed on the Strategy Map as the town board's Strategic Priorities. The FY19-21 budget and financial plan is full of programs, initiatives, and resources intended to carry out the 19 strategic objectives. These objectives, listed on the Strategy Map, serve as the foundation of the town's Balanced Scorecard that drives operational priorities throughout the year.

There is no one right path to achieving goals, especially in dynamic environments. Hence, questions, deliberation, alternate suggestions, and debate on prioritization of the limited resources is an essential part of effective budget and operational planning. In addition to input from the town board and employees, feedback from the advisory boards, citizens, business community, and other key stakeholders is an important part of helping achieve long-term strategic priorities.

Please do not hesitate to contact me, Budget Director Emily Bradford, Assistant to the Town Manager Jen Della Valle or Finance Director Daphna Schwartz if you need additional information. Town staff will make every effort to respond quickly and objectively to help you develop a budget that you feel best addresses the needs of the community!

Sincerely,

Eric J. Peterson

Eric J. Peterson
Town Manager

Source: Town of Hillsborough, N.C.

Appendix B. Police Patrol Budget Page
(Hillsborough, Fiscal Year 2020)

POLICE - PATROL

Account Name	FY18 Actual	FY19 Estimate	FY20 Budget	FY21 Projection	FY22 Projection	$ Change	% Change	Comments
Personal Services								
Overtime	15,980	18,000	30,000	30,000	30,000	12,000	66.7%	Regular overtime
Salaries - Regular	1,100,859	1,125,752	1,124,382	1,124,382	1,124,382	(1,370)	-0.1%	FY19-21 vacancy rate = 0%
Bonus Pay	2,854	3,500	3,500	3,500	3,500	0	0.0%	
FICA	83,468	88,683	88,578	88,578	88,578	(105)	-0.1%	
Hospitalization	180,483	194,743	189,191	202,434	216,604	(5,552)	-2.9%	
Life/Disability/Vision	6,709	7,121	7,378	7,447	7,447	257	3.6%	
Dental Insurance	6,550	7,261	7,102	7,741	8,438	(159)	-2.2%	
Retirement	89,220	98,536	112,315	126,209	140,104	13,779	14.0%	
Supplemental Retirement - 401K	53,613	57,963	57,894	57,894	57,894	(69)	-0.1%	
Personal Services Subtotal	1,539,735	1,601,559	1,620,340	1,648,185	1,676,947	18,781	1.2%	
Operations								
Training/Conferences/Conventions	6,185	6,560	6,560	6,560	6,560	0	0.0%	
Miscellaneous		4,000	4,000	4,000	4,000			
Train 2 Defend		2,560	2,560	2,560	2,560			Firearms training & qualifications
Telephone/Internet	4,959	6,300	6,300	6,300	6,300	0	0.0%	
Smartphone Reimbursement		4,200	4,200	4,200	4,200			5 phone stipends @ $70/stipend/mo
Verizon Wireless Service		2,100	2,100	2,100	2,100			
License Fees	0	0	0	0	0	0	0.0%	
Maintenance - Equipment	1,371	2,000	3,000	3,000	3,000	1,000	50.0%	Miscellaneous repairs (i.e. radio repair)
Maintenance - Vehicle	0	205	150	150	150	(55)	-26.8%	
Gasoline	33,084	35,572	39,130	43,043	47,346	3,558	10.0%	
Supplies - Office	352	0	0	0	0	0	0.0%	FY19 - Transferred to Police-Admin Supp.
Supplies - Departmental	112,659	95,624	46,279	17,724	17,724	(49,345)	-51.6%	
Patrol Equipment		7,800	7,500	7,500	7,500			FY19-increased ammunition and other costs
Replace Tasers		4,224	4,224	4,224	4,224			FY19-22 Replace 16 Tasers. 5 yr pmnt plan
Body-Worn Cameras		8,600	0	6,000	6,000			Replacing body worn cameras & dock
Active Shooter Kits		0	16,055	0	0			Ballistics equipment for Patrol officers
Replace Patrol Rifle Optics		0	8,500	0	0			Need sights that are for day & night use
Vehicle Storage Vaults		5,000	0	0	0			FY19 - 2 storage units for Chevy Tahoes
Replace Handheld Radios		70,000	10,000	0	0			FY19 - Replace 14 radios; FY20 - 2 radios
Supplies - Data Processing	0	0	0	0	0	0	0.0%	FY18 - Moved to IT buget
Uniforms	14,305	13,150	18,150	7,400	7,400	5,000	38.0%	Annual boots plus ~$250/officer
Uniforms		10,150	6,650	6,650	6,650			FY19 - Training uniforms
External Load Bearning Vest Carriers		0	10,000	0	0			Transition away from duty belts
Replace Body Armor/Vests		3,000	1,500	750	750			5-year cycle. 4-FY19, 2-FY20, 1-FY21
C.S. - Mobile Data Terminals	3,808	4,400	4,400	4,400	4,400	0	0.0%	Connectivity to County/RMS/Internet
Misc MDT Maintenance		500	500	500	500			Drop ALEN service due to new RMS system
MDT Aircards		3,900	3,900	3,900	3,900			
Data Processing Services	6,834	8,000	0	9,500	9,500	(8,000)	-100.0%	
Body Camera Video Storage		17,500	0	9,500	9,500			FY19- includes FY19 & FY20 storage expense
Miscellaneous	324	1,000	1,000	1,000	1,000	0	0.0%	Increased for emergency/disaster/
Vehicle Tax & Tags	8,121	0	0	0	0	0	0.0%	special events
Miscellaneous - Police Dog	2,409	4,000	4,000	4,000	4,000	0	0.0%	Supplies for 2 K-9s
Operations Subtotal	194,411	176,811	128,969	103,077	107,380	(47,842)	-27.1%	
Capital Outlay								
Capital - Equipment	0	0	0	0	0	0	0.0%	
Capital - Vehicles	407,089	0	47,500	47,500	0	47,500	0.0%	
Replace Vehicles 194 and 195		0	47,500	47,500	0			Replace 2 2010 Dodge Chargers
Capital - K9	0	15,071	0	0	0	(15,071)	-100.0%	FY18 - K-9 Grant of $11k
Capital Outlay Subtotal	407,089	15,071	47,500	47,500	0	32,429	215.2%	
Debt Service								
Capital Lease	0	99,970	99,969	99,970	99,970	(1)	0.0%	
Police Vehicles		99,970	99,969	99,970	99,970			Debt retired in FY23
Debt Service Subtotal	0	99,970	99,969	99,970	99,970	(1)	0.0%	
Police- Patrol Total	**$2,141,235**	**$1,893,411**	**$1,896,778**	**$1,898,732**	**$1,884,297**	**$3,367**	**0.2%**	
% Change	*35.1%*	*-11.6%*	*0.2%*	*0.1%*	*-0.8%*			

Source: Town of Hillsborough, N.C.

Appendix C. Wastewater Treatment Plant—Budget Highlights (Hillsborough, Fiscal Year 2019)

WASTEWATER TREATMENT PLANT – BUDGET HIGHLIGHTS

KEY OPERATIONS/FUNCTION:

- The Wastewater Treatment Plant treats wastewater from the Hillsborough wastewater service area, then discharges treated effluent to the Eno River, as regulated by the NC Department of Environmental Quality-Division of Water Resources-Water Quality Permitting Section, and in accordance with the Town's NPDES Discharge Permit. Water quality analyses are performed by an outside laboratory and its in-house state certified laboratory.

FY18 MAJOR ACCOMPLISHMENTS:

- Completed Effluent Reaeration Project: This new structure ensures the Dissolved Oxygen concentration of the water discharged to the Eno River will protect the aquatic life and maintain permit requirements.
- Continued Excellent Water Quality: The wastewater plant has had no water quality violations since the year 2006 and discharges water that far surpasses requirements.
- A risk assessment was completed to ensure all safety, security procedures, and facility infrastructure meet all State and Federal requirements and guidelines.

FY19 MAJOR BUDGET CHANGES/NEW REQUESTS/FOCUS AREAS:

- Purchase a utility vehicle with a trailer and hoist to transport personnel, tools, parts and equipment around the plant for repairs and maintenance.
- Replace access/support bridge on grit removal basin. The failing bridge creates both safety and capital risks.

FINANCIAL FORECAST: KEY ISSUES & HIGHLIGHTS:

- Design of New Flocculators: This project will greatly help with the reduction in chemical use and improve effluent quality. This will be needed as flows to the plant increase.
- The wastewater Bills as % of Median Household Income remains high. This is mostly due to debt incurred from the plant upgrade completed in 2014. We will continue to look for ways to reduce costs wherever possible.

ACTION PLAN PRIORITIES (OBJECTIVES & STRATEGIES):

- Staff has been able to delay the very expensive phase 2 plant upgrade. We are now forecasting design to begin in FY22 and construction in FY23. However, we continue to work towards delaying the project even further into the future.
- The risk assessment identified several areas of improvement needed. We will now be working on a schedule and budget for the improvements.

BUDGET & BALANCED SCORECARD HIGHLIGHTS:

Cost Area	FY17 Actual	FY18 Estimate	FY19 Budget	FY20 Projection	FY21 Projection	$ Change	% Change	Comments
Personal Services	450,723	472,980	486,773	496,505	507,549	13,793	2.9%	
Operations	515,274	532,196	593,007	555,630	586,055	60,811	11.4%	
Capital Outlay	28,232	61,232	28,500	0	0	(32,732)	-53.5%	FY19-Utility vehicle w/trailer & hoist
Debt Service	1,284,012	1,262,151	1,240,289	1,218,428	1,196,566	(21,862)	-1.7%	
Transfers	0	0	0	100,000	100,000	0	0.0%	FYs20-21-WWTP Ph II Master Plan
Total	**$2,278,241**	**$2,328,559**	**$2,348,569**	**$2,370,563**	**$2,390,170**	**$ 20,010**	**0.9%**	
% Change	*-4.2%*	*2.2%*	*0.9%*	*0.9%*	*0.8%*			
FTE	6.00	6.00	6.00	6.00	6.00			

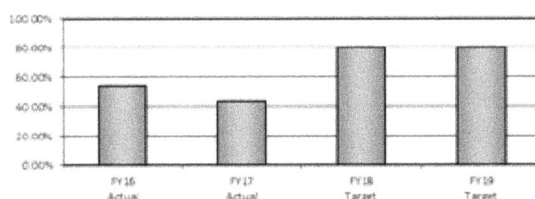

Peak Monthly Demand as % of Wastewater Treatment Capacity

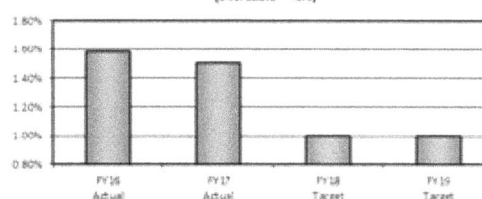

Wastewater Bills as % of Median Household Income (MHI) (affordable = <1%)